AN INTRODUCTION TO EFFECTIVE PARENTING EDUCATION:

EXPLORING CONTEXT, CONTENT, AND STRATEGIES

FIRST EDITION

Dr. Kathleen Dyer

Bassim Hamadeh, CEO and Publisher
Michael Simpson, Vice President of Acquisitions
Jamie Giganti, Senior Managing Editor
Jess Estrella, Senior Graphic Designer
Jennifer McCarthy, Acquisitions Editor
Gem Rabanera, Project Editor
Alexa Lucido, Licensing Coordinator
Berenice Quirino, Associate Production Editor
Joyce Lue, Interior Designer

Copyright © 2018 by Dr. Kathleen Dyer. All rights reserved. No part of this publication may be reprinted, reproduced, transmitted, or utilized in any form or by any electronic, mechanical, or other means, now known or hereafter invented, including photocopying, microfilming, and recording, or in any information retrieval system without the written permission of Cognella, Inc. For inquiries regarding permissions, translations, foreign rights, audio rights, and any other forms of reproduction, please contact the Cognella Licensing Department at rights@cognella.com.

Trademark Notice: Product or corporate names may be trademarks or registered trademarks, and are used only for identification and explanation without intent to infringe.

Cover image copyright © Depositphotos/mikdam.

Printed in the United States of America

ISBN: 978-1-5165-0502-9 (pbk) / 978-1-5165-0503-6 (br)

Contents

Acknowledgments — v

Introduction — vii

Part I: Parenthood: The Context of Parenting Education

Chapter 1. Contemporary Parenting — 3

Chapter 2. Contemporary Parenthood — 33

Part II: The Pyramid Model: The Content of Parenting Education

Chapter 3. Relationships — 69

Chapter 4. Communication for Teaching New Skills — 119

Chapter 5. Communication for Problem Solving — 149

Chapter 6. Consequences — 197

Chapter 7. Applied Behavior Analysis — 233

Part III: Teaching: Strategies for Parenting Education

Chapter 8. The Grief of a Parent — 287

Chapter 9. Effective Teaching — 301

Chapter 10. Parent Education Interventions — 325

Index — **349**

Acknowledgments

The writing of this book has dominated my life for more than a year. It has been a great joy to have this opportunity to share my vision for the Parent Education class that is "mine" as surely as are my own children. I love the course, I have deep affection for the students who have shared it with me for the past 17 years, and I have great hopes for its future. I am delighted to share this vision with other Child and Family Science scholars and students beyond my own university.

I must acknowledge those who have made this experience possible and those who have contributed to this book. The California State University, Fresno—Fresno State—is the academic home I have chosen, and it has nurtured my aspirations as a scholar in Child and Family Science. Thank you, Fresno State, for that support, and specifically for the sabbatical release that allowed me to get this project off the ground. Thank you, Fresno State students in Child and Family Science, for taking this journey of discovery with me.

Furthermore, I have colleagues whose influence is visible in these pages: Dr. Richard Berrett, professor extraordinaire, who created this course 40 years ago at Fresno State, who trusted me with his students and his vision, who has mentored me through all my years of teaching so far, and who created the Pyramid Model used in this book. Thank you, Rich.

I was trained by amazing family scholars at Mizzou, and I am fortunate to work in a vibrant department at Fresno State, and therefore have had many supportive mentors and colleagues, all of whom have influenced my work here. One colleague in particular, Dr. Sharlet Rafacz, made valuable contributions to my understanding of Applied Behavior Analysis, and her influence is to be found in these pages. My husband, Dr. Ray Hall, a consummate scholar (albeit in an unrelated discipline), served as a reader to provide general feedback on this manuscript. All mistakes are my own, of course, and reflect my own imperfections, despite the influence of these amazing academic professionals.

To most readers, my family will be more visible in these pages than my professional colleagues. The lives of my husband and children are a bit exposed in the pages of this book. While I only do so with their permission, this book opens up our personal lives to the examination and critique of unknown others. I believe that examples are powerful, and real-life examples are far better than artificially constructed ones. Therefore, I have used true examples from my own life to exemplify many of the concepts in this book. I have also used photographs of my family, the people most precious to me in the world. I offer my deepest gratitude to my husband, Ray; my children, Gabby, Letty, Ellie, and Sofie; my mother, Maren Dyer; my father, Don Dyer; and my sisters Kerry Borawski and Shannon Tiemeyer, and my brother Joe Dyer for allowing me to describe our family life in these pages.

Introduction

This book is intended to be used as a textbook in college classes on parenting or parent education. I have been teaching such a class at a state university in California for 17 years. It has been one of the most meaningful professional experiences of my career.

At the time I first accepted the course assignment, the focus was exclusively on parenting strategies, the techniques that parents and others use for child guidance. "Parenting Strategies" is typically a single chapter in most parenting textbooks, but the tradition in my department was to really unpack those ideas, and we had dedicated this entire course to them. I saw immediately that the content was wildly valuable and deserved the in-depth treatment. I had a toddler and was pregnant with my second child at the time. I gave birth midway during that first semester and took my newborn to class with me for the rest of the semester. I have taught the class virtually every semester and every summer since then. Each semester, I have thought about my own parenting through the lens of the course content, and every semester, some different aspect of my own life as a parent has come into focus for me due to my immersion in this course content. My understanding of and appreciation for the content of this class have deepened as my children have grown and I have matured as a parent.

Through the years, students who are parents tell me that the course changes much about how they approach their own children. Students who are aunts and uncles tell me that they use ideas from the course with their beloved nieces and nephews. Students who work in preschools and after-school programs tell me that they use material from the class in their place of work. Many students through the years have told me that they shared copies of our textbook (a book of readings) with family and friends. They often ask me for advice about how to talk to their relatives and friends about parenting now that they have some insights they think would be valuable. Being consistently reminded of the immediate practical applications of the course content has encouraged me to consider how the parenting class might help prepare students not just to think about parenting more deeply, but to teach this content to parents.

I started reading the published literature about parent education and looking into published parenting programs. I had opportunities to teach parenting classes in my community, and I worked with former students who taught parenting programs as part of the jobs that they acquired after graduation. I became a Certified Family Life Educator and deepened my commitment to the provision of evidence-based and compassionate parent education. To help me address parent education more directly, the collection of readings I used in my parenting class kept shifting. I finally decided it was time to share my vision of an introductory parent education book, to put it all into my own words. This book is, therefore, the product of nearly two decades of course development.

This book is designed to serve as an introduction for those who may find themselves in the position of providing parent education. They may not start out with parent education as a career goal, but it develops that way. I envision this book to serve as a resource for that student or professional, someone who has a background in Child and Family Science, who wants to apply their knowledge and skills in the domain of parent education. It is a textbook that provides three things: an overview of the context of parenthood in the United States, a fairly in-depth look at what family scientists know about parenting strategies, and a brief review of teaching strategies specific to parenting education.

PART I
Parenthood: The Context of Parenting Education

It was little more than a century ago, around the turn of the 20th century, that the scientific study of child development emerged, and scientists began to recognize that what happens in a family early in the life of a child is important for the future development of that child. A few short decades later, the discipline of family science emerged as scientists in various other disciplines (for example, sociology, psychology, anthropology, and counseling) converged to study the social institution of the family. As a result, parenthood is now studied from the point of view of the child and of the parent.

During the century that these related disciplines of child development and family science were developing and focusing on parenthood, we saw drastic changes in parenthood in the United States and worldwide. These social changes continue to shape the context within which parenting occurs and may have increased the need for direct application of science to the goal of helping parents navigate their responsibilities to their children. This is the work of parent education.

A minor controversy exists in the field of parent education over what we should call the work that we do. Is it "parent education" because we educate people who are parents? If so, then who exactly qualifies? Or is it "parenting education" because we deal with the job of parenting, regardless of who does it? I hesitate to enter the fray and will use the terms interchangeably. I believe both terms are subject to the same problem: the lack of a definition for "parent."

Very often, parents both biologically produce a child and provide the home environment for his or her upbringing. But some parents biologically produce a child and do not participate in the care and rearing of said child (for instance, sperm and egg donors, parents who die before their child is fully grown, parents whose children die in childhood, fathers who were never told that they had impregnated a lover, those who release an infant for adoption); while other parents provide the care and rearing without having biologically produced the child (for instance, stepparents, adoptive parents, foster parents, grandparents raising grandchildren). People in all three of these categories are generally considered parents. But other people may do a significant amount of work toward the care and rearing of children but are not granted the title of "parent" (child care providers, babysitters, older siblings, grandparents, teachers, coaches, and so on). A conclusive definition seems elusive.

For the purposes of this book, we will leave the term *parent* inexactly defined. Let us embrace the ambiguity and allow the terms *parent* and *parenting* to be subjectively defined; that is, to be decided upon personally by the subject. I have no interest in deciding once and for all who is allowed to claim the status of parent and consequently who is actually parenting. People with an interest in the care of children can decide for themselves. And if they want to read a parenting book or come to a parenting class, then I applaud their commitment and hope to help them with the task that lies before them—whatever exactly that is.

The forthcoming chapters in Part I of this book will review the context within which parenting occurs and parenting advice is offered. Chapter 1 focuses on what science can tell us about effective parenting. It addresses questions such as: Why is parenting an important topic for professionals in child and family science? What do we know about the way parents approach the job, and the effectiveness of those styles? Is there such a thing as "good" parenting? Why do human beings need help with parenting? Does parenting advice reflect scientific knowledge about effective parenting or something else?

Chapter 2 centers on the determinants of parenting. It addresses questions such as: What are the life circumstances of parents in the United States today? How have changes in birth rates changed the experience of parenthood? Are parents of different racial/ethnic groups different from each other, or does everyone want the same thing for their kids? Does it matter if children are raised by single or married parents? Does it matter what kinds of romantic relationships parents have?

1. Contemporary Parenting

Introduction

We start our journey of preparation for parent education by considering contemporary parenting in the United States. Parenting is an important job, one that directly shapes the lives of both children and parents. It is all-consuming; children are more or less completely dependent on their parents for 18 years or longer, and parents' lives are completely overwhelmed with the task of parenthood for at least that long, more if they have multiple children. The job is long, arduous, and full of uncertainties. No wonder parents seek help! We will start with the importance of parenting, then we will examine the various styles parents adopt as they face this difficult job, as well as what the experts say about contemporary parenting.

Importance of Parenting

Those of us who study parenting do so because we think it is wildly important. Acknowledging the importance of adults in the lives of children, and vice versa, is why students generally come to a university program in child and family science. They want to make a difference in the world, and so they are drawn to study what might be the relationship most capable of making a difference, that between a parent and a child.

For Children

It seems intuitively true that parents are very, very important for children. The most important people in my early life, without a doubt, were my parents. (See Figures 1.1 and 1.2.) My siblings and grandparents were important, too, but those relationships were largely mediated, at least at first, through my parents. I suspect that every reader of this text would say

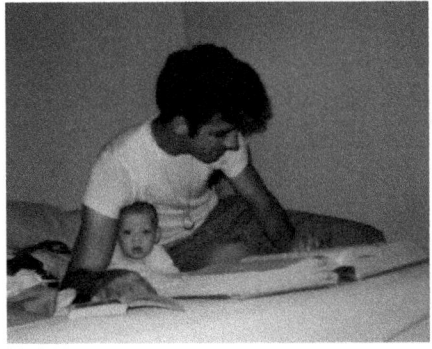 

Figure 1.1 My Dad and I with dictionary **Figure 1.2** My Mom and her Granddaughters

the same for their own early life. For good or for bad, parents are important in shaping the lives of their children.

It is quite likely that we are prone to assign more credit or blame to parents than is justified. It is quite likely that parents and children alike are the products of environmental forces that are outside of the control of an individual parent, such as forces shaping the economy and the political climate. And it is also quite likely that the outcome of a person's life has as much to do with random chance (that is, luck) as it does with the parenting experienced early in life. Yet most of us in the discipline of child and family science would still assert that it is the closest of intimate relationships, such as that between parent and child, that have any chance at all of having a meaningful impact on the life of a child. And so we want to support those relationships as best we can and do everything possible for the good of our society to nurture healthy parent-child relationships.

Do we have any evidence that the quality of parenting can actually produce desirable outcomes in children? Well, that is a question that we will tackle piece by piece throughout this text. Briefly, family scientists can state with confidence that some aspects of parenting are associated with better or worse outcomes in children. Many aspects of parenting reflect the diversity in cultural and personal beliefs and are not associated with better or worse outcomes. However, we can identify some parenting practices that seem to be counterproductive or even destructive. And we can identify some principles of parenting that seem to produce the best outcomes. These will be identified at the end of this chapter and then addressed systematically in each future chapter.

That said, there is likely to be a threshold effect. A half-century ago, a pediatrician named Winnicott (1953) suggested that there is such a thing as a **good enough** mother. Winnicott argued that a good enough mother was not perfect and needn't be perfect. While he did not use the language of attachment theory (which had not yet been fully articulated), he described a parent who offered sensitive responsiveness adequate for a secure attachment, and one who avoided abusive behaviors. He suggested that the parent's imperfections were actually helpful to the child, allowing him or her to learn to adapt to the realities of the world.

If Winnicott was right that sensitive caregiving without abuse is good enough, and there is no particular benefit to improving upon good enough, then parent educators might take this to heart. When we teach in a setting that is voluntary and full of what are likely to be good enough parents, we might adopt an approach that offers more parent support than anything else. But when we teach in a setting with parents who are already at high risk for parenting challenges, we might target the abusive and insensitive practices and simply leave the rest alone. One of the most important tasks of a parent educator, therefore, is to differentiate which parenting practices are likely to cause harm (so that we can help parents find alternatives) from other parenting practices that simply and harmlessly reflect diversity in style or belief.

For Parents

Subjectively, parents have a lot to say about how parenthood changes them. The reader might casually inquire of relatives and friends who are parents, "How do you think parenthood has changed you?" Only do so if you have time, though, because your friend or relative will probably have a lot to say about this. So many things change with parenthood, I will say for myself, that my life can only be understood as two separate lives: before I was a parent, and after I was a parent. (See Figure 1.3.)

One can try to prepare—but it is really impossible to fathom in advance—what it might be like to have every single moment in time (including the time when one is asleep) dominated by a helpless and beloved infant. There is simply nothing else in life that can hijack every moment of one's life as thoroughly as a baby. And those changes persist even when the baby grows into a child, a teenager, and an emerging adult.

Subjectively, those changes are simultaneously joyful and painful. One heartwarming essay (Bourke, 2012) puts it this way: "I want to tell her that the physical wounds of childbearing heal, but that becoming a mother will leave her with an emotional wound so raw that she will forever be vulnerable." This resonates with me as a mother. Every story of a child lost or hurt makes me identify with

Figure 1.3 My Family

the pain of that child's parents. Every siren I hear when my children are not with me gives me pause. When they start driving, the sirens become far scarier than before. It is something like a wound. But the only reason parents are so vulnerable to the threat of loss is because of how deeply they love their children.

Most parents say that parenthood is the most meaningful thing they have done with their lives. Among adults in the United States who are parents, the vast majority (85%) rank their relationships with their children as maximally important (10 on a scale from 1 to 10) to their personal happiness and fulfillment (Taylor, Funk, & Clark, 2007). (See Figure 1.4.)

Not only does parenthood subjectively change the way one experiences life, family science research has documented the ways that parenthood affects parental health, employment, finances, family relationships, and personality (Ambert, 2001) and how it shapes the context and processes of adult development (Palkovitz, Marks, Appleby, & Kramer Holmes, 2002).

Perhaps no one is surprised to learn that parenthood is not good for a parent's health. It is difficult to find time to prepare healthy meals when caring for a child and harder still to get out of the house to exercise. It's also not surprising that parenthood is hard on the pocketbook. The United States Department of Agriculture regularly produces a report on the cost of raising a child, the most recent of which (Lino, 2014) concludes that a middle-class family with a child

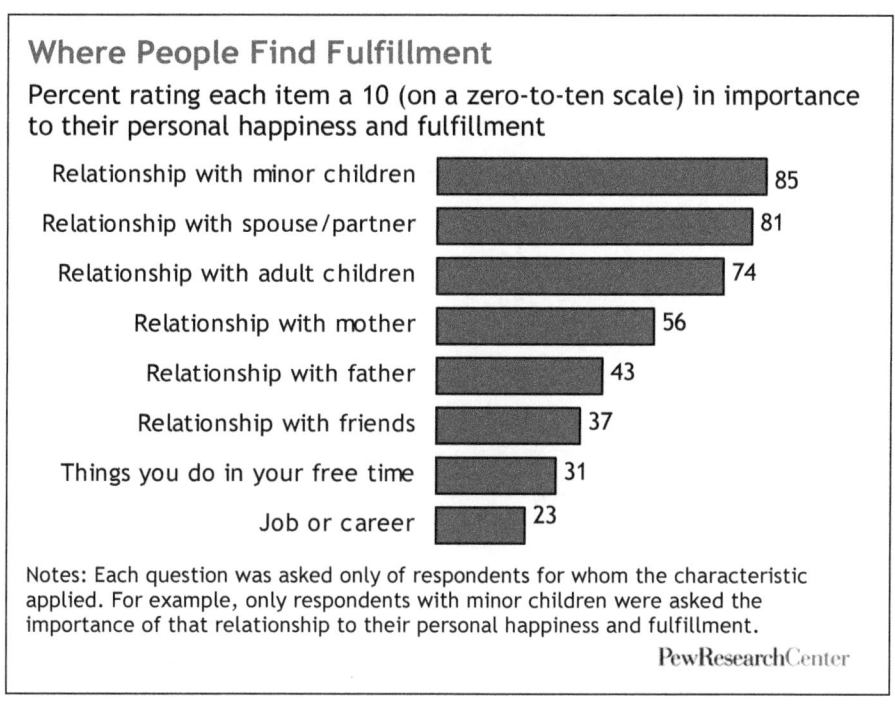

Figure 1.4 Where People Find Fulfillment

born in 2013 will likely spend $245,340 in current dollars for food, housing, child care and education, and other child-rearing expenses up to age 18. Wow. That's got to sting, but it's not exactly a surprise.

What often surprises students of family science is the revelation that parenthood doesn't make people happy. All of the data suggest that parents, if they are different at all, are less happy than adults who are not parents (Hansen, 2012). (See Figure 1.5.) People who think they're doing a great job as a parent report the highest levels of happiness, with 40% saying they are "very happy." Of those who judge that they are doing a fair or poor job as a parent, only 11% report being "very happy" (Parker, 2014). And sadly, as children get older, parents are progressively less likely to report that they are doing a good job (Parker, Horowitz, & Rohal, 2015). While we don't have longitudinal data to confirm this, it appears that parents grow less happy as their children grow up.

If, as it seems, it is true that personal happiness takes a hit with parenthood (Medina, Lederhos, & Lillis, 2009) and then declines as children age, that would mirror the relationship between marital satisfaction and parenthood. It has been well documented that marital satisfaction declines fairly dramatically at the birth of a couple's first child (Medina, Lederhos, & Lillis, 2009).

Contemporary Parenting 7

Marriage, Parenthood and Happiness

% saying they are ... with their life

	Married		Not married	
	Parent	Non-parent	Parent	Non-parent
Very happy	36	39	23	22
Pretty happy	49	51	46	62
Not too happy	13	9	25	15

Note: Parents include those with children of any age. "Don't know/Refused" responses not shown.

Source: Pew Research Center survey Nov 28-Dec 5, 2012, N=2,511

PEW RESEARCH CENTER

Figure 1.5 Marriage, Parenthood, and Happiness

Incidentally, there is evidence that this decline in marital satisfaction can be significantly mitigated by interventions provided during pregnancy to help new parents anticipate how their roles will change (Schulz, Cowan, & Cowan, 2006). This is an example of timing parent education for maximal effect. Nevertheless, after the transition to parenthood, marital satisfaction continues to decline as children age (Hirschberger, Srivastava, Marsh, Cowan, & Cowan, 2009). Parenthood is simply hard on parents' well-being.

Parenting Styles

We have established that parenting is an important yet difficult task. Now let us turn to the styles with which parents approach the job. **Parenting style** is the overall pattern, or general approach, toward parenting. It is different from specific parenting practices in that it is more global in nature. A single practice does not a style make. A style is the whole picture, the way several pieces fit together, and it refers to the manner in which those behaviors are implemented (Darling & Steinberg, 1993). For instance, a parenting practice is breastfeeding. But the style is something bigger than the practice. It is the manner of the breastfeeding: Is it done sensitively, or on a strict schedule? Is it done with tenderness, or with a businesslike attitude? Furthermore, we still wouldn't know the parenting style until we know how that particular form of breastfeeding fits with other parenting practices employed by the same mother. The overall picture is the parenting style.

Diana Baumrind's Parenting Styles

Diana Baumrind was a clinical and developmental psychologist at UC Berkeley in the mid-20th century. She proposed that two aspects of parenting processes were critically important: **parental responsiveness**, sometimes called *nurturance* or *warmth*, the level of parental sensitivity to the child's needs; and **parental demandingness**, sometimes called *guidance* or *control*, the parent's expectation of behavioral control. One might think of responsiveness as the emotional component of parenting and demandingness as the behavioral component of parenting. Based on these dimensions, she identified three parenting styles (Baumrind, 1967):

1. **Authoritarian** parenting is characterized by high demandingness with low responsiveness. These are the classically "strict" disciplinarians whose rules are inflexible and who resort to punishment for infractions of those rules. They are restrictive and inflexible. They have high expectations for behavior, but they do not show affection or support the children's interests.

2. **Permissive** parenting is characterized by low demandingness but high responsiveness. These parents want to be pals with their children. This type is sometimes known as "indulgent" because they indulge their children's wishes without restriction. They are very loving, but they do not discipline their children or expect mature behavior.

3. **Authoritative** parenting is characterized by high demandingness and high responsiveness. These parents have rules, but those rules are somewhat more flexible than authoritarian parents. They are also emotionally nurturing. Baumrind saw this as an intermediate option between the opposite extremes of Authoritarian and Permissive parenting and believed it to be the healthiest balance.

Later, based on empirical evidence, Maccoby and Martin (1983) proposed adding a fourth style to the typology:

Table 1.1 Parenting Styles (Baumrind; Maccoby & Martin)

	Low Level of Demandingness	High Level of Demandingness
Low Level of Responsiveness	Neglectful	Authoritarian
High Level of Responsiveness	Permissive	Authoritative

4. **Neglectful** parenting is characterized by low demandingness and low responsiveness. These parents meet their children's basic physical needs, but are otherwise unengaged in the process of parenting. They place no restrictions on children's behavior, often not even supervising it, nor do they nurture a warm relationship with the children. This has been called uninvolved or withdrawn parenting.

This parenting typology (see Table 1.1) has proved to be a very useful tool for examining the processes of parenting. Baumrind was not the first to propose the two dimensions of parenting (an emotional dimension and a behavioral dimension), but she worked tirelessly for four decades collecting empirical evidence about these parenting styles, testing the model and expanding scientific understanding of these parenting styles. It is a remarkably useful way to conceptualize parenting, and one that has been validated by extensive research.

Issues with Parenting Styles

Before we discuss the child outcomes associated with these parenting styles, let me acknowledge the limitations of the Baumrind/Maccoby and Martin model of parenting styles.

First of all, each dimension (responsiveness and demandingness) is conceptually divided into "high" and "low" when they are, more truly, continua. Parents do not fall neatly into the category of high responsiveness (or demandingness) or low responsiveness (or demandingness). Instead, responsiveness and demandingness are continuous, such that a parent might be very, very high, or just somewhat high, or higher than average, or right in the middle, etc. Therefore, the dividing line between what is considered "high" and what is considered "low" is arbitrarily drawn. And it forces the researcher to take parents who fall on the middle of the continuum and lump them into one category or the other, when the truth is that they are in the middle of the range and may not belong in either the high or low categories. Therefore, there is bound to be some error built in. It is an imprecise indicator. People in the mid-range on these dimensions will not be well described by the categories in this model. It is possible, furthermore, that the outcomes of parenting that fall near the middle of the continua are different from outcomes of children whose parenting style is nearer the extremes, but we cannot identify that.

Secondly, several family scientists have proposed that the component of demandingness is really made up of two parts. When Baumrind says "demandingness," she includes indicators of psychological control along with behavioral control. Others have proposed that these are two completely separate dimensions. Psychological control includes things like intrusiveness and control through guilt. These are aspects of parenting that almost anyone would recognize as emotionally toxic. A model that explicitly separates these from control that is purely behavioral (for example, supervision, limits on behavior, consequences for behavior) has shown promise as an improvement upon the four-type model (Barber, Stolz, Olsen, Collins, & Burchinal, 2005).

Thirdly, parenting style is rarely perfectly consistent. One parent may use a particular style, but the child's other parent adopts a different style. This very often happens when parents disagree about parenting; each parent becomes more extreme in reaction to their perception that the other parent is doing things wrong. Or more complicated, a parent is likely to use one style with one child and another style with his or her sibling. Students often tell me that they believe the gender of the child determines the parenting style they are subjected to. These students are frequently girls who say that they experienced authoritarian parenting, but that their brothers experienced permissive parenting. Or older siblings whose younger siblings were parented more permissively. Then there is the parent who adopts one style when the child is young but a different style when the child is older. And yet more troubling for the erstwhile researcher: a parent may even adopt one style at one moment of the day, or with a particular issue, but a different style later in the day when the topic is different. And even in the same encounter, a parent may bounce between styles when he or she is unsure how to handle something.

Fourth, and finally, this particular conception of parenting style may be culture bound. While it has been applied to parents from many places in the world and has been remarkably robust across cultures, it doesn't *always* work well outside of the United States, or even on nonwhite samples within the United

States. Sometimes the four styles themselves simply don't seem to map onto local styles so that most parents are unclassifiable. Other times, the styles do seem applicable, but the associated outcomes are different from what we find in white families in the United States (Dewar, 2010). While these two dimensions (responsiveness and demandingness) seem to be culturally relevant in the United States, there may be other dimensions of parenting that are more relevant in other cultures.

These issues illustrate the inherent difficulty of studying the process of parenting rather than the more objective, structural variables such as gender, age, ethnicity, and marital status that we will tackle in Chapter 2. Process is messy and complicated. It is not nearly as objective and clear as those structural variables. Structural variables are clean, but they are less helpful to people who seek advice. A parent seeking help with her parenting cannot change her age or ethnicity, for instance. Those variables are often beyond a parent's control. But parenting style is something that adults can reflect on and adjust. It gets to the heart of what we really need to know. It gets to the question of every parent in a parenting class—"What should I do?" What approach is the right one? What approach has the best chance of success?

Child Outcomes

Nothing has been quite so helpful in answering the parenting question "What should I do?" as the concept of parenting style. And despite the issues described above, Baumrind's typology has been a remarkably robust and useful way to study parenting styles, at least in the United States. We know that it's imprecise, and the details are messy, but still, this model has given us some answers that can be translated into practical and evidence-based advice for parents.

What have we learned? Essentially, the authoritative parenting style consistently produces the most desirable child outcomes (Steinberg, 2001; Baumrind & Larzelere, 2010). To understand specific outcomes of the various types, it is helpful to recall that responsiveness generally reflects the emotional component of parenting, and demandingness generally reflects the behavioral component of parenting. Therefore, responsiveness is related to emotional outcomes and demandingness to behavioral outcomes. Parents who offer a high degree of responsiveness (both authoritative and permissive parents do this) will produce children who are emotionally strong. They feel secure, and they have good relationship skills. Parents who offer a high degree of demandingness (both authoritarian and authoritative parents do this) will produce children who are behaviorally disciplined and mature.

Notice that authoritative parenting offers both emotional and behavioral support, and therefore, children who are parented with this style will benefit in all possible domains. They tend to be well behaved and academically successful, while also competent interpersonally and well liked by others. Adolescents with authoritative parents have the lowest rates of use of illicit drugs (Baumrind, 1991), as an example of typical outcomes. Life still presents challenges to these children, obviously, but what characterizes children with authoritative parents is that they are well equipped to deal with challenges, so they are less likely to be derailed completely. They have the social supports necessary to cope with difficulty because they have the social skills necessary to forge strong relationships. And they have the discipline required to approach a challenge constructively because they are accustomed to disciplined behavior.

Children of permissive parents, alternatively, are generally capable of warm interpersonal relationships and are happy, but their behavior is immature and somewhat uncontrolled. They may take a while to mature, but they are emotionally healthy and do eventually get there. They are nice kids who have friends, but they get into minor trouble in high school. Their parents say things like: "I know he's smart, but he just doesn't apply himself." They might get caught smoking pot or cutting school, but they are not committing crimes that hurt other people. I think of the young people who avoid getting a full-time job because it just doesn't appeal to them, or the kids who have the resources for college but are simply not disciplined enough to succeed there. Their parents might refer to them as good kids who just don't know what they want to pursue in life. They remain in their parents' home into their twenties and beyond and seem to be taking a long time arriving at adulthood. They take advantage of their parents, and they know it. They don't feel good about it, but they are simply not disciplined enough to do differently.

Authoritarian parenting produces somewhat worse outcomes. The children's behavior is controlled, and they tend to be obedient conformists. But they suffer emotionally, often being unhappy. Perhaps because their parents have stereotypically hierarchical relationships with them, conflict cannot be resolved, so they have more frequent conflict with their parents, which is very stressful for both child and parent (Dixon, Brooks-Gunn, & Graber, 2008). Because they are emotionally unhealthy, they have trouble with relationships. Their parents never listened to their needs and desires, and so they relate to others on a superficial level, never forming deep and meaningful intimate relationships. But they do behave. These kids are not skipping classes generally. They follow the rules or at least they are vigilant about the rules, knowing how to avoid getting caught for their misbehavior. Honesty and authenticity in relationships have not served them well because their parents would hear no reason or emotional pleas. Therefore, they resort to sneakiness when they must. But they generally conform and work hard, in an attempt to try to please their parents. Parents might refer to these as good kids who will "thank me later" for making them work so hard.

And finally, the worst outcomes are found in children whose parents used a neglectful style. Despite having their physical needs met, they were not nurtured emotionally, nor guided behaviorally. They have neither emotional stability nor well-controlled behavior. Their problematic outcomes seem to be exaggerated and extreme because they lack the skills needed to regulate their responses, either emotionally or behaviorally. When these kids act out, their misbehavior is likely far more extreme than kids raised with any of the other parenting styles. For instance, children with neglectful parents are the most frequent and extreme users of illicit drugs (Baumrind, 1991). In fact, children with neglectful parents are the most likely to engage in deviant and criminal acts more generally (Spraitz, 2011).

Given this review of outcomes, it's not surprising that parent education programs are largely concerned with promoting the authoritative parenting style. But there are other ways to think about parenting styles.

Parenting Style Matched to Context

While authoritative parenting is overall the most effective approach to the care of children, there are nuances. There are several ways that parenting style may need to be matched to the context.

A lot has been written about the cultural transferability (or not) of the Baumrind/Maccoby and Martin typology of parenting styles. Steinberg (2001) argues that the model works cross-culturally but notes that children in African American and Asian American homes in the United States do not respond as badly to authoritarian parenting as do white American children. Speculation about findings like these generally concludes that parenting styles are more or less effective given their context. Perhaps if the environment is relatively high risk, then authoritarian parenting is more effective because it offers some protections from the risky environment. Perhaps if authoritarian parenting is normative in the cultural environment, then it is not perceived quite so negatively and is thus less harmful.

Another aspect of context that may be relevant is the age of the child. An infant, for instance, does not really need behavioral discipline quite yet. Therefore, permissive parenting in infancy might be quite appropriate. And as children age from adolescence into emerging adulthood, they may need less parenting of any sort, so a neglectful approach might be perfectly acceptable.

One model in the literature offers a way to systematically think about matching the parenting style to the child's needs. Rich Berrett (2006) proposes that, just as there are two dimensions of parenting behaviors (responsiveness and demandingness), we might consider two dimensions of children's behaviors as well. He suggests that those two dimensions are motivation and ability. Notice that these dimensions are highly context specific and apply only to a given task or behavior rather than being used to generally describe a whole person. **Motivation** is the emotional dimension; it is the energy with which a child approaches the task at hand. A highly motivated child is eager and enthusiastic, or at least sincere and committed. A highly motivated child approaches a given task with an honest desire for the experience. **Ability** is the behavioral dimension; it is skill. A highly skilled child has become proficient at the task at hand. This is not an emotional state; this is an objective level of competence at the task.

If we divide each continuum into "high" and "low" as was done with parental sensitivity and demandingness, we can classify a child's state on a 2 × 2 table. Refer back to Table 1.1. Note that these classifications are context dependent. A child who is forced to go to school but doesn't believe it is useful could be classified as low on motivation and low on ability with regard to school. The child's position might change over time if he begins to enjoy school or if he masters some of the content in his classes. But at any one time, the child could be classified, for a given task, as falling into one of the four categories.

According to Berrett's model, an unmotivated child needs parental responsiveness. The emotional dimension of behavior requires the emotional dimension of parenting. Similarly, an unskilled child needs parental demandingness; the behavioral dimension of the child's behavior requires the behavioral dimension of parenting. The implications of this pairing are specified on Table 1.2.

Table 1.2 Berrett's Dimensions of Children's Behavior

	Low Level of Ability	High Level of Ability
Low Level of Motivation	Requires Authoritative Parenting.	Requires Permissive Parenting.
High Level of Motivation	Requires Authoritarian Parenting.	Requires Negligent Parenting.

Let us consider some examples. Athletes often describe their very best, most beloved and effective coaches in a manner that sounds quite authoritarian. "He wouldn't let me get away with slacking off." "She pushed me hard. Even when I didn't know if I could do it, she insisted." I've said the same things of amazing professors I've had. Why is it that an authoritarian style, in the context of coaching or teaching, can produce good effects as well as affection and gratitude? Berrett's model can explain this. If a young person is playing a sport that he or she had to try out for, then that must mean he or she is already quite motivated to play the sport. But as they progress in their sport, they lack the required abilities for each new level. That means they have low ability (relative to the specific task) and high motivation (relative to the specific task). Therefore (consult Table 1.2), they would require authoritarian parenting (or coaching). Similarly, if a student seeks out a class because they have chosen their own major, that student will be motivated to succeed in the class. But their ability in that specific subject is low, which is why they need the class in the first place. Again, that student would require authoritarian parenting (or teaching).

But the very same high school or college student, when faced with a different task, might require a different style of parenting/coaching/teaching. If the young person likes a clean room and is therefore highly motivated to keep a clean room and has developed habits of consciousness that we could say reflect the ability to keep a clean room, then the parent could adopt a negligent parenting approach in that area.

This model might help to explain exceptions to the general rule, which is that under most circumstances children could use help with both motivation and ability. This is simply due to their status as children, which necessarily infers lack of experience and perspective. They don't know what they don't know, and they don't know why they need to know it. Consequently, most of the time, authoritative parenting (or teaching or coaching) is the most appropriate approach.

So Berrett's model is a proposal for how parenting style might be nuanced. The tenets and hypotheses have never been tested empirically, so I cannot say if it works or not. But the proposal itself is an example of how complicated the issue of parenting style is. It is likely that there is a lot that remains to be discovered about the role of context in parenting.

Expert Parenting Advice

We see that there are several possible approaches that parents use to meet the demands of the job of parenting. This is different from what happens in most other species. Other animals seem hard-wired to know how to care for their young. Readers may have seen cats or dogs give birth, and they seem immediately and automatically to know how to clean their young and nurse them. We don't see other adult cats hanging around offering advice and assistance. We don't see the new mama dog looking up in terror and confusion, at a loss for what to do. They just do the job. But we, on the other hand, are often plagued by the realization that we don't know what we're doing and fear of what to do next.

After the birth of my oldest child, it seemed I was toting her in to the doctor's office every couple of days for her to be weighed and checked. It seemed that the good doctor was just checking in on things to make sure everything was proceeding as it should. Until I got the surprising news after one such visit that they would see me "in a couple of months." I couldn't believe it. I didn't feel like I'd succeeded, I felt terrified. I may have even said out loud "You're going to trust me with her for that long?" Which was absurd. I had a PhD in Human Development and Family Studies; you'd think I would feel confident taking care of a baby. But somehow, I didn't. It was scary. She was so vulnerable. So precious and breakable (Figure 1.6). And I didn't know what I was supposed to be doing.

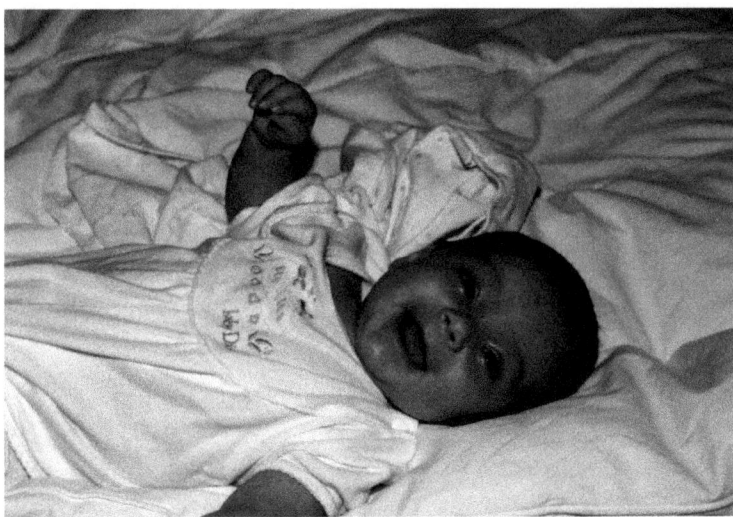

Figure 1.6 First Baby

Perhaps this emotional vulnerability, tied to a new baby's physical vulnerability, drives the demand for parenting advice. But whatever the reason, parents seek out a lot of advice to help with child care. And everyone seems willing to oblige. The pediatrician hands out flyers on typical questions for the child's age. The church offers parenting classes. Older members of the family sometimes descend upon the new parents, so much so that the stereotype of a helpful mother or mother-in-law showing up when a new baby is to be born is well known, as is the stereotype of an intrusive grandparent or in-law offering advice that the new parent doesn't want. As if that's not enough, perfect strangers in public places often pipe up with suggestions as well.

Human Evolution

One way to look at this is to consider the evolutionary history of our species. Some species (**specialist species**) evolve to live in a very specific environment, and they can only live in that particular environment. They may be spectacularly successful there, but their success is tied to the details of the place, the food sources of the place. For instance, some birds have very specialized beaks that allow them to exploit a very specific food source. Examples include the spoonbill, the shoebill, and the red crossbill. Their names include descriptions of the unique features of their bills that are specialized to a particular environment and food source. For example, the sword-billed hummingbird (see Figure 1.7) has an unbelievably long beak, longer than its body, in fact, which allows it to feed on flowers unavailable to other birds.

Figure 1.7 Sword-billed Hummingbird

This is evolution working through specialization. These specialist species become endangered or go extinct when the climate changes, when their habitat is reduced or altered, or when their primary food source is depleted. They are unable to migrate to new locations because they have adapted so perfectly to the place where they are. The koala is another good example of a specialist species; it only has one food source: eucalyptus. Another classic example is the duck-billed platypus, an animal so specialized that it can only live in a particular environment in Australia.

A different evolutionary strategy, however, is to generalize, which is the strategy used by humans (**generalist species**). Our bodies are generalized such that we can adapt using culture to virtually any environment in the world. The human species lives comfortably on every single continent except Antarctica. Instead of specializing to the cold by growing a heavy fur coat, we adapt culturally by using other animals' fur coats. When we go to warmer climes, we take off the fur coat and find ways to stay cool. Our bodies are generalized enough that they can adapt to both the very cold of the Arctic Circle and the intense heat of the tropics. We can exploit virtually any food source available because we have not grown specialized appendages (such as bills), but we instead use tools. This strategy of generalization means that, as a species, we are very flexible. We can live almost anywhere.

As a generalist species, however, humans must rely less on instinct and more on learning and innovation. We are not specialized to a given environment; we have to learn how to live there, and we share what we learn with other members of our species. Therefore, our collective knowledge is immense and can be passed on to others. As a group, we make progress because of that shared knowledge and the processes we have for sharing it. This can be extended to parenting. We are not hard-wired to care for our babies in any one particular way; we must be flexible enough to care for them in a way that matches our environment. As a result, our reliance on parenting advice, and even drastic changes in parenting advice over time, and the variety of parenting advice offered in different contexts is all natural and necessary.

Traditional folk wisdom was the essence of parenting advice for millennia, and certainly the advice varied from one locale to another, from one culture to another, from one type of economy to another. However, most people did not encounter such diversity in their daily lives. They lived in homogeneous communities and received the local folk wisdom about the care of children.

Industrial Revolution

The **Industrial Revolution**, when manufacturing replaced agriculture as the foundation of the world's most powerful economies, gradually transformed the culture, economy, and families of the United States. One marker of the effect of industrialization is urbanization. In the late 1800s, the US population was mostly rural; only about 20% lived in cities. But currently, the numbers are exactly reversed; now, only 20% of the US population live in rural areas (US Census Bureau, 2012).

With the shift into population centers, most parents were raising children in a totally different environment from where they had grown up. Furthermore, people lived close to one another in the cities and interacted regularly with people who were culturally different from themselves. Therefore, folk wisdom became less useful as parents and grandparents had no advice for the specific circumstances of people's lives.

Such drastic changes in living conditions prompted concerns about parenting. Middle-class mothers started meeting in maternal associations to discuss child-rearing. A call went out to experts in the brand-new fields of psychology and child study to apply science to child-rearing (Hulbert, 2003). And the experts answered the call, essentially inventing the discipline of parent education (Croake & Glover, 1977). Academic programs in Home Economics emerged after the land grant university system was created in 1862, and these programs began to disseminate parenting advice (Stolz, 2011).

However, parenting education from outside of the academic discipline of Home Economics gained a foothold in popular culture and was found more compelling than the professional advice based on the science of child study. Hulbert (2003) notes in her history of parent education that the most successful advisers were not necessarily the ones who were most measured and careful, but instead, the bombastic and extreme advisers captured a larger audience. This was the heyday of the behaviorists (whom we will discuss at length in Chapter 7). Not surprisingly given the era, the first best-selling expert parenting advice recommended a behaviorist approach. The very first in a series of best-selling parenting manuals was *The Care and Feeding of Children: A Catechism for the Use of Mothers and Children's Nurses* (1894) by Luther Emmett Holt, a pediatrician. He recommended regularity and discipline, but was not supportive of affection and warmth in parenting. Consider this line from his book: "Babies under six months should never be played with: and the less of it at anytime the better for the infant." He recommended what Baumrind would later classify as an authoritarian approach.

John Watson's 1928 book *The Psychological Care of Infant and Child*, the next in the series of best-selling parenting advice manuals, also recommended an authoritarian parenting style: strict behavioral control with little emotional warmth. For instance, John Watson famously recommended that parents "Never let them sit on your lap. If you must, kiss them once on the forehead when they say good night. Shake hands with them in the morning. Give them a pat on the head if they have made an extraordinary job of a difficult task" (Watson, 1928). All of this came from a chapter of his book entitled "The Danger of Too Much Mother Love." That's pretty harsh!

Why did the early experts recommend the authoritarian style, a style that today we regard to be harmful? Well, both Holt and Watson were out of their depth. They wrote parenting manuals but had no expertise in parenting. Holt was a pediatrician. Watson was a psychologist who studied learning. What they offered was simply bad advice that reflected their theoretical leanings but had no empirical support.

But, it is also possible that industrialization had created an economy within which authoritarian parenting was more effective than it is now. The goal of parenting, after all, is always to produce children who are capable of becoming productive members of the society. After the Industrial Revolution, that meant being capable of working in factories or doing other kinds of wage labor that required obedience and conformity (see Figure 1.8.). Children with authoritarian parents may have benefited by their employability, and the style may have been less harmful simply because it was more normative than it is today. At the very least, this would have made sense to parents of the time, and this might have made them open to hearing the advice offered by Holt and Watson.

Nazi Holocaust

The **Nazi Holocaust**, the genocide perpetrated in western Europe under Germany's Third Reich, changed the way the parenting experts considered their advice. As the world tried to make sense of the horrific crimes against humanity (see Figure 1.9) that had been committed in Germany, everyone wondered how this could possibly have been done on such a scale. Millions of people had been brutally killed. Yes, there were some very evil people who served as masterminds, but their plans only came to fruition because of many ordinary

Figure 1.8 Assembly Line

people who obeyed immoral commands to execute innocent people. Perhaps that sort of obedience to authority and conformity—just the sort promoted by authoritarian parenting—was dangerous.

Political opposition to Fascist (authoritarian) governments naturally translated into a suspicion of authoritarian parenting as well. The cultural tide in the United States turned against obedience and conformity as goals of parenting. The changes were epitomized in one of the best-selling books of all time, a new best-selling parenting advice manual by the pediatrician Benjamin Spock (1946) entitled *The Common Sense Book of Baby and Child Care*. His advice contrasted with the behaviorists from early in the century because he essentially gave parents permission to be affectionate and loving, and he promised them that they could trust their instincts. "Don't be afraid to trust your own common sense," he wrote. "What good mothers and fathers instinctively feel like doing for their babies is usually best" (Spock, 1946). It was a clear repudiation of the earlier behaviorist body of parenting advice (Pace, 1998).

Dr. Spock's advice, when compared to what had come before it, may be considered permissive, although Spock himself rejected this characterization (Reed, 1983). This move toward permissive parenting in expert advice can be seen as a reaction against the authoritarian parenting recommended previously. If it had produced obedience to the degree that otherwise decent human beings would participate in something as awful as the Holocaust, then it makes sense that the pendulum would swing decidedly in the opposite direction.

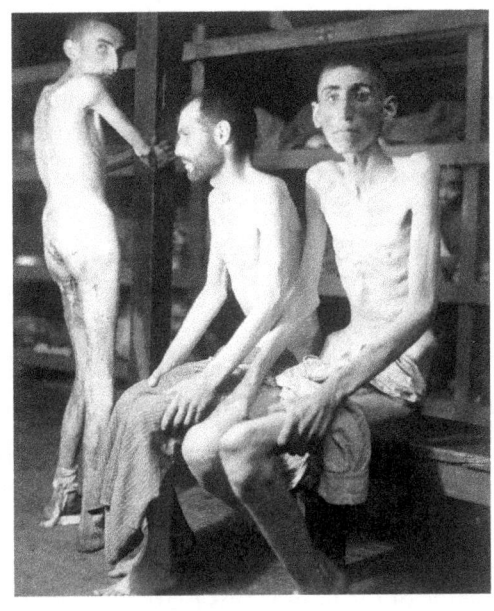

Figure 1.9 Nazi Holocaust

Spock's book was the undisputed leader of parenting advice manuals for decades. Spock revised the book multiple times, holding firm to the principle that parental hesitancy is the biggest barrier to effective parenting. He wanted parents to stop relying on experts telling them to do things that felt wrong and to instead rely on their instincts (Hulbert, 2003). The irony, of course, is that many parents relied on his advice rather than their own instincts. I've met many parents who confess to having kept multiple copies of Spock's book around the house so that they could refer to it on the spot whenever a parenting problem arose. My own mother lost faith in the parenting experts fairly early into her role as parent, but I still have the copy of Spock's book that I found on a shelf in the basement of my childhood home. Spock was ubiquitous for several decades of the mid-twentieth century.

Just as there is an economic explanation for the ubiquity of advice recommending authoritarian parenting early in the century, there is a similar explanation for the move toward more permissive parenting mid-century. Thanks to new computer technology, the economy of the United States was moving toward a reliance on creativity and ideas rather than the mechanization of the Industrial Revolution. Instead of each person doing their part on an assembly line of a factory, now the valuable employees were the ones who could work creatively with knowledge and ideas. And they had to be able to work with each other; interpersonal skills were becoming more important in the workplace. It is possible that permissive parenting fosters these characteristics more than authoritarian parenting did, or at least that such an argument would have made sense to parents at the time.

Social Revolution

The permissive parenting recommended mid-century occurred at the same time that a social revolution was brewing in the United States. (See Table 1.3 for a summary of these historical eras.) During World War II, a wave of women had moved into the work force. Black women had been engaged in paid employment for nearly a century; immigrant women had worked as household servants for just as long, but for the first time, it became normative for white women to work outside of the home. This marked a sea change in the dominant US culture. The women's rights movement, the civil rights movement, the LGBT rights movement, and the peace movement all converged over decades and exploded in the 1960s and 1970s in a social revolution. Collectively, this social revolution drastically changed US culture.

Some blamed the social upheaval of the 1960s on permissive parenting. In fact, some blamed it directly on Dr. Spock. The Reverend Norman Vincent Peale, a religious leader who supported the Vietnam War and resented Dr. Spock's opposition to the war, was one of his most vocal critics. Children raised by the principles of Spock's advice have been called "the Spock generation." These were the kids who, according to Peale, "were Spocked when they should have been spanked!" Peale asserted that the anti-Vietnam War movement was

Table 1.3 History of Parenting Advice

Historical Event	Parenting Style Recommended	Predominant Parenting Advice Manual(s)
Industrial Revolution	Authoritarian	*The Care and Feeding of Children*, Lester Holt (1894) & *The Psychological Care of Infant and Child,* John Watson (1928)
Nazi Holocaust	Permissive	*Common Sense Book of Baby and Child Care,* Benjamin Spock (1946)
Social Revolution	Authoritative	None—explosion of self-help literature, multiple books in competition and contradiction

a disgrace, and further stated that "the US is paying the price for two generations that followed the Dr. Spock baby plan of instant gratification of needs" (Pace, 1998).

Decades later, it seems foolish to suggest that Dr. Spock single-handedly caused the social revolution of the 1960s. But an observer of history might note how remarkable it is that expert parenting advice had taken on such a prominent role in society that it was even remotely plausible that a book on baby care could have forged political and cultural change. But the social revolution did usher in a time of an explosion of parenting advice and scientific research on parenting. Diana Baumrind first published her model of parenting styles at this time, in the late 1960s. Research soon established that the authoritative parenting style is associated with better outcomes than either authoritarian or permissive parenting. While parenting advice had been big business for several decades already, the field of evidence-based parent education emerged as a professional discipline in the 1970s.

Baumrind's model of parenting styles reflected and shaped a scientific consensus about the effectiveness of authoritative parenting. Finally, the experts converged around science instead of ideologically driven advice. Finally, the experts had a consistent message about balance between the prior extremes. True experts, family scientists who empirically study parenting, generally agree on fundamental principles that will be expounded below. But first, what happened to the parenting advice industry when science intervened?

Current State of Parenting Advice

The parenting advice industry had grown to be such big business that it was largely unaffected by the progress of family science. In fact, availability of parenting advice from those posing as experts but without expertise exploded along with the whole self-help movement of the 1970s. A search of "parenting" on amazon.com in late 2016 yielded more than 237,000 hits. Gone are the days of a single parenting manual dominating the market. Now we have thousands of parenting manuals available at any given time, and most are written by people with little or no qualifications. One review of parenting advice books pertaining to infant sleep (Ramos & Youngclarke, 2006) found that half of the books had authors with no professional credentials of any sort, and the vast majority (75%) had authors who had never published in the academic literature.

Despite the lack of a clear front-runner analogous to Dr. Spock from a half-century ago, there are still some big names in the parenting advice area. Many of these have a medical background, similar to the earlier parent advisers Drs. Holt and Spock. This includes T. Berry Brazelton (*The Brazelton Way* and *Touchpoints*) and William Sears (*The Baby Book*, *The Discipline Book*, etc.), both medical doctors with no family science background. Still others have no professional credentials at all, such as Heidi Muroff, the author of the *What to Expect* series, and Faber and Mazlish of *How to Talk So Kids Will Listen* fame. Much of what they write is wonderful and consistent with the scientific consensus about parenting. But these so-called experts coexist, sharing the spotlight with each other and often competing with and contradicting each other and other parent advisers who are writing books that fill the bookshelves in the *Parenting* section of the local bookstore.

So the quantity of parenting advice has expanded, but the quality of advice coming from those without expertise is as mixed as it ever was. Some of it is admirable. A review of parenting advice in *Essence* magazine found that parenting advice in the magazine clearly advocated authoritative parenting and denounced physical punishment (Prusank & Duran, 2014). But a content analysis of parenting advice on *Yahoo Parenting* found it to be fear based with almost no references to published empirical research (Ram, Seiler, & Rickman, 2016). No wonder parents feel overwhelmed by "expert" advice and mistrust it.

Current Scientific Consensus

While the mainstream parenting advice business is a hopelessly tangled mess of the reliable and the ridiculous, a scientific consensus has developed in family science regarding parenting education. Ann Hulbert, who has written a history of parenting advice in the 20th century (2003), argues that parenting advice reflects a fundamental tension in the job of parenting: the tension between power and intimacy. She argues that the parenting pendulum swings back and forth between an emphasis on parental power and control (a parent-centered approach) and meeting children's need for warmth and intimacy (a child-centered approach) because the two are in constant—and inevitable—tension.

Family scientists have arrived at the same conclusion and call parenting that achieves balance between these extremes authoritative parenting. Successful parenting is not a matter of finding out which side is right, because both are right. Parenting is a matter of balancing these two opposing forces. The balance is bound to look different at different points in time, for different parents, with different children, living in different cultural and family contexts. But there are few principles that professional parent educators, experts who actually have expertise, generally agree on.

First, **authoritative parenting** produces the best outcomes. Children need both behavioral control and emotional support, and authoritative parenting offers both. While there might be nonexperts writing books promoting either authoritarian parenting or permissive parenting, this is no longer truly a debate. What exactly that balance looks like will vary, but the fact that a balance is needed is universally endorsed. Every subsequent chapter of this book addresses the balance between the behavioral and emotional demands of parenting.

Second, **psychological control** is damaging to children. Psychological control tactics include the use of shame, guilt, or withdrawal of affection to control behavior. These techniques are manipulative and destructive of both the child's psychological health and the parent-child relationship (Barber, 1996). More on this especially in Chapter 5.

Third, **secure attachment** in infancy and early childhood lays the foundation for emotional health and relationship success later in life. Tender and sensitive caregiving of young children is necessary for all children in all cultures. Infants cannot be spoiled. Crying should not be ignored. While some nonexperts still say that babies shouldn't be held or kissed, and while our stores are full of objects to replace parental affection, no expert supports this nonsense. This idea is addressed in great detail in Chapter 3.

Fourth, **harsh punishment** is harmful. While the research on corporal punishment is quite complicated the one thing family science experts agree on, unequivocally, is that frequent and/or harsh physical punishment is problematic (Gershoff, 2013). More on this in Chapter 7.

Fifth, **parental supervision** and monitoring help prevent problem behaviors. Kids simply do better when parents know where they are and who they are with. This seems true even when such monitoring does not coincide with restrictiveness or permissiveness. Independently of behavioral control, then, parental awareness seems to reduce high-risk behaviors. This is addressed more specifically in Chapter 7.

Part II of this text contains specific strategies that all work toward these ends. These are the guidelines around which our discipline has professional consensus. There is still plenty of room for diversity, but these points represent the knowledge in which we are secure. These are the principles that do not change.

Conclusion

Thus we can conclude, here at the beginning of our study of parent education, that parenting is important and deserving of serious consideration. There are multiple parenting styles that parents adopt when they approach this very difficult job, and these styles are shaped by the historical and economic context. The most effective parenting reflects a balance of emotional nurturing and behavioral guidance.

There is no one *single* thing that is good parenting. The scientific consensus is that authoritative parenting, secure attachment, and parental supervision are indicators of "good" parenting. However, note that each one describes a balance rather than a specific practice. Authoritative parenting is a balance of control and nurturing, but there are no specific practices required of authoritative parenting, and the balance will look different in different contexts, as we will discuss in Chapter 2. Secure attachment is also on the list, but as we will discover in Chapter 3, secure attachment is formed through care that is sensitively responsive. That does not require a specific practice; it varies based on the needs of the specific child. And finally, parental supervision is on the list. Supervision implies involvement in the details of a child's life, but there are many possible ways to do that. In short, good parenting comes in many forms but within some constraints. This understanding lays the foundation for our exploration of parent education.

Review and Reflection Questions

1. What is "good enough" parenting? Do you think there is a reason to educate good enough parents?

2. What are the positive and negative effects of parenting on parents? How does this match what you would have thought were the effects of parenting?

3. What are the two dimensions of parenting? The four parenting styles? Outcomes of each? What style did your parents use? Does the outcome match your experience?

4. How does Berrett propose matching parenting style to the needs of the child?

5. Why do humans need parenting advice even though other animals parent by instinct?

6. What parenting style was advised by experts after the Industrial Revolution? Why?

7. Why did the Nazi Holocaust change the minds of parent advisers? What style did they recommend afterward?

8. Why did the social revolution of the 1960s change the opinions of parent advisers? What style did they recommend afterward?

9. What is the current scientific consensus about effective parenting? What implications does this have for parent educators?

Terminology to Know

- Authoritarian parenting
- Authoritative parenting
- Generalist species
- Good-enough mother
- Industrial Revolution
- Nazi Holocaust
- Neglectful/uninvolved/withdrawn parenting
- Parental demandingness/guidance/control
- Parental responsiveness/nurturance/warmth
- Parenting style
- Permissive/indulgent parenting
- Social revolution
- Specialist species

Names to Know

- Baumrind
- Berrett
- Holt
- Spock
- Watson
- Winnicott

References

Ambert, A.M. (2001). *The effect of children on parents, 2nd edition*. Routledge.

Barber, B.K. (1996). Parental psychological control: Revisiting a neglected construct. *Child Development, 67,* 3296–3319.

Barber, B.K., Stolz, H.E., Olsen, J.A., Collins, W.A., & Burchinal, M. (2005). Parental support, psychological control, and behavioral control: Assessing relevance across time, culture, and method. *Monographs of the Society for Research in Child Development, 70, 4,* i–147.

Baumrind, D. (1967). Child care practices anteceding three patterns of preschool behavior. *Genetic Psychology Monographs, 75, 1,* 43–88.

Baumrind, D. (1991). The influence of parenting style on adolescent competence and substance abuse. *Journal of Early Adolescence, 11,* 56–95.

Baumrind, D., & Larzelere, R.E. (2010). Effects of preschool parents' power assertive patterns and practices on adolescent development. *Parenting: Science and Practice, 10,* 157–201.

Berrett, R.D. (2006). An exploration of human behavior. In R.D. Berrett & K.D. Ramos (Eds.), *Engaged Parenting.* Pearson Custom Publishing.

Bourke, D.H. (2012). It will change your life, in *Everyday Miracles.* Bonfire Books. http://www.dalehansonbourke.com/it-will-change-your-life-2/ Retrieved 12/19/2016.

Croake, J.W., & Glover, K.E. (1977). A history and evaluation of parent education. *Family Coordinator, 26, 2,* 151–158.

Darling, N., & Steinberg, L. (1993). Parenting style as context: An integrative model. *Child Development, 113,* 487–496.

Dewar, G. (2010). Parenting styles: A guide for the science-minded. *Parenting Science.* http://www.parentingscience.com/parenting-styles.html Retrieved 12/19/2016.

Dixon, S.V., Brooks-Gunn, J., & Graber, J.A. (2008). The roles of respect for parental authority and parenting practices in parent-child conflict among African American, Latino, and European American families. *Journal of Family Psychology, 22, 1,* 1–10.

Gershoff, E.T. (2013). Spanking and child development: We know enough now to stop hitting our children. *Child Development Perspectives, 7, 3,* 133–137.

Hansen, T. (2012). Parenthood and Happiness: A review of folk theories versus empirical evidence. *Social Indicators Research, 108,* 26–64.

Hirschberger, G., Srivastava, S., Marsh, P., Cowan, C.P., & Cowan, P.A. (2009). Attachment, marital satisfaction, and divorce during the first fifteen years of parenthood. *Personal Relationships, 16, 3,* 401–420.

Holt, L.E. (1894). *The care and feeding of children: A catechism for the use of mothers and children's nurses.*

Hulbert, A. (2003). *Raising America: Experts, parents, and a century of advice about children.* Knopf.

Lino, M. (2014). Expenditures on children by families, 2013. US Department of Agriculture, Center for Nutrition Policy and Promotion. Miscellaneous Publication No. 1528–2013.

Maccoby, E.E., & Martin, J.A. (1983). Socialization in the context of the family: Parent-child interaction. In Mussen, P.H., & Hetherington, E.M. *Manual of child psychology, Volume 4: Social development*. New York: John Wiley and Sons, pp. 1–101.

Medina, A.M., Lederhos, C.L., & Lillis, T.A. (2009). Sleep disruption and decline in marital satisfaction across the transition to parenthood. *Families, Systems, and Health, 27, 2*, 153–160.

Pace, E. (1998). Benjamin Spock, world's pediatrician, dies at 94. *New York Times*, March 17, 1998. Retrieved 12/24/2016.

Palkovitz, R., Marks, L.D., Appleby, D.W., & Kramer Holmes, E. (2002) Parenting and Adult Development. Faculty Publications and Presentations. Paper 9. http://digitalcommons.liberty.edu/ccfs_fac_pubs/9 Retrieved 12/19/2016.

Parker, K. (2014). Parenthood and happiness: It's more complicated than you think. http://www.pewresearch.org/fact-tank/2014/02/07/parenthood-and-happiness-its-more-complicated-than-you-think/ Accessed 5/17/2016.

Parker, K., Horowitz, J.M., & Rohal, M. (2015). Parenting in America: Outlook, worries, aspirations are strongly linked to financial situation. Pew Research Center. http://www.pewsocialtrends.org/2015/12/17/parenting-in-america/ Retrieved 12/22/2016.

Prusank, D.T., & Duran, R. (2014). Walking the tightrope: Parenting advice in *Essence* magazine. *Howard Journal of Communications, 25*, 77–97.

Ram, A., Seiler, A., & Rickman, A. (2016). Mediated realities: Identifying themes in digital parenting news magazine content. Poster presentation at the 37th Annual Central California Research Symposium, Fresno, California, April 20, 2016.

Ramos, K.D., & Youngclarke, D. (2006). Parenting advice books about child sleep: Cosleeping and crying-it-out. *Sleep, 29(12)*, 1608–1615.

Reed, R. (1983). Dr. Spock, at 80, still giving advice. *New York Times*, May 2, 1983.

Schulz, M.S., Cowan, C.P., & Cowan, P.A. (2006). Promoting healthy beginnings: A randomized controlled trial of a preventive intervention to preserve marital quality during the transition to parenthood. *Journal of Consulting and Clinical Psychology, 74, 1*, 20–31.

Spock, B. (1946). *The common sense book of baby and child care*. Duell, Sloan, & Pearce.

Spraitz, J.D. (2011). Parenting styles and criminal involvement: A test of Baumrind's theory. (Unpublished doctoral dissertation). Indiana University of Pennsylvania.

Steinberg, L. (2001). We know some things: Parent-adolescent relationships in retrospect and prospect. *Journal of Research on Adolescence, 11, 1*, 1–19.

Stolz, H. (2011). Parenting Education. In S.F. Duncan & H.W. Goddard (Eds.), *Family life education: Principles and practices for effective outreach, 2nd edition*, pp. 191–210. Thousand Oaks, CA: Sage.

Taylor, P., Funk, C., & Clark, A. (2007). As marriage and parenthood drift apart, public is concerned about social impact. Pew Research Center. http://www.pewsocialtrends.org/files/2007/07/Pew-Marriage-report-6-28-for-web-display.pdf Retrieved 12/18/2016.

US Census Bureau (2012). *United States Summary: 2010. 2010 Census of Population and Housing, Population and Housing Unit Counts*, CPH-2-5. US Government Printing Office, Washington, DC.

Watson. J. (1928). *The psychological care of infant and child*. New York: W.W. Norton & Co.

Winnicott, D. (1953). Transitional objects and transitional phenomena: A study of the first not-me possession. *International Journal of Psychoanalysis, 34, 2*, 89–97.

Credits

- Fig. 1.3: Copyright © 2015 by Raymond Hall. Reprinted with permission.
- Fig. 1.4: Source: Pew Research Center.
- Fig. 1.5: Source: Pew Research Center.
- Fig. 1.7: Copyright © 2013 by Drferry / Wikimedia Commons, (CC BY-SA 3.0) at https://commons.wikimedia.org/wiki/File:Male_Swordbilled_Hummingbird.jpg.
- Fig. 1.8: Copyright in the Public Domain.
- Fig. 1.9: Pvt. H. Miller / Copyright in the Public Domain.

2. Contemporary Parenthood

Introduction

So far, we have established that parenting is an important area of study, one that is a primary force shaping the lives of both children and their parents. Scientific study of parenting in the 20th century has finally brought us some degree of expert consensus about the components of effective parenting. They are guidelines rather than strict rules, and we know that parents implement them differently based on the specific context of parenthood.

Parent educators may see parents in a very narrow and artificial environment, that of a classroom, only once, or spanning just a few weeks of time. It is difficult to have a sense of perspective, to understand the broader circumstances under which the parents are operating. But a narrow focus that is not appropriately cognizant of the broader context is dangerous because it lends itself to a judgmental and condescending attitude, and that is counterproductive in a parent educator. So we must ask ourselves, What brings parents into that classroom? Why are they behaving as they do? This will help us construct advice that will meet them where they are.

Demographics of Parenthood

Now that reliable and effective contraception is widely available, birth rates are dropping, not just in the United States but around the world. Where we once worried about overpopulation, now industrialized countries are very concerned about birth rates that have fallen below replacement level. This creates an aging population without the economic resources of a younger generation to support it (Turner, 2009). Birth rates have declined to unprecedented lows. Even so, a large majority of adults in the United States still become parents. But while most adults become parents, they are having significantly fewer children than just a few decades ago.

Fertility Rate

In order to see how I reached these conclusions, let's consider what we mean by *birth rate*. The birth rate is a measure of how many babies are born in a given time period relative to some standard. The most widely used and most precise birth rate is a **general fertility rate**, which is the number of babies born per year relative to the number of people who could possibly have given birth. "People who could possibly have given birth" are women of childbearing age; that is, past puberty but who have not yet reached menopause. This is generally considered as ages 15 to 44. This is the standard format for the general fertility rate. If we consider the previous century (see Figure 2.1), it is clear that the general fertility rate in the United States is currently much lower than it has been historically.

The birth rate dropped during the Great Depression and then rose with the post–World War II baby boom, when the birth rate rose drastically higher than it had been, and remained high for about two decades. Then came the birth control pill (invented in 1960) and the end of the postwar economic boom. The birth rate plummeted to new lows and has remained fairly constantly low ever since. We are currently hovering around 65 births per year per 1,000 women of childbearing age.

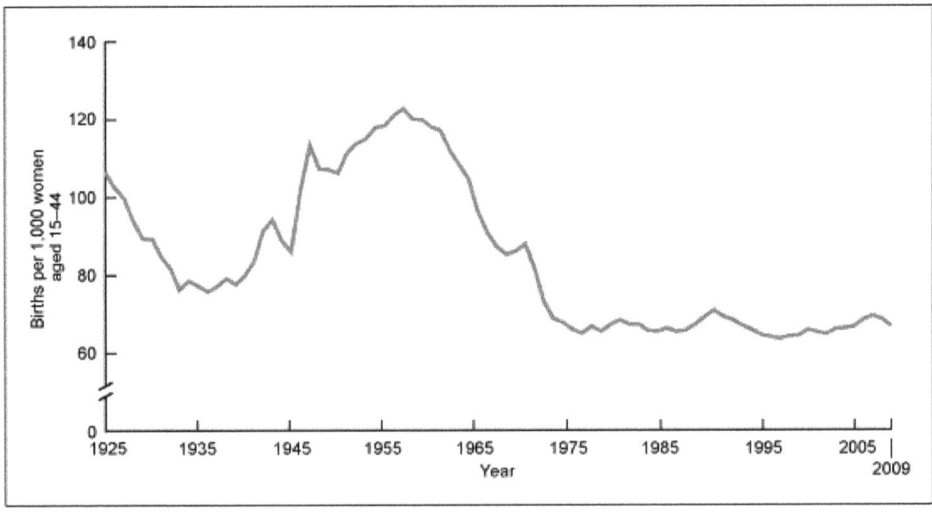

Figure 2.1 Fertility Rate: United States 1925–2009

Notice that this number is absolutely precise. Once a year is over, demographers can simply get a count of how many births occurred that year, and a count of how many women were of childbearing age. As long as we have reliable counts (and we do, given the Bureau of Vital Statistics and the Census Bureau) then it is simple math to determine the general fertility rate. We can easily compare one year to another to see historical trends. We can also compare one ethnic group to another, one family structure to another, etc.

But first, let's consider another way to conceptualize the birth rate. While the general fertility rate is precise, it is not intuitively meaningful and it doesn't tell us much about the experience of a typical woman. Therefore, another option is the **total fertility rate**, which is the average number of babies born to women while they are in their childbearing years (that is, aged 15 to 44). This number is appealing because it is far more intuitive, and it adds information about typical family size. At the peak of the baby boom in the late 1950s, the total fertility rate in the United States was 3.7 children born to each woman. The total fertility rate in the United States had dropped to 1.9 by 2014 (Mather, 2014). When the total fertility rate drops below 2.0—**replacement level**—then the population is not producing enough babies to replace itself and will start to age and then shrink. The United States also attracts immigrants, so our population is not shrinking yet, but many other industrialized countries around the world are below replacement level and therefore dealing with the many problems of an aging population.

Stop for a moment to consider how this number is determined. We said that the total fertility rate in the United States was 1.9 in 2014. To be absolutely precise, the number could not have been calculated until women in 2014 reached the age of 45 years, so that we know how many children they actually gave birth to. But a lot of women in 2014 were only 40, or 30, or 20 years old. So how do demographers know how many babies they *will* have before they reach age 45? They don't know exactly, so the total fertility rate is an informed guess. Demographers do this by starting with the general fertility rate discussed above. They calculate a general fertility rate for women of a given age. They extrapolate that, if those numbers remain the same into the future, they predict how many babies each woman will have by the time she reaches age 45. Therefore, the total fertility rate, while intuitively meaningful and useful because of the information about family size, is more of a projection than a precise rate.

The total fertility rate is appealing because it tells us something about the typical experience of women, but it involves projection, and it also has the feature of providing a statistical mean, an average. As stated above, a woman in the US currently has, on average, 1.9 babies in her life. But notice that the average is somewhat nonsensical. Nobody actually has 1.9 children because there is no such thing as nine-tenths of a baby. A statistical mean is also problematic because it doesn't tell us anything about the range. We might want to know if there are many people whose number of children is meaningfully different from the average. For instance, how many people have 0 children? Has that number been changing? Has the total fertility rate declined because more people are opting out of parenthood altogether? Or is it because everyone is just having fewer children?

To answer these questions, we turn to a third way of considering birth rate, which is simply the percentage of women who meet a specific criterion. For instance, to answer the questions raised above, the percent of women at the end of their childbearing years who remain childless hovered at about 10% in the 1970s, then rose gradually to a high of 20% by 2005, and then declined again to 15% by 2014 and seems to be continuing that downward trajectory (Livingston, 2015). (See Figure 2.2.)

We can conclude therefore that a very large majority (85%) of women in the United States become parents. By and large, what seems to be driving the trend of lower birth rates is that people are having fewer children, rather than an increase in the number of people avoiding parenthood altogether. To illustrate, in 1976, 40% of mothers had four or more children, but in 2014, that number was down to 14% (Livingston, 2015).

What are we to make of these general demographic trends? Well, we live longer but spend far less time actively caring for children. As family sizes have gotten smaller, people have less exposure to younger siblings, and they become aunts and uncles at later ages. Consequently, they may come to the job of parenting less prepared and less comfortable with children than did their parents and grandparents. It may not be unusual for a new parent never to have held and cared for a baby before holding his or her own newborn child. Additionally, parents are increasingly likely to have only one or two children, so that we simply have fewer experienced parents raising children. Smaller family size also means that parents offer more individual attention to each child (Strohschein, Gauthier, Campbell, & Kleparchuck, 2008). So this trend appears to have some advantages (parents have fuller lives with diverse aspects and they have more time to spend with each child) and some disadvantages (parents are less experienced and prepared for parenthood).

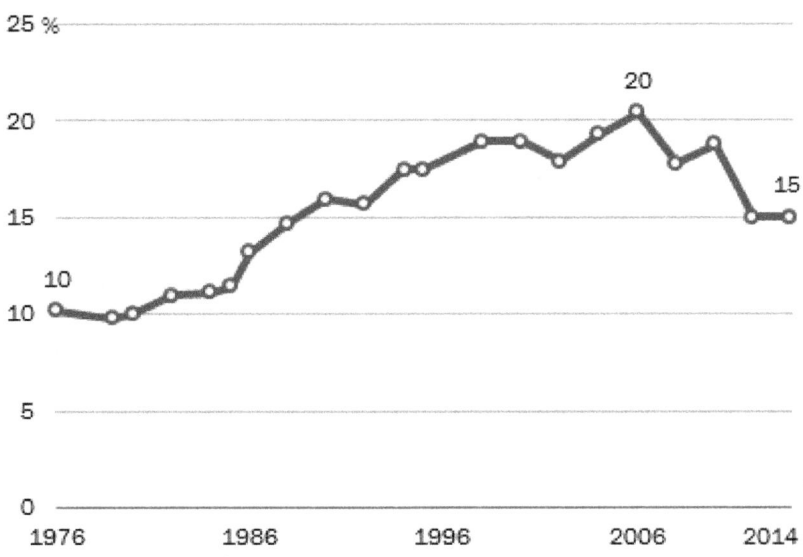

Figure 2.2 The Rise and Fall of Childlessness

Ethnicity and Age

We can use the general fertility rates discussed above to compare racial/ethnic groups to each other with regard to birth rates. It is clear (see Figure 2.3) that Hispanics have the highest general fertility rate in the United States (although it drastically declined between 2005 and 2010), and Asian Americans have the lowest (Martin, Hamilton, & Osterman, 2015).

In addition to Hispanics' higher general fertility rate than other groups, they also have the largest family sizes, as measured by total fertility rate (at

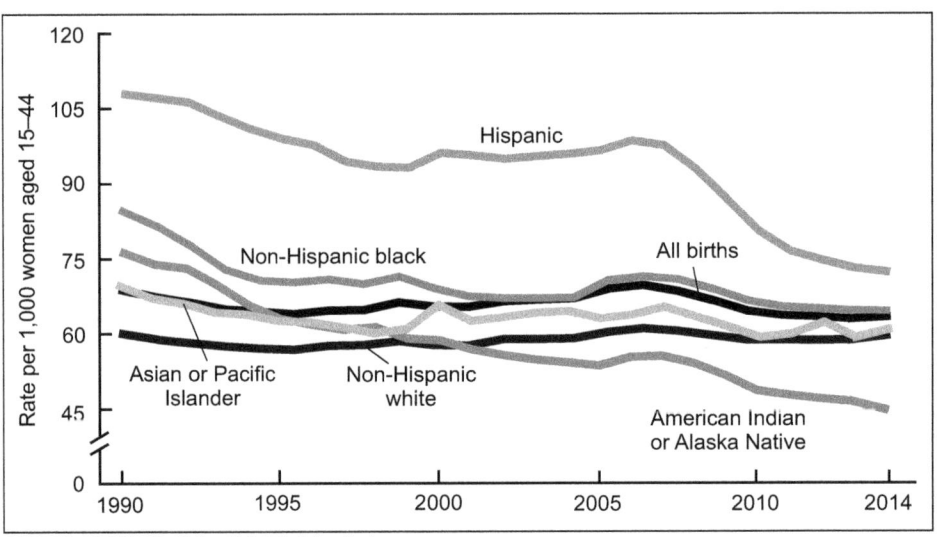

Figure 2.3 General Fertility Rates by race and Hispanic origin of mother: US, 1990–2014

2.4, compared to 2.1 for African Americans, and 1.8 for both Asian and white Americans) (Passel, Livingston, & Cohn, 2012). Fully 40% of Hispanic women have four or more children (compared to 18% of black women and 10% of Asian and white women) (Livingston, 2015). And finally, they are the least likely (10% chance) of all ethnic groups to remain childless (compared to 13% of Asian women, 15% of black women, and 17% of white women) (Livingston, 2015). Note that all three measures of fertility rate lead us to similar conclusions. There are robustly different fertility patterns across racial and ethnic groups.

Another demographic trend that is often reported in the news is that people are becoming parents at a later age than ever before. This has been associated with benefits for children; when parents are older, they are more economically stable and emotionally mature. Children whose parents are stable in these ways face a lifetime of advantage, as each challenge can be met more effectively by parents who have resources (Martin, 2002).

But it is also true that the change is not terribly dramatic. Transition to parenthood still generally remains the business of the twenty-somethings. First, let us consider births to very young women: teenagers. While becoming a parent as a teenager is a dramatically life-altering event and one that puts a woman and her new baby at risk in many ways, this is not a problem that is spiraling out of control, as we are sometimes told.

The teen birth rate is substantially lower than the birth rate for adult women and has been declining for decades (Office of Adolescent Health, 2016). For the sake of comparison, remember that the general fertility rate for all women is about 65 per 1,000. The general fertility rate for women aged 15–19 was significantly lower in 2014 at 24 per 1,000. For the sake of comparison, it was about 120 for women in their twenties. Teen birth rate in the United States has been creeping downward continuously for at least two decades. Another way to consider this is that 11% of adolescent females in the United States give birth before reaching age 20. The risk is highest for Hispanic women (17%), then for black women (16%), and lowest for white women (8%). So teenagers becoming parents is not exactly uncommon in the United States, but neither is it typical. And it is on a pronounced decline.

What, then, of the opposite extreme, the one we hear so much about in the news, that people in the United States are postponing parenthood until late into their childbearing years? The average age of a woman's first birth has steadily been climbing in the United States. It currently stands at about 26 years of age (Mathews & Hamilton, 2016). The clear reason for the increase in age at first birth is the fairly drastic decline in teen births. For instance, from 2000 to 2014, the percentage of first births to women under 20 years old declined from 23% to 13%. However, the percentage of first births to women over 35 was small and barely changed, from 7% to 9%. The big story here is <u>not</u> that many women are postponing childbirth until they are near the end of their childbearing years; it is that they are postponing childbirth until they are out of their teens (Mathews & Hamilton, 2016).

The average age at first birth varies by race/ethnicity according to the same patterns described above, with Hispanics having the lowest age at first birth, then African Americans are slightly older, whites slightly older than that, and Asian Americans with the oldest average age at first birth.

What does all of this mean for parent education? It is a reminder to recognize that there is still a lot of diversity with regard to parenthood. We can generalize to say that family sizes are small and parents are mostly in their late twenties when they enter parenthood. And yet, we should not be surprised by racial/ethnic diversity. If the population we serve is Hispanic or black, we might expect parents to be younger and families to be larger. Both of these factors are likely to increase parenting stress (Nomaguchi & House, 2013). If the population we serve is white or Asian, we might expect the opposite. To know that these patterns are systematic can be a reminder to consider context and not just assume that a person's age and number of children reflect something about them personally.

Family Structure

Just as we have seen significant historical changes in birth rate, we have also seen significant historical change in the family structures into which children are born in the United States. Specifically, children are more likely than ever before to be born to unmarried parents. And children today experience a very wide range of potential family living arrangements, including the likelihood of joint physical custody between two parents' homes and the likelihood of both parents living with new partners and the children of those new partners.

A few demographic trends interact with each other to produce conclusions about family structure that are not entirely intuitive. Let us begin with some of the facts. The general fertility rate of unmarried women in the United States is about half the general fertility rate for married women (44 compared to 86). The general fertility rate of unmarried women rose dramatically from 1980 (at 29) through 2006 (at 50), and it has been declining since then. So the birth rate of unmarried women is low comparatively and is dropping (Hamilton, Martin, Osterman, Curlin, & Mathews, 2015).

Now, here's where it gets interesting. Despite the relatively low and declining birth rate among unmarried women, the proportion of children born to unmarried parents is increasing, and rather drastically so. In 1960, only 5% of babies were born to unmarried parents, but that number stood at 40% in 2014 (Child Trends Databank, 2015). This is possible because of a demographic trend that we haven't discussed yet, that of later age at marriage. As people delay marriage into their late twenties and thirties, there are simply far more single people of childbearing age. So while their birthrate is low comparatively, there are so many single people in their twenties that they are the parents of a large proportion (almost half) of the babies born in the United States. A majority (58%) of those unmarried parents are cohabiting couples at the time of their baby's birth (Child Trends Databank, 2015).

The racial/ethnic differences in the proportion of babies born to unmarried parents are striking and differ a bit from the pattern of ethnic differences in birth rate. Black children are the most likely (71%), followed by Hispanic babies (53%), and white babies are the least likely (29%) to be born to unmarried parents. Hispanic unmarried mothers are the most likely to be cohabiting with the child's father at the time of the birth, and black mothers are the least likely to be doing so (Child Trends Databank, 2015). (See Figure 2.4.)

What does this mean for children and for the task of parenting them? Children born to unmarried parents (whether cohabiting or not) have poorer outcomes than do children born to married parents. Those outcomes include poverty, household instability, social and emotional problems, and low educational attainment, as well as lower incomes and higher divorce rates in adulthood (Child Trends Databank, 2015). Causation cannot be determined, so we do not know exactly why this is. The circumstances of the births may put parents at an economic disadvantage from which they find it virtually impossible to escape, and that might explain poor outcomes in the future. Or the parents may have already been suffering economically before the birth, which is why they had not gotten married, and so their trajectory progressed after the birth just as it had already been going. We simply don't know what came first, the economic struggles or the child's birth.

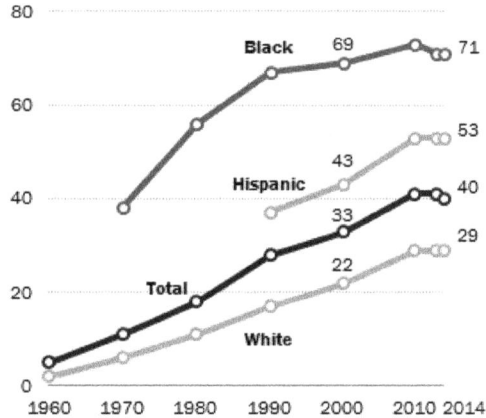

Figure 2.4 The decoupling of marriage and childbearing

As the parent educator arrives on the scene after the babies have been born, the causal relationship may not be relevant. Suffice it to say that it is now normative for children to be born to unmarried parents. This will become an important fact when we begin to consider parenting classes for parents who are not in a romantic relationship with their parenting partner. A generation ago, we may have been safe to assume that those parents were divorcing, and many of these parenting classes are referred to as **divorce parent education**. But now the children are just as likely to have been born to parents who were never married to each other. Therefore, there is a shift from divorce parenting education to the more generic **coparenting education**.

This is somewhat problematic, as divorce education deals prominently with the experience of loss and upheaval, but coparenting education need not necessarily share that focus. It is not clear whether parents would benefit from coparenting education that is specific to separation/divorce, or if a one-size-fits-all approach is adequate.

Contemporary Parenthood 41

Another issue related to family structure is that the legal system has been changing to allow a much broader range of living arrangements for children whose parents are not married or living together. Reports of census data are that 16% of children in the United States live with a stepparent, stepsibling, or half sibling (Parker, Horowitz, & Rohan, 2015). It is not new that children have stepfamilies. But as little as 100 to 150 years ago, life expectancy was much lower, such that marriages commonly ended when children were still living at home, but the end of the marriage was due to the death of one partner, and stepfamilies were formed when the remaining parent remarried. In that case, there would be no shared custody. Now, children are far more likely to be born to unmarried parents, and when marriages end it is by divorce rather than death (Coontz, 2016). Now there are two parents remaining alive and potentially involved in the child's life. All in all, this is great news for children, that they are far more likely to reach adulthood with both of their parents still living. But it might mean some extra complication of living arrangements as children spend time with both of those parents.

In addition to the fact that children are quite likely to grow to adulthood with both of their parents still living, our courts in the United States have also shifted toward a preference for custody of children to be shared. The legal system of the United States was originally based on English common law, which considered children to be the property of their father so that fathers would always get exclusive custody of children whenever there was a question. After the Industrial Revolution, the role of mothers as the emotional center of families was emphasized, and the courts shifted in the opposite direction, assuming that mothers would get exclusive custody of children whenever there was a question (Folberg, 1991).

But thanks to a large and convincing body of child and family science research, courts in the United States have gradually shifted toward an assumption that children's best interests should drive custody decisions and that it is usually in children's best interests to have regular contact with both parents (Parkinson, 2011). As a result, children are more likely to live part time with one parent and part time with another. This has been called a **binuclear family**, one that allows children to have a place in families with more than nucleus (or center). Outcomes are better for children who experience shared custody, and this remains true even when the parents maintain a high level of conflict with each other (Nielsen, 2014).

See Figure 2.5 for a summary of how these changes have affected the living arrangements of children in the United States. Essentially, the proportion of children who live with parents who are married to each other is now less than half. A third of children live primarily with a single parent, and 15% live primarily in a stepfamily (Livingston, 2014). Binuclear families are not reflected in this graphic, so we can infer that actual living arrangements are even more complicated than what is depicted here.

What all of this means for parent educators is that we must simply abandon any notion we might have that nuclear families with married parents are somehow normative. Subsequently, we must rethink our tendency to view other family forms through a deficit lens. No one family structure is normative. No one family structure (even the much-maligned single-parent home) is inherently problematic. Instead, we must forge deeper; we must examine the processes that play themselves out inside of families. We must look at the behaviors and relationships directly, rather than assuming we know what's going on just by naming the family structure. Such processes of parenting are the parenting styles described in chapter 1.

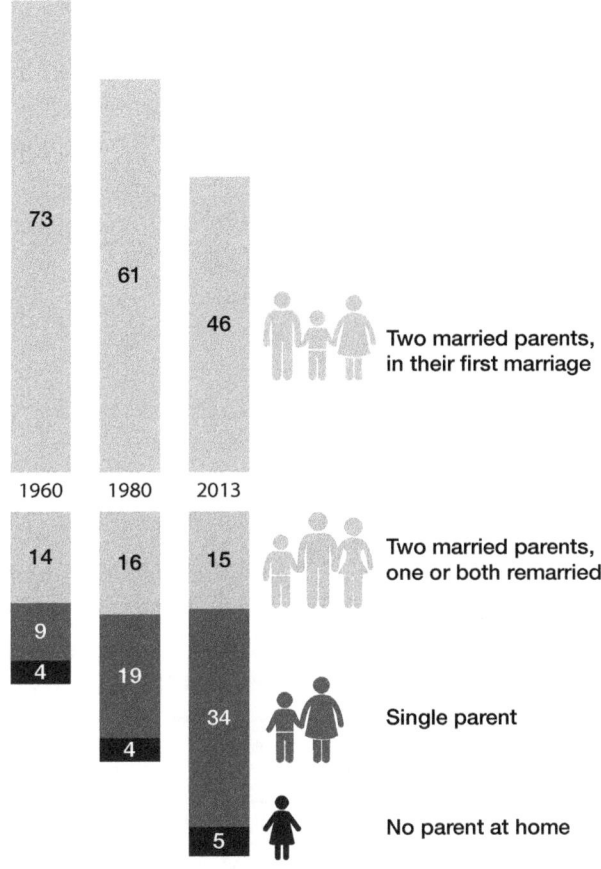

Figure 2.5 How the American Family Has Changed

Sociocultural Context of Parenting

Just as family size and marital status vary widely among parents, so too do parenting styles. But the sociocultural context shapes parenting styles in predictable ways.

Parental Goals

One way to conceptualize social and cultural diversity in parenting is to consider **parental goals**; that is, what qualities parents would like to foster in their children. Parental goals can be considered a measure of personal and cultural values. There is a great deal of similarity among parents in the United States. For instance, over 90% of parents in this country say that "being responsible" and "hard work" are especially important to teach children. Virtually all parents are very likely, additionally, to endorse independence, helping others, and good manners. But there is considerable disagreement over whether some other qualities are important to teach children. For instance, tolerance, obedience, religious faith, and curiosity are considered very important by some, but not all, parents (Parker, 2014). (See Figure 2.7.) Parental goals for children do produce predictably different parenting practices and styles (Fox, 2005; Luster, Rhoades, & Haas, 1989) and so are a useful way to conceptualize why there is diversity in parenting.

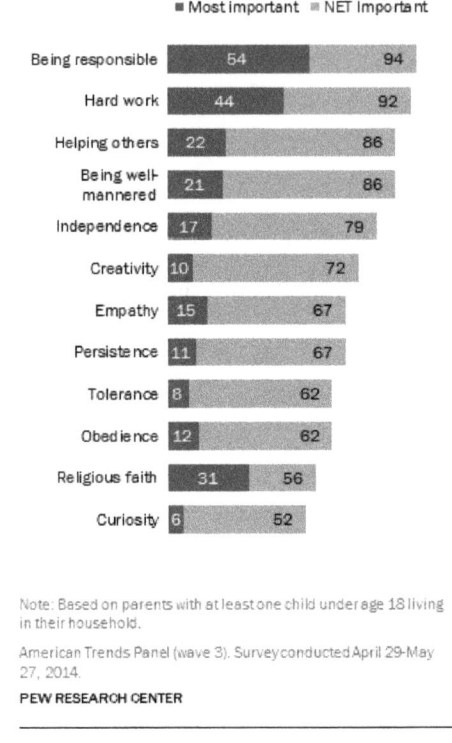

Figure 2.6 Parents See Responsibility, Hard Work, as Most Important to Teach Children

Patterns of difference are apparent with regard to politics and socioeconomic status. Conservative parents are significantly more likely to endorse teaching religious faith and obedience, while more liberal parents are significantly more likely to endorse teaching tolerance, empathy, and curiosity (Doherty, Funk, Kiley, & Weisel, 2014). (See Figure 2.7.)

Similarly, social class is relevant to parental goals. It was discovered several decades ago that middle-class parents highly value independence in their children, whereas working-class parents more highly value obedience and conformity (Kohn, 1979). More recent research continues to find these differences. Highly educated parents are more likely to endorse empathy, curiosity, persistence, and tolerance and less likely to endorse obedience and religious faith as essential values to teach to children (Doherty, Funk, Kiley, & Weisel, 2014).

With that in mind, we look back over the list of parental goals on which parents differ. Two jump out as possibly related to parenting style: empathy and obedience. Remember that we have a scientific consensus that authoritative parenting produces the best outcomes. Empathy is a trait that is nurtured by the emotional aspect of parenting style, and obedience reflects the behavioral aspect of parenting style. Therefore, parent educators might attend to those parental goals and consider how to talk to parents about those.

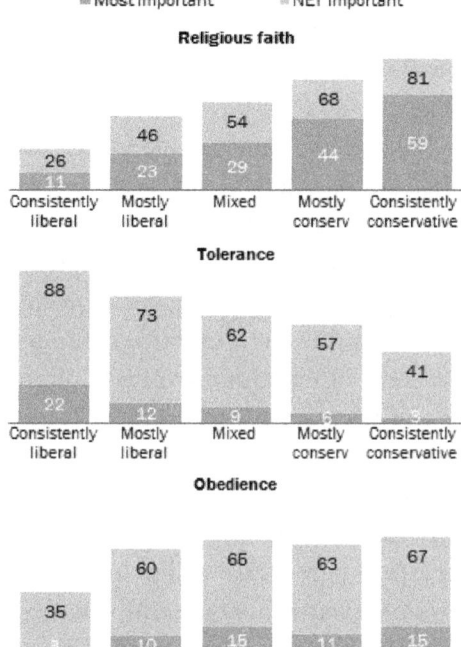

Figure 2.7 Conservaties Prioritize Teaching Faith, Obedience; Liberals Value Tolerance

Race/Ethnicity

Research on parental goals finds surprisingly little variation by race/ethnicity (Doherty, Funk, Kiley, & Weisel, 2014). But there are some differences, and

Contemporary Parenthood 45

those pertain mostly to indicators of parenting style, so they are relevant to parent educators. There are always exceptions to these rules, as well as considerable diversity within each racial/ethnic group, so a parent educator should never assume that a given parent will match the profiles described below. But these patterns represent a starting place, a place from which to consider how the context of a parent's life could be shaped by his or her racial/ethnic background.

Black parents are notable for the value they place on obedience and respect, which suggests a tendency toward the authoritarian parenting style. They tend to be stricter than parents in other ethnic groups and are more likely to rely on physical discipline (Chao & Kanatsu, 2008; Dixon, Graber, & Brooks-Gunn, 2008; Gershoff et al., 2012). Latino parents also have more authoritarian beliefs and values and exercise a higher degree of behavioral control than do parents in other ethnic groups (Bulcroft, Carmody, & Bulcroft, 1996), but they are not necessarily more likely to use corporal punishment (Gershoff et al., 2012). Asian American parents emphasize loyalty and obedience, also consistent with authoritarian parenting, but are not necessarily more likely to use corporal punishment (Chao & Kanatsu, 2008; Gershoff et al., 2012). European American parents score the lowest on behavioral control but the highest on emotional warmth, suggesting a tendency toward permissive parenting (Chao & Kanatsu, 2008).

Research has consistently shown that racial/ethnic minority parents are exposed to greater stress than are white parents. The source of the stress appears to be primarily structural in nature, meaning that the extra stress comes from things like their younger age, higher rate of unemployment, immigration status, and lower income. But parents also experience increased parental stress when they endorse beliefs related to an authoritarian parenting style. Authoritarian parents tend to struggle more than others do with their children's nonconformity and disobedience, causing them distress at even normal and healthy children's behavior (Nomaguchi & House, 2013).

Socioeconomic Status

Social class, also known as **socioeconomic status**, is a social status based on income, education, and prestige of one's employment. The financial circumstances of the family determine the neighborhood the family can live in, and that shapes the parent's outlook on their children's prospects, which alters the way they interact with them. For instance, parents earning less than $30,000 a year are far more likely than parents earning at least $75,000 a year to say that they worry their child will be shot (47% versus 22%), be kidnapped (55% versus 44%), or get in trouble with the law (40% versus 21%) (Parker, Horowitz, & Rohal, 2015). These anxieties are likely to profoundly shape their judgments of their children's behavior, and thus the parenting practices they deem to be necessary to maintain their children's safety.

One prominent example of research on social class and parenting is Annette Lareau's study of how social class affects parenting (Lareau, 2011). She found that middle-class and higher-income parents use close supervision and organized activities to actively and directly teach their children the skills they will need to deal with the demands of adulthood, whereas working-class parents give their children more time for free play and independence in their daily activities. As it turns out, the working-class kids are happier in childhood and closer to family members, while the wealthier children are more likely to be bored and less capable of solving their own problems. But as they move into adulthood, the working-class kids stagnate and do not get as far, whereas the wealthier children move into adulthood with skills that pay off in the work world.

Socioeconomic status not only shapes parental goals, but the stress of economic hardship pushes parents toward a more authoritarian parenting style. Parents who face economic stress tend to become more punitive and less sensitively responsive. They resort more quickly to physical punishment and offer less affection (Garrett, Ng'andu, & Ferron, 1994). When families' incomes rise, punitive behaviors decrease (Hashima & Amato, 1994). It is important for parent educators to understand why this authoritarian parenting appears in economically stressed families. It does not appear to be a "culture of poverty" issue, whereby poor people somehow have different values from wealthier people. Instead, it is a behavioral response to environmental stressors, one that is reduced when the environmental stressors are relieved.

Personal and Familial Context of Parenting

Cultural beliefs and one's status in society are important considerations for a parent educator. So, too, are more individual characteristics of the parent-child dynamic.

Individual Characteristics of the Parent

In some important ways, men and women parent differently. For one thing, mothers still do more of the work of parenting, despite big changes in the participation of fathers in the home (Parker & Wang, 2013). Mothers simply spend more time with their children than do fathers (Cabrera, Tamis-LeMonda, Bradley, Hofferth, & Lamb, 2000; Wall & Arnold, 2007). There are exceptions, of course, but by and large, mothers do most of the direct caregiving. (See Figure 2.8.) Mothers are also more likely than men to consider parenthood essential to their identity (Rogers & White, 1998). An **intensive mothering ideology**, the belief that women should find their identity in motherhood and should devote themselves tirelessly to the job, pervades US culture (Hays, 1996).

This might explain why mothers are more likely than fathers to say that parenting is tiring most or all of the time (Parker, Horowitz, & Rohal, 2015). However, a **polarization of fatherhood** has been documented in recent decades (Coontz, 2016). That is to say that fathers are both more likely to be totally absent from their children's lives and more likely to be directly and deeply engaged in their children's daily lives as compared to the mid-20th century. Some fathers are totally absent, leaving their children to be raised entirely by their mothers, but the ones who remain engaged are doing more than the generations of men that preceded them.

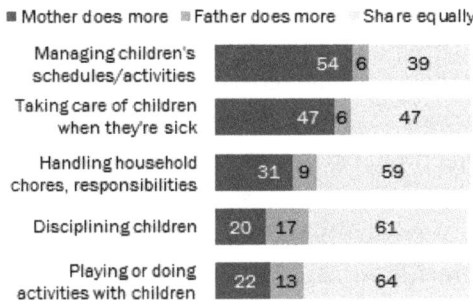

Figure 2.8 Division of Labor in Households with Two Full-Time Working Parents

These dynamics are relevant to parent education. Mothers are more likely than fathers (twice as likely, in fact) to seek out parenting advice (Parker, Horowitz, & Rohal, 2015). Single mothers—and we know that there are more of them than ever before—are looking for help with a role that is overwhelming. They need practical solutions that reflect their actual circumstances. Often, that means the parent educator must abandon gender-specific notions of parenthood and recognize that a mother or (less commonly) a father is doing all of the parenting.

The polarization of fatherhood also means that fathers who show up to a community-based voluntary parenting program are likely to be eager for tools to help them with what is a sincere desire to engage in a way that their own fathers may not have. In voluntary parenting programs, both men and women are typically eager for a transformation of traditional gender roles in parenting.

Similarly, courts are ordering fathers to parenting classes in order to enable them to step into roles that may be unfamiliar to them. I live and work in California, where courts default to joint physical custody for children when custody is contested. This means that fathers are assuming the tasks of parenthood after a divorce or separation, and it is sometimes new and unfamiliar to them. Mothers that I work with in a postdivorce parenting program are very nervous about relinquishing parenting tasks to their former partners and resentful because they feel that all their prior years of hard work are not being recognized. This is a subtext of court-ordered parenting education that the parent educator should know is there. We are in the middle of drastic cultural changes for fatherhood, and parent educators are poised to help equip men embrace the new form of fatherhood that they seek and help women embrace a new form of motherhood that they often did not ask for.

Parental Relationships

One aspect of the familial context that has a big effect on parenting is the relationship of the parents with each other. This includes both family structure and the quality of the parents' relationships with each other and with new romantic partners. We should by now mistrust the ubiquitous bifurcation of single-parent or married-couple family types. There are many subtypes of each of these and many other possibilities as well.

We have learned already that nearly half of children in the United States are born to parents who are not married to each other at the time of the birth. Some of those unmarried parents are cohabiting, with relationships of varying quality; some are attempting to coparent while living apart, with relationships of varying quality; and some have left the parenting to only one partner. And parents repartner with predictable frequency, introducing new coparents into the child's life. Parents who are married to each other at the birth of their child also have relationships of varying quality. Some will later separate, sometimes establishing coparenting relationships and others not, and many repartner.

Coparenting

Coparenting is the sharing of parental responsibilities in order to meet the needs of children (Gable, Crnic, & Belsky, 1994). Regardless of whether parents are married or not, cohabiting or not, if they participate in the care and rearing of their children, then they are coparenting. The concept of coparenting can apply to a wider range of adults than just the child's biological parents. Stepparents often actively coparent, as do grandparents and older siblings.

Belsky (1990) notes that **supportive coparenting** (also known as **cooperative coparenting**) is when those involved actively collaborate with each other to enact a shared model of care. Maccoby and Mnookin (1992) define this as having frequent interaction that is low in discord. (See Table 2.1) Supportive coparents are in frequent contact whether or not they live together, consulting about the child's behavior and considering what response they will both agree to implement and enforce. Couples with high relationship satisfaction are the most able to practice supportive coparenting. They trust each other's perceptions and judgments, often relying on the other for guidance as well as support.

To envision supportive coparenting, imagine what happens after a child throws a fit and storms out of the room. When the parents turn to each other and say, "What just happened here?" and each shares their perception, this is one aspect of supportive coparenting because they are relying on one another to help with their interpretation of the behavior. Then one might say, "Do you think I should go after her? Are we being too rigid, should we allow her to do it?" They discuss how to act, they decide jointly, and then they convey their decision to the child. This is another aspect of supportive coparenting, the joint decision making. Finally, they may comfort one another if the decision was painful, or the child's behavior worrisome, or when the outcome was different from what had been anticipated.

Table 2.1 Types of Coparenting

	Low Discord	High Discord
Infrequent Interaction	Parallel Parenting	Conflicted (Unsupportive) Coparenting
Frequent Interaction	Cooperative (Supportive) Coparenting	

Couples who share values, are emotionally mature enough for self-reflection, and who trust one another are the most likely to be able to do this. I personally believe that my parenting decisions are better when I can talk them over with my husband in advance. He can sometimes offer a perspective on the child's behavior that I had not considered. He sometimes guides me in a direction different from my initial inclination, and I appreciate the opportunity to consider multiple options. Mostly, he acknowledges the difficulties and lets me talk through my parenting struggles. The comfort he provides to me allows me to face the difficult parts of parenting. Supportive coparenting is clearly the ideal circumstance, and in fact, it is associated with the best outcomes in divorced families (Amato, Kane, & James, 2011). But it is not always possible.

Unsupportive coparenting (also known as **conflicted coparenting**) is when those involved act against one another, undermining or criticizing the other parent and sabotaging the other's parenting strategies. Maccoby and Mnookin (1992) define conflicted coparenting as having infrequent interaction but high levels of discord. (See Table 2.1.) This may come in the form of one partner simply retreating and refusing to participate in parenting, leaving all of the work and decisions and the difficulty to be faced by the other parent, alone and without support. Or it comes in the form of active hostility between the parents, reversing or refusing to enforce the other's decisions. Parents sometimes actively subvert the other's rules by facilitating children's violations of those rules or hiding infractions from the other parent. Either way, parents are not offering one another assistance in the job.

Why would anyone do this? Unsupportive coparenting is likely to be bad for kids, damaging their relationships with both parents and requiring of them undesirable behaviors such as deception. Furthermore, the parents will feel frustrated, angry, and alone in the job of parenting. It has been assumed that unsupportive coparenting is more common after divorce, when parents are so angry with each other that they are blinded by their own rage and cannot see the futility of, and damage caused by, such hostile patterns of relationship. Unsupportive, highly conflicted parental relationships postdivorce are in fact associated with poor outcomes for children (Buchanan, Maccoby, & Dornbusch, 1996). Conventional wisdom is that those parents must separate their feelings about their failed marriage from their job as coparents and step up to the plate for their kids, and just grow up.

From my experience teaching postdivorce parenting classes, I can affirm that I've seen this pattern. But I also question the utility of telling bitterly angry people that they should simply learn how to practice supportive coparenting for the sake of their children. In order to practice supportive coparenting, those involved must trust one another's perceptions and judgments and must exhibit emotional maturity and kindness under pressure. I am not sure that this is possible when one or both people are untrustworthy in some essential way or lack the requisite emotional maturity. These qualities may be what led to their divorce in the first place.

I've also witnessed unsupportive coparenting among people who are still in a romantic relationship with each other. Sometimes they have profound disagreements about appropriate parenting despite an otherwise happy relationship. Sometimes they are unsatisfied in their relationship but have chosen to stay together, and they act out their battles with each other through their children. I suspect that the core of unsupportive coparenting is the lack of trust in the other parent. Supportive coparenting simply is not an option so long as a fundamental mistrust between the parents remains.

A third option for coparenting, identified empirically in research on postdivorce coparenting, has been called **parallel parenting** (Maccoby & Mnookin, 1992). (See Table 2.1.) It is defined as infrequent interaction with a low level of discord. The parents stop fighting and sabotaging one another by avoiding one another. Parallel parenting is when the adults coparent by dividing up responsibilities or time, and each one parents alone, but without interference or sabotage from the other. Maybe the children alternate weeks between parents. When they are with Mom, she makes all the decisions, she enforces all decisions, she provides all transportation, she responds to all problems. But she can only make decisions that pertain to her week. Similarly, Dad is fully responsible for the kids during his week, but he cannot make decisions about what happens during Mom's week. Neither can sign the children up for extracurricular activities during the other's time unless the other parent explicitly agrees. Neither can inflict a grounding or punishment that extends into the other's time with the children. Neither disparages the other parent or attempts to interfere in any way with the other's relationship with the children. Surely, children know that their parents do not get along. But they are protected from the direct assault of parental conflict.

Parent educators must consider these types of coparenting because they are in a position to advise parents about how to move forward. Should they push supportive coparenting, or it more realistic to suggest parallel parenting? Children whose parents use supportive coparenting seem to have the best outcomes. But the data are correlational so we cannot determine causation. Presumably, those who use supportive coparenting are more trustworthy and mature in the first place. It remains unknown if it is possible to coach adults into supportive coparenting and thereby improve outcomes for their children. Frankly, it seems more likely to me that supportive coparenting is simply not an option for people who arrive at a parenting class, often court mandated, because of their high-conflict relationship. In fact, Maccoby and Mnookin (1992) followed families for three years postdivorce and found that the general pattern was to move in the direction of parallel parenting. More recent data also suggest the same, that parents move toward parallel parenting over time (Amato, Kane, & James, 2011). Supportive coparenting certainly happens after divorce in some cases, and those children seem to benefit. But the parent educator may need to assess how likely that is for families that he or she is working with.

Coparenting was first subjected to scrutiny when the divorce rate skyrocketed in the 1970s and 1980s. Concern for the well-being of children triggered serious consideration of whether divorce hurts children. It is clear from decades of research that children of divorced parents have more problems than children whose parents remain married (Amato, 2000; Amato, 2010). However, decades of research have revealed two important caveats about the outcomes of divorce that are critical for the parent educator to understand.

First, the effect size of divorce on child outcomes is quite small. On average, the difference between children of divorced versus non-divorced parents is very small, and it disappears for almost everyone within two years (Amato & Anthony, 2014; Barber & Demo, 2006). But among some children, their school performance and mental health do not improve, and it seems that they have been permanently damaged by the parental divorce.

The second caveat is that it is very difficult to determine what causes those poor outcomes. Here we have a confusion of correlation and causality. Just because divorce is correlated with bad outcomes, do we know that the divorce caused the bad outcomes? No, we don't know that at all. In fact, decades of research suggest that the real culprit is hostile conflict between the parents (Kline, Johnston, & Tschann, 1991; Amato, 2000; Gager, Yabiku, & Linver, 2016). Children whose parents engage in hostile conflict but who stay married have the same poor outcomes as children whose parents engage in hostile conflict and get divorced. Similarly, children whose parents get divorced amicably do not display these poor outcomes. So we have reason to believe that it is the hostile conflict between parents that is really hard on kids, not necessarily parental divorce.

All of the work on coparenting is very important for parent educators who work with postdivorce parenting programs to appreciate. It is true that the issue of coparenting has only been studied in the context of divorced parents, and so we are forced to infer the degree to which these findings apply to coresidential parents. However, the results pertaining to parental conflict are so consistent that it would be foolish for a parent educator to ignore them. Hostile conflict between parents is damaging for children. A primary goal of parent education, therefore, must be to help people coparent with as little hostile conflict as possible, whether that be through supportive coparenting or parallel parenting.

Same-Sex Relationships

Another aspect of parental relationships that has received a lot of attention in politics and in the research is the sexual orientation of the parent. It has been hypothesized that children learn different things from male and female parents and so need one of each to be fully rounded in their development. This idea has been used to deny LGBT parents access to their children and the right to form families, but it has not been supported empirically.

Early research on children raised by LGBT parents typically studied the biological children of lesbian women who had babies in heterosexual relationships but then came out, and retained custody of their children through the courts' preference for mother-custody arrangements. (Johnson, 2012). Family science research revealed that such children were similar in outcomes to other children of divorced parents raised by a single mother (Tasker, 2005).

Prior to the 1990s, many gays and lesbians opted to sacrifice their desire for family relationships in order to be true to their sexual orientation. "Family" was seen by many, including many in the LGBT community, as antithetical to their sexual orientation. But the 1990s saw the **lesbian baby boom**, when an unprecedented number of lesbian women used artificial insemination to become parents. Family scientists noted the trend, and studied the children born to same-sex parents in this manner. The research was clear: the babies of the lesbian baby boom had identical outcomes to their age-mates raised by heterosexual parents (Patterson, 1994).

LGBT couples were legally prohibited from adopting children until very recently. For instance, Florida had a law explicitly preventing gays and lesbians from adopting children that was not overturned until 2010 (Ramos, 2010). Currently, there are no longer any legal barriers to LGBT men and women becoming parents. As laws started changing with regard to adoption, the 2000s brought the **gayby boom**, when gay men launched family formation through adoption or surrogacy. It is estimated that among LGBT adults under age 50, 48% of lesbian women and 20% of gay men are raising a minor child (Gates, 2013).

The limited research that has been conducted on families with LGBT parents that were formed by adoption suggests that children adopted by LGBT parents have very similar outcomes to children of similar social class. They are no more likely to be LGBT themselves and no more likely to suffer depression or anxiety than other children (Anderssen, Amlie, & Ytteroy, 2002).

The take-away message for parent educators is the imperative to support LGBT parents in just the same manner that they would support straight parents. Sexual orientation of parents seems utterly unrelated to the effectiveness of parenting.

Individual Characteristics of the Child

Perhaps the most compelling individual characteristic of the child that shapes parenting advice—and parenting itself—is the child's age. Mother's knowledge of child development has been linked to effective parenting and desirable child outcomes (Benasich & Brooks-Gunn, 1996). The effect of knowledge remained significant even after controlling for socioeconomic status. Research such as this supports the argument that parent education should include education about normative child development.

I once spent a couple of hours as a passenger in the cab of a tow truck late at night, trying to make casual conversation with the tow truck driver. After he learned what I do for a living, he started asking me about how to get his kids to do their chores. "They just won't obey. They do everything they can to get out of work and don't seem to respect me the way I think they should." He was very upset by what he saw as their sense of entitlement, that they took him for granted and did not easily acquiesce to his authority. I had some ideas about this. These are common complaints about teenagers. But imagine my surprise when I learned that his children were only three and five years old! For such young children, this seems to be developmentally appropriate and not problem behavior. In fact, the true problem is that the father was placing completely unrealistic expectations on his young children. But it is fair to argue on his behalf that he really had no way of knowing. He works with cars. He has never really been around small children since he was one himself. How is he supposed to know?

Another example: Because I study infant sleep, I talk to a lot of parents about their baby's sleeping habits. Parents tend to think that their success as a parent depends on having a baby who sleeps all night long at a very young age. When I explain that more than half of babies still have regular night wakings at

12 months of age (Scher, 1991), they breathe a sigh of relief. They thought something was wrong because they believed their baby to be abnormal. Knowledge of child development can help.

How do adults learn about normal child development? Many adults have a sense of developmentally normal behaviors by being around family members with children or by babysitting. But recall that as the total fertility rate falls, families are smaller, and many people have less exposure to children than they did a generation or more in the past. This also means that most folks get a culturally narrow view of development because they get it only from one cultural context: their own. Heaven help the adult who gets his ideas about normal development by watching television or movies, as children are typically depicted in very unnatural ways.

Therefore, if parents (like the tow truck driver or the parent of a wakeful infant) are going to learn about child development, they need a reliable source. This is one role of a parent educator, to have a good understanding of normative child development and to use that information to help parents construct developmentally appropriate expectations and responses to child behavior.

Conclusion

Contemporary parenthood is shaped by structural features of families, including historical influences on birth rate and family size, ethnicity, family structure, and socioeconomic status. We have addressed each of these incompletely, but this brief review demonstrates that parenting behaviors reflect external circumstances and parental belief systems. Since people have varied circumstances and beliefs, it is no surprise that parenting behaviors and parenting advice should vary. Parent advisers must take these contextual issues into account in order to be effective.

Let us consider a very common parent education scenario. A father is referred to Child Protective Services (CPS) for possible abuse of a child. The investigating CPS social worker notes that the parent has unrealistic expectations for his child's behavior and lacks skills for behavior management, and so resorts to physical punishment frequently. The parent is then ordered to take a parenting class.

Notice that the social worker has identified only factors that are immediate to the father's personal circumstances (the dad's state of mind and level of skill). We might not be surprised to learn that this is a recently separated dad who has never done much of the caregiving because when he was married, his wife did it. Now, he is highly stressed due to the conflict with his ex-wife and the difficulty of his new role as direct caregiver. This helps provide an important context. It may also be true that the father has taken a new job as a result of the divorce, and now he works overnight. This is an especially stressful work situation, which is affecting his ability to provide care to his child. Why did he take that particular job? Maybe it was because the housing market crashed so he couldn't get another job in construction like he had held previously. He would like to request that the court alter the custody order to reflect his new job where he works nights, but the court will not accept a request for modification of custody so soon after the current order was made, so a law is directly affecting his parenting.

Could this father benefit from a parenting class? Yes, most certainly. He and his child need help if they are to make this transition successfully. But when he arrives at the first class, how will the teacher regard him? If the teacher considers only the most immediate context, she might see this father as a bad guy, impatient and insensitive and unskilled. She might see him as a hopeless case, because she sees his personal failings without context and assumes that they reflect his entire identity. But if the teacher considers the broader context of this man's life, she will have compassion for his circumstances and will thus be more likely to find ways to help him. And please notice that the way she helps will consist of educating him about his child's needs and offering him new skills, but she might also help him find ways to reduce conflict with his ex-wife and find ways to adjust the visitation schedule or his work schedule. She may even advocate for reasonable reforms of the family court system. Clearly, a broader perspective helps the educator fully understand the dynamic in order to better serve the family.

Parenting behaviors are not only the product of the parent's skill, they often reflect circumstances bigger than the parent. So a parent educator sometimes becomes an advocate to change forces outside of the parent himself. Skill building is important and helpful, and we will move on to that next, but it is not the only significant thing.

Review and Reflection Questions

1. What is the difference between a general birth rate and a total fertility rate? How do they differ in precision and in the kind of information they include?

2. Why is the birth rate falling in the United States? Is it falling for everyone?

3. What can we infer about parents based on the historical and comparative review of birth rates?

4. Is there a typical family structure that children live in? What has caused that to change in the last half-century? What does that mean for parent educators?

5. What parenting goals are virtually universal? Which ones vary by politics? By social class? By race? How might these differences in parenting goals produce different parenting? Should a parent educator be worried about this?

6. How do mothers and fathers differ in their parenting? What implications are there for parent education?

7. What are the three options for coparenting styles? Which did your own parents use? What do you think should be recommended for divorced couples?

8. Does the parent's sexual orientation have any impact on parenting?

9. How does it help parents to understand child development?

Terminology to Know

- Binuclear family
- Coparenting
- Coparenting education
- Divorce parent education
- Gayby boom
- General fertility rate
- Intensive mothering ideology

- Lesbian baby boom
- Parallel parenting
- Parental goals
- Polarization of fatherhood
- Replacement level
- Socioeconomic status
- Supportive/cooperative coparenting
- Total fertility rate
- Unsupportive/conflicted coparenting

References

Amato, P. (2000). The consequences of divorce for adults and children. *Journal of Marriage and the Family, 62*, 1269–1287.

Amato, P. (2010). Research on divorce: Continuing trends and new developments. *Journal of Marriage and the Family, 72*, 650–666.

Amato, P., & Anthony, C.J. (2014). Estimating the effects of parental divorce and death with fixed effects model. *Journal of Marriage and the Family, 76, 2*, 370–386.

Amato, P.R., Kane, J.B., & James, S. (2011). Reconsidering the "good divorce." *Family Relations, 60, 5*, 511–524.

Anderssen, N., Amlie, C., & Ytteroy, E.A. (2002). Outcomes for children with lesbian or gay parents: A review of studies from 1978 to 2000. *Scandinavian Journal of Psychology, 43*, 335–351.

Barber, B. L., & Demo, D.H. (2006). The kids are alright (at least, most of them): Links between divorce and dissolution and child well-being. *Handbook of divorce and relationship dissolution*. M.A. Fine & J.H. Harvey (Eds.); pp. 289–311. Mahway, NJ: Lawrence Erlbaum Associates Publishers.

Belsky, J. (1990). Children and marriage. In F. Fincham and T. Bradbury (Eds.), *The psychology of marriage: Basic issues and applications*, pp. 172–200. New York: Guilford.

Benasich, A., & Brooks-Gunn, J. (1996). Maternal attitudes and knowledge of child-rearing: Associations with family and child outcomes. *Child Development, 67*, 1186–1205.

Buchanan, C.M., Maccoby, E.E., & Dornbusch, S.M. (1996). *Adolescents after divorce*. Cambridge, MA: Harvard University Press.

Bulcroft, R.A., Carmody, D.C., & Bulcroft, K.A. (1996). Patterns of parental independence giving to adolescents: Variations by race, age, and gender of child. *Journal of Marriage and Family, 58, 4*, 866–883.

Cabrera, N.J., Tamis-LeMonda, C.S., Bradley, R.H., Hofferth, S., & Lamb, M.E. (2000). Fatherhood in the twenty-first century. *Child Development, 71, 1*, 127–136.

Chao, R., & Kanatsu, A. (2008). Beyond socioeconomics: Explaining ethnic group differences in parenting through cultural and immigration processes. *Applied Developmental Science, 12, 4*, 181–187.

Child Trends Databank (2015). Births to unmarried women. http://www.childtrends.org/?indicators=births-to-unmarried-women Retrieved 12/18/2016.

Coontz, S. (2016). *The way we never were: American families and the nostalgia trap, revised edition.* Basic Books.

Dixon, S.V., Brooks-Gunn, J., & Graber, J.A. (2008). The roles of respect for parental authority and parenting practices in parent-child conflict among African American, Latino, and European American families. *Journal of Family Psychology, 22, 1*, 1–10.

Doherty, C., Funk, C., Kiley, J., & Weisel, R. (2014). Teaching the children: Sharp ideological differences, some common ground. Pew Research Center. http://www.people-press.org/2014/09/18/teaching-the-children-sharp-ideological-differences-some-common-ground/ Retrieved 12/28/2016.

Folberg, J. (1991). *Joint custody and shared parenting.* Guilford Press.

Fox, G.E. (2005). Incorporating parental goals in parenting programs through collaborative relationships with parents. *Journal of Extension, 43, 1.* https://joe.org/joe/2005february/iw2.php Retrieved 12/28/2016.

Gable, S., Crnic, K., & Belsky, J. (1994). Coparenting within the family system: Influences on children's development. *Family Relations, 43*, 380–386.

Gager, C.T., Yabiku, S.T., & Linver, M.R. (2016). Conflict or divorce: Does parental conflict and/or divorce increase the likelihood of adult children's cohabiting and marital dissolution? *Marriage and Family Review, 52, 3*, 243–261.

Garrett, P., Ng'andu, N., & Ferron, J. (1994). Poverty experiences of young children and the quality of their home environments. *Child Development, 65*, 331–345.

Gates, G.J. (2013). LGT parenting in the United States. Executive summary of a report of the Williams Institute. http:///wiliamsinstitute.law.ucla.edu/wp-content/uploads/LGBT-Parenting.pdf. Retrieved 1/3/2017.

Gershoff, E.T., Lansford, J.E., Sexton, H.R., Davis-Kean, P., & Smeroff, A.J. (2012). Longitudinal links between spanking and children's externalizing behaviors in a national sample of White, Black, Hispanic, and Asian American families. *Child Development, 83, 3*, 838–843.

Hamilton, B.E., Martin, J.A., Osterman, M.J.K., Curlin, S.C., & Mathews, T.J. (2015). Births: Final data for 2014. National Vital Statistics Reports, 64, 12. https://www.cdc.gov/nchs/data/nvsr/nvsr64/nvsr64_12.pdf Retrieved 12/18/2016.

Hashima, P., & Amato, P. (1994). Poverty, social support, and parental behavior. *Child Development, 65, 2*, 394–403.

Hays, S. (1996). *The cultural contradictions of motherhood.* New Haven, CT: Yale University Press.

Johnson, S.M. (2012). Lesbian mothers and their children: The third wave. *Journal of Lesbian Studies, 16, 1*, 45–53.

Kohn, M.L. (1979). *Class and conformity: A study in values, 2nd edition.* Chicago: University of Chicago.

Kline, M., Johnston, J.R., & Tschann, J.M. (1991). The long shadow of marital conflict: A model of children's post-divorce adjustment. *Journal of Marriage and the Family, 53, 2*, 297–309.

Lareau, A. (2011) *Unequal childhoods: Class, race, and family life*, 2nd edition. University of California Press.

Livingston, G. (2014). Fewer than half of US kids today live in a traditional family. Pew Research Center. http://www.pewresearch.org/fact-tank/2014/12/22/less-than-half-of-u-s-kids-today-live-in-a-traditional-family/ Retrieved 12/18/2016.

Livingston, G. (2015). Childlessness falls, family size grows among highly educated women. Pew Research Center. http://www.pewsocialtrends.org/2015/05/07/family-size-among-mothers/ Retrieved 12/17/2016.

Luster, T., Rhoades, K., & Haas, B. (1989). The relation between parental values and parenting behavior: A test of the Kohn Hypothesis. *Journal of Marriage and the Family, 51*, 139–147.

Maccoby, E.E., & Mnookin, R.H. (1992). *Dividing the child: Social and legal dilemmas of custody.* Cambridge, MA: Harvard University Press.

Martin, J.A., Hamilton, B.E., & Osterman, M.J.K. (2015). Births in the United States, 2014. NCHS Data Brief, number 216. Centers for Disease Control, US Department of Health and Human Services. https://www.cdc.gov/nchs/data/databriefs/db216.pdf Retrieved 12/18/2016.

Martin, S.P. (2002). *Delayed marriage and childbearing: Implications and measurement of diverging trends in family timing.* College Park: University of Maryland, Department of Sociology, and Maryland Population Research Center.

Mather, M. (2014). The World Population Data Sheet 2014: Decline in US fertility. Population Reference Bureau. http://www.prb.org/Publications/Datasheets/2014/2014-world-population-data-sheet/us-fertility-decline-factsheet.aspx Retrieved 12/18/2016.

Mathews, T.J., & Hamilton, B.E. (2016). Mean age of mothers is on the rise: United States, 2000–2014. Centers for Disease Control and Prevention, National Center for Health Statistics. https://www.cdc.gov/nchs/products/databriefs/db232.htm Retrieved 12/18/2016.

Nielsen, L. (2014). Shared physical custody: Summary of 40 studies on outcomes for children. *Journal of Divorce and Remarriage, 55*, 614–636.

Nomaguchi, K., & House, A.N. (2013). Racial-ethnic disparities in maternal parenting stress: The role of structural disadvantages and parenting values. *Journal of Health and Social Behavior, 54, 3*, https://www.ncbi.nlm.nih.gov/pmc/articles/PMC3836435/ Retrieved 12/28/2016.

Office of Adolescent Health (2016). Trends in teen pregnancy and childbearing. US Department of Health and Human Services. https://www.hhs.gov/ash/oah/adolescent-health-topics/reproductive-health/teen-pregnancy/trends.html

Parker, K. (2014). Families may differ, but they share common values on parenting. Pew Research Center. http://www.pewresearch.org/fact-tank/2014/09/18/families-may-differ-but-they-share-common-values-on-parenting/ Retrieved 12/28/2016.

Parker, K., Horowitz, J.M., & Rohal, M. (2015). Parenting in America: Outlook, worries, aspirations are strongly linked to financial situation. Pew Research Center. http://www.pewsocialtrends.org/2015/12/17/parenting-in-america/ Retrieved 5/17/2016.

Parker, K., & Wang, W. (2013). Modern parenthood: Roles of moms and dads converge as they balance work and family. Pew Research Center. http://www.pewsocialtrends.org/2013/03/14/modern-parenthood-roles-of-moms-and-dads-converge-as-they-balance-work-and-family/ Retrieved 12/22/2016.

Parkinson, P. (2011). *Family law and the indissolubility of parenthood*. Cambridge University Press.

Passel, J.S., Livingston, G., & Cohn, D. (2012). Explaining why minority births now outnumber white births. Pew Research Center. http://www.pewsocialtrends.org/2012/05/17/explaining-why-minority-births-now-outnumber-white-births/ Retrieved 12/18/2016.

Patterson, C.J. (1994). Children of the lesbian baby boom: Behavioral adjustment, self-concept, and sex-role identity. In B. Greene & G. Herek (Eds.), *Contemporary perspectives on lesbian and gay psychology: Theory, research, and application* (pp. 156–175). Beverly Hills, CA: Sage.

Ramos, V.M. (2010). Florida won't challenge end to gay adoption ban. *Orlando Sentinel*, October 10, 2010. http://articles.orlandosentinel.com/2010-10-22/news/os-gay-adoption-florida-20101022_1_gay-adoption-ban-martin-gill-gay-advocates Retrieved 12/30/2016.

Rogers, S.J., & White, L.K. (1998). Satisfaction with parenting: The role of marital happiness, family structure, and parents' gender. *Journal of Marriage and the Family, 60, 2*, 293–308.

Scher, A. (1991). A longitudinal study of night waking in the first year. *Child: Care, Health, and Development, 17*, 295–302.

Strohschin, L., Gauthier, A.H., Campbell, R., & Kleparchuk, C. (2008). Parenting as a dynamic process: A test of the resource dilution hypothesis theory. *Journal of Marriage and the Family, 70,* 670–683.

Tasker, F. (2005). Lesbian mothers, gay fathers, and their children: A review. *Journal of Developmental and Behavioral Pediatrics, 26, 3,* 224–240.

Turner, A. (2009). Population ageing: What should we worry about? *Philos Trans R Soc Lond B Biol Sci, 364, 1532,* 3009–3021.

Wall, G., & Arnold, S. (2007). How involved is involved fathering?: An exploration of the contemporary culture of fatherhood. *Gender and Society, 21, 4,* 508–527.

Credits

- Fig. 2.1: Centers for Disease Control / Copyright in the Public Domain.
- Fig. 2.2: Source: Pew Research Center.
- Fig. 2.3: Centers for Disease Control / Copyright in the Public Domain.
- Fig. 2.4: Source: Pew Research Center.
- Fig. 2.5: Source: Pew Research Center.
- Fig. 2.5(1): Copyright © by Depositphotos / leremy.
- Fig. 2.5(2): Copyright © by Depositphotos / agesxe.gmail.com.
- Fig. 2.6: Source: Pew Research Center.
- Fig. 2.7: Source: Pew Research Center.
- Fig. 2.8: Source: Pew Research Center.

PART II
The Pyramid Model: The Content of Parenting Education

Parenting advice and education are ubiquitous. Doctors, in-laws, friends, even strangers in public places all feel compelled to offer advice. Parent advice books number in the hundreds of thousands. Parenting classes are offered in churches, hospitals, and community centers. Parenting programs are required before adoption, after divorce, and a multitude of other circumstances. There is no shortage of instruction in parenting strategies, so much so that parents (and parent advisers) face the question of which strategy to use when.

Richard Berrett (1982) proposed a way to organize the breadth of parenting advice available. This organization of strategies was developed even more deeply in two editions of the *Engaged Parenting* reader (Berrett & Ramos, 2006; Dyer and Berrett, 2015). It is presented here as the Pyramid Model of Parenting (Figure P2.1). This is the point of the pyramid model, to help parents (and those who advise them) identify the most appropriate strategy for a given need. Since parents and their children live in complicated families, since they change over time and often have several issues to deal with simultaneously, they need something better than a piecemeal approach, better than an unorganized jumble of tools. To answer the question of how various parenting strategies relate to each other and might all be used, Berrett and Dyer (2015) propose that parenting strategies be considered using the model of a pyramid (see Figure P2.1).

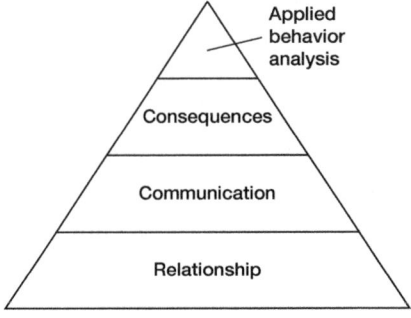

Figure P2.1 Parenting Pyramid

The structure of the pyramid suggests two important things. First, those strategies at the base are really the foundation upon which all else rests, and they are necessary to support the structure. Strategies higher up the pyramid simply won't work unless strategies lower down have already been established. Second, those parenting behaviors near the top of the pyramid are much smaller than those at the bottom and thus should be used much more sparingly. The apex of the pyramid is not the "best" or most respectable; instead, strategies at the apex have a place in the structure but a much smaller role than those near the base of the pyramid.

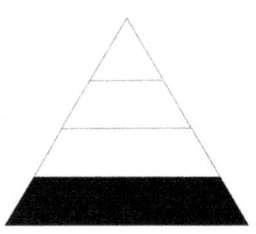

Figure 3.1

At the base of the pyramid, the largest section is the foundation of **attachment relationships**, the focus of Chapter 3. Without a strong relationship, no parenting technique can possibly be successful. Furthermore, when parents have difficulty with their children, a first point of examination is the nature of the relationship. Children who are repeatedly disobedient, disrespectful, and problematic may be angry, hurt, or disappointed and resentful toward the parent. Building the foundation of a loving, caring relationship will prevent many parent-child problems and resolve many others. While parent-child attachment relationships are first constructed in infancy, relationship-building is omnipresent through all stages of parenting. It is never left behind in favor of other strategies; it is always operating even when other approaches are added to it. It is the foundation on which all other strategies rest.

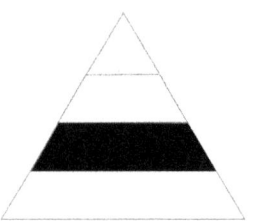

Figure 5.1

Communication is the next area of the pyramid and occupies a space just smaller than the foundation. Obviously, communication is part of building relationships, so we refer here specifically to communication to teach skills (Chapter 4) and solve problems (Chapter 5). One of the main jobs of a parent is to teach, including both concrete skills (how to brush one's teeth, how to ride a bike and drive a car, how to write a check, and so forth) and more abstract emotional and relationship skills (how to share a room with someone who is more/less neat, how to cope with disappointment). Chapter 4 addresses the former and Chapter 5 the latter. Parents and children who are capable of listening to each other and capable of confronting one another with kindness can resolve many issues.

When problem solving using communication leaves issues unresolved, it is valuable to turn to **consequences** (Chapter 6). Children instinctively know that part of their job is to grow up and out of their parents' direct influence. Therefore, they will occasionally challenge, even defy, parents, despite a good relationship and clear communication. In short, they will sometimes push parents beyond the comfort of that warm and supportive relationship. Furthermore, sometimes parents need to push them out of it in order to teach them skills they will need as they grow increasingly independent. Natural and logical consequences are the best way to teach children responsibility. Natural and logical consequences are the third section of the pyramid and are used less frequently than communication. Of the two, natural consequences should be tried first, so they are lower on the pyramid. But it is sometimes necessary to use logical consequences instead.

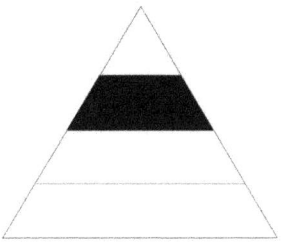

Figure 6.1

If communication and consequences are insufficient to ease a parent-child issue, we turn to the final and smallest section of the pyramid: **Applied Behavior Analysis** (Chapter 7). Analysis of behavior problems may indicate that antecedents can be used more effectively, and those changes are recommended. But reward and punishment have limitations and risks that restrict their utility. Applied behavior analysis approaches are widely used in our society, but this model suggests that they should be used far less than they are.

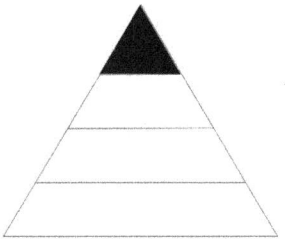

Figure 7.1

Each of the forthcoming chapters will fully define these strategies. Each chapter will answer questions such as: Where did the idea for this strategy come from? What are the best practices for use of this approach, and what are the pitfalls to watch out for? Under what conditions, and with what children might this strategy be used? How do parents react when they learn about this? Are there any formal parent education programs that include these strategies, and has evaluation found that it works?

References

Berrett, R.D. (1982). *The pursuit of family strength*. Statewide Publications.

Berrett, R.D., & Ramos, K.D. (Eds.) (2006). *Engaged parenting*. Pearson Custom Publishing.

Dyer, K.D., & Berrett, R.D. (2015). *Engaged parenting, 2nd edition*. San Diego, CA: Cognella.

3. Relationships

Introduction

Here we are at the base of the parenting pyramid: relationships. What we do here is what everything else rests on. Therefore, this may be the most important part. No matter what the issue or the parenting strategy used, relationships are always in the background creating a foundation on which all else rests. So we must explore the quality of parent-child relationships and what we know about how to make them strong.

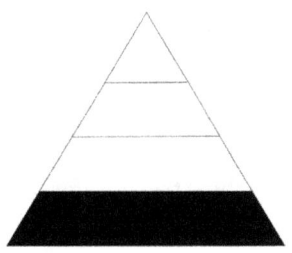

Figure 3.1 Attachment on Pyramid

Attachment Theory and Background

The theory we will use to approach relationships is **attachment theory**. It was articulated in the mid-20th century by John Bowlby (1969) and expanded significantly by Mary Ainsworth (Ainsworth, Blehar, Waters, & Wall, 1978). The tenets of attachment theory have been supported by a very large body of research evidence in recent decades. While attachment theory is being actively and vigorously researched, it is already one of the best-supported theories in family science. Bowlby and Ainsworth wrote about parent-child relationships in infancy, so that will be the basis of this exposition. As escaped slave and abolitionist Frederick Douglass wrote: "It's easier to build strong children than to repair broken men." However, we will discover quickly that the principles of attachment relationships can be expanded rather easily to inform all close personal relationships.

Fundamentally, attachment theory asserts that one's earliest relationships with caregivers in infancy shape identity and create relationship expectations that have impacts that guide one's life far into the future. But before we get to the details of how that happens, let's start with a bigger picture.

Environment of Evolutionary Adaptedness

To understand attachment theory, we begin by putting the history of the human species in context. The genus *Homo* appeared in Africa approximately 2.8 million years ago (Stringer, 1994). The agricultural revolution, which enabled humans to live in large, settled groups, occurred about 11,000 years ago. That means that the vast majority of time during which our species was evolving, we lived by foraging and hunting and moving through a vast landscape. John Bowlby knew less than we do today about early hominid history, but he called those millions of years on the African safari the **Environment of Evolutionary Adaptedness** (EEA). What he meant by that term is that those were the conditions under which our human species evolved and for which we are best suited (Bowlby, 1969). Every species is evolved to survive within a particular environment, and the environment within which our species evolved is the African savanna of the Pleistocene. Therefore, if we want to consider why our species has certain traits, we must consider how those traits may have afforded a survival advantage in the EEA.

What was that environment like? It was characterized by a wet season and a dry season, just as the sub-Saharan African savannas are today (see Figure 3.2).

Figure 3.2 African Savannah

We can look to fairly contemporary reports of foraging humans for an understanding of what life was like for our ancestors. The !Kung San are one such group, still living a nomadic, foraging life on the African savanna. Small groups travel about following large game during the dry months. They meet up in larger groups during the wet season, when there is enough water to sustain large groups (e.g., Shostak, 2000). All of this means constant mobility in small bands through a terrain that was dangerous due to insecure food availability and predators. Life was indeed tenuous for our ancestors.

Infant Care in the Environment of Evolutionary Adaptedness

We can reason out a few guesses about how babies were cared for in the EEA, and these logical conclusions have largely been confirmed by ethnographic study of contemporary groups who live much like our ancestors did (Konner, 2005). These characteristics of parenting in the EEA are summarized in Table 3.1. For one thing, human babies were (and are) unbelievably vulnerable and incapable of caring for themselves in even the most rudimentary way for some time after birth. This is the result of being a big-brained species that is also bipedal. Mothers need to give birth while the baby is still small enough to make it through the birth canal, but in order for that to happen, human babies must be born before their brains are fully developed. Otherwise, the head would simply be too big for birth. Therefore, human babies are different from other large mammals in that their young are born completely helpless. In addition, humans (like other large mammals) require years of care before reaching adulthood and being able

Table 3.1 Parenting in the Environment of Evolutionary Adaptedness

Parenting in the Environment of Evolutionary Adaptedness
Bonding
Grief
Attachment
Multiple Caregivers
Constant Physical Contact
Immediate Response to Crying
Cosleeping
Frequent Breastfeeding
Long Duration of Breastfeeding

to care for themselves. Human babies thus are extraordinarily needy, and their only chance of survival is to somehow convince an adult to care for them (Small, 1999). Consequently, babies have evolved all kinds of behaviors that elicit adult attention, called **attachment-promoting behaviors**, such as crying, clinging, and reaching, which inspire caregiving from adults (Bretherton, 1992). These behaviors generally signal distress and broadcast a need for intervention.

In the EEA, this neediness could only have been accommodated by forging very strong interpersonal bonds that inspire adults to invest heavily—and for many years—in the care of the young. The only way a baby could survive was to have adults willing to make big sacrifices on his or her behalf. The strong feelings of love and devotion on the part of the parent is referred to in attachment theory as **bonding** (Benoit, 2004). Bonding must happen very early in the child's life, maybe even before birth, if the child is to survive. A parent who does not experience bonding might not adequately care for the baby. Bonding occurs before the baby has a sufficiently developed brain to form a reciprocal attachment relationship, so bonding is a precursor of attachment, and it is something that happens to the adult. The process of bonding means that adults who love children are vulnerable to intense grief when harm does come to the child. In the EEA, infant mortality must have been very high, so grief is a normative part of the experience of parenthood.

The mutual relationship that forms over time between the committed adult and the child being cared for is **attachment**. Attachment relationships were essential in the EEA because they kept the vulnerable young close to trusted caregivers in a dangerous world. Since all human babies are born before their brains are fully matured, for the first four to six months after birth the survival of a baby was dependent on the bonding of adults around him. Infants instinctively send signals that tug at adult heartstrings (attachment-promoting behaviors) and thus help to promote bonding. But after those first few months, the baby's brain is adequately developed to also feel bonding toward the main caregivers. This point, when the bonding becomes mutual, is the beginning of attachment relationships.

Bonding, and then attachment, which kept babies alive in the EEA, were not necessarily exclusive to one caregiver. In fact, it makes far more sense that human babies anticipated multiple caregivers, at least in part because maternal mortality was quite high in the EEA. If the bond between biological mother and infant was unique and irreplaceable, then babies would automatically die when their mothers did, and our species could never have survived. Human adults do seem to instinctively respond to babies, and it's not just biological parents who demonstrate the instinct. So the babies most likely to survive would have been the ones who had multiple caregivers who experienced bonding to the baby. Those babies had a back-up, so to speak. If one bonded caregiver died, there was another who could step in. So it is natural, even typical, for human babies to be cared for by more than one person, and they develop attachment relationships with each of those caregivers (Schaffer & Emerson, 1964).

Since the EEA was dangerous, with our human ancestors preyed upon by other large animals, it seems likely that babies were kept in constant physical contact with caregiving adults. It would not make sense to set a baby down, as it would be hard to find the exact location again. If being left alone was dangerous, then human babies would have evolved the instinct to cry when left alone. Those who survived would have been the ones who had caregivers who responded immediately to the infant's cries. To allow a child to cry would have alerted predators to the child's exact location, not good for the child or the adults in proximity. Therefore, minimal crying with immediate response to crying and an immediate cessation of crying once a caregiver arrived certainly evolved as normative for our species. It also means that babies were never left alone to sleep. Adults would not have slept in privacy either, as they would be incredibly vulnerable to predators while asleep, so it would only be safe to sleep in the presence of other members of the tribe. The baby's brain is still wired to behave as it did on the African savanna. And that means that contemporary babies "expect" to be held constantly and never to be left alone, even during sleep. When they are set down, and left alone, they have evolved to cry, and to expect an immediate response from an adult, at which they stop crying (Small, 1999).

One more implication that deserves some consideration is feeding. Babies in the EEA were sustained by human milk, of course, as it evolved specifically for that purpose. But breastfeeding most likely was done very differently than it is done in contemporary US culture. For one thing, human babies were nursed very frequently. Human milk is relatively low-fat, and therefore does not sate a human baby's appetite for very long. It is also low-protein and not calorically dense. Therefore, babies need to nurse often for satiety and for adequate nourishment. Some mammals (called spaced feeders) produce very high-fat, high-protein milk and nurse infrequently. Rabbits are spaced feeders. They leave their young in a nest while they go out to find food and return infrequently to nurse. Young rabbits are sustained by the dense milk, which is 18% fat and 14% protein (Jenness, 1974). But other mammals (called continual feeders) produce low-fat, low-protein milk and thus are compelled to nurse frequently. Humans clearly belong to this second group, the continual feeders. Human milk is only 4% fat and 1% protein (Jenness, 1974; Institute of Medicine, 1991). Contemporary human parents might think it would be convenient to stash their babies in a nest and only nurse them infrequently, but that is clearly not how our ancestors evolved in the EEA. We evolved to nurse frequently, day and night. In addition to frequent (and thereby basically unscheduled) nursing, babies in the EEA nursed for a long duration, probably on the order of five to seven years. So breastfeeding was a major part of parenting babies and young children for our ancestors. This pattern of breastfeeding is still seen among the !Kung San (Konner, 2005), which confirms the speculation that this pattern was typical of our human ancestors.

Implications for Contemporary Parenting
What does all of this discussion of evolution and the EEA mean for contemporary parenting? Are we obligated to parent just as our ancestors did? No, of course not. With the agricultural revolution and later the Industrial Revolution, daily life for most members of the human species has altered drastically. The changes have happened so fast on an evolutionary scale, however, that we have launched into modern civilization with bodies that are exquisitely evolved for an earlier time. Our babies, therefore, "expect" care such as that described above. Most importantly for our purposes here, the attachment system evolved in the EEA and is still the primary mechanism to keep babies alive. Our instincts don't necessarily tell us what to do, but we do have an instinct that drives us toward attachment relationships. Understanding this can help us make sense of behaviors that otherwise seem nonsensical. For instance, when a baby is sleeping with great contentment in someone's arms, but then wakes up crying upon the slightest movement in the direction of setting him down, adults are often flabbergasted and wonder why he protests. "He's asleep … why does he care if I'm holding him or not!?!" Well, he has finely tuned instincts that say to be put down, especially while sleeping, poses a grave threat to his safety, so of course he protests. I believe that once we understand this, babies start to make sense to us. And to understand someone's distress softens our heart to them, and better enables us to have loving relationships.

A second implication for contemporary parenting is that the dynamics of attachment formation actually still operate in the exact same way they must have operated in the EEA. After all, Bowlby wrote about the concept of the EEA because he was trying to understand and explain contemporary attachment behaviors. His explanation offers us a way to understand why attachment works the way it does. Bowlby proposed this in 1969. Let's go back just a little bit before that, when contemporary work on parent-child relationships began.

Origins of Attachment Theory

Prior to any modern scientific investigation into the nature of parent-child relationships, Freudian psychoanalytic theory offered a hypothesis about why babies love their mothers. Freud asserted that humans are compelled by a drive to continue living (duh!) and called that a **primary drive** (specifically, libido). He then suggested that there are **secondary drives**, things we want not for their own sake but because they allow us to fulfill a primary drive (Freud, 1930). Freud's psychoanalytic theory produced the argument that an infant's love for its mother was a secondary drive, that infants love their mothers because mothers feed them (Miller & Dollard, 1941). This was really the only hypothesis on the table when scientists started to explore the issue.

Among the first such scientists was Konrad Lorenz, who, in 1935, documented the imprinting that occurs between goslings (baby geese) and their caregiver (usually, the mother goose). It turns out that geese will **imprint** on the first moving thing they see when they hatch. Imprinting obliges the gosling to follow that figure around at all costs. The gosling will continue to follow the target of its imprinting, even if that figure does not provide food and protection. Imprinting appears to be instantaneous, instinctive, and unalterable. Presumably, this works often enough, as the gosling's mother is quite likely to be the target of the imprinting (Burkhardt, 2005). Evidence about imprinting directly challenged the Freudian secondary drive hypothesis because the goslings' behavior remains intact regardless of whether the object of the imprinting provides food. This raised the question of whether human babies are the same way. There are some obvious similarities. Human babies also have relationships with their mothers, seemingly immediately at birth, that children seek to maintain, even if the relationship is not a good one. Just as with goslings, this system usually works well enough, as most parents care for their children and children do seem to love their parents no matter how neglectful or abusive the parents are.

However, there are some differences relevant to our discussion here. The most important difference between imprinting in geese and attachment formation in humans is that geese imprint on a caregiver instantly upon hatching, which is unalterable, but human babies take months to form attachment relationships. Babies do not even begin to form attachments until a few months after their birth, and attachment relationships can be changed when caregiving changes. The smaller difference, still meaningful for our purposes, is that imprinting is exclusive; a gosling imprints on only one figure. Human babies, though, form attachments with multiple caregivers. Therefore, we distinguish between two methods of forging a connection between the young and their caregivers which enables survival: imprinting (found in birds) and attachment (found in humans and presumably in some other mammals as well).

So human attachment relationships are different from imprinting in birds in some very profound ways. After Lorenz's work, we were left with a serious challenge to the secondary drive hypothesis but without an alternative explanation for the very close relationship found between most human parents and their children. Next on the scene came Harry Harlow, in Madison, Wisconsin (pictured in Figure 3.3). Harlow wanted to study primates but needed to produce a population of monkeys for use in his lab. He wanted to study learning in infant macaque monkeys, so he started to raise them by hand, rather than allowing them to be reared by their mothers. He noticed that those monkeys were very different from the others and so developed a scientific curiosity about the effects of mothers and maternal deprivation on the young. This, unexpectedly, was the work for which he would become famous (Suomi & Leroy, 1982).

The maternally deprived monkeys behaved similarly to the very young human children who were separated from their parents through hospitalization and institutionalization. René Spitz very famously made a film in 1947 about grief in those maternally deprived children. Bowlby's colleague James Robertson studied children separated from their parents during World War II (Bretherton, 1992). The issue of human children separated from their mothers was prominent, therefore, at the time that Harry Harlow studied this phenomenon with monkeys (see Figure 3.3), and it was already a major focus of John Bowlby's research lab in London, England.

Harlow experimented with the maternally deprived infant macaques. Since humans are much more closely related to monkeys than to geese, it is reasonable to assume that this is a better model for human attachment than is imprinting. Harlow provided various surrogate mothers for the baby monkeys. He discovered that the babies showed a clear and strong preference for a terrycloth-covered surrogate mother rather than a wire mother that provided food. Notice (Figure 3.3) that the terrycloth-covered mother also had physical features that made it more realistic, including a round face and big eyes, but that it did not provide access to food.

Figure 3.3 Harry Harlow

For our purposes here, we will focus on three conclusions of Harlow's work (Harlow, 1958).

1. Early attachment relationships shape functioning all through life. Maternally deprived baby monkeys were damaged socially and were always incapable of normal macaque relationship behavior. This suggests that early attachment is critical for healthy future development.

2. Attachment is related to **contact comfort** rather than feeding. That is, a baby monkey prefers to spend much of its time with a surrogate mother who is soft and fuzzy, with whom he can snuggle, rather than a cold wire mother that provides food. This suggests that touch is a central element of attachment relationships.

3. Attachment relationships are characterized by proximity seeking when frightened. When frightened, infants use their surrogate mothers to feel safe and protected. Harlow discovered it by purposefully frightening a baby monkey, who would then run to the cloth mother (never to the wire mother that provides food) and seem to draw confidence from contact with the surrogate mother, turning back to face the perceived threat. Bowlby will later call this *secure base behavior*; it is one of the primary indicators of an attachment relationship.

At the same time that Harlow was doing his research with mother substitutes, John Bowlby was in England studying human children's separation from their parents (Bretherton, 1992). An American researcher named Mary Ainsworth worked in his research lab with him. Bowlby focused on finding an explanation for the close relationship between mother and child and turned to the work of Lorenz and Harlow. From 1958 to 1960, Bowlby published papers outlining his new theory (Bretherton, 1992). Bowlby's attachment theory asserts that:

1. Babies are born with an innate need to form an attachment to a caregiver for all of the reasons described above in the section on the EEA. **Secure base behavior** is the primary indicator of an attachment relationship. It is the child's use of the adult as a place to return to when distressed and a launching pad for exploration when secure.

2. Babies need continuous care from an attachment figure for about two years. This is a **critical period**, meaning that it is developmentally required at that specific time. Delay or interruption of the attachment relationship during this period is damaging to the baby's development (McLeod, 2007).

3. The consequences of long-term deprivation of an attachment figure are serious and affect all domains of life, perhaps especially the ability to have affectionate relationships with others (McLeod, 2007).

4. The quality of the attachment relationship that forms between baby and caregiver is the product of the interaction between the two and produces differences in personality later in life (Sroufe, 2005).

5. Attachment is a behavioral system, one that is triggered when the child is having an emotional need, when the child is distressed in some way. It is only during these specific moments in the relationship that the attachment relationship is formed and when it can be observed. Emotional needs, also called **tender needs**, include fear, anger, sadness, and any other painful emotion that would, in the EEA, put the young child in danger such that they would need to seek proximity to a caregiver. Fear signals danger in an obvious way; the child is afraid of a perceived danger. Anger and sadness both make a person less attentive to their environment, less able to perceive threats. Therefore, in the EEA, it would

have been safest to be in the presence of others while feeling angry or sad (Bowlby, 1969).

6. Attachment relationships shape the way a child thinks about the nature of the world, which Bowlby calls the **internal working model**. This model becomes the prototype of all future relationships. A secure internal working model sees others in the world as trustworthy, views oneself as valuable, and sees the self as capable of interacting with others effectively (McLeod, 2007).

All of these points have been supported by subsequent research on human attachment and are generally accepted to be true. Further development of the theory was accomplished by Mary Ainsworth. She moved Bowlby's theory from the realm of speculative supposition into an empirical science. Her observational research on mother-infant pairs in Uganda (begun in 1953) was the first empirical study of attachment theory. This is where Ainsworth identified three different types of attachment relationships and made the discovery that maternal sensitivity is the likely mechanism by which attachment is formed. She then launched the Baltimore study, where she studied mother-infant pairs in that city, and developed a procedure that can be done in a laboratory during a short time (approximately 20 minutes) called the **Strange Situation**, which is considered the gold standard for measurement of attachment. She collected data that she analyzed with a thoroughness and carefulness that distinguish her as a truly great scientist (Bretherton, 1992).

Attachment Patterns and Their Outcomes

Because the attachment system is only activated when the child is having tender needs, the Strange Situation procedure is designed to gradually increase the infant's distress. The observer notes the pattern of behavior between caregiver and child as the child's discomfort increases. First, a stranger is brought into the room, which puts children of this age (12–18 months) on edge. Then, the stranger talks to them. Then the mother leaves the child alone with the stranger, and finally, the mother and stranger leave the child alone. Each of these events ratchets up the child's emotional distress so that the observer can be certain that the attachment system is activated. The three attachment patterns described by Ainsworth (Ainsworth, Blehar, Waters, & Wall, 1978) are:

1. **Secure Attachment**: Babies in these relationships explore the environment but use the parent as a secure base when they feel stressed. They become distressed when the parent leaves the room, and use attachment-promoting signals upon the parent's return. The dynamic between the parent and child works to soothe the child, who is then able to return to play. In Ainsworth's Baltimore study (Ainsworth, Blehar, Waters, & Wall, 1978) and in a meta-analysis of strange situation studies from around the world (Van Ijzendoorn & Kroonenberg, 1988), secure attachment is the most prevalent pattern, representing slightly more than half (approximately 60–65%) of baby-caregiver pairs studied.

2. **Insecure Avoidant Attachment**: Babies in these relationships do not necessarily display distress overtly when the parent leaves the room, although their play becomes diminished in quality. But upon the parent's return, they characteristically minimize attachment-promoting behaviors rather than seeking comfort from the parent. They may even avoid interaction with the parent should it be offered. In Ainsworth's Baltimore study (Ainsworth, Blehar, Waters, & Wall, 1978) and in a meta-analysis of strange situation studies from around the world (Van Ijzendoorn & Kroonenberg, 1988), avoidant attachment is the most prevalent insecure pattern, representing about one-fifth (15–20%) of baby-caregiver pairs studied.

3. **Insecure Resistant Attachment**: Babies in these relationships are least likely to explore the environment, even when the parent is present. They become extraordinarily distressed when the parent leaves the room and maximize attachment-promoting behaviors upon the parent's return. Furthermore, and most characteristically, the dynamic between the parent and child does NOT work to soothe the child when the parent attempts to respond. The child might escalate attachment-promoting signals even while the parent attempts to soothe him, or he might angrily reject those attempts. (Note: This is sometimes called an *ambivalent attachment* because it appears that the child is ambivalent, sometimes wanting the parent's attention and at other times rejecting it.) In Ainsworth's Baltimore study (Ainsworth, Blehar, Waters, & Wall, 1978) and in a meta-analysis of strange situation studies from around the world (Van Ijzendoorn & Kroonenberg, 1988), resistant attachment is somewhat less prevalent (10–15%) than avoidant attachment among the baby-caregiver pairs studied.

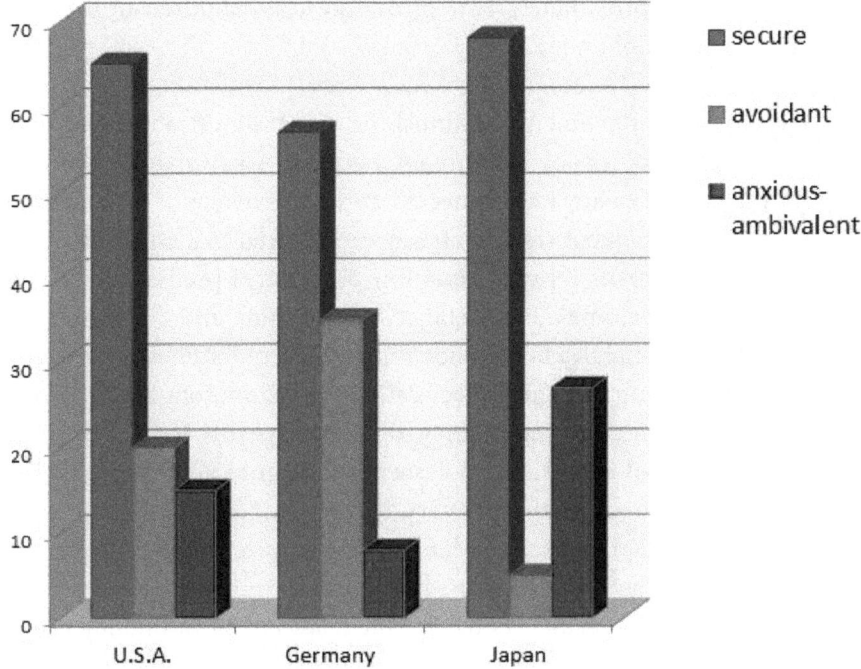

Figure 3.4 Prevalence of Patterns of Attachment

The prevalence of these three types of attachment in various cultures is noted in Figure 3.4. When Ainsworth was conducting research, she found in every sample a small but not insignificant proportion of relationships that did not fit into any of these three patterns. She called them "Unclassifiable." Her student, Mary Main, spent her career studying the so-called unclassifiable attachment relationships, and as a result of her work, we now call this type of insecure attachment *Disorganized* (Main & Hesse, 1990).

4. **Insecure Disorganized Attachment**: Babies in these relationships show characteristics of more than one of the patterns described by Ainsworth. For instance, they might show clear signs of avoidance combined with clear signs of resistance, or a secure pattern interspersed with moments of clear avoidance. Sometimes these babies show what appears to be fear, or they "still" and do not do anything during critical moments of reunion with the parent after being stressed. These disorganized behaviors are often very bizarre and perplexing. After this category was added, it has been

identified in approximately 12% of middle-class children in the United States (Main & Solomon, 1990).

These four types of attachment relationships are a significant expansion of Bowlby's conceptualization of attachment because Ainsworth demonstrated that, while attachment of any kind is necessary for survival, not all attachments are equally good. Subsequent research has demonstrated that attachment status (as defined by Ainsworth's Strange Situation procedure) predict future cognitive and emotional outcomes. For instance, Alan Sroufe and colleagues at the University of Minnesota have been following a group of families since the early 1970s, an intensive longitudinal project called the Minnesota Study. After assessing attachment status during infancy, they measured outcomes during the preschool years, school-age years, adolescence, and into adulthood. Children with a secure attachment to the primary caregiver in infancy demonstrated greater happiness, social skills, compliance, empathy, emotional health, more friends, leadership behavior, and more satisfaction in romantic relationships. In short, the security of the primary attachment relationship in infancy is a very important predictor of good outcomes in all areas of life for decades at least (Sroufe, Egeland, Carlson, & Collins, 2005).

Best Practices

The implications of attachment theory for parenting are both profound and fairly obvious. If we accept attachment theory—and it has so much support in the research that, frankly, it would be foolish not to—then we must conclude that sensitive responsiveness should be the most important principle of all parenting guidance. Mary Ainsworth's description of sensitive responsiveness should be the set of instructions given to new parents. It is the key to success in the job of parenting.

Sensitive Responsiveness

Ainsworth's remarkable contribution to science, in addition to devising a method to identify and classify attachment relationships (the strange situation), was to provide an explanation for what produces these four patterns of relationship. What does determine the quality of attachment relationships? Ainsworth identifies it as maternal sensitivity, also called **sensitive responsiveness**. Sensitive responsiveness is a pattern of interaction by which the caregiver tailors his or her behavior to the signals of the child. The parent is responsive to the child's expressed tender needs (rather than ignoring them) and changes the response based on the child's reaction to each behavior. Therefore, sensitive responsiveness is dependent on reciprocal interactions between parent and child. Subsequent longitudinal research (Sroufe, 2005), as well as a meta-analysis of research on this question (DeWolff & Van Ijzendoorn, 1997), have confirmed that sensitive responsiveness does, in fact, predict the pattern of attachment. Ainsworth describes sensitive responsiveness (Ainsworth, 1969) as having four components and one underlying feature:

1. **Awareness of signals:** The sensitive parent detects when the child is sending a signal about his or her tender needs. First, the parent must make him- or herself reasonably available so that these signals will get through. Second, the parent must have a fairly low threshold to detect even low-intensity signals rather than ignoring them and waiting until the child is so distressed that signals are persistent and intense. For instance, a sensitive parent will notice whimpers rather than waiting until a child is crying outright. *Please note that sensitive responsiveness is only called for when the child is in distress. Tender needs must be present to observe attachment patterns as in the Strange Situation, but they also must be present for the attachment pattern to be formed as well.*

2. **Accurate interpretation of signals:** The sensitive parent interprets the signals in a way that is consistent with the child's development and resists the temptation to distort the message to fit a preconceived notion of what is going on. This is often characterized by empathy in the parent's description of the child's behavior.

3. **Prompt response to signals:** The sensitive parent responds quickly to the child's signal. Ainsworth measured this very simply, by counting the seconds or minutes from the time the signal of distress is received until the parent goes to the child. She said that sensitive parents respond immediately. The wait-and-see approach so commonly endorsed, where parents are instructed NOT to jump when the baby cries but instead to

Table 3.2 Patterns of Attachment

Attachment Pattern	Characterized By:	Produced By:
Secure	Secure base behavior, contact fully resolves distress	Consistent, sensitive responsiveness
Insecure-Avoidant	Minimized attachment promoting signals	Consistent non-responsiveness
Insecure-Resistant	Maximized attachment promoting signals	Inconsistent responsiveness
Insecure-Disorganized	No clear pattern; fear; stilling	Drastic change in responsiveness; Frightening parental behavior

wait and see if she can soothe herself, directly contradicts this principle of sensitive responsiveness.

4. **Appropriate response to signals:** The sensitive parent responds in a way that works to soothe the child. There is no one correct response, as circumstances and children vary. If the response soothes the child, then it was an appropriate response. Sensitive parents try different things to soothe the baby, each time watching carefully to see if the effort is working. If it's not working, they try something else. If it does work, they use that strategy again in the future. Secure attachment is not a product of any particular caregiving practice; it is a product of the sensitivity with which the practice is employed.

5. **Rhythmicity:** The daily rhythm of life seemed to Ainsworth to be a feature underlying the four components described above. She noted that sensitive parents tend to be mid-range on a scale of how structured their caregiving is. She asserted that sensitive care acknowledges that babies need rhythm and structure to help shape their lives, but that structure cannot be rigid, as babies' needs do change as a result of development and other circumstances in their life. So a middling amount of rhythmicity is optimal.

The patterns of attachment that result from various patterns of responsiveness are summarized in Figure 3.4. Sensitive responsiveness, consistently applied when the child has tender needs, is thus the ideal parenting approach. It produces secure attachment. The reader may recall that sensitive and responsive caregiving in infancy is one of the points on which family scientists have achieved a consensus. The degree of support for this argument in the research literature is so extensive that there is no justification for disagreement.

Babies who have a sensitively responsive parent develop an internal working model that says that the caregiver can be trusted in times of need, that the child is valuable, and that the child is capable of getting what he needs if he asks for it. This model will then be applied in all new relationships, which is why these children grow up to have social skills that enable them to do well in life. Babies with secure attachments in infancy grow up to be demonstrably more self-reliant, able to regulate their own emotions, more persistent and flexible in problem solving, display more positive emotions while with peers, and have greater social competence. When they move into childhood, they pursue peer relationships and manage those relationships largely independent of adult intervention. When stressful events befall their families, these children are resilient and much less likely than other children to develop behavior problems or psychiatric diagnoses such as depression or anxiety by the late teen years. When they do develop behavior or psychiatric problems, they recover more quickly than insecurely attached children (Sroufe, 2005).

Insecure-avoidant attachment is the product of **consistent non-responsiveness** to the child's tender needs. This is when parents do not respond to attachment-promoting signals sent by their child. The child cries or reaches to the parent and is rebuffed. Who would do this to a baby? These are sometimes parents who have been socialized to believe that children need to be toughened up, so they purposefully ignore signals of need. A mother once reported to me that she left her babies to lie on the floor while she worked around the house. "Oh, eventually they stop crying." Yes, of course they do. They learn that there's no point in asking, as requests for assistance are never answered. That parent didn't realize what a sad story she was telling. Parents with severe depression or addiction problems are also at increased risk of producing insecure-avoidant attachment relationships with their children. The parent in these cases is simply not capable of the first component of sensitive responsiveness, being aware of the child's signals of tender needs. The internal working model that develops is the belief that the parent will not meet their needs, that they are incapable of getting their needs met, and that they are not worth the caregiver's time and attention. These children grow up to have difficulties in relationships because they do not trust that they will ever get what they need or that they can possibly effect a change in their own circumstances. Longitudinal research has found that children with insecure-avoidant attachments in infancy have great difficulty with interpersonal relationships. They are characterized by others as isolated and not sociable. They appear not to want peer relationships. If they develop behavior problems in adolescence, it is generally with anger and explosive conduct (Sroufe, 2005).

Insecure-resistant attachment is the product of **inconsistent responsiveness** to tender needs. These parents sometimes respond sensitively but sometimes do not. Parents fall into this inconsistent pattern of behavior when their impulses are good, but they are constrained by outside circumstances. For instance, very young parents are at great risk of this attachment pattern, simply because they lack the maturity to respond with sensitivity every single time their baby needs attention. They can do it sometimes, but then the immaturity of their youth overcomes their good intentions. Longitudinal research has found that children with insecure-resistant attachments in infancy grow up to be hesitant to play and explore, easily frustrated, quick to give up in the face of challenge, and perceived by others as passive. They tend to hover near adults for guidance and are easily upset. They intently seek out peer relationships but are not very effective at maintaining friendships. If they develop problems in adolescence, it is generally with anxiety (Sroufe, 2005).

Mary Main and her colleagues spent years videotaping parents and children who have insecure-disorganized attachments trying to identify a causative factor, and they discovered that **frightening parental behavior** is likely the cause (Hesse & Main, 2006). Subsequent longitudinal research has confirmed that

Table 3.3 Emotional Availability (Biringen, 2004)

Characteristics of Emotional Availability
1. Parent is emotionally recruitable by the child.
2. Child is emotionally recruitable by the parent.
3. Parent is sensitive to the child.
4. Interactions are appropriately structured.
5. Parent is available without being intrusive.
6. No overt or covert hostility is present.
7. Child is responsive to parent.
8. Child allows parent to be involved in his/her life.

intrusive interactions and maltreatment predict insecure-disorganized attachment (Sroufe, 2005). Abused and neglected children are very likely to display a disorganized attachment with the maltreating parent, but even in non-abusive families, harshly insensitive parenting practices can be perceived as frightening and therefore produce a disorganized attachment (Van Ijzendoorn, 1999). Longitudinal research on children with insecure-disorganized attachment in infancy reveals that they are the group most likely to have a psychiatric diagnosis by late adolescence, especially the very serious disorders that involve dissociation and personality disorders (Sroufe, 2005).

Emotional Availability

One popularized version of sensitive responsiveness that is admirably consistent with empirical evidence is contained in Zeynep Biringen's 2004 book on creating a secure attachment. She outlines the features of a parent-child relationship characterized by **emotional availability** (see Table 3.3), which is clearly a reworking of Ainsworth's notion of sensitive responsiveness. Biringen has conducted research on sensitive responsiveness and settled on the following characteristics as demonstrated in the behavior of securely attached parent-child pairs (Biringen, Derscheid, Vliegen, Closson, & Easterbrooks, 2014; Ziv, Aviezer, Gini, Sagi, & Koren-Karie, 2000).

1. Parent is emotionally recruitable by the child. This is Ainsworth's notion of being available to receive signals of attachment needs, combined with her notion of accurately interpreting those signals. Biringen says that the parent must see the child's attempt and know that it means that the child needs him or her. The parent must be willing to respond when the child calls.

2. Child is emotionally recruitable by the parent. This is the mirror image of the first item. Attachment, as I've said already, is a reciprocal relationship. This means that the signals go both ways, and they must be detected and interpreted correctly, both ways. A popular parenting adviser, William Sears (2001), calls this ***mutual sensitivity***. He points out that securely attached children are remarkably sensitive to the signals sent by the parent.

3. Parent is sensitive to child. Sensitivity refers to the specific details of the individual child in exactly the same way that Ainsworth uses the term. A sensitive parent knows their child, recognizes their particular signals, is familiar with their tastes and preferences, and can read their nonverbal signals. The parent responds to the child according to the particulars of the child and the circumstances. There is also an element of liking one's child and therefore consistently displaying genuinely positive affection for the child. Biringen specifies, however, that the parent's affect must be appropriate to the circumstances; that is to say, it must be authentic. And of course, part of authenticity is that the parent's verbal and nonverbal expressions should match.

4. Interactions are appropriately structured. The parent sets reasonable limits while acknowledging the shifting needs of the child and finds a balance of these competing interests. This may be the same as what Ainsworth called *rhythmicity*. Biringen explains that providing a supportive framework can create a sense of safety necessary for exploration to occur.

5. Parent is available without being intrusive. It is possible for well-meaning parents to be intrusive through overstimulation, overprotection, and over-directiveness, something Ainsworth also noted in her Maternal Sensitivity Scales (1969). These parents might want so much for their child to be happy and learn what is necessary that they may try to force these lessons and prevent the child from making his or her own decisions that could possibly teach the desired lessons. Another version of intrusiveness is an unwillingness to accept imperfection in our children. Sometimes the best thing that an emotionally available (i.e., sensitively responsive) parent can do is to let the child make a mistake and help the child process what happened after the fact. But an intrusive parent is unwilling to allow the mistake to happen in the first place, thereby depriving the child of the learning experience. The contemporary concept of helicopter parenting might be identifying what Ainsworth and Biringen would have called intrusive parenting. The term *helicopter parenting* was coined by Cline and Fay (1990) in a book that we will discuss at length in a later chapter of this book. But it seems that attachment theory would see helicopter parenting as overinvolved, so much so that children are prevented from learning.

6. No overt or covert hostility is present. Children can annoy and anger their parents. That's the nature of the job. It would be unrealistic to expect parents never to be angry or upset. But parents must have sufficient maturity to be able to control themselves and to prevent hostility from creeping—or exploding—into their interactions with children. This is similar to Ainsworth's description of accurately interpreting the child's signals. She notes that empathy for the child is required in order to make an accurate interpretation of the child's signals.

7. Child is responsive to parent. Children of emotionally available parents will respond positively and eagerly when the parent makes a gesture to initiate interaction. Through years of interaction, the child has come to see the parent's involvement as a positive and desirable event and wants to connect to the parent. These children are generally happy and respond with positive affect to their parents. Ainsworth did not directly measure the child's behavior when identifying sensitive responsiveness because she wanted to operationalize the sensitive responsiveness of the parent by looking only at the parent's behavior. Biringen has accepted decades of research showing that these two things are connected, so much so that if you see the outcome in the child's behavior, it can be taken as a sign that the parent has done something to produce it.

8. Child allows parent to be involved in his or her life. The healthiest parent-child relationship strikes a balance between the capacity for autonomy and the desire to connect. Again, this is based on the assumption that the child's behavior reflects the parenting practices that produced it.

One implication of attachment theory and research is that attachment relationships are always operating in the background, no matter what else is going on. In my work doing parenting education, no matter what parenting problem walks through the door, the first thing I ask myself is how to determine the level of sensitive responsiveness in the situation. If the parent is sensitively responsive, then I know that the parent is likely to be open to suggestions, and the child is likely to be resilient. Whatever strategy is suggested will rest on a solid foundation. But if I detect that the parent is not sensitively responsive, I know that nothing I suggest will work until that problem is resolved.

Sensitive responsiveness (as defined above by Ainsworth and Biringen) is the guiding principle for creating and maintaining healthy parent-child relationships. One implication of this concept is that parents simply must respond to children's emotional needs. This clearly reveals a lot of "common wisdom" as pure bunk. Every variation of "just let the baby cry" is obviously nonsense. When the children have emotional needs, parents must respond in some way. Attachment theory doesn't tell parents what exactly to do, but we know that to do nothing is a bad idea.

So how must they respond? Should they always give the child exactly what the child is asking for? Well, Ainsworth says that sensitive parents respond appropriately, so the difficult task is to figure out what is appropriate. And she says that parents must respond sensitively, so parents must tailor their response to the particular child and the particular circumstances. Based on attachment theory, there is no single intervention that is best for everyone and should always be done. To create strong relationships, parents must respond to their child as a unique individual and honor the relationship as a unique interaction. There are no specific rules about how to do that, as it will be different with every relationship. This is big news. It means that the job is harder than we ever imagined. It means that there is no set of instructions because the instructions are different every time and can only be "read" in the relationship itself.

When Should Sensitive Responsiveness Be Used?

Their placement on the parenting pyramid says everything. Attachment relationships form the base of the pyramid. The principles of attachment formation and maintenance are operating at all times as the context within which all else happens. Sensitive responsiveness, also known as emotional availability, is always the goal. There is no risk of being too sensitive or being sensitive too often. Literally, the more sensitively responsive, the better.

However, it should be noted that the attachment system is only activated when the child is having tender needs, which is when they are experiencing painful emotions. Consequently, anytime fear, sadness, or anger are operating, the parent should be thinking in terms of sensitive responsiveness.

Developmental Connections

Sensitive responsiveness is appropriate for children of all ages. It may even be appropriate in all human relationships. Most adults want friends, siblings, and romantic partners who use these guidelines with them (be available, interpret signals with empathy, respond promptly, fully resolve distress, for instance); I know that I do. So the concept itself is not limited to just one time in life. However, there are some peculiarities of attachment relationships at different ages.

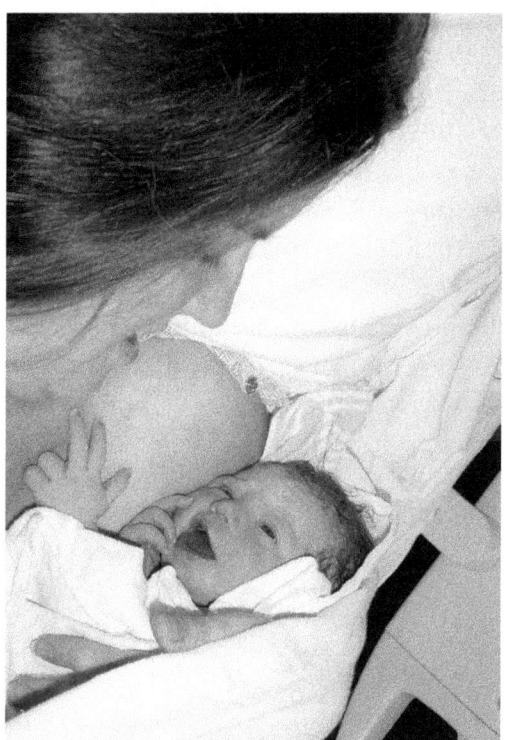

Figure 3.5 Newborn Baby Elicits Parental Bonding

Newborn Babies: Pre-attachment

Attachment formation is developmentally all consuming in the first few years of life. But very early on, from zero to seven months of age, babies do not have adequate brain development to form attachment relationships yet. Bowlby wrote that this early **pre-attachment phase** is much shorter, zero to six weeks (Bowlby, 1969), but the ages he specified represented a wild guess with no empirical foundation. But around the same time, two researchers (Schaffer & Emerson, 1964) empirically measured relevant behaviors in babies using a longitudinal design, and they provided age estimates with more validity. Babies in the pre-attachment phase have instincts that promote bonding in their adult caregivers. Their vision allows them to lock eyes with an adult who is holding them. They smile. They curl their fingers around the adult's finger placed in their palm. All of these behaviors cause adult hearts to melt. The adults fall in love, and the baby's survival is secured at least until attachment formation. (See Figure 3.5.) Babies in this early stage do show signs of recognizing familiar adults, especially after about three months of age. They may even display some preference for familiar adults, but they do not display secure base behavior or the mutual sensitivity that characterize attachment relationships.

The fact that attachment does not form until the second half of the first year means that babies are somewhat indifferent as to who provides their care early on. They will often happily go to anyone who offers to hold them. This means that newborn babies are not damaged by the loss of a mother very early in life so long as a mother substitute provides adequate care. Babies adopted in the first months of life are in no danger with regard to attachment formation. It also means that birth experiences and early breastfeeding are probably not related to attachment. If they promote bonding, then that might lead to a better attachment relationship later, but this has never been demonstrated to be the case. There might be good reasons to have a natural childbirth, and there are definitely lots of good reasons to breastfeed, but those reasons do not include promotion of secure attachment.

Late Infancy and Toddlerhood: Attachment Formation

Attachment formation, when true attachment relationships form most actively, occurs between seven and ten months (Schaffer & Emerson, 1964). Stranger anxiety develops around six months after birth and separation anxiety around ten months. Babies start to notice exactly who their caregivers are and to develop a strong preference for their regular caregivers. Grandparents, aunts and uncles, and friends of the family may lament: "She used to love for me to hold her, but now she cries when she sees me! What happened?" The truth is that nothing happened that has anything to do with the disgruntled friend or relative. It's just that the baby's brain developed sufficiently to form relationships, and human babies have evolved to be afraid of people unfamiliar to them. At this point, attachment relationships form in a most dramatic way.

Many infants in the latter half of the first year turn into "Velcro babies." They want to be physically attached to their main caregivers constantly and protest strenuously when handed over to anyone else or even set down to be alone. During this time, they develop attachment relationships with a small number of people, but they will have a hierarchy of preference for those attachment figures. If a baby is attached to Mom, Dad, and the babysitter and all three are in the room when she gets hurt (which triggers a tender need), there is probably one of those three people she will prefer as her first choice. It is very often, but not always, the mother.

In my work as a parent educator, I talk to mothers who are heartbroken because the baby seems to prefer its grandmother or babysitter. I talk to fathers who feel jealous and hurt that the baby seems to prefer its mother. I believe this stems from a fundamental misunderstanding of how attachment works. If we believe that attachment is exclusive, then we will feel displaced by the child's attachment relationship with another caregiver. But attachment is NOT exclusive. The baby really can have attachment relationships with all three of those caregivers. Sometimes a parent educator can help the parent reframe the situation by pointing out how lucky the child is to have multiple attachment figures, all of whom are completely devoted to the child's health and happiness. And how lucky the parent is to share the work with those collaborators. Bowlby himself asserts strongly (Bowlby, 1988) that one person really cannot alone do all of the work of caring for a child. It is an exhausting job and simply must be shared.

This is especially hard to swallow when the adults who have attachment relationships with the same child do not have an amicable relationship with each other. Parents who are in the process of divorcing, for instance, sometimes suffer terrible angst because of a misunderstanding of the child's attachment hierarchies. Here is a scenario I often encounter when doing court-mandated parenting education for divorcing parents: Mom says that the young child doesn't want to go to Dad for visitation because the child clings to her and cries when Dad arrives to pick up the child. Mom worries that the child is being mistreated at Dad's house and that's why the child doesn't want to go. Mom doesn't believe Dad when he says that as soon as she leaves, the baby clings to him like that, and it would be fine if Mom just lets go. Dad sees Mom's resistance as evidence that she is purposely trying to turn the child against him by treating him as a threat. (I'm using "Mom" and "Dad" this way because this is a very common pattern, but any two caregivers could develop a dynamic like this regardless of gender or their specific relationship to the child. For instance, I've seen nannies and moms get into this cycle as well.)

Both adults in this scenario are evaluating the situation based on a misunderstanding of how attachment works, and it is causing each one of them to think the worst of the other parent, increasing conflict—and thus stress—in the child's world. It is far more likely that, because of mutual sensitivity, the child is picking up on the stress that the parents are feeling, so the child is distressed, and that is triggering the attachment system. The baby simply has a hierarchy of attachment figures, with the mother higher than the father (because Mom probably spent more time with the baby prior to the divorce), and so in her distress, she is preferring the attachment figure at the top of her hierarchy. Because of the hierarchy of multiple attachment figures, Dad is probably telling the truth that the child calms and uses him as a secure base when Mom is not around. And the mom is probably sincerely concerned, not maliciously trying to turn the child against him. A parent educator who can help the parents understand this dynamic will relieve a lot of anxiety and reduce conflict in that family, which is good for parents and child alike.

Attachment formation is somewhat malleable during the early years of development. Changes in caregiving in the toddler years can change the attachment relationship. An intervention at 12 months designed to improve the parent's sensitive responsiveness can change an insecure attachment relationship to a secure one by 18 months of age (Sroufe, Egeland, Carlson, & Collins, 2005).

Later Childhood and Adolescence

Once children get through the attachment formation process, which may be complete by three or four years of age (a specific age has not been identified by research, but it seems to be in this range), then attachment relationships are resistant to change, and children retain some characteristic behaviors of their first attachment relationship pattern, even when change is effected (Sroufe, 2005). From a cognitive point of view, what happens is that children start to project the internal working model they assumed during attachment formation onto new people, and they develop what might be called an **attachment style** that is applied beyond just the relationship that produced it. The attachment style elicits corresponding caregiving from teachers and shapes all relationships in a self-fulfilling prophecy.

Unless the parent educator is teaching a transition to parenthood class for brand-new parents, they will mostly encounter parents with school-age or adolescent children. Therefore, the parents formed attachment relationships with their children several years ago, and those relationships are very resistant to change. However, the principles of sensitive responsiveness can be employed with children of any age. Even if the parent has not been consistently responsive in the past, it is possible to start now. There's no way this would damage a relationship, and it's a better way to live than to continue in the isolation or intrusiveness of insecure attachment relationships. The tender needs of a child may be better hidden when they are older than when they were babies. And the attachment-promoting behaviors (which are efforts to signal tender needs) will be different. Instead of crying and lifting his arms to be picked up, an older child might roll his eyes and look away. The parent of an older child will need to learn to see these as signals of tender needs. Older children also need to be comforted differently than babies, obviously. Harlow's notion of contact comfort is easier to implement with babies than with older kids who might resist getting a hug. But the basic principle remains the same: an intervention is appropriate if it fully resolves the distress.

Intergenerational Transmission of Attachment

Bowlby and Ainsworth both speculated that parents would have a similar attachment relationship with their own children that they had with their own parent as a young child. In other words, attachment would be transmitted intergenerationally. Mary Main (Main, Kaplan, & Cassidy, 1985) developed a method for identifying an adult's internal working models through an interview. The interview is coded in such a way that some adults are classified as having a **secure-autonomous model** of relationships, meaning that they value close relationships and talk about their own past attachment relationships without defensiveness. These adults are quite likely to have secure attachment relationships with their own infants. Others have a **dismissing model**, which means they dismiss the importance of attachment relationships and either can't remember their own past attachment relationships or they idealize those relationships, and so have no true memories. These parents are likely to have insecure-avoidant attachments with their infants. Some reveal a **preoccupied model**, meaning that they are preoccupied with anger or confusion regarding their past attachment relationships. These are likely to have insecure-resistant attachments with their infants. Finally, some have an **unresolved model**, indicated by a disorganization or disorientation in their narrative about their early attachment relationships. These parents are likely to have insecure-disorganized attachments with their infants. This was taken as indirect evidence, but strong evidence nonetheless, that early attachment relationships shape the way people think (their internal working models) about relationships, and those models make them better or worse at sensitively responding to the tender needs of their own children.

It has been confirmed since then that internal working models of relationships in adulthood are in fact related to one's attachment status in infancy (we have some longitudinal studies that have verified this), and that the adult's internal working model is in fact related to the quality of attachment relationships with the adult's children. However, there are lots of exceptions so that these relationships are smaller than expected (Verhage et al., 2015). Hence, these are tendencies but should not be taken as predestination. Adults can explore their own attachment histories and decide to change the way they think about relationships. As a result, no one is doomed to a life of insecure relationships and passing that legacy on to their own children. In fact, those who adopt a secure attachment style as adults are called *earned secure*, and they display the same relationship satisfaction as those who were continuously secure (Roisman, Padron, Sroufe, & Egeland, 2002). How exactly to get into that earned secure group is a topic for a different book, but suffice it to say that intergenerational transmission of attachment status does occur, but it can be interrupted.

How Parents React

In my experience, this is very emotional content to teach to parents. If they have babies or young children, they are amazingly attentive. I believe that thinking about relationships in this way validates the overwhelming emotions they have toward their little one. It's as if they've longed for someone to tell them that it's okay to love and nurture the baby to their heart's desire, and now, here is an expert who says just that. Parents hate to hear "just let him cry," but they've been told it so many times, they are afraid it might be the best answer. But then I come along and tell them to always respond to their crying baby. They are relieved, and they desperately want this to be true. Parents of young children sometimes ask the following questions:

> **Question: Won't all of that responding to baby's cries just make baby cry more?**
> Answer: No; in fact, the opposite is true. More responsive parents have babies who cry less (Bell & Ainsworth, 1973). This is not what their mother-in-law is likely to tell them, but it is true nonetheless. It makes sense if you think in terms of security. A secure baby does not have to maximize his attachment-promoting behaviors because he is totally confident that when he needs his caregiver, all he has to do is signal. Therefore, he only signals when he has a tender need, and he stops signaling quickly when he receives a response.
>
> **Question: What if I work outside of the home? Won't my baby automatically have a resistant attachment to me because I'm not consistently with her?**

Answer: Mothers who are employed outside of the home are no less likely to have secure attachments with their babies than mothers who stay home (Harrison & Ungerer, 2002). It turns out that in a baby's mind, out of sight is pretty much out of mind. If the parent is present and responds coldly or inappropriately, the baby takes note, and an insecure attachment begins to form. But if the parent isn't present, then attachment is not forming.

Question: What if the baby's other parent and I have different levels of sensitive responsiveness? (Note: It is always the *other* parent or caregiver who lacks sensitivity!)
Answer: This certainly happens. The child will forge a secure attachment relationship with the parent who is sensitively responsive and an insecure attachment relationship with the one who is not. Consequently, the child will then behave very differently while in the care of one parent from the other. These inconsistencies are not at all surprising. It would be wonderful if all children could have multiple secure attachment relationships, but sometimes they don't get that. It turns out that if they have just one, then they are far better poised to follow the trajectory of a securely attached child. If they have two, they're better off still, but the main effect comes from having *one* secure attachment relationship. Incidentally, sometimes it is a grandparent or babysitter who provides the secure attachment relationship, and that is very beneficial to the child. When I am asked this question, the questioner is almost always no longer in a romantic relationship with the other parent and is worried about the child being treated insensitively while in the other parent's home. I believe that such a parent needs to be reassured that what she does in her home is the only part of this that she has control over, and that if she can provide sensitive care, her child will profoundly benefit from that, regardless of what happens in the other home.

Those who no longer have an infant in the home sometimes appear to be stricken as they listen. They tell me afterward that everything I said makes sense, and now they worry that they have damaged or alienated their children because they have NOT acted with sensitive responsiveness. They tend to ask:

Question: Can the course be changed?

Answer: Bowlby argues that attachment is just an initiating condition that puts a child on a trajectory. Therefore, the attachment does not directly cause outcomes in the future; it just puts a person on a path toward some outcomes being more or less likely. However, as the trajectory gets more and more established over time, it gets progressively harder to deviate. In fact, data from the longitudinal Minnesota study found that change is possible when caregiving changes, but that there always remains a strong tendency to revert back to the original pattern (Sroufe, 2005). However, some researchers have found that continuity into adulthood is not as strong as theorized (Verhage et al., 2015). Studies of interventions demonstrate that it is clearly possible for attachment relationships to be improved (Letourneau, Tryphonopoulos, Giesbrecht, Dennis, Bhogal, & Watson, 2015). Therefore, becoming more sensitively responsive is always a good strategy, no matter how late in the game.

Question: Shouldn't I do fun things with my child? Won't that help us have a better relationship?
Answer: Yes, I imagine that it would be good. People in loving relationships should enjoy one another's company regularly. But it will not help with an attachment relationship. Remember that the attachment system is activated only by tender needs. So parents want to be on the lookout for signals that their child is distressed and respond to those signals in a sensitive way. To be lots of fun without tending to emotional distress is the stereotype of the Disneyland Dad, and it is seriously lacking.

Then there are the parents who simply do not see why attachment is relevant to their concerns. They are laser focused on the specific issue that brought them into the class (perhaps their child is failing math and they need to get him to do his homework; the court referred them because of a divorce and they don't think they need a class at all) and since their child is no longer an infant, this is not what they're here for. If I can't convince a parent that this is relevant, then it's time to move on. Adult learners will invest in learning only when they perceive that they have a real need. Not everyone will see this as important. A parent educator will have a chance to return to some of the foundational ideas of attachment theory with active listening in Chapter Six. We can do it without calling it attachment, but the parent educator should be familiar enough with attachment theory to see the parallels.

Programs and Critique

Very few parenting education interventions address attachment relationships. This seems a gross oversight to me, as the quality of the parent-child relationship is the basis upon which all else rests. Do we just assume that people know how to have healthy relationships? If so, it seems a foolish assumption, given the evidence of relationship difficulty that abounds in our world. But like it or not, attachment is generally only addressed formally in parenting programs for new parents.

Programs that do attend to the issue of sensitive responsiveness have found promising outcomes. For instance, a study that involved videotaping fathers with their infants and analyzing those videos as a means of teaching them about sensitive responsiveness found significant improvements that were maintained for at least eight months (Magill-Evans, Harrison, Benzies, Gierl, & Kimak, 2007). Furthermore, one analysis of factors that allow parenting programs to be effective suggest that both internalizing and externalizing problematic child behaviors are reduced by means of improving the parent-child relationship (Tein, Sandler, MacKinnon, & Wolchik, 2004).

Standardized Intervention Programs

Two attachment-based formal interventions have been documented in the literature. One is called **Circle of Security**. It is an intensive intervention (generally lasting months) conducted with clinically referred families that includes the conduct of a Strange Situation, which is then analyzed in depth with the parent to enable understanding the child's signals and the patterns of behavior that are counterproductive. One study of 83 parent-child dyads who participated in Circle of Security found fewer indications or disorganized attachment, and overall, more dyads classified as secure after the intervention than before (Huber, McMahon, & Sweller, 2015). Additional research with special populations has found evidence of effectiveness at increasing sensitive responsiveness and attachment security (Cassidy, Ziv, Stupica, Sherman, Butler, Karfgin, Cooper, Hoffman, & Powell, 2010; Cassidy, Woodhouse, Sherman, Stupica, & Lejuez, 2001). So this is promising, but it is an intervention, not a primarily educational program.

Another is called **STEEP** (Steps Toward Effective, Enjoyable Parenting) (Egeland & Erickson, 2004) and is an intense and multifaceted intervention, lasting for more than two years, designed to promote secure attachment with infants. It begins before the baby's birth, targeting high-risk families, and relies heavily on home visits with review of videotaped interactions between mother and baby. The program also uses mother-infant play groups and a support group for mothers. It also involves family nights that include other family members. One evaluation of the program reported that mother/infant pairs who received the intervention were significantly more likely than controls to be classified as having a secure attachment at 12 months (Suess, Bohlen, Carlson, Spangler, & Frumentia Maier, 2016).

Attachment Parenting

While it is not a formal parenting education program, the **attachment parenting (AP) movement** is a force in contemporary culture of the United States. Parents identify themselves online as *AP* to signal to others that they buy into a set of practices that, nominally at least, are derived from attachment theory. There are some popular parenting advisers who write AP books that guide this movement, the most prominent of whom is William Sears, a California pediatrician. He has written more than 30 parenting advice books, often with his wife Martha, including *The Attachment Parenting Book*. He also runs a website called "Ask Dr. Sears." His definition of AP is not the only one out there, but due to his prominence, we will consider what he has to say in order to critique the attachment parenting movement. A video on his website lists the 7 B's of attachment parenting. They include:

1. **Birth bonding:** The first days after birth are a sensitive period for parental bonding to occur. Therefore, he promotes natural childbirth without medication and immediate physical contact between mother and baby.

    CRITIQUE: Attachment cannot form at birth. A newborn's brain is simply not adequately developed to create an attachment relationship until six or seven months after birth. Therefore, the only thing happening at birth is bonding, which is something that happens to the mother. No researcher has ever documented a relationship between the circumstances of birth and maternal bonding (e.g., Eyer, 1994). There may be good reasons to have a natural childbirth (I personally had three natural births without any pain medication and highly recommend it), but natural childbirth does nothing to promote secure attachment.

Figure 3.6 Baby Wearing

2. **Breastfeeding:** Breastfeeding promotes sensitivity by focusing the mother's attention on the child's signals and that breastfeeding promotes hormone changes that enhance attachment.

   CRITIQUE: On the surface of it, I would not expect breastfeeding to be related to attachment for three reasons. 1. Most breastfeeding happens in the pre-attachment phase, when attachment is not forming. 2. Harry Harlow's research determined rather conclusively that attachment is not related to feeding behavior, but it has to do with contact comfort. 3. Mary Ainsworth reminds us that there are no specific behaviors necessary for secure attachment; the deciding factor is how sensitive the care. Researchers have empirically explored Dr. Sears's assertions about both sensitivity as a result of proximity and about hormonal influences and not found any evidence to support these claims (Jansen, de Weerth, & Riksen-Walraven, 2008). A recent large study of breastfeeding and attachment found that breastfeeding itself is not related to security of the attachment relationship, but that breastfeeding duration is correlated such that those who nursed for many months were more likely to have secure attachment relationships (Tharner et al., 2012).

3. **Baby-wearing:** Parents should keep the baby in close physical proximity virtually all day long with the assistance of slings and other baby-wearing devices. (See Figure 3.6.)

   CRITIQUE: There has been one study of the effects of baby-wearing on attachment; only one, but it's the most reliable and valid study design possible: a randomized controlled trial (Anisfeld, Casper, Nozyce, & Cunningham, 1990). They recruited a sample of at-risk parents: poor teenaged mothers. At birth, they were randomly assigned to receive either a baby-carrying device called a Snugli or a bouncy seat. Researchers assessed attachment at 12 months of age and found that the comparison group (the bouncy seat) had a 38% rate of secure attachment. (This is a reasonable expectation in such a high-risk group.) But in the group of mothers given Snuglis, the rate of secure attachment was 83%, which is even higher than the national average of about 60%. This is a truly remarkable finding. The explanation goes like this: When parent and child are in close physical proximity, the parent is far more likely to notice the baby's signals, even the small ones. If they are in such close proximity during the first year, the parent and child will develop a "dance"—a back-and-forth exchange that will usually be far more sensitive than would be possible with the baby stashed farther away in a swing or playpen. The positive outcome of baby-wearing also harkens back to Harry Harlow's observation that contact comfort is a primary mechanism of attachment formation. Perhaps Harlow was right!

4. **Bedding close to baby:** Parents need to sleep very near their baby because tender needs must be responded to, day or night. Co-sleeping facilitates close physical contact and breastfeeding.

   CRITIQUE: This is my area of research and one I care about deeply. When I was finishing up my doctoral degree in Family Science in the late 1990s, I was a new mother, one very interested in sleep research and one who was reading about the newly emerging attachment parenting movement. I read what William Sears had to say about what he calls *nighttime parenting* and noticed that his assertions in this area were very consistent with attachment theory, but that they had not exactly been empirically tested. But his argument made so much sense to me, and I enjoyed sleeping with my own baby so much, that I really wanted this to be true. I started my

Table 3.4 Attachment Parenting Movement

Sears' 7 B's of Attachment Parenting	Supported by Attachment Theory?	Evidence of Relationship to Secure Attachment?
Birth Bonding	No—too early for attachment formation, necessity of multiple caregivers	No
Breastfeeding	Probably not—was necessary in EEA, but too early for attachment formation, contact comfort not feeding	Duration of breastfeeding only
Baby-wearing	Maybe—was necessary in EEA	Yes
Bedding close	Maybe—was necessary in EEA	No
Belief in the language value of baby's cry	Yes—this is the essence of sensitive responsiveness	Yes
Beware of baby trainers	Yes— sensitive responsiveness excludes ignoring cries	Probably
Balance	No—theory says nothing about this	Maybe

research agenda on infant sleep then, and I'm still pursuing it today. I'm sorry to report that to date, I have found no relationship between sleep location and attachment. And it's not for lack of trying. In one study, I conducted strange situation attachment assessments, and even using the gold standard measurement of attachment found no relationship at all between sleep location at any point in the first year and attachment at 12 months (Dyer, Reid, & Matson, 2009).

5. **Belief in the language value of baby's cry:** Baby will cry when he has a need. Parents should trust that and respond immediately—always—when baby cries.

CRITIQUE: Anyone who has read this chapter will recognize that this is the only assumption of AP that is totally in line with attachment theory. This one could have been written by Mary Ainsworth herself! She also provided quite a lot of research evidence (all cited earlier in the chapter) that this is true.

6. **Beware of baby trainers:** Parents should not trust those who tell them to let the baby cry it out. They are offering a convenience that will produce long-term damage to the parent-child relationship.

   CRITIQUE: The study I conducted and cited above as evidence that sleep location is not related to attachment (Dyer, Reid, & Matson, 2009) had a surprise result for me: that attachment is related to cry-it-out sleep training. I found that babies who had been sleep trained with a cry-it-out method were more likely to have an insecure-resistant attachment. I speculate that this is the result of a daytime/nighttime inconsistency whereby parents may be sensitively responsive during daytime hours, but totally nonresponsive during nighttime hours. At this point, my study is the only one that uses a direct measure of attachment (strange situation) to answer the question of whether crying it out damages attachment, and it turns out it does.

7. **Balance:** Parents must not neglect their own needs or the needs of their adult romantic relationship, but instead balance these against the demands of the baby.

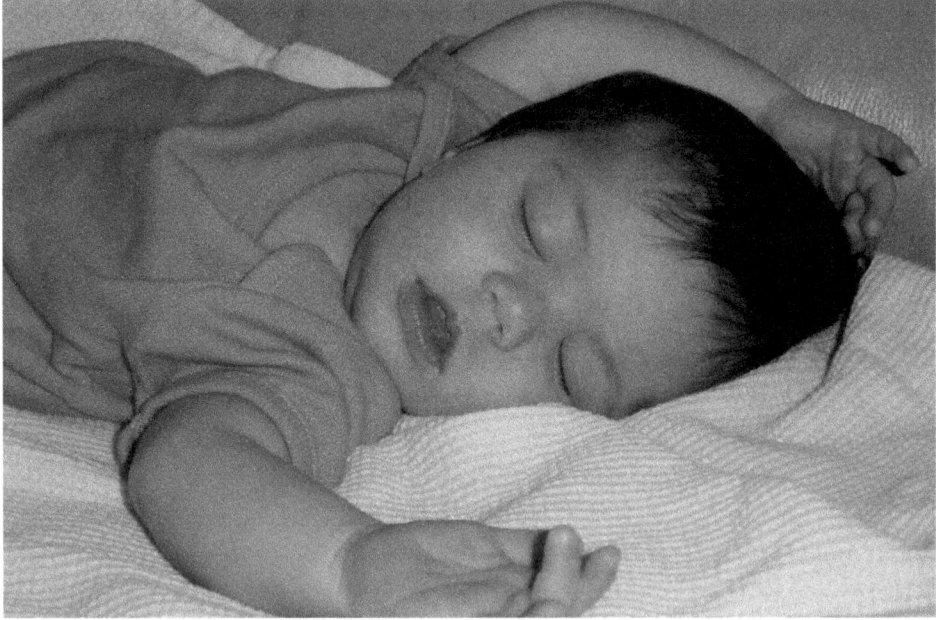

Figure 3.7 Newborn Sleep

CRITIQUE: This is not something that attachment theory addresses. However, I found one published study on precisely this issue. The sample includes 79 black urban families living with high stress. The authors report that high levels of parental conflict are associated with low maternal sensitivity and insecure mother-infant attachment (Finger, Hans, Bernstein, & Cox, 2009). This is only one small sample, but the finding is congruent with the assertion of AP.

So on the whole, what can we say about attachment parenting? As Table 3.4 illustrates, it's problematic that many of the assertions of AP are not even addressed in the theory it is named for. It is also problematic that some of the assertions of the movement are demonstrably false. But some of them are spot-on. And some seem to be true even if they were not tenets of the theory. So it's a mixed bag.

Application: Infant Sleep

After the congratulations, well-meaning friends often asked of my newborn, "Is she a *good* baby?" As a new mother, I had to interpret the meaning of this question. I learned that appropriate answers ranged from "Oh, she's wonderful ... she's been sleeping through the night since she was two weeks old!" to "Well, she's still keeping me up most nights!" I discovered that this was really a question about sleep. How well is the baby sleeping at night, and thus how well are the parents sleeping at night?

As the mother of four children, I appreciate the important role of sleep in the lives of young families. However, I also marvel at the absurdity of placing moral judgment on an infant based on his or her sleeping habits. This convention of asking about infant sleep by asking if the baby is "good" reveals a discourse on children's sleep that is profoundly value laden. The perceived moral implications of children's sleeping arrangements complicate parents' approach toward the issue and make it unnecessarily difficult. Assuming that a child's moral goodness is not related to his or sleep habits allows parents to adopt a policy of nighttime responsiveness, thereby assuaging sleep problems and enhancing the parent-child attachment.

Normal Development of Sleep in Children

In order to avoid assigning moral meaning to sleep habits, it is necessary to know what developmentally normal sleep is for children. Newborns have no established circadian rhythm. They eat when they are hungry and sleep when they are tired, and there is no pattern to these behaviors. (See Figure 3.7.) This places the baby's parents in a position of being constantly called upon, and it can be exhausting. Newborn babies do sometimes sleep for long bouts in the first week after birth, which probably reflects their physiological exhaustion from the birth. These sleep episodes may coincidentally occur at night when the parents also want to sleep. However, this is not the marker of a "good" baby; it is a stroke of good luck for the parents. Similarly, there is nothing wrong with a baby who sleeps only for 20-minute bouts both day and night, although the parents could be considered unlucky. I have been blessed with both experiences in the extreme. My oldest daughter slept in stretches of six hours at night during the first week after her birth. I thought I must be the perfect mother! However, when my third cried fairly continuously and slept only in short bursts at night during her first week, I realized that it was simply the luck of the draw.

By six weeks after birth, a baby's brain has developed to the point that it can start to establish patterns of sleep behavior. Sleep starts to consolidate into predictable chunks rather than being spread out randomly throughout the day. Babies will typically sleep for several hours during the night, for a couple of hours in the afternoon, and for perhaps an hour mid-morning. This pattern is often established by three months after birth. This sleep consolidation provides the parents with some predictability and some reasonable expectation for nighttime sleep and is thus highly valued by tired parents. However, the relatively consolidated sleep cycle is imperfect. Babies are still prone to wake up during these sleep periods and typically need help falling back to sleep. Nonetheless, the process of sleep consolidation gradually continues until the vast majority of sleep occurs during nighttime hours. This is when children give up daytime naps, typically between the ages of three and five years.

There are individual differences in the rate of sleep consolidation and no reason to believe that these differences reflect "goodness" or the lack thereof in the child's character. Some babies consolidate their sleep relatively quickly, while others take longer; some fall asleep easily at the beginning of the night, but others require intense parenting at bedtime. Furthermore, some babies calm themselves back to sleep (i.e., self-soothe) after a night waking even at very young ages, while some babies are not able to self-soothe after waking until they are much older. These differences are at least partly related to the child's inborn temperament. Some children naturally have more stable physiological rhythms than others, and some are simply less easily stimulated to fear. This is temperament: unchangeable and morally neutral.

Not only do children's sleep habits vary by temperament, there are developmental issues to consider as well. Near the end of the first year (approximately 9 to 12 months after birth), many babies experience a temporary interruption in the consolidation of sleep. They experience renewal of or an increase in night wakings. Evidence suggests that sleep becomes disrupted when the child is on the brink of a major developmental accomplishment, such as when the child is learning to cruise around furniture or to walk. Once the milestone is achieved, the child returns to more predictable sleep. Babies and young children also tend to experience transitory disrupted sleep when they are sick, teething, or when they are experiencing emotional stress. While this may be inconvenient and difficult for parents, it only means that the child is developmentally normal.

Nightmares and the so-called irrational fears become issues during the preschool years. Children may become afraid of monsters under their beds, the creaking of floorboards, being alone, or the dark itself. This is a product of cognitive development sufficient to imagine things that have not happened and to remember those imaginings, without enough life experience to put the fears into context or emotional regulation skills necessary to quell them. Because such fears are seen by adults as being irrational, they are often interpreted as unimportant at best and manipulative at worst.

Bedtime struggles typically occur in slightly older children. They may fight going to bed because they don't feel tired, or because they don't want to stop an enjoyable activity or miss something exciting that they anticipate may be enjoyed by those who remain awake. Staying up late may be viewed as a privilege, and therefore being sent to bed feels like exclusion or punishment. Sometimes they are simply tired of their utter powerlessness, eating what someone else says to eat, getting in the car when told without knowledge of the destination, and so they try to claim some power over their lives by asserting the power that they do have, power over their own bodies. Bedtime struggles are not well understood because they are typically interpreted as power struggles in which children attempt to defy legitimate parental authority.

Behavioral Approach

Professional advice about child sleep abounds. Since the ideology of the dominant culture in the United States is that good children are sleeping children, parents feel a tremendous pressure to report that their charges are sleeping through the night, both to illustrate their child's goodness and their own competence as parents. This intrusion of a question of moral character makes the entire process much more difficult than it needs to be.

The approach recommended by most advisers and most members of the medical profession is one that assumes that good children will sleep whenever their good parents want them to be doing so. In order to achieve this—and to pretend it is the case even when it isn't—most of the books on the subject recommend some form of cry-it-out sleep training. Parents are encouraged to place as much distance between themselves and the child as possible and then simply not respond to the child's calls for help in order to "teach" the child to fall asleep and stay asleep on their own. The most popular variation on this technique (called **Ferberizing** after the author of the best-selling book that outlined its practice, Dr. Richard Ferber) does allow parents to verbally soothe their crying baby at increasing intervals, but parents should never pick up the crying baby, and the baby should never, ever be allowed to fall asleep in the comfort of the parent's arms.

Sleep training is based on the principles of applied behavior analysis. Ignoring children's pleas for comfort at night is a form of extinction, whereby undesirable behavior (i.e., night waking and subsequent crying for the parent) will disappear if it is not reinforced. In many cases, this does in fact work. If babies are not attended to when they express needs, they will stop expressing those needs. Studies of sleep training demonstrate that babies do stop crying during the night after learning that their cries will not be answered. The problem with this approach is that the baby stops crying only after learning that his or her cries are not considered important, and that the parents or other caregivers cannot be relied upon. Children learn not only that their behavior is unproductive, but that their feelings of fear are not acceptable to the parents. This may be the beginning of a serious rift in the parent-child relationship. If the parents cannot be trusted at night, why then should they be trusted in the day? If nighttime feelings are unacceptable, mightn't daytime feelings also be unacceptable?

Attachment Approach

An alternative approach to nighttime parenting is one that emerges from a focus on attachment, at the bottom of the parenting pyramid, instead of behaviorism, which is the very top of the pyramid. An attachment approach validates the child's feelings, regardless of whether or not the parent thinks the feelings are logical, and responds with empathy to the child's call for help, even if the call comes in the middle of the night. This alternative approach is quite simple. Unlike sleep training approaches, it does not require intense instruction, it doesn't ask the parents to ignore their parental instincts, and it can assume any number of forms. It is not limited to correct and incorrect implementation. This alternative approach to sleep is simply to respond sensitively to a child's nighttime needs just as one responds sensitively to a child's daytime needs.

Ainsworth's research identified five features of sensitive responsiveness: 1) awareness of the child's signals; 2) accurate interpretation of those signals; 3) prompt response to signals; 4) appropriate response to signals; and 5) rhythmicity.

Awareness of nighttime signals means listening for a child's calls. Research in sleep laboratories indicate that mothers' sleep is greatly altered, especially during the first few months after giving birth. Mothers sleep lightly and are easily aroused by the sounds of their babies fussing. (The sleep of fathers has not been studied.) Apparently, biology has predisposed us to be aware. We can enhance our awareness by keeping babies closer to us so that we hear and notice more during the night. The American Academy of Pediatrics recommends that infants sleep in the same room as the parents during the first few months after birth. Whether or not the baby should be in the same bed as the adults is a subject of great controversy, but the recommendation that the baby be close by to enhance awareness is universal. Awareness of signals doesn't always mean responding to the baby's nighttime movements and sounds. Those signals must be accurately interpreted first.

Accurate interpretation of signals requires some knowledge of child development. The overview of the development of child sleep provided above is lengthy because it is my belief that many parents misinterpret normal sleep behavior as evidence of moral corruption, and this is the root cause of insensitive nighttime parenting. Nighttime crying of an infant can be misconstrued as manipulation, which virtually guarantees an inappropriate response. Bedtime resistance can be misinterpreted as rejection of parental authority, also prompting an

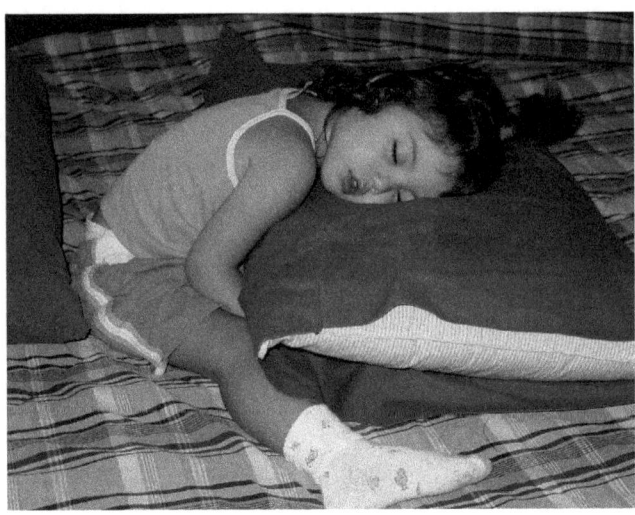

Figure 3.8 A "Good" Sleeper

inappropriate response. Therefore, it is important to consider that separation from parents triggers feelings of anxiety in children, and that this is normal.

Once sleep behaviors are interpreted accurately, parents must choose how to respond, and they must do so promptly. What is appropriate will depend on their cultural context and their personal belief systems. For instance, some parents choose to bring a wakeful child into the parental bed for comfort while others find this option completely unacceptable. Some do not even have a parental bed; instead they have one family bed for all members of the family to share. Others consider this a violation of the sanctity of the marital bed. The actual sleep location of the various members of the family is not terribly important compared to the degree of responsiveness to the child's expression of emotion.

The notion of rhythmicity applies to sleep most directly in parental beliefs about how strictly to schedule sleep. Insensitive parents go in one of two directions: 1) they will have a rigid bedtime and waking time and not be willing to alter those based on signals from the baby; or 2) they will have no bedtime and wake-up structure at all. Either way, the specific needs of the baby are ignored. The most sensitive parents will be willing to create a sleep routine, but they will also be willing to alter it when the baby's needs change due to sickness or developmental changes.

When I began my research on infant sleep I was also beginning my life as a parent. I shared my bed with my newborn daughter and found the experience intoxicating. Her warm body wriggling during REM sleep, her slow steady breathing and the drool in the corner of her slack mouth during deep sleep, her sweet milky breath in light sleep after she nursed in the middle of the night, her light cooing after waking contentedly in the early morning ... these were for me the most precious moments of motherhood. Professionally, I began to explore whether or not my personal experience could be generalized, that sharing sleep would enhance attachment. I have not yet answered this question conclusively, but I have come to believe that nighttime responsiveness to emotional needs is more important than sleep location. My research suggests that nighttime responsiveness enhances attachment but may also delay sleep consolidation. Conversely, my research suggests that cry-it-out sleep training (such as Ferberizing) very young children produces "good sleepers" who have disturbed relationships with their parents.

Now, 18 years later, all four of my children are what could be called "good sleepers," even though that could not have been said of all of them in their early years. Currently, they all go to sleep in their own beds when tired, and they do so without a struggle. One of my daughters once went to bed very early after a long fun day. She said in explanation, "My brain is telling me I'm sleepy" (Figure 3.8). I believe that their ability to read the signals of their own bodies and respond appropriately is the consequence of my doing this for them when they were younger. In other words, this is the reward for early responsive nighttime parenting.

Review and Reflection Questions

1. What is the basic argument of attachment theory?

2. What were the characteristics of parenting (as far as we know) in the Environment of Evolutionary Adaptedness? Should we try to parent the same way today?

3. How is attachment different from imprinting? Why do humans use attachment while birds use imprinting?

4. What did we learn from Harry Harlow's research with baby monkeys?

5. What do the four types of attachment look like? What parenting behavior produces each one? What are the outcomes of each?

6. What are the components of Ainsworth's notion of sensitive responsiveness?

7. What are the characteristics of emotional availability? What does this concept add to our understanding of attachment that builds on Ainsworth's notion of sensitive responsiveness?

8. At what age is attachment forming? What implications does that have for infant adoption? Natural childbirth? Postdivorce coparenting?

9. How does the quality of infant attachment relationships become an adult attachment style? How does that shape parenting behaviors and cause an intergenerational transmission of attachment? Can this ever be changed?

10. Does working outside the home affect the parent-child attachment?

11. What are the arguments of the attachment parenting movement? Are they consistent with empirical evidence about attachment?

12. How might we understand behavioral sleep training through the lens of attachment theory?

Terminology to Know

- Attachment
- Attachment formation
- Attachment parenting movement
- Attachment style
- Attachment theory
- Attachment-promoting behaviors
- Baby-wearing
- Birth bonding
- Bonding
- Consistent non-responsiveness
- Contact comfort
- Critical period
- Dismissing model
- Emotional availability
- Environment of Evolutionary Adaptedness
- Frightening parental behavior
- Imprinting
- Inconsistent responsiveness
- Insecure avoidant attachment
- Insecure disorganized attachment
- Insecure resistant attachment
- Internal working model
- Mutual sensitivity
- Pre-attachment phase

Names to Know

- Ainsworth
- Biringen
- Bowlby
- Ferber
- Freud
- Harlow
- Lorenz
- Main
- Sears

- Preoccupied model
- Primary drive
- Rhythmicity
- Secondary drive
- Secure attachment
- Secure base behavior
- Secure-autonomous model
- Sensitive responsiveness
- Sleep training/Ferberizing
- Strange Situation
- Tender needs
- Unresolved model

References

Ainsworth, M.D.S. (1969). Maternal Sensitivity Scales. http://www.psychology.sunysb.edu/attachment/measures/content/ainsworth_scales.html Accessed 1/24/2016.

Ainsworth, M.D.S., Blehar, M.C., Waters, E., & Wall, S. (1978). *Patterns of attachment: A psychological study of the strange situation.* NJ: Erlbaum.

Anisfeld, E., Casper, V., Nozyce, M., & Cunningham, N. (1990). Does infant carrying promote attachment? An experimental study of the effects of increased physical contact on the development of attachment. *Child Development, 61, 5,* 1617–1627.

Bell, S., & Ainsworth, M.D. (1973). Infant crying and maternal responsiveness. *Child development and behavior, 2nd edition.* F. Rebelsky, L. Dorman (Eds.). Oxford, UK: Alfred A. Knopf.

Benoit, D. (2004). Infant-parent attachment: Definition, types, antecedents, measurement and outcome. *Paediatric Child Health, 9, 8,* 541–545.

Biringen, Z. (2004). *Raising a secure child.* Penguin Group USA.

Biringen, Z., Derscheid, D., Vliegen, N., Closson, L., & Easterbrooks, M.A. (2014). Emotional availability (EA): Theoretical background, empirical research using the EA Scales, and clinical applications. *Developmental Review, 34, 2,* 114–167.

Bowlby, John (1969) *Attachment.* Basic Books.

Bowlby, J. (1988). *A secure base.* London: Routledge.

Bretherton, I. (1992). The origins of attachment theory: John Bowlby and Mary Ainsworth. *Developmental Psychology, 28,* 759–775.

Burkhardt, R.W. (2005). *Patterns of behavior: Konrad Lorenz, Niko Tinbergen, and the founding of ethology*. University of Chicago Press.

Cassidy, J., Woodhouse, S., Sherman, L., Stupica, B., & Lejuez, C. (2011). Enhancing infant attachment security: An examination of treatment efficacy and differential susceptibility. *Journal of Development and Psychopathology, 23*, 131–148.

Cassidy, J., Ziv, Y., Stupica, B., Sherman, L.J., Butler, H., Karfgin, A., Cooper, G., Hoffman, K.T., & Powell, B. (2010). Enhancing maternal sensitivity and attachment security in the infants of women in a jail-diversion program. In J. Cassidy, J. Poehlmann, & P.R. Shaver (Eds.), *Incarcerated individuals and their children viewed from the perspective of attachment theory*. Special issue of *Attachment and Human Development*.

Cline, F.W., & Fay, J. (1990). *Parenting with Love and Logic: Teaching children responsibility*. Pinion Press.

DeWolff, M.S., & Van Ijzendoorn, M.H. (1997). Sensitivity and attachment: A meta-analysis on parental antecedents of infant attachment. *Child Development, 68, 4*, 571–591.

Dyer, K., Reid, K., & Matson, M. (2009, April). Crying themselves to sleep: Relationship of infant sleep training to sleep quality and attachment. Paper presentation at the biennial meeting of the Society for Research in Child Development. Denver, Colorado.

Egeland, B., & Erickson, M.F. (2004). Lessons from STEEP: Linking theory, research and practice for the well-being of infants and parents. In A.J. Sameroff, S.C. McDonough, & K.L. Rosenblum (Eds.), *Treating parent-infant relationship problems: Strategies for intervention* (pp. 213–242). New York: Guilford.

Eyer, D.E. (1994). Infant bonding: A scientific fiction. *Human Nature, 5, 1*, 69–94.

Finger, B., Hans, S.L., Bernstein, V.J., & Cox, S.M. (2009). Parent relationship quality and infant-mother attachment. *Attachment and Human Development, 11, 3*, 285–306.

Freud, S. (1930). *Civilization and its discontents*. Internationaler Psychoanlytischer Vertag Wien.

Harlow, H.F. (1958). The nature of love. *American Psychologist, 13*, 673–685.

Harrison, L.J., & Ungerer, J.A. (2002). Maternal employment and infant-mother attachment security at 12 months postpartum. *Developmental Psychology, 38, 5*, 758–773.

Hesse, E., & Main, M. (2006). Frightened, threatening, and dissociative parental behavior in low-risk samples: Description, discussion, and interpretations. *Development and Psychopathology, 18, 2*, 309–343.

Huber, A., McMahon, C.A., & Sweller, N. (2015). Efficacy of the 20-week Circle of Security intervention: Changes in caregiver reflective functioning, representations, and child attachment in an Australian clinical sample. *Infant Mental Health Journal*, http://dx.doi.org.hmlproxy.lib.csufresno.edu/10.1002/imhj.21540

Institute of Medicine, National Academy of Sciences (1991). Nutrition during lactation. Washington, DC: National Academy Press.

Jansen, J., de Weerth, C., & Riksen-Walraven, J.M. (2008). Breastfeeding and the mother-infant relationship—A review. *Developmental Review, 28, 4,* 503–521.

Jenness, R. (1974). Biosynthesis and composition of milk. *Journal of Investigative Dermatology, 63,* 109–118.

Konner, M. (2005). Hunter-gatherer infancy and childhood: The !Kung and others. In *Hunter-gatherer childhoods: Evolutionary, developmental, and cultural perspectives.* B.S. Hewlett & M.E. Lamb (Eds.). New Brunswick, NJ: Transaction Publishers.

Letourneau, N., Tryphonopoulos, P., Giesbrecht, G., Dennis, C.-L., Bhogal, S., & Watson, B. (2015). Narrative and meta-analytic review of interventions aiming to improve maternal-child attachment security. *Infant Mental Health Journal, 36, 4,* 366–387.

Magill-Evans, J., Harrison, M.J., Benzies, K., Gierl, M., & Kimak, C. (2007). Effects of parenting education on first-time fathers' skills in interactions with their infants. *Fathering, 5, 1,* 42–57.

Main, M., & Hesse, E. (1990). Parents' unresolved traumatic experiences are related to infant disorganized attachment status: Is frightened and/or frightening parental behavior the linking mechanism? In *Attachment in the Preschool Years: Theory, Research, and Intervention.* M.T. Greenberg, D. Cicchetti, & E.M. Cummings (Eds.). Chicago: University of Chicago Press, 161–182.

Main, M., Kaplan, N., & Cassidy, J. (1985). Security in infancy, childhood, and adulthood: A move to the level of representation. In I. Bretherton & W. Waters (Eds.), Growing points of attachment theory and research. *Monographs of the Society for Research in Child Development, 50,* 66–104.

Main, M., & Solomon, J. (1990). Procedures for identifying disorganized/disoriented infants during the Ainsworth Strange Situation. In M. Greenberg, D. Cicchetti, & E.M. Cummings (Eds.), *Attachment in the preschool years,* pp. 121–160. Chicago: University of Chicago Press.

McLeod, S. A. (2007). Bowlby's attachment theory. www.simplypsychology.org/bowlby.html Retrieved 1/28/2016.

Miller, N., & Dollard, J. (1941). *Social learning and imitation.* New Haven, CT: Yale University Press.

Roisman, G., Padron, E., Sroufe, A., & Egeland, B. (2002). Earned-secure attachment status in retrospect and prospect. *Child Development, 73, 4,* 1204–1219.

Schaffer, H.R., & Emerson, P.E. (1964). The development of social attachments in infancy. *Monographs of the Society for Research in Child Development, 29, 3,* 1–77.

Sears, W., & Sears, M. (2001). *The attachment parenting book: A commonsense guide to understanding and nurturing your baby.* Little, Brown and Company.

Sears, W., & Sears, M. (n.d.). Attachment parenting babies are raised the way nature intended. http://www.askdrsears.com/topics/parenting/attachment-parenting/attachment-parenting-babies Accessed 1/31/2016.

Shostak, M. (2000). *Nisa: The life and words of a !Kung woman, 4th edition*. Harvard University Press.

Small, M. (1999). *Our babies, ourselves: How biology and culture shape the way we parent*. Anchor.

Sroufe, L.A. (2005). Attachment and development: A prospective, longitudinal study from birth to adulthood. *Attachment and Human Development, 7, 4,* 349–367.

Sroufe, L.A., Egeland, B., Carlson, E., & Collins, W.A. (2005). *The development of the person: The Minnesota study of risk and adaptation from birth to adulthood*. New York: Guilford.

Stringer, C.B. (1994). The evolution of early humans. In S. Jones, R. Martin, & D. Pilbeam (Eds.), *The Cambridge encyclopedia of human evolution*. Cambridge, UK: Cambridge University Press.

Suess, G.J., Bohlen, U., Carlson, E.A., Spangler, G., & Frumentia Maier, M. (2016). Effectiveness of attachment based STEEP intervention in a German high-risk sample. *Attachment and Human Development, 18, 5,* 443–460.

Suomi, S.J., & Leroy, H.A. (1982). In Memoriam: Harry F. Harlow (1905–1981). *Am. J. Primatol., 2*:319–342.

Tein, J.Y., Sandler, I.N., MacKinnon, D.P., & Wolchik, S.A. (2004). How did it work? Who did it work for? Mediation in the context of a moderated prevention effect for children of divorce. *Journal of Counseling and Clinical Psychology, 72, 4,* 617–624.

Tharner, A., Luijk, M. P. C. M., Raat, H., Ijzendoorn, M.H., Bakermans-Kranenburg, M.J., Moll, H.A., Jaddoe, V.W.V., Hofman, A., Verhulst, F.C., & Tiemeier, H. (2012). Breastfeeding and its relation to maternal sensitivity and infant attachment. *Journal of Developmental and Behavioral Pediatrics, 33, 5,* 396–404.

Van Ijzendoorn, M.H. (1999). Disorganized attachment in early childhood: Meta-analysis of precursors, concomitants, and sequelae. *Development and Psychopathology, 11, 2,* 225–249.

Van Ijzendoorn, M.H., & Kroonenberg, P.M. (1988) Cross-cultural patterns of attachment: A meta-analysis of the strange situation. *Child Development, 59,* 147–156.

Verhage, M.L., Schuengel, C., Madigan, S., Fearon, R.M.P., Oosterman, M., Cassibba, R., Bakermans-Kranenburg, M.J., & Van Ijzendoorn, M.H. (2015). Narrowing the transmission gap: A synthesis of three decades of research on intergenerational transmission of attachment. *Psychological Bulletin*. Advance online publication. http://dx.doi.org/10.1037/bul0000038 (retrieved 1/31/2016).

Ziv, Y., Aviezer, O., Gini, M., Sagi, A., & Koren-Karie, N. (2000). Emotional availability in the mother-infant dyad as related to the quality of infant-mother attachment relationship. *Attachment and Human Development, 2, 2*, 149–169.

Credits

- Fig. 3.2: Copyright © 2011 by Kev Moses, (CC BY 2.0) at https://commons.wikimedia.org/wiki/File:Acacia_Kenya_Savannah.jpg.
- Fig. 3.3: Copyright © by Al Fenn / Time, Inc.
- Fig. 3.4: Copyright © 2015 by Stilfehler / Wikimedia Commons, (CC BY-SA 3.0) at https://commons.wikimedia.org/wiki/File:Attachment_types_-_USA_Germany_Japan.JPG.
- Fig. 3.6: Copyright © 2001 by Michael Borawski. Reprinted with permission.

4. Communication for Teaching New Skills

Introduction

So far, we have established that relationships form the base of the parenting pyramid and that the key to secure attachment relationships is sensitive responsiveness. The next level of the pyramid is communication. As we are still very close to the bottom of the pyramid, it is still true that the methods described in this chapter are intended for very broad use. And so we begin with something that virtually all parents see as one of their primary duties: teaching their children.

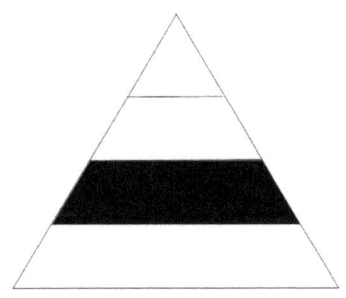

Figure 4.1 Communication on Pyramid

The list of things to teach them is overwhelming, really. They are born so desperately helpless. They have to learning how to dress themselves, how to hold a spoon, use a knife, tie their shoes, use the toilet, wash dishes, and so on. The need for instruction is seemingly endless. They need to learn how to operate the stovetop, the washing machine and clothes dryer, how to brush their teeth, how to place a phone call, address an envelope, how to problem solve why their computer is acting funny, how to fill out a job application, how to drive a car. And that doesn't even address all of the skills they need to learn for success in school and work: how to write letters and numbers, how multiplication works, when to cite a source, how to pronounce a word. Some of these tasks they bring to me with the preface "Mom, how do I ... ?" and others are tasks that I decide they need to know (for instance, how to load the dishwasher properly, how to operate the lawn mower, how to thoroughly vacuum the carpet in their bedroom). And then there are the things they want to know how to do for fun: how to play soccer, how to ride a bike, how to bait a hook, how to build a fire and pack a tent. No matter how you look at it, the need for instruction is ubiquitous. A parent is a teacher.

So as we move up the pyramid, we turn to the issue of using communication to teach new skills. How should a parent approach these tasks? How to address children when they fail? When they succeed? When they are struggling? When they say that they don't want to keep trying?

Theory and Background

The psychology of learning is informed by multiple theories and thus is a bigger topic than we will be able to fully address here. Learning is inextricably tied to the concepts of intelligence, motivation, and pedagogy. A full review of these topics is beyond the scope of this book. Therefore, we will briefly review some of these topics that have been directly linked to parenting education.

Self-Esteem Movement: Learning Through Believing

The **self-esteem movement** is the remnant of a discredited theory. It did, in its day, generate testable hypotheses, so it could have been called a theory. The theory proposed that **self-esteem** (a person's sense of self-worth) is a critical aspect of a person's identity and personality that determines much of their future life outcomes (Mruk, 2006). It started in 1969 with the publication of *The Psychology of Self-Esteem* by Nathaniel Branden (1969). Scientific research was conducted. But the evidence did not support it. The arguments made by the self-esteem movement are, quite simply, wrong. That is why I call it a movement rather than a theory at this point. Unfortunately, the fact that it is clearly wrong has not stopped it from forcefully moving through society shaping parenting practices and parent education programs.

Once scientists started to measure self-esteem systematically in large groups of people, the research confirmed that people who are successful have high self-esteem. For instance, high self-esteem is observed among those with good school performance and job performance (Baumeister, Campbell, Krueger, & Vohs, 2003). Furthermore, high self-esteem is one of the strongest predictors of happiness and overall life satisfaction (e.g., Baumeister et al., 2003). So far, so good. But then a story was invented (one without any evidence to support it, unfortunately) that high self-esteem is what allows people to succeed in life; it is the causal agent. The argument goes like this: if kids feel good about themselves, then they will have the courage to try new things. They will project confidence, they will take risks, and those qualities and experiences will lead to greater success in life. Parenting education (a field that was coming into its own in the 1970s) was profoundly affected by the self-esteem movement. Raising kids' self-esteem was seen as a primary goal of good parenting. And all of it was based on this proposed mechanism by which self-esteem would produce success. For instance, the Active Parenting program, even in its most recent iteration (Popkin, 2014), describes the "Think-Feel-Do Cycle" to explain how self-esteem (what kids think about themselves) can shape their feelings, which then shape their behaviors, either for success (if they think highly of themselves) or failure (if they think poorly of themselves). This was widely accepted because it just made so much sense.

This led to nothing short of a social movement in which every effort was made to boost kids' self-esteem. Every child on the team got a trophy. An award for everyone at the end of the class. No more red pens used to mark up written assignments for school in the fear that being corrected might damage a child's self-esteem. And at home, parents had to relentlessly tell their child that he or she was wonderful, amazing, the best, the most spectacular child ever born, beautiful, smart, and funny. Nothing short of gushing praise at every turn, no matter what, to help shore up the dangerously fragile self-esteem of children of all ages.

My life experiences illustrate the pervasive influence of the self-esteem movement. When I was in elementary school (before the self-esteem movement) I played soccer in the fall, basketball in the winter, and softball in the spring. I played on each of these teams every year. When our team did well for a season, the team as a whole earned a trophy. That trophy was then displayed in the trophy case in the hallway of our school. It didn't happen every year; in fact, it happened very rarely, that a team from my school brought home a trophy. It was a big deal. By the time my own children were in school, the self-esteem movement had fully transformed school sports. When the kids started the soccer season, before a single game had been played, I had already paid for an individual trophy which would be purchased for every single child, regardless of how her team performed during the season. Thanks to the self-esteem movement, each and every child got a trophy, no matter how they or their team came out.

The trophies are big business for someone. But from the kids' point of view, they were dime a dozen, soon filled up the shelves, and one by one were thrown

Figure 4.2 Soccer Trophies

away. Did my kids like getting them? Maybe. Probably. (See Figure 4.2.) Were they inspired to keep playing soccer? No. Definitely not. Did it hurt them in any way? Well, maybe not, but I do have a serious question about this. In addition to the trophies, one of my children had a soccer coach who gave medals out after every game to anyone who scored a goal. My daughter played defense, and so never, ever had the slightest shot at earning a medal. After every game, she cried in disappointment that she hadn't earned a medal. She imagined that she was the only person on the team to never, ever, not-even-once get a medal at the end of the game. It caused her anxiety. Soon, she hated going to a soccer game because she anticipated that she would not win a medal yet again. It was sad. After the season was over, she never wanted to play soccer again. I had loved soccer for many years of my early life. My fondest childhood memories were of playing soccer. I wanted to share my love for the game with my daughter, but by first grade she had decided that she hated it, and I blame it on the stupid medals.

This is just my personal observation about the effects of the self-esteem movement. In academia, there were also hints of a problem. For instance, there was the logical inference that if high self-esteem produced success, then low self-esteem must produce failure. It was believed to be the reason that some kids bully others, abuse drugs, or commit acts of violence. The argument went that they don't feel good about themselves, so they try to feel better about themselves by putting other kids down or by escaping through drugs and alcohol. Low self-esteem became the go-to explanation for all of the things that could go wrong in a life. But the problem was that this argument simply was not supported by evidence. Low self-esteem does not, in fact, predict violence, bullying behavior, delinquency, racism, or drug and alcohol abuse (Emler, 2001). And maybe most surprisingly, violent criminal offenders have significantly *higher* self-esteem on average than do noncriminals (Woessner & Schneider, 2013). In fact, an artificially inflated self-esteem may even produce narcissism and cause criminally violent behavior (Walker & Bright, 2009).

While efforts to promote self-esteem raged in the dominant culture, scientific research kept falsifying the tenets of the self-esteem movement. Psychologists concluded that, while self-esteem is correlated with some forms of success, it is just as likely that success causes high self-esteem rather than the other way around (Baumeister, Campbell, Krueger, & Vohs, 2003). For instance, longitudinal research, which follows the same children through time, measuring things like self-esteem and grades in school at multiple times over multiple years, found that self-esteem in young children was mostly unrelated to academic achievement later (Pottebaum, Keith, & Ehly, 1986). That is to say, having self-esteem first does not predict success later, so it seems unlikely that self-esteem *causes* later success.

Furthermore, some correlations between self-esteem and good outcomes disappear when objective measures of those good outcomes are used. For instance, when people rate their self-esteem, and also rate their own physical attractiveness, the scores are positively correlated (when one is high, the other is also high). But when objective measures of physical attractiveness are used (i.e., when attractiveness is rated by other people) then the correlation disappears (Deiner, Wolsic & Fujita, 1995). Similar results are found with popularity and interpersonal skills; when people rate their own popularity and people-skills, they are correlated with self-esteem, but when others report these things, the correlations disappear (Buhrmester, 1988; Baumeister et al., 2003). Thus, it seems like people with high self-esteem think highly of themselves, but other people don't necessarily think as well of them. It might all be in their mind.

As if this were not all bad enough for the self-esteem movement, several studies have specifically explored the effects of praise on behavior and found it to be wanting. A systematic review of 41 empirical studies comparing praise to other methods of behavioral control concludes that praise does not reliably produce compliance. Even worse for the movement, criticism does produce compliance (Owen, Slep, & Heyman, 2012). So regardless of what praise might do for self-esteem, it does not get kids to do what adults are asking of them. And even if criticism damages self-esteem, it does improve behavior. Furthermore, rewards (and praise is, by definition, a verbal reward) most definitely reduce internal motivation for kids to want to learn (Deci, Koestner, & Ryan, 1999). Kids who are praised for their efforts at soccer, or painting, or music, become gradually less interested in pursuing those activities. This is terrible news!

And one more thing: it turns out that children older than 12 can read between the lines. When adolescent children witness a teacher praising another student, they take it to mean that the student really isn't that bright and has done as well as he can do. But when they witness a teacher criticizing, they interpret that the recipient of the criticism has potential and isn't living up to it. So they are interpreting both praise and criticism differently than adults anticipated (Meyer, 1992). This shouldn't surprise students of child development, who know that children around this age enter the stage of formal operations (according to Piaget's theory).

All of this is very bad news for the self-esteem movement, which at this point is a thoroughly discredited theory. And yet as a social force, the self-esteem movement powers on. Interventions are designed to raise children's self-esteem, even though those interventions have been shown to raise self-esteem but not improve any of the behavioral outcomes of interest (e.g., Guo, Wu, Smokowski, Bacallao, Evans, & Cotter, 2015). Despite the lack of evidence that this works in any way, parents have been left with the clear message that they need to praise their children incessantly to build their self-esteem and never criticize them in order to protect their self-esteem. And many parenting education programs promote self-esteem-building practices recommended by the self-esteem movement.

Social Development Theory: Learning Through Relationship

So a discredited theory is still shaping parenting education programs. That's disheartening. Knowing what we know, then, what are we to replace it with? If gushing praise produces an artificially inflated self-esteem, which leads to narcissism and violence but doesn't actually help children learn useful skills, then how do parents teach their kids? One learning theory that has been supported by empirical research is Lev Vygotsky's social development theory, developed in the 1930s but not widely appreciated outside of his home country of Russia until the 1970s. Vygotsky asserted that learning is deeply tied to the socio-cultural context and especially that learning happens in the context of interpersonal relationships. As the parenting pyramid assumes that relationships form the foundation for all else, this recognition of the important role of relationships resonates with our model.

Vygotsky's theory stresses the important role of a More Knowledgeable Other (which obviously could be a parent) who presents tasks that are in the child's **Zone of Proximal Development** (ZPD). The ZPD includes tasks that the child is not yet capable of doing alone, but could do with assistance. According to this model, the parent's role is to present tasks in the child's ZPD to promote learning and then provide the necessary assistance so that the child can learn the tasks. Once those tasks are learned, the ZPD shifts toward more difficult ones. In that way, the ZPD is constantly shifting as learning happens, so that teaching requires sensitivity to the specific—and changing—state of the child's skills. In fact, Vygotsky stressed the importance of following a child's cues about his or her interests, and providing instruction only when the child is engaged and interested in the task (Crain, 2005).

Later Vygotskyan theorists (Wood, Bruner, & Ross, 1978) introduced the term **scaffolding** (see Figure 4.3) to describe the temporary assistance that directs the child toward steps to complete a task in his or her ZPD. The idea is that more support should be offered when the child is having difficulty with the task, and support should be gradually removed as the child makes progress.

A very clear example of scaffolding is putting training wheels on a child's bicycle when the child is learning to ride. The training wheels support the child while he or she learns the basics of bicycle operation. But the training wheels prevent the child from becoming totally proficient at balancing the bike, so they have to come off at some point. The adult needs to monitor the child's skills to determine the child's ZPD in order to know when to take off the training wheels. And then, the child might require some additional scaffolding in the form of a parent running alongside the bike as the child takes off for the first time. The moment that the parent lets go and

Figure 4.3 Scaffolding

Communication For Teaching New Skills 125

Figure 4.4 Learning to Ride a Bike

the child rides independently is often captured in a photograph and hailed as the moment the child learned to ride (see Figure 4.4). But it was preceded by, and made possible by, weeks of scaffolding.

So we've seen it in action with bike riding and other motor skills, but the principle of scaffolding is the same for all kinds of learning. Research has supported the argument that scaffolding is a mechanism to enhance learning. For instance, one study found that parental scaffolding during naturalistic observations in the preschool years predicts academic competence while in elementary school (Neitzel & Stright, 2003).

A review of the literature (Hogan and Pressley, 1997) suggests the essential elements of scaffolding in educational settings. These best practices include forms of tailored assistance such as:

1. **Modeling**—doing the task for the child to watch, suggesting that they pay particular attention to specific aspects

2. **Cues and Prompts**—reminders of what the child already knows that is relevant, suggestions of areas to consider or things to try

3. **Questions**—asking about the procedure in order to help the child talk through a problem

4. **Discussion**—talking about successes and failures to help the child identify the strategies to determine what worked and what didn't work

It also requires specific feedback to the child on his or her progress, as well as mechanisms for controlling the child's frustration level so that he or she remains motivated to continue work. Our objective for the rest of this chapter is to identify the communication approaches that serve as scaffolding for children working on learning new tasks. What kind of feedback on progress is helpful? What mechanisms help children remain motivated?

Implicit Theories of Intelligence: Learning Through Mindset

What kind of feedback is helpful when providing scaffolding to help children learn a new task? The self-esteem movement recommended unrestrained praise and a total lack of criticism, but that doesn't seem to work to facilitate learning. Self-esteem does accompany happiness, and all parents want happiness for their children, so no one is against self-esteem in any way. But self-esteem simply does not help children learn new tasks. That leaves us with this nagging question: what kind of feedback as part of scaffolding is useful?

Orientations to Learning

Only very recently has science produced an answer that does have empirical support. Carol Dweck is a psychologist who studies motivation. For decades, Dweck (e.g., Dweck & Leggett, 1998) studied the differences between children who avoid challenge (a **"helpless" orientation**) and those who are persistent in the face of challenge (a **"mastery" orientation**). Those who have a mastery orientation, regardless of their initial skill level at the task, end up performing better than those with a helpless orientation, regardless of their initial skill level. They learn effectively.

Dweck has discovered that those with a helpless orientation tend to have **performance goals**, in that they are motivated by a desire to gain a favorable judgment of their competence. They want to put on a performance, a good show, and have someone tell them how good it was. They are paying attention to external sources of approval or disapproval. While they engage in a difficult task, they interpret difficulty and challenge to mean that they are failing, and they believe that their personal inadequacies are the explanation for the failure, saying to themselves things like "I'm just not smart" or "I'm just a klutz." They predict that they will continue to fail. "I'm never going to get this right." Emotionally, they report being bored or anxious about the activity; they do not enjoy it. Their self-talk during the activity is often not relevant to the task itself; for instance, they sometimes talk about how they are good at something else. And over time, their performance on similar tasks declines. They do not learn how to solve the problem, and they increasingly avoid even trying.

By contrast, those with a mastery response tend to have **learning goals**, meaning that they are motivated to increase their competence. They are paying attention to internal markers of success rather than external ones. They do not perceive failure when they struggle; instead, they tend to think about strategies they could try next, or remind themselves of methods for focusing their effort. They predict that they will eventually succeed at the task. Many of them enjoy the challenge; they find it exciting and fun. Their self-talk is all about the task at hand, talking themselves through possible solutions. Over time, their performance at such tasks remains stable or improves. They actively learn new strategies and enjoy the challenge.

Mindset

Obviously, then, a mastery orientation is the key to learning. But where does it come from? Why do some children have a helpless orientation while others have a mastery orientation? Dweck (2006) has discovered that these orientations come from the way people believe intelligence works. She calls it a *mindset*.

Children with a helpless orientation have the mindset that intelligence is an entity, a "thing" that people either have or they don't. It can't be changed, it's just there. They imagine that those who have intelligence know how to do things and never have to work to learn how to do those things. This is a **fixed mindset**. If intelligence is fixed, then there is nothing they can do to get more of it. Since they believe that intelligence is immutable and set, they are happy with evidence that they have it (for instance, when they perform well on a task without trying), but they are fairly devastated by evidence that they don't have it (that is, when a task is challenging and they don't immediately know how to perform). They certainly don't want anyone else to discover that they don't have intelligence, so

Table 4.1 Mindsets

	Fixed Mindset	Growth Mindset
Approach challenges:	By avoiding (Helpless Orientation)	With persistence (Mastery Orientation)
Motivated by goal of:	Performance	Learning
View challenge as:	A threat	An opportunity
Believe intelligence is:	An entity, a trait (you have it or you don't)	Incremental (measured on a continuum)
Can intelligence change?	No, it is fixed	Yes, it is malleable
Self-cognitions during challenge:	Negative, failures attributed to personal inadequacy, predict failure	Strategy, effort, predict success
Emotional response to challenge:	Boredom or anxiety	Excitement
Verbalizations during challenge are:	Task-irrelevant (diversionary or self-aggrandizing)	Solution-oriented self-instruction
Performance:	Declines over time	Improves or remains stable over time
Produced by:	Person-centered feedback	Process-centered feedback

they resist trying new things. Thus, they do not take risks and therefore cannot learn new skills.

Children with a mastery orientation, on the other hand, have the mindset that intelligence is measured incrementally, that it's possible to have a lot or a little or anywhere in between. And since it's made up of parts like that, it could be increased or decreased incrementally. This is accompanied by the belief that it takes effort and strategy to increase one's intelligence. This is a **growth mindset**. With a growth mindset, children see challenges as valuable opportunities to improve their intelligence; not knowing how to do something is not a threat—it is an opportunity. They seek out such opportunities, and they enjoy them. They feel smart when they are working hard. These two mindsets are summarized in Table 4.1.

Consider how frustrating it is to an adult when their beloved child says something like "I guess I'm just stupid" or "I'm ugly!" The adult hates to get a glimpse of the fixed mindset because it is unnecessarily defeatist. However, the adult often responds with something that also reflects fixed mindset: "No, you're not! You're a very smart kid!" or "No, you're very beautiful!" The adult inadvertently reinforces the child's fixed mindset.

Incidentally, people can have a mindset about intelligence, but they can also have a mindset about other traits as well. A fixed mindset about artistic or musical skills is the belief that these are talents that people either have or they don't, whereas a growth mindset about these is the belief that such talents can be developed with work. A fixed mindset about moral goodness is the belief that people are either good or honest or kind, or they are not; whereas a growth mindset is the belief that prosocial qualities can be developed.

Furthermore, mindsets are just as likely to affect adult learners as young children. Parent educators should take note that parents will come in to a parenting class with either a fixed mindset about their parenting skills (which will produce a helpless orientation to challenge), or a growth mindset about their parenting skills (which will produce a mastery orientation to challenge). We will return to the topic of mindsets in Chapter 11 for a discussion of how parent educators can apply these concepts in their work with parents.

Types of Feedback

In what is already considered one of the most ground-breaking advances in developmental psychology in decades, Dweck and her colleagues have discovered evidence that mindset is shaped (and can be changed) by communication, by the way that adults give feedback to children who are facing a challenging task. Her research method was to first give children a fairly easy task, and then (by random selection) either praise them for their intelligence or praise them for their effort. Then the tasks got harder. Dweck and her colleagues discovered that, when faced with a challenge, those who had previously been praised for their intelligence had developed a fixed mindset about their ability to do the task and adopted a helpless orientation. Those who had been praised for effort reflected a growth mindset as the tasks got more difficult and adopted a mastery orientation toward them (Mueller & Dweck, 1998). Mindsets were created with only a single sentence of praise: either "You must be really smart at this" (praising intelligence) or "You must have worked really hard" (praising effort). Those are powerful words! And more recently, the findings of these laboratory experiments have been observed in longitudinal studies of naturalistic parenting behaviors in the home (Gunderson, Gripshover, Romero, Dweck, Goldin-Meadow, & Levine, 2013; Pomerantz & Kempner, 2013), supporting the assertion that the way that parents talk to children about their tasks matters far into the future.

While this procedure specifically praised for intelligence or effort, Dweck notes that these are examples of two general types of praise: person centered and process centered. Furthermore, this distinction can apply equally well to criticism.

1. **Person-centered** feedback focuses on traits of the person (for example, ability, intelligence, moral goodness). Person-centered feedback treats qualities of the person as if they were fixed and unchangeable. The child's trait is judged by the adult to be good (this is praise) or bad (this is criticism). Dweck has proposed that person-centered praise creates a sense of contingent worth, that the judged person feels that they are only worthy because of their success, and that future failures could invalidate the praise.

2. Alternatively, **process-centered** feedback focuses on the way the task was approached (either effort or strategy). Process-centered praise and criticism imply that performance is the product of what was done rather than the identity of the person doing it. The behavior is described; the person is not judged.

The self-esteem movement had hypothesized that positive feedback (praise) was helpful and negative feedback (criticism) was harmful, but that turned out to be wrong. Now we have an alternative hypothesis, one which has garnered quite a lot of support in the last decade. It seems that feedback is useful when it is process oriented, whether it is praise or criticism, but harmful when it is person centered, whether it is praise or criticism (Kamins & Dweck, 1999). This is a major breakthrough!

Best Practices

Work on mindset and how it is shaped is still under way and still in its infancy as an area of psychological research. But it seems clear that we can finally offer some evidence-based advice about how to talk to kids when they are trying to learn a new skill. The implications for parenting are pretty obvious: reject the self-esteem movement, avoid person-centered praise, and use scaffolding of new tasks with process-centered feedback.

Reject the Self-Esteem Movement

The self-esteem movement is still operating as a force in society. Parents need to reject advice that comes from it. Beware of advice designed to "raise your child's self-esteem." Don't fall for the argument that low self-esteem causes bullying and violence; these problems have more complex causes and solutions.

This doesn't mean that self-esteem is terrible and we should knock it out of anyone who has it. People are happier when they have high self-esteem, and happiness is worth pursuing. But what we are going for is an accurate self-concept, which is actually useful to people as they navigate the world. An accurate self-concept allows people to make good decisions and achieve genuine success, which brings happiness (e.g., Marques, Pais-Ribeiro, & Lopez, 2011). High self-esteem, just for its own sake, is not helpful.

Avoid Person-Centered (Evaluative) Praise

Most importantly, rejecting the self-esteem movement means avoiding the ubiquitous person-centered praise that it demands. Not only does person-centered praise not work to produce desirable behavior and academic achievement, but it actually sets the recipient of the praise up for failure by producing a helpless orientation when they face difficulty. Parents must, therefore, reject the impulse to constantly tell children that they are wonderful, beautiful, special, and smart.

An Israeli schoolteacher turned clinical psychologist and parent educator named Haim Ginott wrote extensively about the problems with praise in the late 1960s. His arguments were not supported by evidence at the time, but he also concluded that person-centered praise was harmful for children. He had observed that this simply did not have the effect the parents hoped for. It does not work. He asserts that it does not work because the kind of praise parents generally offer is **evaluative praise**, which judges or evaluates the character or personality of the child. Evaluative praise says things like: "You're such a generous kid!" or "You're really thoughtful!" or "What a great artist you are!" Even though these are positive evaluations, they are still evaluations. Clearly, evaluative praise is the same thing as person-centered praise.

Ginott argues that evaluative (i.e., person-centered) praise does not work to make the child feel good about him- or herself or to keep working on the task at hand, for several reasons (Ginott, 1961. First, evaluative praise invites dependency. It creates the expectation that children must get approval from others rather than from themselves. Children stop monitoring their progress by their own standards and instead focus outward, on whether an authority figure will approve. This is what Dweck, decades later, would call being motivated by performance goals rather than learning goals. If children are reliant on others to supervise their progress and cannot do it for themselves or are not interested in doing it for themselves, then they are unnecessarily dependent on that authority figure and will be unable to learn effectively on their own.

Second, evaluative praise evokes defensiveness. It may make a child feel inauthentic because the glowing description of their character does not match their secret desires or a past behavior that is not known to the parent (e.g., "My mom says I'm smart, but she doesn't know that I bombed that spelling quiz last week."). Because evaluative praise makes a fully positive evaluation of a person who is truthfully more complex than that, it is essentially a distorted image of the child's character or personality. Consequently, the child is put in a position where he wants to hide the full truth from that authority figure so that he is not discovered to be something worse than what the adult thinks him to be. This is what Dweck would call *contingent worth* decades later. The child gets the message that his value is contingent upon continuing to convince the parent that their unrealistically positive judgment is true. This creates anxiety.

Third, evaluative praise is uncomfortable as a feature of emotionally close relationships. In the context of a close loving relationship, evaluation is uncomfortable because it places the praiser in a position of superior power. A person who has the right and the knowledge to judge another is clearly more powerful than the one being judged. This sets up a hierarchy. The problem is that a power hierarchy makes intimacy difficult. Ginott suggests that we consider how we would feel about getting graded by our lover (an A+ for kissing, say, a B for conversation skills, etc.). Even if the grades were good, we would feel uncomfortable about it because getting evaluated establishes a power hierarchy, and power is antithetical to intimacy.

Ginott's explanations have not so far been tested empirically. I offer them here as possible further explanation for the findings about person-centered/evaluative praise.

But all of this so far is what NOT to do. A good start—but what SHOULD parent educators recommend?

Scaffolding for Learning

Figure 4.5 Learning to Drive a Car

Vygotsky's theory informs us that when a child is learning a new task, it is important to gauge exactly where her skills and interests lie because the parent's approach will have to be tailored a bit to the specific conditions. The task will have to be in the child's Zone of Proximal Development (ZPD), and it will change over time as the child's ZPD changes.

In principle, this is really not complicated. Scaffolding is just temporary support and instruction that is withdrawn as the child acquires the skill. It includes demonstrations, instruction, cues, prompts, and feedback. Having just taught my oldest daughter to drive a car (Figure. 4.5), this comes readily to mind as an example where I certainly did use scaffolding. In the weeks preceding her going to driving school, I verbally pointed things out to her while we were in the car together. I said things like: "Notice that I stop at the white line, so the hood of my car is not in the crosswalk at all," and "Notice that I have to pull the car out into the intersection about this far before I start turning left." This is demonstration with instruction. When she was ready to get behind the wheel, I first took her to an empty parking lot where she could get the feel of the vehicle first before we dealt with traffic. She drove the car through the empty lot, feeling how the car reacted when she moved the steering wheel, getting the hang of turning while in reverse, and such things. She also practiced pulling into and out parking spaces. It was lots of practice with instruction. There was also feedback in the form of direct observation. After pulling into a parking space, I encouraged her to get out to visually inspect how close she was to the white lines marking the parking space. We went out on the roads once I judged that her ZPD had moved forward a bit.

Once she was driving on the streets, at first I only asked her to make right-hand turns because I wanted to keep the task in her ZPD. The first time I instructed her to turn left at the light, she looked a little panicked and said she was afraid she wouldn't know how to. So as we approached the light, I gave her instructions the whole time, little reminders of things she knew already. "Remember, when the light turns green, the oncoming traffic has the right of way, so you will have to wait for a break in that traffic before you turn left," and "Remember to pull out into the intersection before you start turning the wheel to the left." Eventually, her ZPD had moved forward enough that I stopped giving instructions while she was driving unless she asked or we encountered a problem.

At this point, she has her license and is a very competent driver. Months of scaffolding produced her driving skill. Research on driving safety has concluded that scaffolding is the most helpful technique for those learning to drive, and thus graduated drivers' licenses are standard practice in California and in many other states (National Highway Traffic Safety Administration, 2008). Graduated drivers' licenses essentially mandate scaffolding in driving instruction by requiring different levels of intensity of instruction as the young person acquires driving skills. The state requires it, but the parent implements it.

Offer Process-Centered (Descriptive) Feedback

Scaffolding includes feedback. Children need to know how they're doing at the task they are learning. Based on the recent research by Dweck and her colleagues, we now know that positive feedback (praise) can be useful, but so too can negative feedback (criticism). In order to be helpful, both must be limited to the child's behavior and not make generalizations about the person. Dweck called this *process centered*, explaining that it must be about the child's effort or strategies employed. Ginott (1961) calls this **descriptive praise**. It must be specific—the more specific the better—and the feedback should reflect a realistic picture of the child's behavior. These differences are summarized in Table 4.2.

When I taught my daughter Gabby to drive a car, I had to offer lots of feedback, some of it praise and some of it criticism. The praise was always process oriented, or descriptive. Sometimes I offered statements recognizing her effort, including "I'm glad you're making the time to practice today" or "I noticed that you kept working on that parking situation until you got it right." Sometimes the statements were about her strategy; for instance: "I saw you look over your shoulder before putting on your turn signal. That's a good habit to be in." There were also times when I needed to recognize poor effort or a misguided strategy. For a few months, Gabby got discouraged and didn't want to practice, and I

Table 4.2 Types of Feedback

	Person-Centered	Process-Centered
Also known as:	Evaluative	Descriptive, appreciative
Focus on:	Judgment of the person	Description of the effort or strategies employed by the person, or the task itself
Scope:	General	Specific
Nature:	Distorts reality	Realistic
Produces:	Fixed Mindset	Growth Mindset
Effect on relationship:	Threatens relationship, creates contingent worth	No effect on relationship

had to comment on it. I said things like: "Gabby, you haven't agreed to practice driving all week. You need to put more time in, or you won't learn." This was a criticism, to be sure, but it was one that was oriented toward her effort (or lack of it), not toward any quality of her as a person. At one point, I had to make the rule that any time the two of us were in the car together, she would have to drive as I would not. I had to force the issue of effort. I also offered criticisms of her strategies regularly. That is simply necessary when a person is learning a new skill. For instance, knowing which way to turn the wheel when backing up is not intuitive at first. So when she practiced backing out of a parking space, I had to directly instruct her which way to turn the wheel, and sometimes say flat out, "No, that's wrong. Turn the other way." This is also clearly criticism. But again, it is centered entirely on her strategy, not on her as a person. Not only can kids handle this sort of criticism, they need it in order to learn a new task.

Even when one is persuaded to avoid person-centered feedback and instead offer process-centered feedback, old habits die hard. A child proudly holds up her crayon drawing like my daughter Letty is doing in Figure 4.6, and out of long habit, we want to say: "That is so beautiful! What a wonderful artist you are!" We evaluate. We judge. We make generalizations about her talent. Frankly, it's hard to know what else to say. But like all other skills, this one gets easier the more we practice. Saying anything about the process involved in making the crayon scribble artwork is better than evaluating the child.

Dweck specifies effort and strategy as two aspects of the process one might highlight in process-centered feedback. A comment on effort could be: "I noticed that you were working hard on that." One example of noticing strategy could be: "I notice that you used blue here in this part of the picture," or "You put a sun

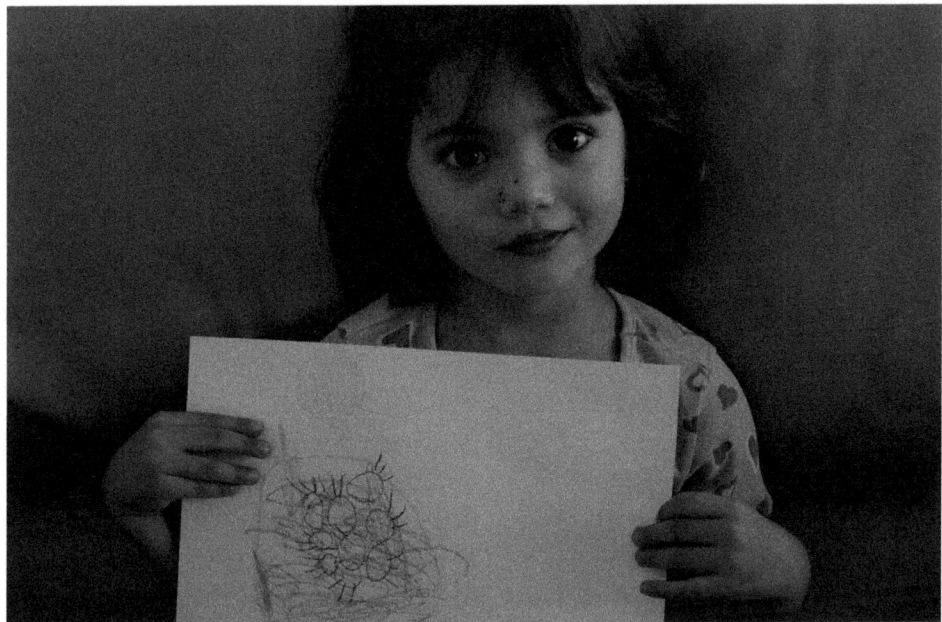

Figure 4.6 Child's Artwork

up in the sky, so this must be during the daytime." Obviously, the harder the child worked on it, the more there is to say about effort, and the more advanced the child's strategy, the more there is to notice with regard to strategy. That's true for praise, anyway. But remember that we can also use process-centered criticism. We might say: "I noticed that you made this drawing very quickly," or "The picture seems to be only on the left side the paper, but the right side is still empty." These statements do not judge the picture as good or bad. It does not even judge the effort or strategy as good or bad. It simply notices these things. This kind of feedback is useful to a child as they learn a new skill. Not only are they being supported by your emotional interest, they are being instructed.

Adele Faber and Elaine Mazlish (1980), who had earlier participated in a parent education group with Haim Ginott, offer suggestions for how to generate descriptive (i.e., process-centered) feedback. One suggestion is for the parent to describe what he sees. Describing what one sees is very similar to identifying effort and strategy, but it is broader still. This is my go-to method for descriptive feedback. I just say what I notice. When my daughter came to me with the artwork in the photo above, I didn't really know what I was looking at. So I just described it back to her. "Hmm. There's a sun up here. And then this has a blue part, with some black things in the blue." She eagerly reported to me that this was a pigpen, and those were pigs playing in the water. She was delighted to tell me about the picture, and my description of what I noticed was simply a way for her to divulge more information.

Many adults are uncomfortable describing what they see without evaluating it. "I see this and I see that" feels flat to them after a lifetime of regularly offering completely over-the-top compliments like "You're a wonderful artist!" But even though the feedback doesn't seem as gushing to the parent, the child notices that this feedback is actually very specific. The parent might say "You're great!" to every presentation of a piece of artwork, but when the parent offers a specific description, the child gets the message that the parent actually looked at the picture. That individualized feedback is quite powerful.

An anecdote of a student perfectly illustrates the power of individualized specific feedback. She reported that, after she learned about descriptive praise in class, she went to a family party. A child in the family drew a picture and brought it to her. In the past, she would have told the child that it was "great" and he was doing "great." Lots of evaluative praise. But this time, she tried descriptive praise instead. The child had drawn a picture of a piece of pizza. She thought to herself "Describe what you see," and so she did. She said: "Oh, this is pizza. I think it has pepperonis on it. It's a pretty big slice, too." And so on. All of the kids noticed this very specific descriptive feedback, and clearly, they all wanted THAT kind of attention, so they all started drawing pictures of pizza slices. And (here's the best part!) they drew different kinds of pizza, using different toppings. Because she noticed details, the details started to matter. That kind of inspiration is what prompts children to spend the time it takes to really develop skills. My student went home with many drawings of pizza slices, and she was astounded. Would this work if you wanted to help a child develop a skill other than drawing? Would it work with math and reading? Could it be used to get a child to practice a musical instrument? To get them to do chores?

I certainly use it for all of those reasons. When I hear my 11-year-old playing the flute, I pop in and say: "I hear that you're practicing!" When the trash bins are out on the curb on the night before trash day, I tell my 18-year-old, "I saw that the trash bins are out. Thank you." Describe what you see. Sometimes acknowledgement of effort goes a long way toward inspiring a person to keep at it.

Sometimes kids will push their parents to make an evaluation with a follow-up question such as: "But is it good?" Those are children who have grown accustomed to external rewards and are seeking to perform in order to get the compliment. That is totally normal in our contemporary culture in which kids are subjected to a lot of evaluative praise. The parent may have to push back a little bit, telling that child that they are not going to offer an evaluation. This could sound like: "I wonder if YOU think it's good?" or "I just hope you enjoy working on drawings like this." Once the adult is comfortable doing this, children start to respond to this sort of feedback with a mastery orientation toward the task.

A second suggestion offered by Faber and Mazlish is for the parent to describe how she feels. This is describing the effect of the child's behavior on another person. With the pigpen drawing above, I could have said: "That has a very happy, lazy, summer feeling to me," or "I used to love drawing when I was little. It's fun to see you doing the same thing." When chores are getting done, I sometimes say to my children: "It is such a relief to me to have help getting the dishes done. Thank you." Or "It's a great feeling to come home to a clean kitchen!" All of these options avoid evaluating the child, which is why they work to encourage learning.

When Should Scaffolding and Process-Centered Feedback Be Used?

Scaffolding and process-centered feedback can be used when the child is learning a new skill. This happens often, of course, so these techniques should always be at the ready.

The tricky part is to remember that scaffolding is, by definition, a temporary support. If the training wheels are never removed from the bike, the child will never be a competent bike rider. But when should scaffolding be removed? Parents have to make judgments about timing, and there are no formulas for doing so. At what point ought they back off and let a child succeed or fail at a task on his own? This is a judgment call for which there are probably no right or wrong answers. The sensitive responsiveness of attachment relationships is still a factor here and should be used to help gauge how the child reacts as scaffolding is removed.

Developmental Connections

Human beings keep learning throughout life. Because of this, the essence of this chapter is not embedded in a single developmental stage. The nature of what they learn changes, of course. My personal observation as a parent is that the stakes keep getting higher and higher as my children approach adulthood. My youngest daughter, Sofie, is learning how to play the flute. I hope that she is learning the value of practice and developing discipline, but her skill at the flute itself is unlikely to have any effect on her life in the future. Contrast that with my oldest, Gabby, who recently learned how to drive a car and is still developing that skill. I often reflect on the fact that her skill at driving is a factor in whether or not she makes it through the day. Literally, her life is at stake. That is terrifying to me. The use of scaffolding and the importance of process-centered feedback are necessary to help with the development of both of these skills. The practices are identical, even as the skills to be learned vary drastically by age.

How Parents React

Parents don't like to hear that the self-esteem movement is wrong. They may recognize some of their mistakes in other areas of parenting, but they believe that showering praise on their child is one of the things that they've been doing right all this time. It feels good to them. It feels like they are offering unconditional love and support, which is what they really WANT to do. Nobody comes to a parenting class to be jolted into a realization that the one thing they thought they were doing right is actually harmful to their child. Therefore, some parents will simply not listen to this "nonsense." It's too different from what they came in believing and too threatening to their identity.

One way to approach this resistance is to offer something new in place of the strategy being taken away. If parent educators convince parents to offer process-centered feedback, those parents will simply have less time to be offering person-centered feedback and so will do it less often. This can be presented as a great new strategy to try that is even better than what they're doing, rather than as a replacement for what they've been doing wrong. But the parent educator must be able to clearly distinguish process-centered feedback from person-centered so that the learners recognize that this is NOT what they've been doing all along. For most folks, this is a dramatic shift.

Some of the questions I am asked include:

> **Q. But it's still bad to criticize kids, right?**
> A. First of all, let's just acknowledge that parents do criticize their children a lot. They know they're not supposed to, so they don't report doing it when they are asked, but in observations of parents with their children, parents criticize far more than they praise (Swenson, Ho, Budhathoki, Belcher, Tucker, Miller, & Gross, 2016). But whether it's

good or bad for kids depends entirely on whether the **criticism** is person centered or process centered. Person-centered criticism (just like person-centered praise) is not helpful. It creates a fixed mindset in the child, which leads to a helpless orientation to challenges. So telling a child that he or she is lazy, thoughtless, stupid, or mean is a destructive way of communicating. It will not produce improved behavior or promote learning. But offering process-centered criticism (commenting on the child's lack of effort or a strategy that was misguided) is actually useful (Kamins & Dweck, 1999).

Q. If I stop praising my child the way I have been, how do I convey to my child that I do love him unconditionally, that I do think he's wonderful?
A. The kind of love an adult feels for a child is really unlike anything else. I remember when my first nieces and nephews were little, and I was smitten with them beyond belief. I have also worked in child care and felt the same overwhelming love for the children in my care. Then my own daughters came into my life, and it was more of the same but a front-row seat and for years on end. Really, the whole world looks different when you love a child. Love for a child is truly unconditional. This is a difficult feeling to express because it is so overwhelming. This is probably why we resort to over-the-top superlatives. It's as if we all live in the fictional town of Lake Wobegon, "where all the children are above average." But I have a suggestion to offer. Perhaps, instead of projecting an unrealistic image of perfection onto the children, we could instead claim OUR feelings of overwhelming love. When I'm tempted to say, "You are such a great kid!" I can say instead how I feel about the child by saying "I love you," or "I feel so lucky to have you in my life," or "I enjoy your company." These are sincere expressions of appreciation and affection, but they are not evaluations of a child.

Q. What happens when we use these strategies to teach our child and they have some kind of setback? They fail a test, they lose a game, they fall off the bike, or they have a car accident. What then?
A. This is going to happen. And one of the most important jobs of a parent is to help children emotionally cope with disappointments. In Chapter 6, the first strategy we will address is active listening, which is the strategy I recommend in this situation.

Programs and Critique

At the time of this writing, there are no formal parenting programs that I know of that are based on Vygotsky's theory or on the concept of mindsets. I look forward to their development. I can imagine parenting programs for parents whose children are struggling in school or parents who simply want to help their kids reach their academic potential. I can imagine parenting programs for parents who want their child to excel at a sport or a musical instrument or any other particular talent.

But until that time, I simply point out that the topics of self-esteem and praise often appear as a side note in some of the parenting programs that we discuss in this book.

Attachment Parenting

William Sears, discussed in the prior chapter as one of the most prominent proponents of attachment parenting, addresses self-esteem in a way that could be straight out of a self-esteem movement manual. He writes (Sears, 2015) that: "Self-esteem is your child's passport to a lifetime of mental health and social happiness. It's the foundation of a child's well-being and the key to success as an adult."

CRITIQUE: Ugh! These statements are simply false, so I'm dismayed to see them on the Ask Dr. Sears website. He is perpetuating the falsified theory that is the foundation of the self-esteem movement. However, I note that this is far afield from the tenets of attachment parenting. It is an aside for him and presumably for the parents who go to his website for guidance. Furthermore, the advice he offers is, by my reading, generally benign, even though the premise is wrong.

Adlerian Programs

Adlerian programs, which will be addressed in Chapter 7, address the issue of self-esteem head on. These include the Systematic Training for Effective Parenting (STEP) program (e.g., Dinkmeyer & McKay, 1996), as well as Active Parenting (Popkin, 2014), Positive Parenting (e.g., Nelsen, 2006), and Love and Logic (Cline & Fay, 2006). Alfred Adler assumed that all misbehavior is the product of a child who wants to fit into the social group but feels discouraged in his efforts to do so. Adler is also the source of the concept of an "inferiority complex," so it is not surprising that he focused his work on helping children feel good about themselves. He didn't use the word self-esteem because it had not yet been coined, but his followers use it.

CRITIQUE: The Adlerian approach is called **encouragement**. The premise sounds a lot like the self-esteem movement. For example, Dinkmeyer and McKay (1996) write: "His parents' goal, then, must be build Fred's self-esteem, his courage to try, and his feelings of adequacy so that he will believe in himself and be willing to make an effort" (p. 57). Cline and Fay (2006) maintain that "Children with poor self-concept often forget to do homework, bully other kids, argue with teachers and parents, steal and withdraw into themselves whenever things get rocky—irresponsible in all they do" (p. 35). These statements could be taken directly from the self-esteem movement playbook.

The recommendation (encouragement) is similar to the self-esteem movement in one way, but very importantly different in another way. The similarity is that parents are instructed to focus on what the child does right (praise) rather than the child's mistakes or failures (criticism). However, we now know that it is the *type* of praise and criticism that really matter, not the positive or negative nature of the evaluation. So on that point, the Adlerian programs are teaching something that is not supported by research.

Adlerian programs differ from the self-esteem movement, though, in their attempt to distinguish encouragement from praise, noting that praise has the potential to discourage a child. They point out that praise generates a desire to please an external authority rather than working toward an internal goal, and they also note that encouragement focuses on effort rather than achievement. These are tantalizing hints that they conceptualize praise to be what Dweck calls *person-centered praise* and encouragement to be what Dweck calls *process-centered praise*. But lacking the insight provided by Dweck's research on mindset, the attempt falls short. They suggest that, while encouragement should be offered for effort, not just achievement, the recommended encouragement often comes in the form of person-centered praise! What they call encouragement focuses entirely on the positive, which means never offering criticism, which means never offering instruction. The terminology is hopelessly entangled. There is plainly a more useful and accurate way to conceptualize the factors that are involved, and that is by using Dweck's notion of mindset rather than Adler's notion of encouragement.

In short, the self-esteem movement has contaminated many parenting education resources. A parent educator needs to be aware of that, and be on guard against it.

Review and Reflection Questions

1. How did the self-esteem movement shape parent-child interactions? How do we know that it was wrong? Did you see any evidence of the self-esteem movement in your own upbringing?

2. What is the primary argument of social development theory?

3. How does scaffolding promote learning? How can it be accomplished in a teaching relationship? Do you ever use scaffolding when teaching a child?

4. What are the features of helpless and mastery orientations? Do these features describe you in any domain of your life? How do these orientations reflect a fixed or growth mindset?

5. How does feedback produce one's mindset? What kind of feedback produces a growth mindset?

6. What is the effect of offering criticism to children when they are learning?

Terminology to Know

- Criticism
- Descriptive praise
- Encouragement
- Evaluative praise
- Fixed mindset
- Growth mindset
- Helpless orientation
- Learning goals
- Mastery orientation
- Performance goals
- Person-centered feedback
- Process-centered feedback
- Scaffolding
- Self-esteem
- Self-esteem movement
- Social development theory
- Zone of Proximal Development (ZPD)

Names to Know

- Dweck
- Vygotsky

References

Baumeister, R.F., Campbell, J.D., Krueger, J.I., & Vohs, K.D. (2003). Does high self-esteem cause better performance, interpersonal success, happiness, or healthier lifestyles? *Psychological Science in the Public Interest, 4, 1,* 1–44.

Branden, N. (1969). *The psychology of self-esteem.* Nash Publishing.

Buhrmester, D., Furman, W., Wittenberg, M.T., & Reis, H.T. (1989). Five domains of interpersonal competence in peer relationships. *Journal of Personality and Social Psychology, 55, 6,* 991–1008.

Cline, F., & Fay, J. (2006). *Parenting with Love and Logic.* Boulder, CO: NavPress.

Crain, W. (2005). *Theories of development: Concepts and applications, 5th edition.* Upper Saddle River, NJ: Pearson.

Deci, E.L., Koestner, R., & Ryan, R.M. (1999). A meta-analytic review of experiments examining the effects of extrinsic rewards on intrinsic motivation.

Deiner, E., Wolsic, B. & Fujita, F. (1995). Physical attractiveness and subjective well-being. *Journal of Personality and Social Psychology, 69, 1,* 120–129.

Dinkmeyer, D., & McKay, G.D. (1996). *Raising a responsible child.* New York: Fireside.

Dweck, C.S. (2006). *Mindset: The new psychology of success.* New York: Random House.

Dweck, C.S., & Leggett, E.L. (1998). A social-cognitive approach to motivation and personality. *Psychological Review, 99, 2,* 256–273.

Emler, N. (2001). *Self-esteem: The costs and causes of low self-worth.* London: Joseph Rowntree Foundation.

Faber, A., & Mazlish, E. (1980). *How to talk so kids will listen & listen so kids will talk.* New York: HarperCollins.

Ginott, H. (1961). *Between parent and child.* New York: Macmillan.

Gunderson, E.A., Gripshover, S.J., Romero, C., Dweck, C.S., Goldin-Meadow, S., & Levine, S.C. (2013). Parent praise to 1- and 3-year-olds predicts children's motivational frameworks 5 years later. *Child Development, 84, 5,* 1526–1541.

Guo, S., Wu, Q., Smokowski, P.R., Bacallao, M., Evans, C.B.R., & Cotter, K.L. (2015). A longitudinal evaluation of the Positive Action program in a low-income, racially diverse, rural county: Effects of self-esteem, school hassles, aggression, and internalizing symptoms. *Journal of Youth and Adolescence, 44, 12,* 2337–2358.

Hogan, K., & Pressley, M. (Eds.) (1997). *Scaffolding and student learning: Instructional approaches and issues.* Cambridge, MA: Brookline Books.

Kamins, M.L., & Dweck, C.S. (1999). Person versus process praise and criticism: Implications for contingent self-worth and coping. *Developmental Psychology, 35, 3,* 833–847.

Marques, S.C., Pais-Ribeiro, J.L., & Lopez, S.J. (2011). The role of positive psychology constructs in predicting mental health and academic achievement in children and adolescents: A two-year longitudinal study. *Journal of Happiness, 12, 6,* 1049–1062.

Meyer, W.U. (1992). Paradoxical effects of praise and criticism on perceived ability. In W. Stroebe & M. Hewstone (Eds.), *European review of social psychology, volume 3,* pp. 259–283. Oxford, UK: John Wiley & Sons.

Mruk, C.J. (2006). *Self-esteem research, theory, and practice, 3rd edition.* New York: Springer.

Mueller, C.M., & Dweck, C.S. (1998). Praise for intelligence can undermine children's motivation and performance. *Journal of Personality and Social Psychology, 75, 1,* 33–52.

National Highway Traffic Safety Administration (2008). Graduated driver licensing system. file:///C:/Users/kdyer/Downloads/810888GradDriverLicense.pdf Accessed 2/20/2016.

Neitzel, C., & Stright, A.D. (2003). Mothers' scaffolding of children's problem solving: Establishing a foundation of academic self-regulatory competence. *Journal of Family Psychology, 17, 1,* 147–159.

Nelsen, J. (2006). *Positive discipline.* New York: Random House.

Owen, D.J., Slep, A.M.S., & Heyman, R.E. (2012). The effect of praise, positive nonverbal response, reprimand, and negative nonverbal response on child compliance: A systematic review. *Clinical Child and Family Psychology Review, 15, 4,* 364–385.

Pomerantz, E.M., & Kempner, S.G. (2013). Mothers' daily person and process praise: Implications for children's theory of intelligence and motivation. *Developmental Psychology, 49, 11,* 2040–2046.

Popkin, M.H. (2014). *Active Parenting: A parent's guide to raising happy and successful children, 4th edition.* Atlanta: Active Parenting Publishers.

Pottebaum, S.M., Keith, T.Z., & Ehly, S.W. (1986). Is there a causal relation between self-concept and academic achievement? *Journal of Educational Research, 79, 3,* 140–144.

Sears, W. (2015). 12 ways to raise a confident child. Ask Dr. Sears. http://www.askdrsears.com/topics/parenting/child-rearing-and-development/12-ways-help-your-child-build-self-confidence Accessed 2/22/2016.

Swenson, S., Ho, G.W.K., Budhathoki, C., Belcher, H.M.E., Tucker, S., Miller, K., & Gross, D. (2016). Parents' use of praise and criticism in a sample of young children seeking mental health services. *Journal of Pediatric Health Care, 30, 1,* –49–56.

Walker, J.S., & Bright, J.A. (2009). False inflated self-esteem and violence: A systematic review and cognitive model. *Journal of Psychiatry and Psychology, 201,* 1–32.

Woessner, G., & Schneider, S. (2013). The role of self-control and self-esteem and the impact of early risk factors among violent offenders. *Criminal Behavior and Mental Health, 23, 2,* 99–112.

Wood, D.J., Bruner, J.S., & Ross, G. (1978). The role of tutoring in problem solving. *Journal of Child Psychiatry and Psychology, 17, 2,* 89–100.

Credit

- Fig. 4.3: U.S. Capitol / Copyright in the Public Domain.

5. Communication for Problem Solving

Introduction

Now we move just a bit higher on the pyramid. We assume that parental beliefs and other aspects of the context are still exerting an influence, and that attachment relationships are shaping up daily life as usual. We've spent time talking about how to use communication to teach children new skills. Now we move on to using communication to solve problems.

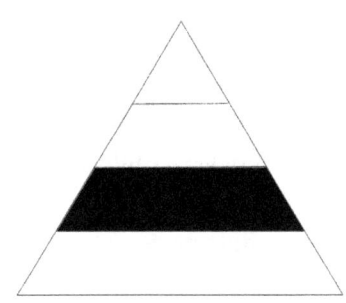

Figure 5.1 Communication on Pyramid

Often, this is why parents sign up for a parenting class. They are encountering everyday problems such as a child who says he'll clean his room but then doesn't do it, or a teenager who sulks but will not acknowledge that anything's wrong. Parents are facing the hard truth that they don't know how to talk to their child, and they come asking an expert for some help. And the request generally comes in one of two forms:

1. How do I get my child to <u>talk</u> to me?

2. How do I get my child to <u>listen</u> to me?

So we are going to tackle these two problems, primarily using concepts popularized by a parenting program called **Parent Effectiveness Training (PET)**. I believe Gordon's book of the same name (Gordon, 2000) is the most generally useful of all parenting advice books I've read. I recommend it to anyone who asks for a good parenting book.

Theory and Background

Parent Effectiveness Training (PET) is based on the principles of humanistic psychology and especially Carl Rogers, one of its founders. Thomas Gordon, who developed PET in the 1960s, was a student of Carl Rogers.

Humanistic Psychology

Humanistic psychology is a theoretical perspective that emerged in the mid-20th century. It focuses on promoting self-actualization, allowing and encouraging all people to express their true selves and meet their full potential. This is a very individualistic philosophy that is also characteristically American. It sees all people as inherently good, and therefore assumes that awareness and understanding will promote positive behavior because it builds on that inherent goodness. Most of my students in Child and Family Science generally believe that it is at least true that *children* are essentially good and therefore typically are predisposed to share this perspective. Parents, too, are generally inclined to see the goodness in their children. They might be angered by misbehavior or heartbroken to feel that communication has broken down with their child, but they trust in the goodness of their child, so they too are generally willing to accept this premise.

In his work as a psychotherapist, Carl Rogers believed that psychotherapy clients can resolve difficulties in their life if they gain adequate insight into their problems, and insight can be gained through a trusting relationship with their therapist (Kramer, 1995). In one of his books describing his theory of client-centered therapy (Rogers, 1951) he explains some of the assumptions of Rogers' client-centered therapy that clearly shape Gordon's PET. These include the following:

1. The way a person perceives the world truly is **reality** for that person. One implication of this is that it makes no sense to try to convince a person that reality is different from their perception. It simply won't work, and it will make them defensive. It creates an adversarial dynamic. Instead, it is best to acknowledge their feelings, whether it is a shared reality or not. Accept that the other person indeed does feel a certain way, and stop trying to talk them out of it. Thomas Gordon will spend a great deal of effort in PET to convince parents to use a **language of acceptance** in the

way they talk to children … to convey that the child, complete with his or her painful feelings, is accepted.

2. People have a natural tendency to **actualize** their potential. That is to say that human beings are naturally striving to be better and to have the most meaningful existence possible. An implication of this statement is essentially to assume the most positive interpretation and expect the best from people. This is a very optimistic attitude. My life experience has taught me that it is not always true, but that it is largely true, and it's better to go through life this way than to go through life expecting the worst. PET assumes this to be true, that both parent and child will naturally want to be better, so it is worth it to emotionally connect and remind the other of internal motivations for doing the right thing.

3. Human emotions are important indicators, both to the person feeling them and to those trying to understand that person, of the person's needs and goals. This becomes important in PET because emotional connections are the ones that drive relationships. Therefore, in everything a parent does, the parent needs to maintain and build the emotional connection to the child. If that is lost, then all is lost. Honoring emotions is the way to intimacy. Emotions are NOT to be squashed, to be overcome, to be ignored. They are to be honored as guides to behavior and the key to intimacy.

4. Change can only be accomplished when a person does not feel that his "self" is threatened. This is related to the language of acceptance referenced in point number 1 above. Only when people feel that they are accepted just as they are do they feel safe to make changes. This has been articulated by others as the paradoxical theory of change (Bleisser, 1970), stating that change cannot be coerced but must be the product of a person's investment in being his or her true self. This notion appears in PET through the avoidance of any kind of coercion. The communication strategies of PET are about making emotional connection, honestly sharing emotions relevant to the decisions, and then allowing each person to make decisions about behavior. People can only do these things if they do not feel that their identity is threatened.

Rogers's practice of therapy, his mechanism of therapy, which honors these assumptions, is **unconditional positive regard**. He argues that the client (and Gordon will extend this to the child) must feel secure in the knowledge that the therapist (or parent) does not question his or her basic value and worth as a human being. When a person is safe in the unconditional positive regard of another person, then he or she is safe to self-actualize. This can be done by exploring emotions, which provide clues that allow others to understand their perception of reality and thus to solve their own problems (Rogers, 1959).

Best Practices

The PET program takes those principles of Rogerian psychotherapy and directly applies them to parent-child relationships. Gordon believes that these tools are widely applicable to all human relationships. In fact, a staple of marriage counseling is to teach adult couples how to use these tools to produce more satisfying and effective communication with each other. But for our purposes here, I will discuss each of Gordon's communication strategies specifically in the context of the parent-child relationship.

Problem-Ownership Principle

Many parents in the United States have heard (and believe) the argument that they need to have good communication with their children. But what exactly is *good* communication? That's a little harder. Gordon (2000) asserts that the most appropriate communication strategy really depends on the nature of the problem. (Seems obvious when I say it like that, right? Of course it depends!)

Table 5.1 Problem Ownership

		Does the CHILD have tangible needs that are not being met?	
		No	Yes
Does the PARENT have tangible needs that are not being met?	No	No Problem	Child-Owned Problem
	Yes	Parent-Owned Problem	Shared Problem

Gordon suggests a method to determine what strategy to use, and it is based on the **problem-ownership principle** (see Table 5.1), which simply says that the most appropriate communication strategy depends upon who "owns" the problem. The person who owns the problem is the person who has tangible needs that are not being met. Please note that this definition is NOT the same as identifying the person who is at fault for the problem. If Mom really needs the dishes done (because if they're not done, she'll have to stay up to do them and thus lose sleep), then she has a tangible need and therefore owns the problem. It may be the child's fault for not doing his chore, but the mom is still the one who owns the problem. This is a parent-owned problem. Alternatively, if the child hasn't completed a school project that is due tomorrow, then the child is at risk of earning a failing grade or losing sleep to get the project done and therefore the child owns the problem. The parent may feel an obligation to help the child with this problem, but still the child is the one who owns the problem. This is a child-owned problem.

The problem-ownership principle is a fairly radical idea in some circles. There are people who inappropriately take on everyone else's problems as if they owned them. This may be happening with the so-called helicopter parents, hovering over their children trying to force solutions to the child's problems. If you recall from Chapter 3, attachment theory offers a different explanation for helicopter parents (i.e., too much intrusiveness, which is not sensitive). And here I am offering another: that helicopter parenting is a failure to understand problem ownership, thereby failing to allow the child to own (and solve) his own problems. At any rate, the idea that all people should be allowed to own their own problems and that no one is required to own anyone else's problems is fairly radical. I believe it directly combats the expectation that parents (and especially mothers) ought to sacrifice all for their children, placing their own happiness as less important than their children's, ultimately sabotaging both causes. Instead, we will assume (in the spirit of humanistic psychology) that all people—parents and children alike—are striving to self-actualize. We will look for opportunities to allow both to succeed.

So as we dive into the nitty gritty, please note that the problem-ownership principle asserts that there are some "problems" that are really not problems at all. A parenting adviser is sometimes able to simply reassure the parent and do nothing else. Because I study infant sleep, parents sometimes come to me asking for advice about that. Occasionally, they ask how to get their baby out of their bed. Considering the problem-ownership principle, I try to find out whose tangible needs are not being met. Is the baby sleeping adequately? Is the sleep space safe for an infant? Sometimes the answer is yes, that he is a happy baby, gets plenty of sleep, the sleeping environment is safe, so the baby's fine. So then I ask about the parent's tangible needs: Are the parents sleeping adequately? Do they feel they have enough opportunity for romantic intimacy? And sometimes the answer is yes, the parents are doing just fine. They love his company in the bed, they enjoy his sweet milky breath and the convenience of breastfeeding during the night without waking up fully, and so on. Pause. This is when the parent blurts out that someone else has a problem with this. A mother-in-law, a pediatrician, the author of a book they read … someone else, someone totally uninvolved in the situation, has conveyed that they should NOT have the baby in their bed. So we shift away from taking about the baby in the bed because by the problem-ownership principle, this is No Problem, and no strategy is needed. Instead, we start discussing the pressure the parent feels to please everyone else. It's a very different conversation, a totally different problem.

However, more often, there really is a problem, and it is important to know what strategy to use to approach it. So what does the problem-ownership principle say specifically about communication? Gordon says that when the child owns the problem, then the parent's task is primarily to listen. The parent wants to listen in such a way that conveys unconditional positive regard, maintains the emotional connection, and allows the child to keep talking through his problem until he arrives at a solution. This is called active listening or emotion coaching. When the parent owns the problem, however, the parent's task is primarily to talk. The parent wants to talk in such a way that the emotional connection is maintained, and the child will be honestly persuaded to change his or her behavior in order to help the parent solve the problem. This is called an I-message. Finally, when the problem is shared, the parents will have to do some listening and some talking. They will use both active listening and I-messages in turn and conclude by finding a solution acceptable to both parties. This is called win-win problem solving. The best practices for these strategies are outlined in Table 5.2, and we will discuss them one by one.

Active Listening/Emotion Coaching

Child-owned problems exist when the child has unmet needs but the parent does not. Let's consider some examples. The child has a science fair project due tomorrow that hasn't been started. The parent may want the child to succeed and may feel tremendous compassion for the child and thus be highly motivated to help with the problem, but the problem still belongs to the child, as the child is

Table 5.2 Best Practices for Communication Strategies

Problem Ownership	Recommended Strategy	Goal of Communication	Best Practices
Child Owned Problem	Active Listening	Connect emotionally. Keep the child talking so that he can solve his own problem.	1. Whole attention 2. Reflect feelings 3. Explore solutions
Parent Owned Problem	I-Message	Connect emotionally. Confront child in such a way that he will want to help parent solve the problem.	1. I feel ___ • True feeling • Specific • Appropriate intensity • Primary feeling 2. When you ___ • Specific • Objective • Without judgment 3. Because ___ • Tangible need
Shared Problem	Win-Win Problem Solving	Connect emotionally. Find a solution that is acceptable to both.	1. Decide not to use power. 2. Active listening. 3. I-Message. 4. Offer possible solutions. 5. Evaluate each based on both people's feelings and needs. 6. Identify solution acceptable to both.

the one who has a tangible need to pass his grade level. The child did not receive an invitation to a peer's birthday party and feels rejected. Again, the parent may be deeply moved by his child's sadness and so want to help, but the problem is still owned by the child. The child misplaced her electronic device and now cannot find it. She is desperately eager to find that toy but cannot seem to locate it. This is a child-owned problem. The child sits down to a chicken dinner but does not want to eat chicken. This is a child-owned problem. The reader can see from this short list that child-owned problems are ubiquitous. Some of them are small (such as the red crayon broke while she was using it), but others are bigger (he got dumped by his first girlfriend), and others are unspeakably big (the death of a classmate). We will start with the small ones because they illustrate how the process works. But be aware that the skills work in exactly the same way with the bigger issues. In fact, if parents use them regularly with small problems, then children are developing skills that they will be able to call upon when they face life's bigger challenges.

Much of what parents do is helping children figure out how to solve their own problems. Gordon (2000) calls this active listening, but I much prefer John Gottman's term for the same thing: emotion coaching (Gottman, DeClaire, & Goleman, 1998). I prefer it because I think "coaching" really captures the parental role. The coach can't go on the field and play the game, right? The coach helps organize the game and then supports the players, but only the players can actually make a play. Similarly, when the child is dealing with his or her own life, the parent simply cannot make the plays. The child has to do that. So parents stand on the sidelines and watch, and if they're lucky, the child gives them a chance to offer support. The better they are at coaching, the more helpful their support is.

Avoid Communication Roadblocks

Gordon states plainly that MOST things parents say in the face of a child-owned problem are not actually very helpful. He calls them **communication roadblocks** because what they have in common is that they shut down the lines of communication (Gordon, 2000). In the face of communication roadblocks offered by parents, children generally stop talking, and they are less and less likely to even initiate a conversation next time. So they shut down communication in the short term about the specific problem, but they also shut down future communication in the long term. Parents who tell the parent educator in exasperation "My child just won't talk to me anymore!" should consider it likely that they have been using roadblocks and that is why the child has stopped sharing.

Parents generally have a very hard time seeing that their reactions—many times offered with a sincere desire to be helpful—are roadblocks. They will be tempted to reassure the parent educator (and themselves) that they never do these things. But they are fooling themselves. In truth, roadblocks are standard issue for parent-child communication.

Let's use an example to illustrate some communication roadblocks. The daughter has come home from school, clearly in a funk, snickering mean things about her friend Kathy. So the parent says, "You sure seem upset with Kathy. What happened?" The daughter explains that she told Kathy about an embarrassing incident, asking Kathy not to tell anyone about it. By recess, everyone in the class knew. The classmates teased her and she feels humiliated by the whole episode, as well as being angry at Kathy for breaking her confidence. Some common roadblocks a parent might use in this situation include:

- **Giving advice**—telling the child how to solve the problem. Parents generally want to be helpful and have their child benefit from their own experience and perspective, so they start offering ideas on how to fix the problem. "Maybe you could invite some kids over after school, and you can make some new friends," or "Perhaps you should just tell Kathy how much it hurt your feelings." Giving advice skips straight to the content of the problem, skipping the emotional connection, sending the message that the emotions are not the important part. But the emotion is the most salient part of the story to the child suffering emotionally, so the child feels like she has not been understood. It also consists of a solution coming from the parent, not the child, which sends an implicit message to the child that she is incapable of solving the problem alone. Plus, it deprives the child of the learning experience of coming up with the solution.
- **Placating**—telling the child that this problem is not worth getting upset over because of other things that are really good. Parents placate because they adore their children and it pains them to see their children suffer. "You're such a sweetheart, I'm sure the other kids don't really think this is a big deal." Or "Well, maybe Kathy isn't a great friend. But there are other girls in the class who like you." Just like giving advice, placating skips over the emotional component of the problem, thereby sending the message that the child's feelings are not important enough to be addressed.
- **Lecturing**—explaining to the child why the problem occurred and what is likely to happen. Parents often lecture because they want to share the lessons they've learned in the hope it will help the child feel better. "You know, girls your age make a big deal about things that are not very important. They will have forgotten all about it by tomorrow." Or "Kathy has always been a little insecure. I think she really wants to be friends with (name a popular kid in class) and she hurt you in order to get it. That makes her a bad friend. Not worth crying over." Just like giving advice and placating, lecturing skips over the emotional component of the child's message, and just like the other roadblocks, it sends the message that the emotions are not important here. The child (for whom this is an emotionally devastating betrayal) may gain information from a lecture, but will still not really feel understood.
- **Sarcasm**—humor at the expense of another person's dignity. Sarcasm is often used to dismiss something deemed unimportant. The parent might say "Oh, I bet Kathy's never done anything embarrassing!" or "I bet the

sun won't rise tomorrow if all the fifth grade girls don't get the news!" The parent might simply be exasperated with this problem that seems so inconsequential that he or she is not even trying to be kind. Or the parent might think that the child will recognize that the problem isn't a big idea and thus feel better. But sarcasm is a roadblock, specifically because it does not take seriously the genuine emotion being expressed—in fact, it ridicules the child for having the emotion.
- **Commanding**—ordering the child to stop expressing the emotion. When parents issue a command such as "I do not want to hear another word about Kathy! Let's move on!" they probably think they are encouraging their child to buck up or grow a thicker skin, which will help them in the long run. But commanding has the same problem of inadvertently disregarding emotions and conveying that the child is not competent to solve the problem.

There are other roadblocks identified by Gordon, but the pattern is already apparent. A roadblock stops communication by its failure to acknowledge and validate the child's emotion. Gottman says that parents develop a pattern of reacting to their children's difficult emotions. Some have an **emotion-dismissing emotional parenting style,** which uses the roadblocks that minimize or ignore children's feelings (advising, placating, lecturing). These parents are generally trying to focus on the positive, trying to be helpful, but they do so by dismissing the importance of their child's painful feelings. Other parents have an **emotion-disapproving emotional parenting style,** which uses roadblocks that criticize the child for having or expressing a painful feeling (sarcasm, commanding). These parents are generally trying to be firm and in control in the hope that they can get their child on the right track.

Process of Active Listening/Emotion Coaching
So what is the alternative? Gordon calls it **active listening**. Gottman calls it **emotion coaching**. It begins with truly accepting the fact that children's painful feelings and experiences belong to them. Parents often have to remind themselves that this is the child's experience and that the parent may coach, but may not play. While Gordon and Gottman describe the process slightly differently, both active listening and emotion coaching boil down to these few steps.

1. **Full and complete attention:** Offering one's full and complete attention seems like such a basic thing that I wouldn't even have to say it. And yet, children very often have a hard time getting the attention of the adults in their lives. Parents of young children are very, very busy. They are trying to hold down jobs to pay the bills, they have to get dinner ready, run to the grocery store, etc. They have to sign report cards, help kids with homework, throw in a load of laundry, drive someone somewhere, and make a phone call. And that's all before bedtime. And that doesn't include the maintenance of the parent's friendships, extended family, and romantic relationships. It is the busiest time of life, the years spent rearing young children. So let's have a little compassion for the parents. This is a hard, hard, job.

   And let's face it, children get upset about truly ridiculous things. One of my daughters wanted to learn how to tie her shoes so badly that when she couldn't do it, she would take her shoe off and bite it! They get upset about siblings looking at them funny. About the balloon being red instead of pink. Or about losing their grip on the balloon and watching it float away. Are parents really going to take these things seriously, given how many other things are going on? Well, by this model, these small frustrations are opportunities to practice. So, yes. They need to take these things seriously. And the first way they convey that is by looking the child in the eye. Anyone who has ever worked with children in any capacity has been instructed to get down on their level. I took a babysitting class offered by a hospital when I was 12, and I remember being told to get down on the floor to play with and talk to smaller children. It seemed so silly when I was 12, but I made a point to do it. Then I overheard my first customer tell my mother that they'd like to have me babysit again, citing the fact that I actually got down on the floor to play with the toddler as evidence that I was a good babysitter. That convinced me. This very simple act of offering full attention is sorely lacking in human relationships. It is a necessary first step to connecting emotionally with another human being.

   Even when the child-owned problems aren't quite so ridiculous, parents are a few years older than their children and thus can put things in perspective better. A friend of mine once described comforting her six-year-old son upon the death of a pet turtle. He held the turtle to his chest, sobbing in sorrow over the loss. The mom, meanwhile, kept thinking about the fact that dinner wasn't ready and the laundry wasn't folded because at her age, she no longer mourned dead turtles. She had learned to cope with small losses like that. Therefore, what a challenge it was for her to take her son's sadness seriously. She had to leave the clothes in the basket, and lie down on the bed to hold her son while he cried. She had to give him every bit of her attention.

We can offer full attention by aligning our bodies with the person we are listening to. Stand next to them if they are standing. Sit next to them if they are sitting. Lean in if they are leaning in. To talk to children, we often have to reduce our size, to get down so that our eyes are on the same level. And if we already have an attachment relationship with the child, we might offer contact comfort as well. This means looking away from smartphones and televisions, moving physically close to the child, and looking them directly in the eye. It also means mentally setting aside whatever was holding one's attention and making a decision to take the child seriously.

2. **Reflect feelings:** While active listening involves all three of these components (full attention, reflecting feelings, exploring solutions), this one—reflecting feelings—is the essence of the idea of active listening. This is the magic. This is the thing that, when a parent does it, it changes everything. Once the parent has given full attention, the parent listens and then reflects back to the child the emotions that are being conveyed. The key to this step is that the FEELING must be reflected, not necessarily the other content of what is being said. Don't worry, we will return to the other content. But first, it is essential to connect emotionally.

The most basic version of this is simple. It means listening to what the child says and noting his or her nonverbal cues as well, and then reflecting back the emotion. "Oh my, you seem very angry about that!" or "This seems to make you very sad," or "I guess this is disappointing for you." In addition to reflecting the feeling with words such as those above, the parent may reflect feelings with his or her facial expression and tone of voice. For instance, when the parent is saying "This seems to make you very sad," he or she is making a sad face and using a dour tone of voice. Thus, the child's emotion is fully reflected. The purpose of this reflection is to convey to the child that he or she is understood. The child is distressed, and when an adult reflects back that distress, it is a way of saying "I hear what you say, I understand, and I sympathize with you." That message helps a person feel understood and accepted. That unconditional positive regard, that acceptance, allows the person to breathe a sigh of relief that their message has been received. It is amazing how often simply being heard and understood is enough to relieve the painful feeling. Very often, the reflection of feelings is met with a literal sign of relief, which can be interpreted as the child saying, "Thank goodness I have been understood!" The intense edge on the emotional distress is often alleviated immediately.

Sometimes the parent can't tell exactly what feeling the child is having, so the initial reflection is something of an educated guess. The parent might say "Oh, that's sad that you didn't get invited," only to have the child respond that she's not sad at all, she's actually very angry. Or the parent might guess that she's angry, and so reflect "Well, that probably makes you angry, huh?" only to have the child look back with tears welling up in her eyes. At that point, the parent will reflect the sadness by saying "Maybe it makes you more sad," which is essentially an invitation to the child to talk about the tears. It's okay that parents guess and okay if the parent makes a wrong guess. The effect of the process is to connect emotionally, so even if the first attempt misses the mark, it still conveys the message that the child's emotion is of interest and is acceptable. So the child will offer clarification, and the pair ends up in the exact same place: a discussion about the child's feeling, in which the child feels that his or her experience is understood and validated.

Reflection of feelings allows the child to expand upon the experience within a context where they feel accepted. They may go on to describe more of the circumstances that made them sad, angry, or disappointed in the first place. The reflecting of feelings continues throughout this process. Nodding sympathetically, offering verbal encouragement such as "Oh, my!" and "I see" serves to acknowledge the validity of the other person's experience; and so the child will generally continue with the story, having found a receptive audience. Sometimes the listener will add a bit more commentary, but it is always for the purpose of acknowledging and validating the speaker's emotions. The commentary might include references back to shared experiences, such as "I remember how angry it made it you when Jason smashed your science project; this must have made you super angry because he interfered with your homework again!" Please note that the commentary should not be a judgment of the situation itself (in this case, the listener should not judge Jason as a good-for-nothing delinquent) but should focus on the feelings of the child telling the story. The listener should not be offering any commentary about what he or she thinks about the situation, but should only be reflecting what the child is conveying.

This portion of active listening (reflecting feelings while the speaker offers more details if he or she chooses) can be over quickly, or it can last quite a while. If the issue is very small, then it may last only a moment ("Oh, how frustrating that your crayon broke!" With a frowny face, the child responds "I know! I wanted to use it!"). But if the issue is bigger, this "venting" may go on longer. It is over when the child (who owns the problem, remember) feels understood. I can usually tell that we've reached the end when my child gives me a signal of such. Sometimes it's raised eyebrows with a wry smile. Sometimes it's a verbal "Oh, it'll be okay, Mom." Because of mutual sensitivity in attachment relationships, each parent learns each individual child's signal, so there can be no standard one. But it is the equivalent of a deep sigh, the kind people make after they've had a good cry and they're ready to move on. There is a sense that the tension has been expelled, then there's a moment of "in-between" time, and then life moves on.

3. **Explore solutions:** Once the emotional connection has been made and maintained through the process of reflecting and validating feelings, sometimes the issue disappears. The child is comforted, and so the issue melts away. It's amazing what sympathetic listening can achieve! But sometimes the question of what to do remains. After the "deep sigh" described above, someone has to say, "Okay, what now?" One of my daughters indicates she's ready to get down to business with a drawn-out "Sooooo …" Sometimes the parent has to be the one to suggest that it is time to explore solutions, by saying something like "Okay, what should you do about the situation with Kathy?"

The essence of exploring solutions is for the listener (the parent) to ask questions. Remember, the goal is to keep the child talking so that he or she can find a solution to his own problem. Therefore, this is NOT the time to launch into giving advice, or delivering a lecture about things the child will understand when he's older. These are still roadblocks if they are offered at this point, just as they were roadblocks if they were offered first thing. Instead, the parent might ask how it could be solved. The child will suggest a course of action, and the parent will ask the child questions about that; for instance, "Yes, you could just go to school tomorrow and pretend nothing happened. How do you think you'll feel all day at school if you do that? Do you think you can still be friends with Kathy after what she did?" Obviously, these questions might be somewhat leading. The parent is trying to get the child to think of things that she hasn't thought of yet. But the parent should not actually offer the answers to any of the questions. This is the child's problem, and the solution must come from her. A good rule of thumb is that the questions the parent asks should help the child zero in on emotions. Emotion coaching helps children learn to recognize their own emotions and the emotions of others and to understand how emotions drive behavior. Therefore, it draws attention to these skills. Another role the parent (the emotional coach) can play here is to ask the child to look for another option, once the first possible solution has been explored. For instance, "I know you'd rather pretend nothing happened, but can you think of another way that you could handle it?"

Active Listening Example

Having gone through the three steps, now let's consider what all of this might look like as it plays out. I was recently in a public park and happened to observe a school-aged boy (I'd guess he was eight years old) playing with an adult man who appeared to be a friend the child's parents. At first, it was playful rough-housing. The boy would run at the man, and they would wrestle around on the ground, sometimes chasing each other. I took note because the adult was gentle and playful, and it was a pleasant scene. But then something changed. I don't know why it changed; I suspect that the boy had been accidentally hurt and the older man didn't realize it. But all I saw was that the boy's face was red and flushed, and his eyes were flashing darkly, not playfully. He was getting ready to run toward the man and tackle him, which he did, and the older man playfully met his tackle, apparently not realizing that the boy's mood had changed. The wrestling continued, and the boy's face got more and more flushed. It was clear to me that he was holding back tears. His face was set hard in anger and hurt.

Let's stop here for a moment. This is obviously a child-owned problem. The child was either physically hurt or embarrassed by some part of the playful wrestling. The child was clearly upset about it, but the adult was fine. The adult was just enjoying some good-natured horsing around and did not have a problem. The child did. If everyone involved was a mature adult, then the person with the problem should be able to say that something had gone wrong and call for the play to be stopped. But the boy did not have the maturity to do that, as he was a child. He needed to learn how to manage the difficult feelings he was facing right then. He needed some coaching to learn how to handle this.

At this point, his dad noticed the boy's angry expression. This is a dad who probably has an attachment relationship with his son, and he noticed the signals that the child was sending. So far, so good. He intervened by physically pulling his son out of the wrangling and looking him in the eye. But as you might imagine, the first thing the dad said was not active listening; it was a communication roadblock. Specifically, it was a command: "Son, you are <u>never</u> to attack out of anger. If you are angry, the game is over." Yes, it's a roadblock. But darn if it's not also a statement that I approve of! I love the message Dad was sending. But did the child hear it? Of course not, because it came in the form of a communication roadblock. There was no acknowledgment of the child's anger and hurt. For the next 10 minutes (until they left the park), he sulked off to the side. At times he was crying and angrily wiping the tears from his face; at other times his face was puffed up with the effort of withholding his tears. I overheard the friend of the family expressing his confusion to the parents: "I thought we were just having fun … I don't know what happened!" The parents dismissed the boy's feelings as utterly unimportant: "It's nothing. He'll get over it. You didn't do anything. Boys are just like that at his age." I overheard it, so the boy must have too. The message he was getting was clearly one of emotion disapproval. His hurt and anger were unacceptable. I suspect that the message the parents intended to send was that his <u>behavior</u> was unacceptable, which of course, it was. But as an outsider objectively observing a scene in which I was not invested, and from that perspective, it was obvious that the child was getting the message that his <u>emotion</u> was unacceptable. Nobody even considered it important enough to ask what had happened, where the emotion came from. Frankly, it was heartbreaking to watch. I realized as it was happening that I was watching loving parents teach their son to hide his emotions, leaving him stranded without any skills for managing his emotions should they grow too powerful to ignore. This is a problem with how we socialize gender in the United States, and it is a larger problem with how we neglect to teach all children (both boys and girls) how to handle emotions.

So what would active listening/emotion coaching have looked like instead? Well, there are three steps outlined above. The friend of the family could have done this. If I noticed the anger and hurt on the boy's face, the friend could have noticed it too. When he saw the hurt and anger, he might have stopped the wrestling. "Whoa, let's take a break." At that time, he could have walked over to the boy, gotten down on a knee to have his eyes level with the boy's. That is listening with his full attention. Then he could have reflected the boy's feelings by saying, "It looks like you may have gotten hurt." Or "I see that you're angry," or even a simple "What happened?" Or "It doesn't feel so playful anymore. What's wrong?" All of this reflects what he sees, that emotions have turned dark. All of these are indicators that he is available to listen. Especially if he mirrors distress nonverbally on his own face as he approaches the boy, these would have signaled that the boy's emotion was important. My guess is that the boy would explain that he got his finger twisted back, had the wind knocked out of him, or some such explanation. Then the man would have comforted him and apologized for accidentally hurting him, and the tension would have melted away.

If relieving the tension were not enough to solve the problem, then the two could consider solutions together. Maybe the boy was injured, and they could discuss what treatment is necessary. They might also discuss how to wrestle so that this injury could be prevented in the future. The solution to the problem cannot be imagined until we know exactly what the feeling is and where it came from. But the third step would happen next, if necessary. They might have left the park happily, the man not feeling so confused, the boy not feeling so alone and ashamed, and the parents not feeling so embarrassed by their child's misbehavior.

The dad could have followed this model in exactly the same way when he intervened to physically separate the son and friend. The mom could have approached the child at any time to initiate this conversation. The process itself is simple; it's just that most adults are simply not in the habit of taking children's feelings seriously. This could really change the world if it became the standard way to address children when they suffer.

Confrontation Through I-Messages

Active listening/emotion coaching is wonderful when the child has a problem, and the parent's job is to listen in a way that facilitates the child thinking through his or her problem. But what about when the tables are turned? When the parent has a problem and needs the child's cooperation to solve it? This is the essence of a **parent-owned problem**, and the communication strategy has to be different. A parent-owned problem is, by definition, when the parent is the person whose needs are not being met. The child is fine, but the adult has unmet needs. Remember that it might be the child's fault, the child might be the cause of the problem, but for our purposes here, we are not talking about blame. We are looking for the best form of communication to use to solve such a problem, and that does not necessitate assigning blame.

A common parent-owned problem is unfinished chores. This is a parent-owned problem because the parent is troubled by the sticky countertops, the overflowing trash can, the unfolded laundry, and the grass that needs mowing, while the child doesn't seem to even notice. When chores go undone, the parent is generally the one who suffers. Parents often tell me that they simply cannot relax in a house that is in constant disarray. They also tell me that they end up doing the chore, which is really no small thing for women who, if they live with young children, are the most tired people on earth. Other common parent-owned problems are kids borrowing their things and not returning them, kids turning up the TV so loud that parents can't have a conversation, children bouncing and yelling in the house when the parent is sick or when the parent is on the phone, or when the parent is talking to someone.

The first step is to accept the premise that parents are, in fact, allowed to have feelings, even unpleasant ones. Parents need not be perfectly happy and poised at all times. Just as children are allowed to feel what they feel but also must limit their behaviors sometimes, so too are parents allowed to feel what they feel but also must limit their behaviors. We might think of it this way: if we practiced active listening all of the time, we would be utterly exhausted. It is a demanding, tiring way of approaching the world. It requires that we be tending, nearly constantly, to other people's emotions. Dealing with painful feelings can be emotionally draining. A person who commits to helping others deal with their painful feelings will only be able to sustain that practice by also taking very good care of herself. Consider the instructions offered at the beginning of every flight on an airplane. In the unlikely event of a loss of cabin pressure, an oxygen mask will drop from the ceiling. Please affix the oxygen mask to your own face before helping others. How selfish, you might think! But there is a good reason for this. The most responsible party must take care of himself; otherwise, he will not be able to help others at all. Similarly, if parents neglect their own emotional needs, then they will simply not be able to sustain the habit of active listening for their children.

Once parents accept that they are allowed to have their feelings and they need to take their feelings as seriously as they take their children's feelings, then they need to know what to do about the parent-owned problems that arise. The parent wants to let the child know that his behavior is having a negative effect on another person, in hopes that the child will want to change his behavior. In other words, the parent must confront the child. Please take note that this is truly a confrontation.

Very few people like confrontations. We don't like to be confronted by someone else, and we don't like to do the confronting either. And this is part of the problem. Since we don't like to confront, we will often avoid doing it, even when a confrontation is called for. We avoid the difficult conversation until we have worked ourselves into a frenzy about it. Let's consider the case of a teenager who repeatedly forgets to get the trash cans to the curb on the night before the trash is due to be picked up. Once it's been forgotten once, or even twice, the trash bin is overflowing and stinky. The parent is irritated every single time he walks past it, or smells it, or tries to shove another garbage bag into it. So next week, the parent reminds the child to take the bin to the curb. It gets done—but only because of the reminder. Now the parent feels annoyed every week upon issuing a reminder and starts steaming silently when the child is already asleep in bed and the parent realizes that the trash didn't get taken out. The parent drags himself out of bed and takes it out himself, reminding himself that the child has been studying for a chemistry test and probably deserves a break. But he doesn't want to confront her about this the next day because, well, at that point, what's done is done. The parent might dislike confrontation so much that he will continue to issue reminders and occasionally do the task himself, resenting every minute of it and feeling quite used because he doesn't want to face an uncomfortable confrontation with the teenager, who is, after all, a darn good kid. Eventually, this parent will explode in anger. Maybe he will forget to remind one week and forget to check to see that it's been done, and trash morning will come and go with the bins still sitting by the side of the house, full of rotting garbage. Then the confrontation will take place, and it will not be pretty. It will be done in anger, not thought through in advance; the child will feel shocked and hurt by the explosion, and the parent will feel ashamed that he lost his temper. Then the parent will silently vow to himself not to blow up at the child again, and so next time be even less willing to confront.

For a parent like the one in this scenario, to avoid a hurtful explosion of anger such as this, he has to learn to confront differently rather than avoiding confrontation altogether. The alternative (but impossible for most people) is to suffer silently and never, ever confront. This is a recipe for martyrdom. It is also not particularly helpful to the child to never be held accountable for the effects of his decisions on others. But most people simply can't silently bear the burden of other people's thoughtlessness without expressing any resentment. Even those who manage to prevent themselves from exploding in anger will generally express their discontent through passive-aggressive behavior, such as sarcastic remarks, eye rolls, and subtle insults. None of this leads to a happy parent (which will also be a better, more loving parent) or to a child who learns responsible behavior and personal accountability in relationships. It is clearly better to learn how to confront differently, and this begins with accepting the need to confront.

Avoid You-Messages

Confrontations often go badly because they begin … well, they begin in a confrontational manner. In PET, these are called **you-messages**. The person who owns the problem generally does one of two things:

1. **Send a put-down:** A put-down message directly states a criticism of the other person. These sentences often do begin with the word *you*, as in: "You are so irresponsible! You just can't seem to remember your chore!" It may be tamer, as in: "You're pretty forgetful!" or "I think that you're just not making this a priority." But what all of these statements have in common is that they directly criticize the other person. Sometimes the put-down starts with the word *why*, as in: "Why in the world didn't you take the trash out last night!?!" or "Why is this so hard for you?" Notice that, even though these are both in the form of a question, they say, loud and clear, "You were wrong (and maybe even stupid) to neglect your task!" Asking a "why" question like this is really just picking a fight because it strongly implies a criticism of the other person.

2. **Send a solution:** On the surface, a solution might seem like a better message to send, but it is also problematic. The solution might be very harsh, as in: "Get your lazy rear off that sofa right now and take the trash out!" or it could be a little more diplomatic, such as: "You need to start making this a priority! Do it BEFORE you watch TV from now on." Parents who are being careful to speak civilly to their children might even phrase it like this: "I would appreciate it if you would start being a little more conscientious about your chore." But notice that all of these are essentially telling the child what he or she has to do to solve the parent's problem.

And all of them carry that same implication as a put-down: that there is something wrong with the child who couldn't get this straight earlier.

The reader may recall from Chapter 1 that a scientific consensus exists that psychological control is a damaging form of control in parent-child relationships. You-messages represent forms of psychological control. Parents use you-messages to essentially shame the child into compliance. This form of control is not only ineffective but also damaging to the child's identity and to the parent-child relationship.

Because of this underlying message ("something is wrong with you") these are all "you-messages." Both put-downs and solutions, no matter how nicely stated or in what tone of voice, are essentially focusing on what's wrong with the other person. As such, they are very likely to make the other person feel defensive. And a person who is feeling defensive is not likely to become an ally who will eagerly try to help solve a problem, which is, after all, the goal. A person who is feeling defensive will try to protect him- or herself from the attack. So you-messages, while they may very well be completely TRUE, they are unlikely to produce the desired effect in terms of changing the child's behavior. Plus, they are likely to damage the parent-child relationship.

At this point in a parenting class, parents usually start to feel indignant, wondering what other option there could possibly be! I suspect that part of their agitation comes from a dawning recognition that, even in the moments that they've tried really hard to be kind and diplomatic, they were STILL offering you-messages! They must be frustrated and feeling discouraged about their parenting. A parent educator should try to have some empathy for them here. They are being told something that is really hard to hear. However, if they do not get at least a little frustrated, then they will not be able to see how amazing an I-message really is. So watch the parent(s) for signs of this kind of frustration.

Process of Constructing I-Messages

An **I-message** is a confrontation, the goal of which is to convince the other person to WANT to help the confronter find a solution to the problem. It does this by focusing the message on what the confronter is feeling, rather than focusing the message on judgments about the other person. An I-message generally has three components:

1. The parent's feeling;

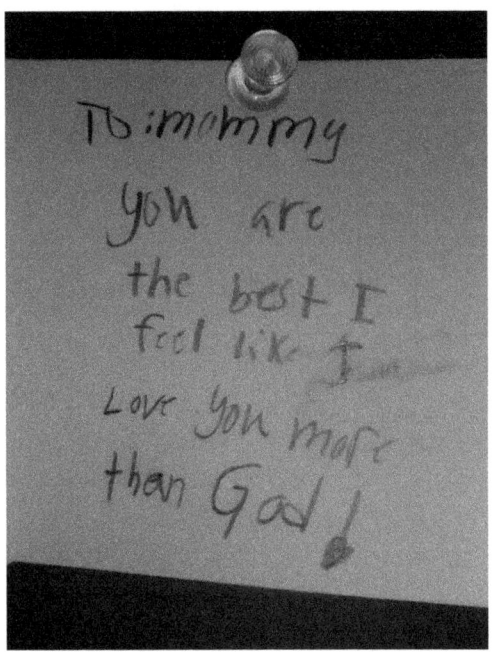

Figure 5.2 Psychological Size

2. The child's behavior that produced the feeling;

3. The effect of the child's behavior on the parent's tangible needs.

Gordon (2000) proposes the following formula to put those components into a sentence: "I feel _____ when you_____ because _____." It is possible to construct I-messages according to this formula, and for someone beginning to use the tool, this is probably a good idea. But once the technique becomes habit, the messages do become less formulaic.

Before we explore the three components in the formula, let's remind ourselves of why we're going to the trouble of writing fill-in-the-blank sentences. It may help to remember the Chinese proverb "Do not use a hatchet to remove a fly from a friend's forehead." What parents are trying to do is correct the child's behavior. They love the child, so they do not want to damage the child in the process. But because adults have so much power over children, and parents in particular have so much power over their own children, there is great potential for children to take things harder than the adult intended. One of my daughters once wrote me a little note, explaining that she loves me more than she loves God (Figure 5.1). This reminds me that parents have immense **psychological size**—that is to say, their importance to a child make them truly massive in terms of the effects of their behavior. Given their enormous psychological size, parents must be very careful with those confrontations.

I could clumsily confront a friend, and that friend (a person of equal power to myself and equal psychological size) would be able to simply tell me that I'm out of line. Those who are equal in power to each other can negotiate such infractions without much harm being done. But someone who has less power than myself may not be able to muster the courage to tell me. Therefore, my unintended slights may go unaddressed and uncorrected, and thus they can do more damage. So when we confront children, we must do it carefully. There is a whole relationship counseling industry trying to teach adults in strained marriages to confront one another with I-messages, so maybe this is good for everyone. But it's definitely true that parents would be more effective in their confrontation with children if they used this technique because it is less likely to trigger the defensiveness or the potential emotional damage of a you-message.

Let us use the example of the trash bins not taken to the curb as an example to illustrate an I-message.

Feeling: The first component of the I-message—arguably the most important part and the most difficult part—is the statement of the parent's feeling. The parent might say that she feels frustrated, sad, afraid, hurt, whatever is appropriate. The idea is that the parent states his or her feeling, so the focus is on the parent, not on an attack of the child's character. Remember, this is an existing relationship. The child loves the parent and so will be emotionally engaged upon hearing that the beloved parent is suffering. We do not want the child on the defensive; we want the child poised and eager to help. And emotions are the language of intimacy, so we start with a recognition of emotions. There are a few guidelines for naming emotions in an I-message:

1. It must be a <u>true feeling</u>. Many adults are not generally very aware of their own feelings. Many were taught as children (like the boy described above who got hurt play-wrestling with a family friend) not to name their feelings, not even to take them seriously. So they try to push their feelings to the background (as the boy in the example tried to do by angrily wiping away his tears); they try to ignore them. They try to rise above them. They rarely take the time to carefully examine the feeling and allow it to be there. So they grow up, become parents, and then find that they don't particularly know what they're feeling at any given time. They might know when they feel good and when they feel bad, but that's it. Consequently, many adults say, "I feel … ," but then they don't name a feeling. They say, "I feel that you were being thoughtless." Which is, of course, not a feeling at all. It's a thought. It's a judgment about the other person. But it is not a feeling. Gordon calls this a **disguised you-message**, a statement that focuses on a character defect of the other person, but simply has "I feel" in front of it. It's not a very good disguise!

Communication For Problem Solving 171

2. The emotion should be as <u>specific</u> as possible. The reason we're naming our emotion is to help motivate the listener to help us. When we name a very general emotion (for example, "I do not feel good about … ," or "I am upset"), then the listener doesn't really have enough information yet. The emotion is too general to act upon. Of course, many adults need to work on recognizing their own emotions. This is an example of how parenting can really help adults grow and develop into better human beings.

3. The stated emotion should be of the <u>appropriate intensity</u>. Sometimes people try to soften a message by understating it: for instance, saying they're annoyed when they're actually furious. This doesn't help. An I-message must be honest and authentic. It should not be mean, but it absolutely must be true. It is sometimes essential to convey an intense emotion without watering it down.

4. When possible, the I-message should include a <u>primary feeling</u> rather than a secondary feeling. This is a concept that comes from the science of development of emotions in infancy. Primary feelings are those that can be observed in all human infants in the first few months after birth. These are believed to be innate and do not require any socialization to shape them. Primary feelings are not necessarily social; that is, they need not be experienced in relation to another person. Primary feelings include joy, distress, sadness, and fear. As babies build relationships and their brains develop, they begin to exhibit the capacity for other emotions, called secondary feelings. Anger appears at about seven months. It is an outgrowth of distress, but anger requires a target (something or someone to be angry at), so it is the first of the secondary feelings. Secondary feelings have also been called the social emotions because they are socialized, and therefore reflect cultural diversity, rather than being universal like the primary feelings. In addition to anger, secondary feelings include embarrassment, pride, and shame. For the purposes of creating an I-message, the difference between primary and secondary feelings is useful, but it has some limits. The main limitation is that parents should be specific when they name their feeling, but the list of primary feelings is rather short and not terribly specific. Newborns display what has been called "distress," but this is a generalized bad feeling without a target. "I am distressed" would not make a great I-message because it is so general. So the way to make this concept useful is to think about whether the named emotion clearly implies a target. "Disappointed" does

not, so I would call it a primary feeling for our purposes here, but "taken for granted" does, so I would call that a secondary feeling.

So how DOES the parent feel when the child forgets to take the trash to the curb? Well, it depends on the circumstances. Sometimes the parent will feel mildly annoyed. I-messages can (and should) be used even when the emotion is fairly mild. Please note that the parent will say "I feel annoyed" rather than "I feel you're being irresponsible" (which is a disguised you-message) and rather than "I don't like it" (which is way too general). "Annoyed" must honestly capture the intensity of the feeling. And finally, the parent will say "I feel annoyed" rather than "I feel disrespected" because the primary feeling is preferable to the secondary feeling.

But sometimes the feeling is more intense than just mild annoyance. What if the trash situation goes on for months? When a parent says (as they often do during a class on this topic) that "annoyed" doesn't cover it, that the feeling is more intense than that, I ask them to try to explain. They typically say that they "feel" that the child is taking them for granted. Well, this a thought, a judgment about the child; it is not a feeling. The parent will agree, but still not know how else to express it. I have to push hard to get them to identify the feeling behind their judgment. "How does it FEEL to have someone take you for granted?" I ask. The inability of most people to identify their feelings is a serious barrier here that should not be underestimated. Eventually, someone will suggest, timidly, that "Maybe this sounds stupid, but I kind of feel unimportant." Whoa, it just got deeper, didn't it? This is almost always what someone comes up with if I push them hard to identify what it feels like to have someone take advantage of them. But other parents start to chime in, agreeing that they also feel unimportant. They feel that their contributions must not be worth very much. They feel useless and worthless. This is a harder one, but it can also be offered as part of an I-message. Consider how powerfully it could affect a child to hear his parent admit to feeling unimportant. I think most children would be able to identify with that feeling, and it could create a powerful connection between parent and child. Of course, it also makes the parent vulnerable, as sharing painful feelings always does. It's a risk. The child could say "Good! You are unimportant!" So it's risky, but it is the way to an authentic and honest relationship, which is what most parents claim that they want to have with their children.

Behavior: Next in the formula is the statement of the child's behavior that produced the parent's feeling. This is delicate. The parent needs for the child to realize that his behavior is affecting the parent, but he doesn't want the child to feel attacked and thus become defensive instead of helpful. There are three rules for the statement of behavior. It must be:

1. **Specific**—Essentially, the parent should stick to one thing, the thing happening at this particular time, without trying to generalize. So she should say, "When I came home tonight to find the trash cans on the side of the house" instead of saying "When you never take out the trash." It seems to the parent that the child "never" takes out the trash, but to say "never" will launch an argument about whether or not they've ever done it once, which is not at all the point. The point is that tonight, the parent came home to find the chore incomplete. It is far less likely to trigger a defensive reaction.

2. **Objective**—The behavior should be described concisely in a way that a perfect stranger, with no emotional involvement or knowledge of the dynamics that led to this situation, would be able to agree is accurate. So instead of saying, "You tried to get out of doing dishes all night," to be more objective, the parent would say, "It's 9:00 p.m., and the dishes are still unwashed." The former is an interpretation. The child might argue back that he didn't try to get out of anything, but he was tempted away by a homework assignment or a great television program, but that he didn't intentionally try to get out of the work. In contrast, the latter is a simple, uncontroversial statement of fact. It is objective. Therefore, it leaves less room for defensiveness to derail the conversation.

3. **Without judgment**—The parent should avoid using judgmental descriptive words that convey an opinion about the morality of the behavior. For instance, words like *messy* or *irresponsible* convey judgment. People have different definitions of these words. I remember telling my own mother that my "messy" room wasn't messy at all, that I knew how it was organized, and it worked just fine! And "irresponsible?" Well, the child might reason that she is perfectly responsible when dealing with things important to her. These words are unnecessary fight-starters.

So putting all of that together, we could end up with a statement such as: "I felt annoyed when I came home tonight and saw that the trash hadn't been taken to the curb." This is a great start to an I-message.

Effect: The final component explains why. The parent explains what tangible effect the child's behavior has on the parent. The more tangible, the better. Most human beings are more motivated to do something when they understand why they're being asked to do it. It might be seen as a sign of respecting the other person when we take the time to explain the rationale. So why is the parent annoyed about the trash cans? Maybe the trash starts to stink and the parent really hates that smell. Maybe the parent will have to do it herself, and she is already tired from a long day at work. Maybe raccoons have been getting into the trash creating a mess in the yard that the parent has had to clean up. Any of these are reasonable, and compelling explanations to offer to the child in order to convince them to help with the problem. Tangible effects are far more compelling than "Because I'm the mom" or "Because I said so." It's no wonder these statements build resistance in children, as they are disrespectful of the child. Adults would never say these things to a friend if they expect to maintain the friendship. Saying these things to children and expecting to continue a warm and loving relationship with those children is folly. It is far better to consider the actual tangible effects of the behavior and conveying that with kindness.

Hence we have several possible I-messages. Here's one: "I felt annoyed when I came home tonight to find the trash hasn't been taken out because I'm going to have to do it myself, but I'm already exhausted." This is giving the child the opportunity to offer cooperation to solve the problem. The child knows that his behavior is having a negative effect on his parent. He has been told this in the spirit of an authentic and honest relationship. Children won't always jump up and run to take out the trash, but this increases the chance of such cooperation. Even if the child does not do it and the parent has to move to use a different strategy (more on that in the next chapter, on consequences), this still lays a foundation of clear understanding with respect.

Win-Win Problem Solving

There is one more tool in the PET bag. If the parent's job is to listen to child-owned problems (active listening) and to confront with parent-owned problems (I-messages), what happens when the problem is both child and parent owned? This happens often. Conflict (called **shared problems** in the language of PET) is normal and present in all families. Quite simply, two people's needs conflict so that each person has tangible needs that cannot be met simultaneously. There is nothing inherently unhealthy about it. But it is unpleasant.

A problem may start in one domain but grow to become a shared problem. For instance, unfinished homework is a child-owned problem, but if summer school is required and the dates conflict with a parent's scheduled vacation, now both parties have tangible needs that are impacted. Other issues right from the start are shared problems. Busy schedules create shared problems when the child's soccer practice conflicts with the parent's work meeting or when the teenager wants the car to get to one event but the parent needs the car for a different event.

Let's face it, just living in close proximity and sharing resources means there will be points of conflict. I have two school-aged daughters who share a room. One is a night owl, preferring to stay up late at night working on craft projects and sleeping until ten minutes before she has to leave for school in the morning, and her sister is a morning lark, often falling asleep by 8:00 p.m. and waking up several hours earlier than the rest of the family in the morning. One child needs the lights on at night for her crafts, the other wants the lights off to sleep. In the morning, the other one has the lights on and blow-dryer blowing, while the other is trying to sleep. It is a true conflict. Neither child is misbehaving. Neither is being selfish or unreasonable. This is simply what happens when people live in close proximity and share resources. I realize that this example is a shared child-child conflict rather than a parent-child one, but it often requires parental intervention to manage these conflicts. The goal is to teach children how to use win-win problem solving in the conflicts they have with siblings and peers. Therefore, we will talk about how to coach a child through a situation like this.

But before we get to win-win problem solving, let us note the alternatives. There are two forms of ineffective problem solving: a solution that allows the parent to win while the child loses, and a solution that allows the child to win while the parent loses.

Avoid Win-Lose Problem Solving

Many points of conflict between parent and child simply require the child to acquiesce to the parent. The parent is in charge. A child really has very little power, after all, while the parent is the sole source of shelter, food, affection, and all other resources. Consequently, very often the parent simply asserts his or her authority, and the child's needs are relegated to a position of lower priority. All parents do this at times. I myself have simply asserted my authority and demanded compliance before. In PET, this is called win-lose problem solving. The parent wins and the child loses.

If this is the primary (or only) strategy for solving shared problems in a family, we might call the style authoritarian parenting. This has be done sometimes, but as an overt approach to solving conflict, it has some problems. First of all, it will take a lot of effort to enforce all of these parental decisions. The child will have to be supervised constantly for compliance; efforts will have to be made to prevent sneaking and cheating since the child has no motivation to cooperate; and punishments will have to be generated to deal with noncompliance. This is a lot of work. Second, the unilateral decisions plus the efforts at enforcement will all damage the parent-child relationship. A child who has no voice in decisions of his or her life will certain grow to resent the parent and to feel that he or she is not known or loved by the parent. Third, while the child's behavior may be in line with what the parent thinks is best, the child will have learned that asserting power is the best way to get what he wants in life. Right now, he has to bend to another's will, but as soon as he gets any power, he will do what was done to him and simply wield power to get what he wants, regardless of the needs and feelings of others. This is not exactly conducive to happy and healthy relationships. A child who acts like this is a brat. A teenager who acts like this is a bully. A coworker who acts like this is soon fired. A boss who acts like this faces a lawsuit. And a spouse who acts like this is soon divorced.

So win-lose problem solving must be used occasionally, but as a general style it is problematic.

Avoid Lose-Win Problem Solving

On the other hand, many points of conflict between parent and child simply require the parent to sacrifice. This is the job that they signed up for when they had a baby, isn't it? If the baby is awake but the parent is tired … well, baby wins, and both stay awake. It's the way it is. If the child is sick, but the parent has to go to work … well, the child's needs supersede the parent's needs, and they both stay home. It's the way it is. Thus, very often the parent simply relinquishes the upper hand, meeting the child's needs while making a sacrifice of her own needs. All parents do this at times. In PET, this is called lose-win problem solving. The parent loses and the child wins.

If lose-win problem solving is the primary (or only) strategy for solving shared problems in a family, we might call the style permissive-indulgent parenting. It is necessary occasionally. With babies, it might even be necessary most of the time. But if it persists into the toddler years and beyond and becomes the standard approach to solving conflict, it has some problems. First of all, this is no way for a parent to live. For a parent to sacrifice continually, for years on end, with no consideration of his or her needs, is devastating to the parent's identity and happiness. Second, this style too damages the parent-child relationship. The parent will certainly resent her children and the burden of parenthood. Children sense that, of course, and the relationship is soured. Children who have been indulged in this way don't usually feel good about their parent's sacrifice, and as they approach adulthood, they feel guilty about it. The parent sees the child as ungrateful, the child sees the parent as a martyr, and neither is eager to continue the relationship. Third, lose-win problem solving is not even good for the children because of what it teaches them about problem solving. They never learn to how to face difficult challenges because they develop a sense of entitlement. They don't know how to cope with disappointment because they've never been emotionally coached through any. They don't know how to work hard because they've had every difficulty smoothed out for them. These children are ill prepared for the challenges of adult life.

Process of Win-Win Problem Solving

Clearly, an alternative approach is necessary: win-win problem solving. The goal of win-win problem solving is to identify a solution that is acceptable to both so that both people win. How to achieve that? It will have to be a combination of active listening (because there are child-owned problems involved) and I-messages (because there are parent-owned problems involved). The process can be broken down into the following steps.

1. **Decide not to use power**—Remember that win-lose and lose-win are options, and they are options that engaged parents sometimes use. It is not a foregone conclusion that a parent will decide to use win-win problem solving. The child knows that the parent might just give in, or the parent might just put her foot down and demand obedience. So to get the ball rolling, the parent must announce her desire to find a solution acceptable to everyone. This is an invitation to participate, in good faith, in negotiation. Personally, I say something like, "Okay, let's figure out something that will work for both of us."

2. **Active listening**—Since both the parent and child have unmet tangible needs—and feelings about those—it is critical to take some time to acknowledge and validate the feelings. Remember the origin of this model is humanistic psychology, so we are assuming that people have to feel

unconditional positive regard and acceptance in order to find solutions to problems. Therefore, as always, we start with emotions. Because the adult is more mature, the adult is capable of temporarily putting his emotions aside to listen to the child's emotions. Consequently, the parent first engages in active listening. This helps to relieve the child's anxiety and brings down the stress level of the conflict.

3. **I-message**—After the child has had a chance to express her feelings, then the parent takes a turn doing the same thing.

4. **Offer possible solutions**—Once both people feel understood and the relevant needs are on the table, then the parent says something like, "Well, what are some options here?" Both child and parent describe options. When they are being described, they should not be evaluated. This is brainstorming, so every idea is taken and explored a bit. This is where something exciting often happens, which is that the pair generates ideas that neither had previously had. There is a kind of creativity that comes from a genuine understanding of one another and a sense of goodwill toward one another that generates ideas. Often, a new idea will make a parent or child gasp in delight. "Oh, oh, oh! I have a great idea! How about …"

5. **Evaluate each based on each person's feelings and tangible needs**—Sometimes the excited epiphany is such a logically good solution that it is unnecessary to continue. But not always. If the solution is not completely obvious after the brainstorming, then the pair start critiquing the solutions offered. Essentially, this means scratching ideas off the list if they are truly unacceptable.

6. **Identify a solution acceptable to both**—The solution may not be perfect. It is a compromise, after all. But it is one that both people are willing to live with. And very often, the solution can be quite good, better than either had anticipated.

This process is not complicated, but it is difficult to do. The hardest part, in my opinion, is for the parent to relinquish power and to decide to approach the problem this way instead. Furthermore, it can be time consuming. Finally, it requires honesty about feelings and about tangible needs. If one person holds back on why exactly they have a problem, then this process will not work. But once a parent decides to commit to the strategy and devote the time, the process itself is smooth.

Example of Parent-Child Win-Win Problem Solving

I have used win-win problem solving frequently with my daughters. I am usually surprised by what I learn about them and gratified by seeing what thoughtful people they are. Let's use a conflict I had with my oldest daughter, Gabby, to illustrate how the process works. My two oldest daughters were with me for the weekend, while the two little ones were visiting their dad. It was early June, so the California rivers were running with snowmelt, and it was the season for river rafting. My brother-in-law is an expert river rafter, owns rafting equipment, and had offered to take us (me, my husband, and my two oldest daughters) on a rafting trip for the weekend. We had been planning it for several weeks, and both girls had agreed that they would like to go. So our story of conflict starts on Friday afternoon, while I was packing up the car to drive to the river. I had asked Gabby to bring me her packed bag, and she had not done so. I found her sitting on her bed with her face set firmly in a "you-can't-make-me" expression. I was surprised that she didn't want to go on the rafting trip, as she told me weeks ago that she was up for it. But that day she insisted that she simply was not going.

I considered a win-lose approach. It would have sounded something like: "Listen here, young lady, we are going on this trip whether you like it or not. You get your little tush in the car right now. If you don't bring a change of clothes, that's fine with me, but you're still going, even if I have to pick you up and put you in the car myself!" I considered this. I was furious that she had changed her mind without telling me. I assumed that I was dealing with her adolescent moodiness and a level of prissiness (not wanting to be without flushing toilets and showers for a day) that I find hard to tolerate. I reasoned that I am the mom, I do a lot for her, and it's not unreasonable to expect her to do something for me once in a while. However, she was a teenager by then and approximately my size, so it would have been difficult to execute such a plan. She would have been furious all weekend, which probably would have ruined my fun too.

I considered a lose-win approach. I could just throw up my hands and give in. It would have been the easiest thing to do, just call off the trip. I might have yelled, "Fine! Thanks for ruining our weekend!" Or I could have taken the silent martyr route, and just sighed deeply, saying, "Okay, Gabby. Have it your way." I would have to unpack all of my camping gear from the car and spend the weekend bitter and angry, as would my second daughter, who would be trapped in the house all weekend with us. My husband and brother-in-law were already at the campsite, with no cell phone signal, so I couldn't even call them to let them know I wasn't coming.

After considering these options, I returned to Gabby's room, where she still sat, stone-faced. I used everything I know about body language to convey that I was listening with my full attention. I sat down next to her and looked her in the eye. I told her that we needed to find a way to solve this problem and that I'd like to find a solution we could both agree to. And then I made an attempt to reflect her feelings. I must have said something like "It's clear from your body language that you do not want to go. You even seem a little angry about it." And then I listened to what she had to say. I was surprised by it. She had worked herself up into an angry state, but behind her anger about being forced to go, she was afraid of river rafting. She had seen whitewater rafting on television, and it looked very dangerous. She envisioned extreme whitewater, and her fear had grown over the preceding weeks. As her fear grew, she started to resent the fact that I was forcing her to do something that she was so afraid of. So by the day we were scheduled to leave, she was quite angry at me for this. I was shocked to hear this—I had no idea that she was afraid! I felt terrible that my darling, precious daughter had been living with this fear and anxiety. I offered contact comfort by hugging her and touching her arm as she talked to me. Obviously, my heart was softened to her, and I understood. I told her so. I didn't explain (yet) that the planned trip was not nearly as dangerous as she had envisioned, but I acknowledged and

Figure 5.3 River Rafting

validated her feelings. At that point, the tension was broken. Her face was no longer hardened; she knew she had been heard and accepted.

Next, it was time for me to share my feelings. Because she knew that she had been truly heard and understood, she was open to hearing me. I explained that I was excited to go on the trip, that I had been looking forward to it for weeks. To discover now at the last minute that I might have to cancel because my child didn't want to go (this is the behavior portion of the I-message, stated objectively and without judgment), I felt very disappointed (this is the feeling part). The semester was just over, and I had been working very hard to get through it. I had been looking forward to this weekend as a stress reliever and as a reward for my hard work (this is the reason part of the I-message). And there was a second I-message too: I felt regretful and embarrassed (the feelings; yes, I know that one is a secondary feeling, but it was true and it had to be said) at the thought of not going because Gabby didn't want to (the behavior), because my husband and brother-in-law were gone already and I couldn't contact them to let them know of my change of plans (the reason). Gabby understood both of these statements, as was clear by the look on her face. I was so proud of her in that moment! I had imagined that she was being a bratty, entitled teenager, but in truth, she was a thoughtful and kind teenager who was also afraid. What a great kid! So the process, so far, had strengthened our relationship. But we still didn't have a solution.

Next, I asked what she thought we should do. She suggested that I could go on the trip and leave her home alone. Given her young age, that was unacceptable to me. But I didn't say so quite yet. (Don't evaluate the options during the brainstorming stage.) She offered that suggestion; I offered a description of the river (explaining that it is not such extreme whitewater) and suggested that she should come as planned because the river is not so scary. At one point, she asked, "If I go to the river, do I have to go on the raft, or could I stay in camp while you go?" That was the moment of creativity for us. Neither of us had considered that option before, and it only came up because she truly understood why it was unacceptable just not to go, and I truly understood why it was unacceptable to force her to do something that frightened her. It was the obvious solution, but neither of us had thought of it until we went through this process.

We agreed that she would go to the campsite with us, but not be forced to go on the river. She agreed that after she saw the river and talked to her uncle, the expert raftsman, she might decide to go, but it would be entirely her decision.

In the end, Gabby did decide to go on the river with us that weekend (see Figure 5.2). It was entirely her decision; she wasn't forced. We had a lovely time. She's even been rafting a few times since. It was a happy ending to a conflict. It took about an hour for us to work through this conflict to arrive at the solution we did. It would have been quicker to use either of the other two strategies, but neither could have produced the emotional connection or the happy weekend. For me, win-win problem solving has always been an investment worth making.

Example of a Parent Facilitating Win-Win Problem Solving Between Children

Most children in the United States have siblings. Learning how to get along with them is difficult. Consequently, much of the conflict in families is between children rather than between parent and child. The parent's role in the case of sibling conflict is to facilitate win-win problem solving between children. This is also something I've done many times, and I offer here an example to illustrate how it works.

My two youngest daughters are only one grade level apart in school. They share a room and are mostly pals, spending most of their time together and playing together, even when one has a friend over. They spend a lot of time together. They are close, which also means that they have a lot of conflict. This story starts with a sobbing child. The younger of the two, Sofie, claimed that her sister, Ellie, had yelled at her and kicked her. I did some active listening: "Oh my goodness, you sound like you really got hurt!" To no one's surprise, Ellie had a totally different version of events. She claimed that Sofie had, for no reason at all, thrown something at her in anger that had hit her on the face and that she had been physically hurt, and that's why she had yelled. No kicking in her version of the story. I used active listening with her too: "Oh my, it hit you right in the face? That must have hurt!" Both children seemed to be hurt by the other's attack as well as indignant because each believed that she had been wronged. Privately, Sofie told me what the triggering event was. She had seen her sister in the cafeteria at school with some new friends whom Sofie doesn't know. Sofie had shouted out a greeting, but, in Sofie's words, Ellie had ignored her completely and just walked past talking to her new friends. That had hurt Sofie's feelings. I encouraged her to tell her sister why she was feeling hurt, but she did not want to.

Only ten minutes later, another argument exploded from their room, this time over what to watch on television. They were clearly unable to get past this conflict. Therefore, I had them both sit down and I told them we were going to find a solution to this problem before we do anything else (step 1, announce the decision not to use power). I could have simply taken one child's side against the other, forcing someone to apologize, or imposing a punishment on the person who I thought was at fault. This would have been a win-lose or lose-win scenario. But in this case, I honestly didn't know whose side I would take. Frankly, it appeared that both kids were behaving badly, but only because their immaturity prevented them from knowing how to handle hurt feelings. I asked who wanted to go first, and neither did. Ellie is a year older, so I told her that, as the older sister, I wanted her to go first, and then I coached an I-message out of her. I asked her what happened. She described walking home from school and being hit in the face with a small piece of a plant when she arrived home. This is the behavior part of an I-message. She may have first said something like "That idiot attacked me with a dirt ball!" It took quite a lot of coaching to get the judgment ("that idiot") and the lack of objectivity ("attacked me") replaced with "I walked into the yard and got hit in the face with something that was either dirt or a plant." I asked how it felt, and she said it hurt, that it hit right next to her eye, and she was worried that her eye had been injured, so she was a little scared in addition to feeling the sting of the object. (This is the feeling and the behavior rolled up together.) So we had accomplished an I-message!

I could see that Sofie, who is a big-hearted little girl, was touched to learn that her sister had been hurt and scared. So I asked her why she had made the attack in the first place. It took a little coaching as well, but she said that when her sister didn't respond to her greeting, she felt ignored. Since "ignored" is not a feeling, I asked her to clarify exactly how it feels when you think you are ignored, and she answered, with tears in her eyes, that it feels very lonely. We had another I-message! Furthermore, I could tell that Ellie had also been softened by the realization that her sister felt lonely. The hardness was gone, and she explained that she simply hadn't heard Sofie. Ellie apologized and said that she would have responded if she had heard.

After both had been heard, I asked what we were going to do about the television. They both laughed it off, saying that they'd work it out. So I didn't even have to engage in the problem-solving part with them this time. Once the tension was reduced and they had connected emotionally, they knew they could come to some agreement about what to watch.

This is a simple process, but it did take 15 minutes or so out of my day. However, if I hadn't done it, I fear they would have been bickering all evening long and would have gone to bed angry with each other. Having a parent coach them through conflict a few times creates kids who know how to get through the conflict next time on their own. And that is, after all, the ultimate goal.

Haim Ginott: Congruent Communication

While Thomas Gordon's PET model was making waves, another parent educator was writing books about communication with ideas that overlapped significantly with it. Haim Ginott began his career in Israel as a classroom teacher. After moving to the United States in 1947, he went back to school to study clinical psychology, but he retained his interest in child guidance.

Ginott argued that the language of psychotherapy helps troubled children heal, so if parents and teachers used that language on a regular basis, children would obviously benefit. His books recommend a style of talking to children that he called "congruent communication." In his own words, **congruent communication** is "communication that is harmonious, authentic, where words fit feelings." The defining characteristics of congruent communication are that the adult's communication is harmonious with the child's feelings; the adult's behavior invites cooperation; and the adult uses discipline rather than punishment (Manning & Bucher, 2001).

Ginott applied this communication approach to parenting (Ginott, 1965; Ginott, 1967) as well as classroom teaching (Ginott, 1972). His advice is similar to Gordon's PET in that Ginott was opposed to using punishment to control children's behavior. They both emphasized accepting children's emotions, in addition to communicating in ways that engender mutually respectful interactions.

John Gottman (Gottman, DeClaire, & Goleman, 1998) acknowledged in his book on emotion coaching that his research on parent-child communication confirmed Haim Ginott's approach. Gottman's book is actually dedicated to Haim Ginott in recognition of Ginott's contribution to emotionally responsive parenting.

Mirroring Emotions

Ginott recommends a way of talking to children that is very similar to active listening. He calls it **mirroring emotions**. Some of his teachings about this include:

- "All feelings are permitted; only actions are limited" (Ginott, 1965). Children are allowed to feel whatever they feel. All feelings thus can be accepted by a loving parent. This does not translate into permissive parenting because children are not allowed to act on all of their feelings, though the feelings themselves can be accepted.

- Acceptance is not the same as approval (Ginott, 1967). Therefore, parents can accept that their children have feelings that they don't necessarily approve of or want to be true.
- "Only after a child feels right can he think right. Only after a child feels right can he do right" (Ginott, 1965). Ginott taught that parents (and teachers) must address children's painful emotions as a way of correcting behavior. Feelings come first in behavioral motivation and in relationship maintenance. Feelings are not to be overcome or ignored. They are to be addressed directly, and before anything else.
- "Strong feelings tend to diminish in intensity and lose their sharp edges when a sympathetic listener accepts them with understanding" (Ginott, 1967, p. 65).

Sane Messages

Ginott offers a technique that is analogous to an I-message that he calls a sane message (Ginott, 1965). **Sane messages** address the child's behavior rather than his or her character and were designed to reduce the possibility of defensiveness. He offers three characteristics of a sane message:

- Children need to hear a verbal message that is consistent (i.e., congruent) with the parent's true feelings.
- It mentions the problem itself rather than the quality of the child that led to the problem. For example, "I see a messy room" rather than "You made a mess in here."
- It limits criticism to a specific event, avoiding the *you always …* or *you never …* assertions that generate so much ill will.

Dealing with Anger

Ginott addresses anger more thoroughly than Gordon. With respect to children's anger, he says, "When attitudes are hostile, the facts are unconvincing" (Ginott, 1967, p. 38). Many parents immediately try to correct children's misstatements or to redefine their perceptions when the child expresses anger. This is understandable. It's reasonable to assume that when the facts are corrected, the feelings will change. However, Ginott observes that it doesn't usually work that way. Instead, it is necessary to acknowledge and validate the anger before trying to offer facts in rebuttal. In other words: active listening first, even in the face of the child's anger—maybe especially in the face of the child's anger.

With regard to parental anger, Ginott argues (1965) that parents should accept the fact that children will on occasion make them angry and accept that they are entitled to anger, without feeling guilt or shame. He wrote that authenticity in relationships is essential, and therefore, if a parent is angry, then the parent's words should reflect the anger. However, just as children are allowed their feelings but must limit their behaviors, adults too must limit their behaviors. They may express anger provided that they do it in a way that does not attack the child's personality or character while doing so. He calls this "anger without insult" (Ginott, 1971).

When Should Communication Strategies Be Used?

The communication strategies described in this chapter should be used frequently. They are in the bottom half of the pyramid, meaning they can be drawn upon frequently. Regular use of these strategies builds parent-child relationships and thus are no threat. They overlap significantly, in fact, with attachment strategies. Active listening, specifically, can be seen as a verbal form of sensitive responsiveness, with parents responding primarily to emotions and then problem solving once the child's emotional state has been soothed. There is really no risk of overdoing it with these strategies. They are used when there are problems (i.e., unmet needs) and conflict in families that need to be solved. Parents can call on them as often as they have time to do so.

If communication strategies do not produce the desired result, the parent should first look lower on the pyramid, asking him- or herself if the attachment relationship is sound. If the attachment relationship is struggling, then the communication strategies will not be as effective as possible. In that case, the parent should focus on sensitive responsiveness when the child has tender needs. But if the attachment relationship feels solid, the parent might need to consider moving up the parenting pyramid to the next level, Consequences, which we will address in Chapter 6.

Developmental Connections

Communication for problem solving is relevant for children of all ages, though it looks a little different depending on the child's age. Many marriage counselors and workplace relationship programs train people in active listening, I-messages, and win-win problem solving. Thomas Gordon himself wrote a book applying these same principles to workplace leadership (Gordon, 2001) and to classroom teaching (Gordon, 2003). Ginott wrote a book applying these concepts to classroom teaching as well (Ginott, 1972). I believe that the skills are transferrable to many circumstances. But since our focus is parent-child relationships, let us consider how these skills vary by the child's age and developmental stage.

Many people assume that communication strategies would only be relevant after children are sufficiently verbal to have a conversation. This is logical, of course, but I think they overstate the case. Babies' receptive language (their capacity to understand language directed toward them) is far more advanced than their productive language (their capacity to produce language to convey a message of their own). Anyone who has ever learned a new language in adulthood can testify that they often know what is being said to them but just can't seem to generate an outgoing message correctly. It's frustrating, but it's a very real fact of language learning. Therefore, we must remember that what we say to babies is important; it is getting through. In fact, the way we speak to babies shapes their learning in profound ways. So if we wait to talk about emotions until the child already has a good grasp of language pertaining to emotions, then we have missed a (literally) once-in-a-lifetime opportunity to shape the way the child thinks about emotions.

One of my students told me that she had a revelation while holding her newborn baby one night while she was enrolled in my class. She heard herself calming her fussy baby by saying things like, "No, no, you're okay, you're fine, it's all right." Then she realized that these things she was cooing to her baby were all communication roadblocks. She realized that she was already in the habit of dismissing her infant's distress. She had grown up with an emotion-dismissing parent, and hadn't appreciated it, so she was dismayed to hear herself doing the same thing. She didn't know if her baby was taking in this emotional dismissal, but she knew that she didn't want to be in such a habit. I couldn't agree more. I have always recommended using active listening with babies on their first day out of the womb! The baby can't convey a messages verbally, obviously, but it's really not hard to tell what a newborn baby is feeling. Those feelings can be reflected verbally, as in: "My baby is so happy to see me!" or "Ooooh, sweet baby is uncomfortable!" or "Darling girl is scared to be left alone!" These verbal messages are good active listening practice for the adult, and they help shape the baby's language development. Active listening is a skill that parents can practice early, and it will be useful for a lifetime.

I-messages, likewise, are a good habit to get into. The more a parent practices identifying his feelings and describing behaviors without judgment, the more his thoughts and emotions are shaped for kindness and compassion. I find that this skill helps me as much as it helps my children. But there is one developmental note about I-messages. Some who teach I-messages (e.g., Popkin, 1987) suggest that they should include an additional component. In addition to the feeling, behavior, and effect, Popkin says that parents should explicitly state their expectation. For example, "I was sad to walk in here and find your books and your stuffed animals on the floor because I'm tired and I don't want to clean it up. I expect you to put away your books before I return." I don't generally recommend this addition because frankly, it seems a little insulting. If the I-message was clear about the specific behavior that caused the problem, then it should be abundantly clear what action is needed to correct it. But here is where I think the age of the child matters. Toddlers may need to have very explicit instructions because of their cognitive limitations. They often need to be given instructions one part at a time because they simply can't hold multiple steps in their mind at the same time. But that's the only situation where I think adding the expectations might be necessary.

How Parents React

Since communication problems are often what bring parents into parenting classes and since there is a strong cultural norm that supports the importance of "good communication," most parents are eager for this content. They see this as important and relevant. Most parents also recognize that these techniques are different from what they've been doing. They generally ask for more on this. More examples, more practice. More discussion of it after learning it and trying it out.

The difficulty, in my experience, is that it is very hard to get out of the habits of using roadblocks, you-messages, and either win-lose or lose-win problem solving. Those strategies are so engrained that parents have a hard time letting go and are sometimes even blind to the fact that they are doing them. Parents will be excited to learn about active listening and I-messages but then go home and are unable to sustain using the techniques because the other habits are so strong. Others have also reported this tendency for the practices to fade (e.g., Taylor & Swan, 1982). Therefore, these skills must be revisited and strengthened after teaching them in the first place.

Some of the questions I commonly get:

Question: Doesn't active listening teach my children to whine and complain about every little thing?

Answer: Paradoxically, no. This is the paradoxical theory of change in action. It turns out a person has to feel accepted as is in order to have the courage to change. We've seen this paradox previously when we studied attachment. A child must feel secure in an attachment relationship in order to feel safe enough to go out and explore the world. Safety at home really doesn't keep them at home. Similarly, allowing a child to have a painful feeling teaches them that they are capable of facing painful feelings and makes them less paralyzed by those feelings.

Question: If I use active listening and allow my child to find a solution to his problem, what if he comes up with a terrible solution?

Answer: Well, this happens. And if we believe that the problem truly belongs to them, then we have to let them try out their solution to see what happens. Personally, I draw the line at a "solution" that would involve an injustice. For instance, I will not stand by when one child concludes that the solution to her problem is to physically hurt her sister. But for the most part, I do let them try out their solutions. I've had children conclude that they will go to bed without finishing their homework or that they will not invite someone to a party and just hope that person doesn't find out. I thought these were bad ideas, but the child must learn that they have the power to make decisions over their own lives.

Question: I look back and see times when I totally sent a you-message. Have I screwed up my kids already? How perfect do I have to be?

Answer: Thankfully, relationships are dynamic and flexible. And especially when an attachment relationship is in place, parents' mistakes are taken in stride. I don't mean that parents can't damage children; I believe they can. But almost always, improvements are welcomed and appreciated. Late truly is better than never. And apologies after the fact can be very powerful. Parents should consider revisiting an issue if they believe they mishandled it the first time through.

Question: I'm uncomfortable with the "I feel____ when you _____ because _____" script. Won't my kids look at me funny and wonder why I'm talking in such a scripted way?

Answer: When you first start to use I-messages, yes, they might look at you funny, and ask why you're talking like that. It's okay to explain: "I want to try a new way of talking to you. I'm not happy with the way I've been doing it because I haven't been respectful of you. So I'm going to try this instead." When I recommend to parents that they say this, they generally report back to me that the child said "Okay," and that was that. Yes, it can be awkward to learn a new skill. But it does get smoother. The awkwardness fades and it becomes second nature.

Question: What if I am feeling angry? It's a secondary emotion. Am I not allowed to express it?

Answer: This is a question I struggle with personally. When I'm angry with one of my children, I can usually trace it back to a primary feeling. For instance, when I'm angry at the child for going to a neighbor's house without telling me, I see that the primary feeling is fear for the child's safety. But occasionally, I'm angry and I can't seem to identify the primary feeling behind it. An I-message can be made based on anger. It's possible, and I suspect that sometimes it's necessary. It's a risky prospect because it's very likely to make the child defensive and therefore unable to receive the message. But I suspect that sometimes the anger is so compelling that it simply must be shared. I hope that, even if my child gets defensive and resistant in the moment, that perhaps later they will be able to reflect on my message and hear it. But that won't work if I'm offering angry I-messages all the time. It has to be a rare event for it to be powerful.

Question: Is it bad if I try to use these techniques on my romantic partner?

Answer: Students sometimes report that they tried active listening on their romantic partner, and the response was so amazing that they were afraid that had just used some kind of magic to manipulate their loved one. But no, there's no magic here. That amazing response is an authentic relationship. This is the kind of emotional intimacy that is possible. It is remarkable and wonderful, and yes, you are allowed (even encouraged) to use these tools to create the best relationships you can in all areas of life.

Programs and Critique

Thomas Gordon's Parent Effectiveness Training (PET) program is the most widely used program to teach these communication skills, and it is what I have used as my main source to describe these practices. He has written up the concepts in a book (2001) so that they will be more widely available, even to those who cannot come to a workshop. It remains one of my all-time favorite parenting books.

The PET approach to communication, or pieces of it, have been widely adopted in many domains of contemporary society. The approach is consistent with a democratic approach to life and with the goal of maintaining self-esteem in children. John Gottman has written about emotional intelligence in children, including a book in which he describes active listening but calls it *emotion coaching* (Gottman, DeClaire, & Goleman, 1998). Both the Active Parenting program (Popkin, 1987) and Systematic Training for Effective Parenting (Dinkmeyer & McKay, 1976) combine the communication strategies described here with natural and logical consequences, to be described in the next chapter. Popkin calls active listening *active communication*; Dinkmeyer and McKay call it *reflective listening*. These ideas are so widely accepted that they have been integrated into virtually all human service disciplines. Parenting Wisely is an online parenting education program using video vignettes to teach these communication skills (among others), especially for court-referred parents (Lagges & Gordon, 1997). My students who work in child care centers have been instructed to talk to children this way. My daughter, who is in a peer mediation group in her elementary school, has been trained using these techniques. Marriage preparation programs advise engaged couples to practice these skills with each other. Marriage counselors teach these skills to troubled couples to improve their relationships. This approach is ubiquitous.

Wide adoption of the ideas of PET and the commercial success of the program are both indicators that PET skills are useful. However, scientific evidence is fairly limited. There is research on PET, but much of that was published in the 1970s when the program was new, and the research is methodologically weak. Evaluation research on voluntary educational programs is extraordinarily difficult, which challenges all parenting education research.

That said, a meta-analysis of 26 evaluation studies (Cedar & Levant, 1990) concluded that PET has a beneficial effect on parents' attitude and behavior as well as children's self-esteem. The largest effect was on parental attitudes; PET helps parents understand their children, to have more empathy and respect for them. These effects are sustained for at least six months. Furthermore, small effects on the child's behavior seem to increase over time; if true, this explains why some studies of PET do not report any effect on the child's behavior. In addition, the average effect sizes for these outcomes were fairly small (the largest was about a third of a standard deviation), but effect sizes were larger in the more methodologically sound studies. Overall, we can conclude that the communication skills taught in PET are probably helpful to parents and may be helpful to children as well.

Review and Reflection Questions

1. What is the main argument of humanistic psychology? Do you believe that it is true?

2. What are the aspects of Rogerian therapy that shape PET?

3. Describe the problem-ownership principle. How does one decide whose problem it is? Think of examples of child-owned, parent-owned, and shared problems from your own life experience.

4. Why are communication roadblocks problematic for child-owned problems? Have you had these used on you? How did it feel? How are the roadblocks similar to Gottman's notion of emotion dismissing and emotion disapproving?

5. What is the fundamental goal of active listening/emotion coaching? What are the steps and best practices? When might you have an opportunity to try out this skill?

6. Why do parents have a hard time confronting their children? What is wrong with the you-messages they often send when they have a parent-owned problem?

7. What is the fundamental goal of an I-message? What are the components of it and best practices?

8. Why are win-lose and lose-win problem solving ineffective? Can you think of an example of when these were used in your upbringing?

9. What are the steps and best practices for win-win problem solving?

10. How are Ginott's methods of congruent communication similar to the PET methods of communication?

11. Can PET methods be used with young children or just older ones?

12. Does evaluation research suggest that PET is effective?

Terminology to Know

- Active listening
- Child-owned problems
- Communication roadblocks
- Congruent communication
- Emotion coaching
- Emotion-disapproving emotional parenting style
- Emotion-dismissing emotional parenting style
- Humanistic psychology
- I-message
- Language of acceptance
- Lose-win problem solving
- Mirroring emotions
- Parent Effectiveness Training (PET)
- Parent-owned problem
- Primary emotion
- Problem-ownership principle
- Psychological size
- Sane messages
- Secondary emotion
- Send a put-down
- Send a solution
- Shared problem
- Unconditional positive regard
- Win-lose problem solving
- Win-win problem solving
- You-message

Names to Know

- Ginott
- Gordon
- Gottman
- Rogers

References

Bleisser, A. (1970). The paradoxical theory of change. In J. Fagan & I. L. Shepherd (Eds.), *Gestalt Therapy Now*. http://www.gestalt.org/arnie.htm Accessed 2/9/2016.

Cedar, B., & Levant, R.F. (1990). A meta-analysis of the effects of parent effectiveness training. *American Journal of Family Therapy, 18, 4*, 373–384.

Dinkmeyer, D., & McKay, G.D. (1976). *Systematic training for effective parenting*. Circle Pines, MN: American Guidance Service.

Ginott, H.G. (1965). *Between parent and child*. New York: Macmillan.

Ginott, H.G. (1967). *Between parent and teenager*. New York: Macmillan.

Ginott, H.G. (1971). Anger without insult: Effective method. *Lakeland Ledger, Dec. 22, 1971*, 3c.

Ginott, H.G. (1972). *Teacher and child*. New York: Macmillan.

Gordon, T. (2000). *Parent Effectiveness Training: The proven program for raising responsible children, 30th edition*. Harmony.

Gordon, T. (2001). *Leader Effectiveness Training: LET (revised)*. Tarcher Perigee.

Gordon, T. (2003). *Teacher Effectiveness Training: The program proven to bring out the best in students of all ages*. Three Rivers Press.

Gottman, J., DeClaire, J., & Goleman, D. (1998). *Raising an emotionally intelligent child: The heart of parenting*. Simon & Schuster.

Kramer, R. (1995). The birth of client-centered therapy: Carl Rogers, Otto Rank, and "The Beyond." *Journal of Humanistic Psychology, 35, 4*, 54–110.

Lagges, A., & Gordon, D.A. (1997). Interactive videodisk parent training for teen mothers. *Child and Family Behavior Therapy, 21, 1*, 19–37.

Manning, M.L., & Bucher, K.T. (2001). Revisiting Ginott's congruent communication after thirty years. *Clearing House, 74, 4*, 215–218.

Popkin, M. (1987). *Active Parenting: Teaching cooperation, courage, and responsibility*. Harper San Francisco.

Rogers, C. (1951). *Client-centered therapy: Its current practice, implications, and theory*. London, UK: Constable.

Rogers, C. (1959). A theory of therapy, personality, relationships as developed in the client-centered framework. In S. Koch (Ed.), *Psychology: A study of a science. Vol. 3: Formulations of the person and the social context*. New York: McGraw Hill.

Taylor, P.B., & Swan, R.W. (1982). Parent Effectiveness Training: Adolescents' responses. *Psychological Reports, 51, 1*, 331–338.

Credit

- Fig. 5.3: Copyright © 2012 by Raymond Hall. Reprinted with permission.

6. Consequences

Introduction

So far, we have laid the foundation with sensitive responsiveness for attachment relationships, then we moved on to teaching new skills using scaffolding and process-centered feedback, and finally we addressed problem solving through communication. Now here we are, halfway up the parenting pyramid, approaching the parenting strategies of natural and logical consequences. While they should ideally be used far less often than strategies lower on the pyramid, consequences are perhaps the most overlooked tools in the care of children.

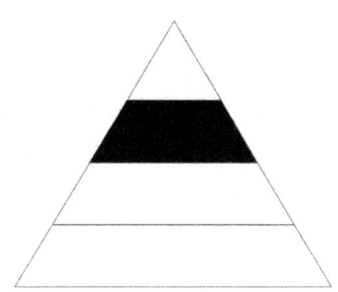

Figure 6.1 Consequences on Pyramid

Consequences help address two main circumstances in family life. First, they can help resolve conflict that was not fully resolved using the I-message communication strategy discussed in Chapter 6. Communication strategies may increase the chance of gaining a child's cooperation, but they don't *always* work. Children instinctively know that part of their job is to grow up and out of the direct influence of their parents. Therefore, they will sometimes push their parents beyond the comfort of the secure attachment relationship and the mutual respect of the PET communication techniques. Sometimes the parent has used I-messages to ask a child to cooperate with the chores, and yet the dishes remain unwashed, or the trash has not been taken to the curb. What then? Many parents keep using communication strategies until they are blue in the face, and then they explode in anger. Fortunately, natural and logical consequences represent a step beyond communication that can help resolve some of those conflicts without driving parents to despair and rage. So for those problems, consequences is the next step in problem solving.

Second, consequences can help teach children about personal responsibility. Some issues of personal responsibility simply do not create child-owned problems (which could be addressed using active listening) or parent-owned problems (which could be addressed with I-messages). However, the parent may see that the child has an important lesson to learn nonetheless and feel an obligation to teach that lesson. The lessons are generally about personal responsibility. For instance, a child might not want to brush his teeth, might feel no tangible need associated with not brushing, and the parent has no tangible need associated with the child not brushing his teeth. And yet the parent wants to guide the child in the right direction because poor dental hygiene can have lifelong consequences for the child. A parent might want to teach personal responsibility with regard to school achievement for those children who do not feel a tangible need to do well in school. A parent might want to teach responsibility with regard to having a clean and orderly bedroom or eating a healthy diet. All of these circumstances can be addressed using the tools of natural and logical consequences.

Theory and Background

The use of natural and logical consequences emerged from the individual psychology of Alfred Adler and the social discipline model of Rudolf Dreikurs.

Alfred Adler: Individual Psychology

Alfred Adler was an Austrian medical doctor who was a colleague of Sigmund Freud. He is one of the original founders of the psychoanalysis movement. But he broke with Freud in 1911, founding his own school of thought about psychology. Adler believed that the individual person is an indivisible whole, tied inextricably to the whole of the cosmos. Therefore, he called his perspective individual psychology. **Individual psychology** is characterized by a focus on the social context in which an individual lives, rather than the interior focus of Freud's psychoanalysis (Orgler, 1976).

Adlerian individual psychology forms the basis of a parenting education model that is widespread in the United States. Tenets of individual psychology that are relevant to the parenting programs they would spawn include the focus on social belonging, inferiority, and encouragement (Stein & Edwards, 1998).

Individual psychology teaches that human beings are capable of profound cooperation, self-improvement, and contribution to the common welfare. This follows from Adler's belief that **social belonging** is the most fundamental goal of our species, and that interconnectedness is essential for optimal development. Human beings are fundamentally interconnected with the entire cosmos. Consequently, the concepts of equality, mutual respect, and cooperation are foundational. This leads to advice to parents to establish equality in family relationships as well as opportunities for children to choose to be cooperative, rather than being forced into cooperation. The goal of Adlerian parenting programs is always to establish interconnectedness, never to isolate or punish.

According to individual psychology, children actively construct and make meaning of their lives. Much of this is done in order to reduce the normal feelings of **inferiority** that arise when the developing child becomes conscious of his or her limitations. Ideally, parents encourage a child to continue reducing feelings of inferiority through cooperation and interdependence. **Encouragement** is thus the primary goal of a parent for his or her child. It produces the courage to overcome inferiority. Adlerian parenting programs address the means by which encouragement of children is facilitated. We addressed this briefly in Chapter 4, concluding that the Adlerian concept of encouragement is similar to Dweck's notion of process-centered feedback but different in some important ways.

When parents or teachers fail to help children cope with feelings of inferiority, children become discouraged, according to Adler. **Discouragement** produces a style of life that seeks to hide inferiority rather than overcome it. Safeguarding devices must be used to protect themselves from failure and the feelings that come with it. These devices include guilt, distancing, accusations, depreciating others, anxiety, and depression. These are the symptoms that must be treated by psychotherapy. Therefore, parenting education was essential in Adler's view of psychology because it can prevent the social ills of discouraged adults who are insufficiently interconnected with society.

Rudolf Dreikurs: Social Discipline Model

Upon Adler's death in 1937, the torch of individual psychology passed to his student, Rudolf Dreikurs. He popularized individual psychology, including parent education based on Adlerian principles. In the process, Dreikurs also contributed significantly to the field in his own right (Shulman & Dreikurs, 1974). His social discipline model is based on the Adlerian assumptions that social belonging is the primary motivator for children and that encouraged children will seek to belong through cooperation. Parenting practices should therefore encourage children and promote belonging, which can only be done by avoiding the use of power for coercion. He added to Adler's ideas, first by identifying parenting styles and second by delineating the concept of natural and logical consequences in his discussion of the goals of misbehavior.

Parenting Styles

Dreikurs (Dreikurs, Cassel, & Ferguson, 2004) identifies three styles of parenting. He calls them:

1. **Autocratic**—Excessively controlling; forcing behavior rather than motivating it. This is clearly the same thing as Baumrind's authoritarian parenting.

2. **Permissive**—No rules; does not facilitate self-discipline. This is analogous to Baumrind's permissive parenting.

3. **Democratic**—Allows freedom of choice, but within limits imposed by responsibilities. It is known in Baumrind's model as authoritative parenting.

This typology is still used by Adlerian programs today. The Active Parenting programs (e.g., Popkin, 2014) call them the dictator (autocratic), the doormat (permissive), and the active parent (democratic). The Positive Discipline program (Nelsen, 2006) refers to them as strict (autocratic), permissive (permissive), and positive (democratic). Love and Logic (Cline & Fay, 2006) calls them drill sergeant parents (autocratic), helicopter parents (permissive), and consultant parents (democratic). By focusing on this typology and clearly promoting the principles of democratic (i.e., authoritative) parenting, Adlerian programs are very much in line with Baumrind's (1971) empirically supported typology of parenting styles. The research is clear that on balance, an authoritative style is the most effective approach (e.g., Masud, Thurasamy, & Ahmad, 2015; Sleddens, Gerards, Thijs, deVries, & Kremers, 2011), and Dreikursian parenting education endorses it.

The reader may recall that there is scientific consensus regarding the superiority of authoritative parenting over other styles. In this way, Adlerian/Dreikursian parenting programs are very much in line with the scientific consensus.

Calling authoritative parenting "democratic" reflects Dreikurs' (and Adler's) commitment to social equality. Incidentally, because of his belief in social equality, Alfred Adler was a staunch feminist. This focus on social equality led to a related concept, the **democratic family**, which is a family system shaped by this democratic parenting style. Dreikurs argues that autocratic parenting may have worked just fine in an autocratic political system, but in our democracy, the family needs to reflect the democratic values of our society. Obviously, it is unrealistic to run a family exactly like a democracy, with everyone voting on issues. Dreikurs defines equality in a democratic family to mean that adults and children have equal claims on dignity and respect. The democratic family ideology leads naturally to an emphasis on problem solving through communication rather than the arbitrary wielding of power. Therefore, contemporary Adlerian/Dreikursian parenting programs generally include the PET communication strategies from Chapter 6 as well as the use of family meetings.

Goals of Misbehavior

While Adler had introduced the idea that children are goal directed and that misbehavior is the product of discouragement, Dreikurs fleshes out this idea and uses it to help parents understand their children's behavior. He suggests that if parents understood WHY their children were misbehaving, they might better be able to craft an appropriate response. Often, children do things that simply mystify adults. Dreikurs proposes four possible goals of misbehavior, each reflecting a greater level of discouragement than the one before. He suggests that parents can identify their child's goal by the feeling that the misbehavior creates in the adult, and for each, he recommends a short-term response (to directly deal with the misbehavior) as well as a long-term response (to reduce the discouragement that produced it). The goals are summarized in Table 6.1.

A mildly discouraged child will misbehave with the **goal of attracting attention**. This is so normal that perfectly healthy, typical toddlers and preschoolers do this every single day. For them, it reflects a temporary state of imbalance. But when parents do not recognize and address the mild discouragement, then this becomes a more constant state: the child's discouragement grows, and other forms of misbehavior follow. Misbehavior for attention typically comes in the form of behaviors such as whining, complaining, begging, and asking for unnecessary help. This misbehavior is caused by the child's faulty belief that the child belongs only when he or she is the center of attention. We want kids to know that they belong all the time, no matter what. Since their belonging is not questioned, they will be interested in making a contribution to the group

Table 6.1 Goals of Misbehavior

	Goal of Misbehavior			
	Attention	Power	Retaliation	Display Inadequacy
Level of Discouragement	Mild	Moderate	Serious	Excessive (may require professional help)
Faulty Belief	I belong only when I'm the center of attention.	I belong only when I'm in control.	I don't belong, and it's your fault.	I don't belong, and I can't belong.
Typical Behaviors	Whine, nag, beg	Confront, scream, disobey, defy	Attack, damage property	Refuse to engage
Adult Feels	Irritated, annoyed	Angry, provoked	Stunned, hurt	Helpless, hopeless
Typical Adult Response	Scolds, reminds	Either overpowers child, or gives in and allows child to win.	Retaliates	Avoids interaction
Recommended Short Term Response	Ignore the irritating behavior.	Sidestep power struggle, or use natural or logical consequences.	Refuse to engage in battle Use active listening.	Be present
Recommended Longer Term Solution	Give attention for positive behavior.	Offer legitimate power.	Attend to relationship building.	Encourage

that they belong to. Therefore, to feel a part of the group only when receiving attention reflects a faulty belief, one that is mildly discouraging.

Adults can identify that the child's goal is attention by their own feelings of annoyance or irritation. A typical response is to scold the child for the annoying behavior. It is a negative form of attention that is unpleasant for everyone involved, but given the child's faulty belief, it does at least assure the child of his belonging. As a result, the misbehavior will continue because it achieves its goal. Consequently, Dreikurs suggests that instead, parents decline to offer attention and ignore the annoying behavior. However, the underlying discouragement must also be addressed, so Dreikurs says that parents should, in addition to ignoring the misbehavior in the moment, also find a way to give attention for some positive behavior. The parent may have to invite some positive behavior in order to give attention for it.

The classic example of the strategy of creating opportunities for positive behavior is when an elementary school teacher turns a troublemaking student into the teacher's pet by giving him or her special helping tasks. One example of how I have used this myself is when one of my children is complaining of boredom or annoyance in the grocery store. I ignore the complaint and say instead that I need help finding something (name a product). For example, "Hmm. Where is the peanut butter? I always forget …" The child almost always alerts, reporting that she knows where it is. I ask her to go get a jar of peanut butter for me, and she's off to complete the task. When she returns, I thank her for helping, and name another product that she can help me find. Her cooperation, her contribution, reflects a return to a sense of belonging.

A moderately discouraged child will misbehave with the **goal of obtaining power**. This is also very normal behavior. Toddlers and teenagers are especially prone to this, as it is developmentally typical for them to be attending to personal power. Typical behaviors that reflect the goal of power include direct confrontation with the parent, disobedience, defiance, and in-your-face confrontation. This kind of misbehavior is based on the child's faulty belief that they belong only when they are in control. Instead of believing that they belong no matter what and that they are responsible for their own decisions and actions, they lose sight of personal responsibility because they wrongly believe that they should focus on being in charge. This faulty belief causes children to be unnecessarily confrontational just to make a point. This produces moments from childhood that are classic, including the "you-can't-make-me" taunt. Or the "no" while looking the parent directly in the eye. Or the over-the-shoulder eye contact, with a bit of a twinkle, and then running away to do the exact thing that was just forbidden.

A parent confronted with a power struggle like this will generally feel angry and provoked. They may think that the child is forcing her into a battle, wondering why the child is pushing them like this. A parent with an autocratic style (what Baumrind calls *authoritarian*) will generally respond by overpowering the child with the same degree of anger that the child used in the power struggle. The autocratic parent will put his foot down and demand compliance. This is analogous to the win-lose problem solving of PET in Chapter 5. Given the power imbalance, the parent will clearly win this confrontation, and the child will be somewhat damaged by the severity of the autocratic response. A parent with a permissive style will generally respond by simply giving in and letting the child have his way. This is analogous to the lose-win problem solving of PET in Chapter 5. Either of these approaches is likely to increase the child's discouragement and lead to misbehavior with the goal of retaliation.

Instead, Dreikurs advises that a parent using the democratic style would use consequences in the short term, combined with offering legitimate power as a long-term strategy to reduce this type of misbehavior. These strategies are described at length later in this chapter as the parenting approaches and strategies that emerged from this theoretical model.

A seriously discouraged child will misbehave with the **goal of retaliation**. This happens to every child at some point, so in that way it is normal behavior. However, it reflects a much more serious level of discouragement than the first two goals of misbehavior. The faulty belief is that the child doesn't belong but that it is the parent's fault. Notice that the first two we discussed saw hope, a path to belonging (even if misguided), while this belief shows no path forward. It is substantially more serious discouragement than the first two. While misbehavior for power might be intense and in-your-face, misbehavior for retaliation is downright mean-spirited. The child wants to hurt the parent. It doesn't even matter if they get caught, they want to make the parent suffer no matter the consequences to themselves. Typical behaviors include outright attacks, verbal or physical, and damaging the parent's property. Hurtful verbal attacks such as "I hate you" or "You're not my REAL dad" are forms of retaliation, as is breaking something that belongs to the parent.

Retaliatory misbehavior might be funny at some level, especially if the child is very young and his or her attacks are ineffective. I know parents sometimes laugh when a very young child puts on a pouty face and says, "I hate you" or some such attempt at a verbal attack. But this is not really funny. The child feels very hurt and is trying to hurt the parent in return. Not funny. When the parent realizes that, or with an older child when the attack is more effective, the parent will generally feel stunned or hurt. Parents are typically shocked because they honestly did not realize that they did anything that would injure their child. They believe that all they do is for the child's well-being, and they just can't believe that the child sees it differently. They feel hurt because their child knows them well enough to choose an attack that will be effective. A student once confessed that she knew nothing made her mom more upset than not being able to find her car keys, so when she was angry with her mom, she would purposely hide her mom's car keys. The worst she ever did was bury them in the backyard, which was probably very effective! I can imagine the parent saying to a friend, "I just don't understand. After all I do for her. Why would she DO this to me?"

Dreikurs suggests that parents avoid the impulse to retaliate back at the child. I've seen parents respond to "I hate you!" with "Oh, yeah? Well, I hate you too!" This is just not very mature. Neither is a slap across the face. These retaliatory responses convey that the parent is simply more powerful than the child and thus will not take the child's sense of injury seriously. Instead, Dreikurs proposes that parents understand that the misbehavior comes from a true sense of injustice. While the parent might be sure that the child misinterpreted their behavior, the parent can still acknowledge that the child genuinely feels that he or she has been wronged. The child feels unjustly injured. Therefore, says Dreikurs, resist the urge to engage in battle. Now that we've studied communication strategies, we can see that active listening would be an appropriate way to respond to misbehavior that comes from a child-owned problem. The parent reflects the child's hurt by saying, "Son, your eyes are welling with tears as if you've been hurt." Or "It seems like you're very upset with me." In the long term, the relationship must be repaired.

A profoundly discouraged child will misbehave with the **goal of displaying inadequacy**. This behavior, it seems to me, reflects depression. Children will get to this point if milder forms of discouragement were not addressed, so there could be a pattern of insensitive parenting that culminates with this. But it also happens that people get depressed for other reasons. Most people experience something like depression at some point in their lives, so in that respect, this is normal. But it is also a serious problem. Depression is very painful for the sufferer, and it affects other aspects of health as well as one's ability to function in school or work and relationships. It is a serious problem that needs to be addressed. Dreikurs describes the display of inadequacy (which I believe to be depression) as behavior that is a refusal to engage. The child believes that he doesn't belong, but the child is no longer angry at the parent about that; the child is simply resigned to the fact. The child won't try to make any efforts toward cooperation or even self-care. The child says things like "No, I don't want to try doing my homework. I'm not good at math," or "I don't see the point of working on this, it's not going to work."

A parent should consider that the misbehavior is the product of depression when the parent feels helpless and hopeless about the situation. The parent might say to a friend, "I don't have any idea how to help him. He won't accept anything I have to offer. I just don't know what to do." These are very unpleasant feelings. The parent will be tempted to avoid further interaction with the child.

Dreikurs suggests that in the short term, the parent should continue to offer his or her presence. To be willing to be with the child conveys that the suffering can be shared and that the parent believes the child is strong enough to endure it. In the long term, Dreikurs says that the parent needs to encourage the child in every way possible. While the Adlerian notion of encouragement has not met with strong support in the research, we can substitute the insights about how to teach new skills that we discussed in Chapter 4 (process-focused feedback to create a growth mindset) as strategies for helping a child emerge from this overpowering feeling of inadequacy.

While these goals of misbehavior are interesting, these ideas are essentially untestable. According to Dreikurs, it is not necessary that children be consciously aware of their goals; in fact, it seems more likely that these processes are not conscious. Unconscious motivations are generally impossible to test. Therefore, this background has been provided primarily because it is in this context that Dreikurs writes about natural and logical consequences, strategies that are widely regarded as helpful tools available to parents.

Best Practices

As described above, Dreikurs maintains that power struggles are based on faulty beliefs. Instead of children believing that they need to gain control in order to be taken seriously, it would be better if children believed that their place in the family was secure and thus spent their energy developing their sense of personal responsibility. He suggests that natural and logical consequences could help a child develop personal responsibility. This aspect of his training agenda has remained very popular as an alternative to violent or manipulative control of children, and it is commonly taught in parenting education programs. Consequently, we will explore the use of natural and logical consequences in more depth.

Avoid Common Excesses

Natural and logical consequences are techniques that allow parents to avoid two very common excesses. Many parents in contemporary society believe that good parents should use communication to solve problems. Therefore, they talk through everything—or at least believe that they *should* talk through problems to find solutions. Their response is always "Let's talk about it"; they ask questions and offer explanations, whether the child participates or not. They may adopt a permissive style because they talk so much that they do not act.

Many other parents in contemporary society believe that it's only the softies who talk through everything and instead assert that kids need more action and less talking. What they often mean by "action" is punishment. This is the neighbor, relative, or stranger who witnesses a misbehaving child and says under his breath, "What that kid needs is a good spanking." They may adopt an authoritarian style because they act harshly and without consultation.

Each position is, from an Adlerian or Dreikursian position, a mistake of excess. While communication can (and should) be used to solve problems in families, it is possible to talk too much. Similarly, while action is sometimes called for, it is possible to jump too far up the parenting pyramid too quickly. The strategies of natural and logical consequences represent an intermediate response, one that avoids both of these excesses.

The excess of talking too much can be a problem because it teaches children not to listen. When words are not followed up with action, then the words lose their meaning. Parents find themselves exhausted from their constant verbal efforts that do not produce any behavior changes, and children adopt a self-centered and disrespectful habit of ignoring their parents. Excessive communication is described in the next section; it has been called "soft limits."

Similarly, the excess of jumping too quickly from communication to punishment can be a problem as well. Children whose behavior is controlled exclusively through punishment (a form of applied behavior analysis) do not internalize the reasons for behavioral controls. Therefore, they moderate their behavior only when they are supervised by a potentially rewarding or punishing authority figure, and they cannot think through how to behave in novel circumstances. We will address these problems (and others) with excessive behavioral approaches in Chapter 7. But for now, let's tentatively accept that sometimes parents must do more than talk: they must act, and that consequences are an option for action that does not carry some of the risks of punishment.

Firm (Not Soft) Limits

The use of consequences in order to avoid the excesses just described is built on the fundamental assumptions that 1) there must be consistency between words and actions; and 2) that parents can communicate with their child in a respectful way while still retaining parental authority. Words that are not supported by actions are essentially meaningless. Mackenzie (1998) calls them soft limits. Parents use **soft limits** when they attempt to verbally describe a rule or convey a boundary, but they do so ineffectively. They actually convey that the rule is optional. Mackenzie says that there are two types of soft limits: when the verbal message itself is unclear and when the verbal message is not supported by actions.

Examples of soft limits where the verbal message is unclear include:

- **Wishes and hopes.** This is when the parent says what he wishes or hopes will happen, rather than directly telling the child what to do. For instance, "I really wish you would come in and eat dinner with us." Or "I sure hope that lawn is mowed before I get home tonight." These are essentially failed attempts at I-messages. They do not share a parental feeling, so they cannot work as an I-message. No emotional connection has been formed; therefore, the expectation simply has no power to motivate. In addition, they cannot work as a limit because the expectation has not been stated clearly.
- **Addenda.** Adding messages onto the end of an original statement makes it seem that the first message can be ignored. These are the "I mean it" and "I said to do it now" comments that parents add on after instructing a child's behavior. When a parent adds "I mean it" after a command, that implies that the parent did not mean it when the command was first offered. As a result, addenda send a destructive double message, one that is simply unclear.
- **Nonspecific instructions.** Sometimes parents are vague in a misguided attempt to be polite; for instance, telling a child not to stay out "too late" or to "be nicer" to a younger sibling. These instructions are easy to violate because kids can always claim not to have understood that "too late" meant "after midnight," since it was never stated. And even if the child is not intentionally violating the rule, most human beings will interpret a vague instruction in the way they want to hear it, so these messages are often genuinely misunderstood.
- **Questions.** Parents sometimes ask a question rather than deliver an instruction, such as "Do you think it's about time for your bath?" Again, this is often in a misguided attempt to be polite. After all, adults asking guiding questions rather than offering direct instruction is a way to soften

a direction. But what works with cognitively mature adults does not always work with children. Cognitive development shapes the way verbal messages are understood. Children in Piaget's concrete operational stage, for instance, will take these messages in the most literal (that is, concrete) way possible, as they are not capable of abstract thinking. Hence, they may really believe that the parent is asking if they want to take a bath, and so truthfully answer no and then be confounded by why the parent is angry with that "smart remark."

While these soft limits are just unclear verbal messages, others are verbal messages that are not supported by action. Examples include:

- **Repeating and reminding.** Parents do this when a problem remains unresolved, but the parent simply keeps offering the instruction without more direct action. It is talking too much. Even if the message was originally offered in the form of a perfect I-message or a textbook example of win-win problem solving, if the issue is not resolved, just repeating the message over again simply does not help. For instance, the kids might be fighting over what channel to watch on the television, and the parent offers an I-message about how their bickering is loud and interfering with her task. She might coach them through win-win problem solving. But the bickering continues. The parent might say "I expect you two to talk about this to find a solution instead of physically fighting," and then later says, "What did I tell you? Talk this through, please!" But the fighting continues and the parent allows it. This is essentially a failed attempt at win-win problem solving. If the parent facilitated the sharing of emotions and brainstorming of solutions, this is more likely to work, but even then, sometimes it just doesn't. In that case, the parent must stop talking and start acting.
- **Ineffective follow-through.** Rules are stated, and then violations are simply ignored. Enforcement is difficult, so parents just let it slide. Parents sometimes bemoan that it's easier just to do the chore themselves than to get the child to do it. Or they see the child eating a cookie before dinner, but they just don't have the energy to deal with the situation, so they pretend not to see. Another form of ineffective follow-through is when parents continually offer explanations for the rule—even while the child is violating the rule—hoping that the explanation will convince them, but it doesn't work. The parent might say, "Honey, if you eat that now, you

won't be hungry for dinner." The child takes a bite. The parent continues, "But then an hour later, you're going to be hungry, because that cookie simply won't fill you up." The child takes another bite. And so on. The parent keeps explaining while the child keeps violating the rule. It is easy for someone on the outside to see that the parent should stop talking and do something about the cookie, but sometimes it's harder to see for the person who is caught in the cycle.

Soft limits are bad for everyone in the family. The parent grows frustrated by his or her ineffectiveness and exhausted by the constant verbal attempts at gaining cooperation. The parent is bound to feel dismissed and unimportant and therefore also feel pushed into an angry, authoritarian stance. In addition, the child adopts behaviors that are incredibly destructive to his or her own wellbeing. Ignoring the instructions or wishes of authority figures is a habit that will interfere with the child's ability to be successful in school and work settings. They may also put themselves into danger if they do not accept the guidance of loving adults.

Therefore, the solution is to use firm limits. **Firm limits** send a clear message about rules and expectations, and that message is consistently supported by both words and actions. Chapter 5 offered PET communication strategies that address the need for clarity in verbal messages. I-messages <u>must</u> describe behavior specifically, objectively, and without judgment. Therefore, the message about behavior is clear when parents use the PET communication strategies. That brings us to the question of how to follow up with action. How do we retain a mutually respectful relationship with children while also asserting parental authority through action?

Natural Consequences

The first option for action (the technique lowest on the pyramid above communication) is the use of natural consequences. A **natural consequence** is simply what happens, without any intervention at all, when the child makes a choice. If a child doesn't eat breakfast, he will get hungry. If he refuses to wear a jacket on a cold morning, he will be cold. If he stays up until 4:00 a.m. playing video games, he will be tired the next day. Natural consequences are less likely to damage the parent-child relationship than are logical consequences because the parent need not be involved directly. The outcome is something that happens without any contrivance whatsoever.

The technique is quite simple in principle. There are only two steps: first, allow the consequence to occur without interference; and second, use active listening afterward to help the child learn from the consequence. The first step, allowing the consequence, means that parents must step back and watch. They must allow their children to make mistakes, obvious mistakes, and "suffer the consequences." That's hard to do for loving parents who have been practicing sensitive responsiveness, nurturing a secure attachment, and tending carefully to their children's needs. It hurts parents to see their children suffer, and many intervene to reduce suffering as often as they can. They simply have a hard time allowing natural consequences. But they might get into the habit of intervening so often that the child is actually prevented from learning valuable lessons. Their natural and admirable desire to protect and nurture might not always be in the child's best interests. The notion of an "overprotective" parent is widely recognized in our society; it is not a new concept. But it is difficult for a parent who is deeply immersed in the situation to recognize, in any given circumstance, if they are being overprotective. That is the difficulty.

The second step is to employ active listening (from Chapter 5) for the resulting child-owned problem. The child who sleeps late and doesn't pack his lunch is hungry all day at school. The child comes home hungry and cranky. This is a classic child-owned problem. The parent wants for the child to actually learn a lesson from this experience; which is to say, the parent wants the child to find a solution to his problem. The solution is obvious, of course: the child needs to pack himself a lunch instead of going to school empty-handed. But the child has to arrive at this conclusion himself. Therefore, the parent empathizes with the child by reflecting his feelings. For example, "Oh, you must have been so hungry! It must have been hard to get through the day!" Once the parent and child have connected emotionally, once they have become allies here, the parent then asks, "I bet you don't want that to happen again. What will you do to prevent it?" This is the problem-solving aspect of active listening, and this where the parent hopes the child will conclude that perhaps he should get up a little earlier or maybe make his lunch at night before he goes to bed. Active listening.

Why is the parent so gentle with the child? Why can't the parent say something like "I have told you dozens of times to get up a little earlier to make your lunch! I told you this would happen!" After all, it's true. Won't a little "I told you so" send the message home more forcefully than sympathy? The answer is no, it won't. A recrimination actually has the opposite effect. It generally eliminates any chance that the child will process the experience at all and learn anything from it. The reason is that the child must face his or her poor decision directly. It can be embarrassing or humiliating. No one likes to admit that they made a stupid decision or made an error in judgment. If instead, they can be angry at someone else for the painful consequence, they will choose that option. So if the parent is recriminating, the child will simply choose to be angry at the parent for his or her coldness and thereby avoid the uncomfortable feelings of embarrassment, shame, or guilt. For the child to learn from his or her choice, the parent must be seen as an ally, to be on the child's side, and emotionally supportive of the child.

Natural consequences work very well for learning responsibility with regard to biological realities. Natural consequences are very effective, for instance, in helping children learn to eat something before heading out on an excursion, to get plenty of sleep before a busy day, to pack a lunch before school, or to wear a coat when it's cold outside.

For example, I grew up in the Midwest, with cold and snowy winters. Even as a teenager, I loved the outdoors and hiked often with my dad, even in the dead of winter. I spent one miserable December day on a hike with my dad, having worn thin socks inside my boots. I could not get warm. My thin socks did not fill the boots, so I chafed in addition to being cold. Plus, snow had gotten in and melted, so my thin socks were also wet. I remember my dad's kindness and sympathy when he learned how miserable I was. He tried to help. Without a spare pair of socks, there was not much to be done except cut the hike short and return home. But we were hiking with other people and did not have our own vehicle, so we had to negotiate with others when we would leave. That meant that I was miserably cold and uncomfortable for a good part of the day. That day was all it took for me to learn the lesson that socks, dry and thick socks, are essential for winter hiking. I still take an extra pair of socks with me when I hike because I learned from natural consequences that lack of preparation makes for an unpleasant hike. Biological realities are easy to learn through natural consequences, when children are allowed the freedom to make the choice that will result in a natural consequence, and parents respond with empathy and kindness.

Another type of problematic behavior that can be ameliorated by natural consequences is carelessness with personal possessions. Toys that are left strewn around on the floor sometimes get stepped on and broken. Toys left lying in the yard get stolen or rained on. Small items are easily lost when insufficient care is taken to protect them. It is sometimes difficult for parents to respond with empathy to these child-owned problems because they repeatedly warned the child of the risks and were ignored. Therefore, opportunities to learn from natural consequences such as these are often missed in a flurry of indignant parental "I-told-you-so" messages and the child's resentment of the parent's coldness. Instead, simple active listening can change the despair over a lost earring into a child-initiated plan to always put earrings where they belong instead of setting them down to take care of later.

Logical Consequences

Despite how effectively natural consequences can teach many lessons, sometimes they are not appropriate and thus should be replaced by logical consequences. One such circumstance is when the natural consequence is simply too extreme or dangerous to be allowed. For instance, parents can't allow their child to ride a bicycle out into the street without proper safety precautions in anticipation that they will learn from the natural consequence of being hit by a car. It's just too extreme. While it may be okay to let a child go to school without a jacket on a mild spring morning, it's probably not okay to let a child go out for the day without a jacket in the driving snow. Playing on a rocky cliff or wading near the top of a waterfall are also simply too dangerous. Some social interactions are also quite dangerous. Early sexual activity places kids at great risk, both emotionally and physically. Secret accounts on social media make them frighteningly vulnerable to adult predators. To their horror, every new parent discovers that the world is quite full of life-threatening dangers. As a result, parents must carefully monitor their children's choices and consciously decide if the natural consequences can be allowed or if intervention (in the form of a logical consequence instead) is necessary.

Another circumstance when natural consequences are not appropriate and should be replaced with logical consequences is when the natural consequence will simply take too long to happen, and thus the child cannot learn from it. Examples include unhealthy eating habits, a refusal to brush one's teeth, regular sun bathing without sunscreen, and avoidance of a particular subject in school. It often takes decades before the natural consequences of overeating and indulging in a high-sugar diet catch up with children. Skin cancer doesn't appear until decades after unprotected sun exposure. Tooth decay takes months, at least, and often years. Poor grades in school or avoiding a particular subject may seem like a good idea to the child until they can't get into college years later or until they are supporting a family on a minimum-wage income and wishing they had tried a little harder in school. All of these behaviors may, therefore, call for logical consequences instead of natural ones.

Logical consequences require parental intervention to be constructed. Instead of simply letting it happen, the parent must actively generate the consequence, and the parent must usually be present to enact and enforce the consequence. The parent is much more intimately involved, and that is the danger. When children see their parent actively involved in producing the consequence, they are more likely to blame the parent and direct their energy toward being angry at the parent.

The best practices for the use of logical consequences are quite a bit more complicated than for natural consequences. The steps are 1) offer choices; 2) enforce consequences; 3) active listening; and 4) give hope.

The first step is to offer choices. It must be obvious to the child that he or she is making a choice, and the consequences of the choices are known to the child in advance. This was not necessary with natural consequences because the outcomes of the choices were, well, natural and therefore automatically implied. But with logical consequences, the parent must spell it out in advance.

The child should be offered limited choices, and the child must be allowed to freely choose between the options. Choices, in and of themselves, often change the dynamic of the parent-child relationship. Remember that Dreikurs said that children sometimes misbehave in order to get power. He asserts that, in a democratic family, children will feel secure in their belonging, but they will want to assume responsibility. Choices allow that to happen. If children do not get choices, they will sometimes try to assert power, not because the issue is all that important to them, but because they simply wish to feel empowered because that helps them feel that they belong. So when a parent says, "It's time for bed," the child hears that the adult has issued the order and is in charge, and so the child realizes that he is not in charge, which makes him feel inferior. Because of his feeling of inferiority, he may try to assert power by saying, "I'm not going to bed! You can't make me!" which is a classic power struggle. The parent can prevent the power struggle by offering choices in the first place, choices that are limited to those acceptable to the parent. For instance, "Do you want to brush your teeth now or after you put on you pajamas?" or "Would you like to wear these pajamas tonight or this other pair?" or "What kind of toothpaste would you like to use tonight?" The child is empowered to be responsible for his own evening and thus has no need to engage in a power struggle.

But choices can also be used when a power struggle has already emerged. It changes the dynamic and sets up for the possible use of logical consequences. For example, if the parent told the child that it is time to brush his teeth, and the child replied that he is not ready to brush, then the parent can essentially ignore the protest and offer a choice of two different toothpaste types. This is an **either/or choice** because both options are equally acceptable to the parent. Examples of either/or choices include:

- "Either you make your lunch tonight before bed or in the morning before you go to school. If you choose to do it in the morning, I'll wake you up at 6:45 a.m."
- "Either you two can alternate who gets to pick a TV show, or you can find something that both of you agree on. I'll keep the television off until you come to a decision."
- "Either you get a ride to school with me, or you walk to school. If you want a ride, I'm leaving promptly at 8:00."

Either/or choices must include choices that are acceptable to both parent and child. There cannot be a "right choice" and a "wrong choice." Choices only work when they are true choices, giving the child the freedom to exercise their personal power. If the parent believes that one option is correct (for instance, "You can clean your room or just live like an animal in a barn for the rest of your life!") that is apparent, and this is experienced as a mean-spirited ultimatum rather than a true choice. The parent must not offer a choice that includes an option that is impractical or even impossible ("Come now, or we are never leaving the house again."). They have to be true options. Both options must also be acceptable to the child to be a true choice. If one "option" is a punishment, then it is not a true choice for the child (for example, "Clean your room now, or come here and get a spanking.").

Sometimes, either/or choices are simply not feasible. Another option is a **when/then choice**, to be used for circumstances when a behavior change is non-negotiable. When a specific behavior is required or a specific behavior must be stopped, the parent can connect that to something else that is logically related. Examples include:

- "When your room has been cleaned, then you may come out of it."
- "When you and your sister stop arguing over what to watch, then you may turn the TV back on."
- "You must stop hitting your sister. When you are ready to be with her without hitting, then you may join us here at the table."

The second step is to enforce the consequences. Whatever was "promised" in the choice must be acted upon. If the parent said that the TV is off until the children come to a decision about what to watch, then the TV must be turned off. This is not always easy. This is where parents heavily invest in the strategy. Their investment must be complete. A half-hearted attempt at using logical consequences will not work; that is what soft limits are. No, these limits must be firm. Parents must mean what they say and must act upon it.

Especially when parents first start using consequences like this after previously using soft limits, the children will test these new firm limits. They will get up and turn the TV back on, in which case the parent must turn it off again, maybe even confiscating the remote control or unplugging the device. If the parent said that toys not put away would be thrown away, then toys must be thrown away. If the parent said, "Stay in your room until …" then parents may have to direct children back into their rooms. For this reason, it is important to carefully consider the choice so as to avoid a potentially destructive showdown. For instance, when a child is throwing a fit in the grocery story, the parent could say: "Either you put the Sugar Bomb cereal back on the shelf now and we can finish shopping, or we're going back out to the car." This is fine for a toddler, but if the child is too old to easily be carried, this is a setup for an epic showdown. Another option might be: "Either you put the Sugar Bomb cereal back on the shelf now and we finish shopping, or I'm going out to the car to wait for you." Once the parent has left the building, the child knows that he doesn't have money to pay for the Sugar Bomb, and the parent is no longer serving as an audience, so eventually he will head out to the car for a ride home.

There are three guidelines with regard to logical consequences that are essential best practices. The first is that the consequence MUST be **logically related** to the misbehavior. What does it mean to be logically related? It must be obvious how the outcome is connected to the misbehavior. Fighting over the TV means the TV is turned off. Fighting over a toy means that the toy is taken away. In both of these cases, the consequence is very clearly related. The child can see easily how the consequence is simply a logical outgrowth of the misbehavior. Sometimes the parent must offer an explanation of how the consequence is logically tied to the misbehavior. The opposite is an outcome that is only arbitrarily (by the whim of the parent) related to the misbehavior, and that is, by definition, a punishment, not a consequence. The fact that speeding in a motor vehicle results in a monetary fine (i.e., a speeding ticket) that's an arbitrary relationship, so it's a punishment. But if misusing the vehicle means that the vehicle is confiscated or one's permission to drive is revoked, that's a logical consequence. It is clearly related. If a child is misusing an object (using a personal device long after bedtime, for instance) and loses her allowance, that is a punishment, because the device has nothing to do with money. On the other hand, if a child misuses the object and as a result has the object taken away, that IS logically related, and is therefore a logical consequence.

Logical consequences are far more powerful than punishments because of the logical connection. Punishments are distanced from the misbehavior and thus are seen as a price that must be paid. Think of parking tickets. Recently, when I was walking to my car (parked in a faculty parking lot on campus), I was walking closely behind a pair who appeared to be students. They were headed toward a car also parked in the faculty lot. One was asking the other how he had permission to park here, and the first explained that he did not, but he gets away with it so often that he's calculated he can afford to get three tickets a semester and it still costs less than if he buys a parking permit for student parking. Therefore, he parks in faculty parking until he gets two parking tickets, and then he starts buying day passes to park in a student parking lot. This is an example of how punishment (a monetary fine for parking, say), which is not logically related, can easily be thought of as a simple cost and not something that teaches a lesson about the misbehavior.

The next guideline for best practice is that the parent's tone during enforcement of the logical consequence MUST be **firm but friendly**. The firmness refers to the parent's steadfastness. The rule is the rule and will not be changed. The limit is firm. However, the friendliness refers to the parent's attitude toward the child during the enforcement of the rule. While the consequence will not

Table 6.2 Best Practices for Natural and Logical Consequences

	Natural Consequences	Logical Consequences
Beforehand	Nothing.	Choice is offered. • All must be acceptable. • No choice is a punishment. • Either/or if both options are acceptable. • When/then choice if unacceptable behavior must stop. • Offered only once.
Implementation	Allow consequence without intervention.	Enforce consequence. • Logically related to the misbehavior. • Firm but friendly tone. • Every time.
Afterward	Active listening.	Active listening. Give hope.

change, the parent can be kind about it. The firm-but-friendly rule is sometimes difficult because, by the time the consequence is enforced, the parent may be very angry and frustrated. But for this to work, the parent must be mature enough to find ways to control his or her behavior.

The "friendly" tone might in fact be neutral, matter-of-fact, but it must never include any hint of a derogatory attitude. The consequence must never be enforced along with criticism of the child's character or intelligence. That effectively changes the consequence into a punishment. Parents are not to set themselves up as an enemy of the child; they are the child's ally, even though the rule must be enforced. The hope is that the child will learn from the consequence, using the parent as an ally to help process the experience, rather than blaming the parent and using that as an excuse not to focus on their own misbehavior.

The final guideline for enforcing consequences is that, once the rule has been stated, it must be enforced **every time**. Enforcing it sometimes but not at other times sends a strong message that this is really something arbitrary, based on the whim of the adult, and thus is not a true rule. If the parent wants it to be taken seriously, the parent must be committed to enforcing it every time. If roller skates are not to be worn in the house, then they must be confiscated every single time the child rolls through the living room. If the parent ignores the behavior once, then the child learns that the true rule is something like "Don't wear roller skates in the house when Mom is in a bad mood, but when she's in a good mood, it's okay." As such, it's not about safety or damage to the wood floors, or anything logically related to the skates. If so, then this is arbitrary, not logical, and is therefore a punishment rather than a logical consequence.

After the logical consequence has been enforced, the next step is to use **active listening** to help the child process what he learned from the consequence. This works, of course, in the exact fashion described in Chapter 5. The child's choice created a child-owned problem. The child's roller skates have been confiscated, or the television has been turned off. Whatever the consequence, it has been enforced, and the outcome is unpleasant for the child. This is a critical moment. Will he cope with his discomfort by growing angry and resentful toward the person he sees as having victimized him, or will he be able to acknowledge that this is the result of his own choice, and is actually both fair and logical? For the latter to happen, the parent has already worked hard to assure that the choice was clear in the first place, that the consequence was clearly logically related, and the parent has maintained a firm but friendly tone in order to secure a position as an ally rather than an enemy. If all of those steps have been taken, then the parent will be able to step in at this critical moment and reflect the child's feelings. If all has gone well, the child accepts the empathy and uses the opportunity to problem solve and thus learn from the logical consequence how to make more responsible choices in the future.

Finally, the parent must **give hope** by specifying when the child will have another opportunity to demonstrate what he or she has learned. The ultimate goal of using this technique is not to make the child suffer, but to teach the child responsibility. Therefore, there must be another opportunity to make a choice. Ideally, the whole episode will end with a success, with the child having accomplished a new level of a personal responsibility. The child should, in the end, feel good about the lesson learned. Thus, after the consequence is enforced and after active listening has been used to help the child problem solve, the child needs another opportunity to make another choice. For instance, the parent should announce that the confiscated toy will be returned or the television remote returned at a particular point so that the child has another chance. "You'll have another chance after dinner," or "You'll have another chance tomorrow."

Example of the Use of Logical Consequences

The basic idea behind logical consequences is simple: people learn their lesson, as my mother used to put it, by "suffering the consequences." Parents have always realized that they might have to take part in constructing those consequences a bit, so as to "teach a lesson." For instance, I have a friend who tried smoking one of her father's cigarettes when she was only nine years old; he caught her in the attempt, and sat with her and forced her to smoke the whole pack. She was sick for days, vomiting and coughing and suffering the worst headache of her young life. Her dad believed he had really taught her a lesson! In truth, she was angry at him, felt rebellious toward him, and saw him as less than trustworthy from that point on. She started smoking that day, and didn't stop for the next 30 years. His lesson didn't work. Why not? Well, the basic idea of logical consequences makes sense, but implementation is tricky. Consequences don't work if the parent just has a general idea of how to do it; it backfires instead. Best practices are critical with this technique.

Since learning the best practices for logical consequences, I have used the technique with great success in my role as parent. I consider it to be one of the most potent tools I have at my disposal. However, I don't use it often. Frankly, I don't need to. The lessons of logical consequences are hard learned and enduring.

One of my great successes with the technique is still remembered by all of my children.

The misbehavior was dawdling in the morning, something that is very typical in households with school-age children. I left for work about the same time every morning that the kids needed to be at school, so I was in the habit of dropping them by school on my way to the university campus. But one of my daughters was, well, not a morning person. She was grumpy about waking up and wanted to stay in bed for a little longer. Then she just seemed to take forever to get dressed and brush her teeth and hair. She liked to daydream, or read a little, or watch something on TV. To eat breakfast and make a lunch? These seemed to be unsurmountable tasks! In her fourth-grade year (so she was about nine years old), this dawdling reached new heights. Not only was she always the last person out of the house, but she was often so late that they would arrive at school as the bell was ringing or shortly thereafter, forcing all the children to scramble to avoid a tardy notice and forcing me to rush onto campus only minutes before my first class. And not only that, but she had an unforgivably bad attitude about it, angrily harrumphing at anyone who said anything with classic preteen indignation. "Jeez! Stop having a cow! I'm coming!" and the like.

I tried I-messages. "Letty, I feel anxious today because you got in the car at 8:17, and so now I won't have time to prepare for my class." I tried facilitating win-win problem solving, helping the other girls to construct I-messages and helping them listen with empathy to Letty's reciprocal complaints. But the behavior did not improve. Finally, I decided that I had simply had enough. My annoyance had been building for months, but communication had not worked, and I wanted to solve the problem without exploding in anger. So I decided on a logical consequence.

Step 1: Offer the choice. One evening, I sat Letty down and told her that the morning routine would be changing, as of the very next day. It's not essential, but when possible, it's helpful to offer the choice when emotions are not already inflamed and when the child has enough time to consider it, which is why I did this the night before. This enhances the feeling of having made a choice, rather than feeling forced into a behavior. I offered an either-or choice: "Either you can ride in the car with me, or you can walk to school. If you want a ride, I will leave the house at 8:00." Either alternative really was okay with me; the school was only a few blocks away and the walk was perfectly safe. I made sure she understood by asking her to repeat it back to me. She understood. Either leave at 8:00 for a ride or leave later and walk herself to school. I was tempted to offer multiple reminders the next morning, but that nagging behavior had exhausted me and was part of why I wanted to do something different, so I toned it down. I reminded her first thing after waking her up, and I reminded her five minutes before departure time. I thought that was fair without being a nag.

Step 2: Enforce the consequence. That morning was difficult for me. I offered the early-morning reminder and then watched her dawdle as usual. Stopping to watch something on the television for "Just a minute, Jeez!" Zoning out while eating her breakfast. So I watched her dawdling but refrained from offering constant reminders. At 7:55 I offered a reminder, and then at 8:00 I announced, "Okay, I'm walking to the car. Anyone who wants a ride needs to come right now."

Is walking to school logically related to the misbehavior of dawdling? Yes, very clearly. If necessary, I would have reminded her of what I had already said in my previous I-messages, about needing to get to my office earlier in order to do my job well. The only way I could do that would be to leave home earlier. Therefore, I needed to leave earlier; she could come or not, it was her choice. This connection was absolutely crystal clear to Letty.

My tone was firm but friendly. I announced that I was leaving, and so I left. I was careful to keep any hint of judgment or anger out of my voice. I simply announced that I was leaving. I walked slowly to the car. As I backed out of the driveway, I watched carefully for any sign that she was coming. I proceeded far more slowly than was strictly necessary because I hoped that she would come. But she didn't. I did not race out of the house quickly in order to deprive her of any chance of choosing to get a ride to make sure she learned her lesson. There was no joy in this for me. No, implementing logical consequences is difficult for parents who have spent years protecting and nurturing their beloved little ones. As I turned the corner at the end of the street, I saw through my rear-view mirror that Letty had flung open the door, and stood aghast at the sight of the family car at the end of the road turning the corner. My heart broke for her. But I could not turn around and go back for her; that would make the whole exercise a textbook example of soft limits.

I drove the other girls to school, dropped them off, and then drove the same route back home, just to check on her. I saw her waiting at the stoplight to cross the street. She had a nervous, almost panicky look on her face. She had been running; I could tell by the way she was panting as she waited for the light. She was safe, but she was a little scared. Normally, she would be walking with her sisters, not by herself. And that's when I noticed that she had forgotten her backpack. I made a judgment call based on my knowledge of that particular child. I decided that getting to school without her backpack was more of a logical consequence than she needed. Please note that parents orchestrate logical consequences, and so parents can adjust them to fit the circumstances. In this case, I had seen the scared look on her face and, knowing my child, I assessed that she was at a level that she could handle, but that any more would not help. I don't know for sure if it was the right call, but it was the call I made, and I would make it again. So I went home and grabbed her backpack and drove it to school for her. Just as she was arriving at school, I pulled up next to her and got out with her backpack.

Steps 3 & 4: Active listening, and give hope. I wanted Letty to consider me an ally rather than the mean person who had done this to her, so the moment that we met was critical to the success of this consequence. I had to maintain my friendly tone. Thankfully, this was no problem. She looked up and saw me. I held up her backpack, and she realized for the first time that she had forgotten it. She gave me a big hug. I could tell she was a little scared, so I reflected her feelings by saying: "You look like you're a little scared." She was still hugging me, but she responded, "Yeah, but I made it to school, Mom!" She actually sounded proud of herself. I said "Yes, you did. Nice job." That's process-centered (descriptive) praise. I could have added "You'll have another chance tomorrow morning" to give hope, but in this particular case, it was unnecessary. She already had a feeling of success about this. She had walked to school by herself, and felt pretty good about it.

The next morning, and every morning for years afterward, Letty was ready to leave the house at 8:00 sharp. I never had to enact that particular consequence again. She still dawdles more than my other children. There are occasionally times when I wait for her in the car and honk the horn to remind her to hurry up. But it is only occasionally, and her attitude about it has greatly improved. Letty has this one pretty much under control thanks to a well-implemented logical consequence.

When Should Consequences Be Used?

As we move up the pyramid, notice that we grow more selective about use of the strategies. Way back down the pyramid, at the relationship level, there were no limits at all. At the communication level, the strategies we discussed are somewhat more selective in terms of when they are needed, but still carry no risk of overuse. But now we've moved onto a level of the pyramid that does carry some risk of overuse.

Rich Berrett (Berrett & Ramos, 2006) argues that moving into the Consequences and Applied Behavior Analysis levels of the pyramid constitute entering a **Danger Zone**. It is a danger zone because these strategies have the potential to damage the parent-child relationship. While I have argued in this chapter that natural and logical consequences require close parental supervision to asses risk and to help children process what they have learned, these strategies do require parents to step back and allow their children to suffer to some degree. This does not come easily when parents have been fostering an emotionally close nurturing and supportive relationship. It requires the parent to temporarily step outside of the relationship and exercise power over the child. The deliberate use of power might be reasoned in the child's best interest and closely monitored, but it is still the use of power, and power is generally antithetical to intimacy. Power threatens intimate relationships. Therefore, the use of power in a parent-child relationship is a dangerous thing. Simply put, it should not be used very much, or it will threaten the foundation of the relationship.

So while it is sometimes necessary to move into the danger zone, parents must be aware of the dangers and attempt to use other strategies instead when possible. That said, there are two basic reasons to move onto the Consequences level of the pyramid. First, to teach personal responsibility; second, when problem solving of parent-owned problems with I-messages was not successful. These circumstances may truly call for the use of natural and logical consequences, and parents should have access to these tools, but their use should remain fairly limited. If a parent notices that he or she is enforcing the same consequence repeatedly, then it is not working and needs to be reconsidered. Perhaps the parent is not following best practices. Or the misbehavior is reflecting a deeper problem than the typical developmental misbehaviors that call for consequences. If a consequence is being enforced frequently, something is wrong, and the strategy should be assessed because overuse is risky. Similarly, if a parent notices that he or she is enforcing multiple consequences several times per day, then that parent should consider the possibility of overreliance on consequences. In that case, the parent should consider using communication strategies instead to address some of the issues because it is risky to be in the danger zone too much of the time.

Developmental Connections

In their first year, babies operate basically on instinct. They do not decide on a course of action and then act that way. They simply act out impulses that are biologically imperative. Developmental psychologists note that **intentionality** (the ability to act with purpose toward a goal that was decided upon in advance), a component of the theory of mind, is really not present until sometime in the second year after birth. Therefore, infants are—and must be—protected from most natural consequences of their behavior. Caregivers must tenderly and patiently respond to their needs without expecting them to learn how to make good choices until at least the second year. And even then, the ability to make choices and follow through with actions is acquired rather gradually. Therefore, the strategies of natural and logical consequences are inappropriate for infants but can be used with toddlers and older children.

Developmentally, toddlers and adolescents are the most likely to push limits. Toddlers are working on a sense of autonomy, seeing themselves as separate from their parents and able to have preferences and skills apart from adults. This is normal and healthy, but it means that they will challenge adult authority as a matter of course. Teenagers too are busy establishing their own identities, and sometimes they do that by pushing back against the identity assumed from their parents. So they will also push limits. This is also normal and healthy. But these are the ages when consequences might be necessary a bit more often.

The best practices, though, do not change based on the child's age. Obviously, some factors vary by the age of the child: the nature of the choices offered and decisions about what consequences are safe and appropriate. But the process stays pretty much the same. One small variation worth mentioning is the final step of logical consequences: the offer of hope. When the child is very young, the next chance must happen quickly. As they get older, the next opportunity can come later. The key is that they must be able to see the events as contingent; they must cognitively be able to connect them as part of the same event. Hence, the timing must reflect the child's cognitive development.

How Parents React

Parents are generally excited to learn about the strategies of natural and logical consequences. Most parents do not like punishing their children but feel that they have been forced into it. They know that communication is not always adequate and believe that they must stop talking and act at times, but they do not feel good about the actions they've been taking so far, which are generally punitive. So the discovery that there are alternative actions to be taken is great news to them.

Some of the questions parents ask when they are just learning about consequences include:

Question: How many times do I have to impose a logical consequence before my child's behavior changes?
Answer: It depends on the age of the child and the nature of the misbehavior, of course, but generally speaking, the first time will have a major impact. Sometimes it is necessary to enforce a consequence two or three times because kids will test a new rule. But that should be it. It will change behavior almost immediately. If the consequence is not effective within two or three attempts, then the parent should explore whether best practices are being followed. The strategy should be reconsidered if it does not work quickly.

However, the misbehavior may gradually creep back into place, so the consequence may have to be enforced again months later. For example, when my children were younger, I had trouble with them leaving their things around the house. I would remind them to pick up after themselves, but sometimes it would get out of hand. So I created a "Saturday box." The choice was something like this: "I'm unhappy with your toys and papers left downstairs. So from now on, I'll give you one reminder. You can either put your things away then, or if you choose to leave your things out, I'll put them in the Saturday box. On Saturday, you'll have a chance to get them back." This is a logical consequence because they have a choice (an either/or choice: either clean up now or lose your personal possession until Saturday) and because the consequence (losing the possession until Saturday) is logically related to the misbehavior. When my children were little, the Saturday box would get a lot of use one week, very little use the next week, and then no use whatsoever for months. But the messiness would gradually creep back into their habits, and so every once in a while I had to break it out again. That seems normal. Messiness is an easy habit to fall into. Therefore, a reboot may sometimes be necessary. But the original boot-up won't take long at all.

Question: It seems like this will take an awful lot of effort! Is it difficult?
Answer: Yes, it will. These are not easy techniques to use, which may explain why they are so underused. In the moment, it is a lot easier to half-heartedly state a rule and then ignore infractions (soft limits;

characteristic of permissive parenting) or to explode in punitive anger (punishment; characteristic of authoritarian parenting). To use consequences requires thoughtfulness, close supervision, and careful consideration.

Plus, consequences for children often have consequences for parents too. I once had a colleague whose child was careless with a personal electronic device, leaving it in a semipublic place where it was stolen. The child took the device against parental advice and with the full knowledge that it might very well be stolen. But he did it anyway. Therefore, the loss of the device was the natural consequence. When the parent asked me what to do about this, I shrugged. It seemed to me that the boy was experiencing the natural consequence of his choice, and he would probably learn a valuable lesson. I suggested that the parents practice active listening. The dad looked at me blankly, clearly disappointed by my answer, but unable to rationally argue. Eventually, he admitted "But next week we're going to drive all the way to Seattle for Christmas with my parents. If he doesn't have something to play with on the car ride, it will be hard on all of us!"

Ah, yes. It is hard on the parents sometimes. And then the active listening can be an emotionally draining process, as we discussed in Chapter 5. So the effort required by the use of natural and logical consequences must be seen as either: a) something we do because parenthood simply requires it, the child simply needs this; or b) an investment that will prevent future problems, and thus make life easier in the long term, even though it is difficult in the short term. I believe it is both.

Question: Is time-out a logical consequence?
Answer: Time-out! It is one of the most beloved alternatives to spanking to arrive in the parenting education world. It is a darling of modern efforts to reduce harsh parenting. I believe parents (as pediatricians, parent educators, etc.) have jumped on the time-out bandwagon because, as I said above, parents really don't like administering harsh punishments. They do it because they feel disempowered, but if they had a better idea, most would happily relinquish punishment. And time-out has been presented as an alternative. As a result, it gets a lot of press.

So what is it? A logical consequence, or a punishment? The answer is it can be either, depending on how it's implemented. I believe that most time-outs are punishments. But the use of time-out as logical consequence can be powerful. In order to be a logical consequence (which is the only way it should be used, in my opinion), it must be:

- The condition on which a choice is made. Examples of when/then choices include: "When you are finished cleaning your room, then you may join us in the living room," or "When you are ready to be with your sister without physical violence, then you may join us in the living room." If children are sent to their room or to a naughty-spot for misbehavior without any element of choice, then the time-out is a punishment, not a logical choice.
- Logically related to the misbehavior. That is feasible if the misbehavior has to do with not dealing with other people in a respectful manner. If a child fights with siblings or talks back to adults, then it is logical to say that they may not interact with other people until they can do so respectfully. Time-out could also be a logical consequence if the misbehavior is not cleaning their room; it seems logical to say that the child must stay in their room until it is clean. But time-out for anything else? Well, I don't see the logical nature, and therefore, it is a punishment.
- It must be administered with a firm but friendly tone. The apocryphal "Go to your room!!!!" is NOT firm but friendly—it is punitive, angry, and judgmental.

Time-outs are used more often as punishment than as logical consequences. In my opinion, that is why they don't work as well as folks wish they would. They are subject to all of the limitations of any other kind of punishment, which we will discuss in Chapter 7. But time-outs can be used as logical consequences instead of punishment. If best practices are followed, they can be successful.

The biggest issue with parents' reactions to learning about natural and logical consequences is that this technique is difficult to use. Parents are excited when they hear about it and go home enthused. But they fall into old habits and continue to use punishments, merely calling them "consequences." They say things like "You have CHOSEN to give up your right to use the car by your poor school performance! You must live with the consequences of your own decision!" They often say this angrily. The "consequence" in this case is not logically related to the misbehavior, it was not freely chosen, and it is enforced in anger. Thus, it is not a consequence; it is a punishment. But the parent uses the language of the democratic family and so convinces himself that he's using a fundamentally new technique when he is not.

Why do so many parents fall into this trap? Natural and logical consequences seem to be really difficult to grasp. Why so hard? I think there are two reasons: 1) Conceptually, it's so simple that parents get the basic idea and just assume it will be that easy to implement, when implementation is actually trickier than they thought; and 2) the use of consequences really does force people to think in a more democratic way than they are used to doing with their children. Parents like being in charge in their own home. Willingly giving up that power in favor of democratic relationships is harder than it would seem. Many parents just can't do it.

I believe that the only way around this challenge is to address the topic of consequences during multiple sessions. The parent educator must teach the idea, let parents go home and try it out, and then process with them what happened when they tried it out. At that point, the parent educator can point out where they have strayed from best practices, assuring them that this is normal so they don't just give up on the idea. But parents need to process this idea more than once.

Programs and Critique

Adler himself is a controversial figure. Among contemporary scientists in psychology, he is tarnished by his association with Sigmund Freud. He shared one of Freud's traits in that he wasn't actually a scientist himself. He theorized about the nature of personality, the self, and child development, but he didn't conduct any research on any of these topics. Unfortunately, neither did his students go on to empirically test his theoretical assertions.

One of Adler's most famous assertions, the inferiority complex, is utterly untestable, and therefore does nothing to advance the science of psychology. It is untestable because there is no way to know if a person actually feels inferior; it is simply not directly observable. Perhaps his other most famous assertion, that birth order affects personality development in specific ways, has been researched with disappointing results. Some say that Adler's notion of birth order effects have been thoroughly discredited (e.g., Watkins, 1992). While it prompted a very important line of research on the effects of family constellation on development, his specific assertions have not been supported. Furthermore, as discussed in Chapter 4, the Adlerian notion of encouragement has not been supported by research and is not entirely consistent with the truly evidence-based concept of process-centered feedback. With these significant reasons to mistrust the Adlerian tenets of individual psychology, the whole argument seems to rest on a tenuous foothold.

On the other hand, Adlerian parenting programs are perhaps the most widespread in popular parenting literature. The all share in common the goals of reducing reliance on punishment while increasing understanding and warm communication, combined with reasonable limit setting (Lindquist & Watkins, 2014). In other words, they promote an authoritative parenting style, which has been clearly demonstrated to produce the best outcomes for children and families. Furthermore, evaluation research confirms that Adlerian programs generally succeed in producing more authoritative parenting practices, especially by reducing harsh punishment (McVittie & Best, 2009) and by helping parents see their children more favorably (Mullis, 1999). Therefore, Adlerian/Dreikursian parenting programs remain widespread and well respected.

Adlerian/Dreikursian parenting programs generally combine the PET communication strategies discussed in Chapter 5 with encouragement (similar to process-centered descriptive praise) and consequences into one package. The programs include Systematic Training for Effective Parenting (http://www.step-publishers.com/), Parenting with Love and Logic (https://www.loveandlogic.com), Active Parenting (http://activeparenting.com), and Positive Discipline Parenting (http://www.positiveparenting.com). These programs offer books directly marketed to parents (e.g., Dinkmeyer & McKay, 1996; Cline & Fay, 2006; Popkin, 2014; and Nelsen, 2006) as well as prepackaged programs for parent educators (even those with little or no training in parenting education) to purchase and facilitate, and online classes available directly to parents.

The main criticism leveled at Adlerian/Dreikursian programs is that the distinction between consequences and punishment is sometimes lost on people, even smart people, who criticize the whole concept. They say that "consequences" is just a way to disguise punishment with a more politically correct label. See Alfie Kohn (Kohn, 2006) for an example of a scathing critique based on a fundamental misunderstanding of the concept. I take from this a huge warning: be careful! People don't easily grasp the distinction. It seems clear enough to me, but watch out, not everyone gets it. As I said above, I think it's not that easy to implement, and it requires a fundamental shift toward a democratic ideology. Therefore, people have a hard time with this. And yet teaching about natural and logical consequences has been shown to shift parenting toward a more authoritative style, and we know that is good. So I come down strongly in support of these programs.

Review and Reflection Questions

1. What are the two reasons for using natural and logical consequences?

2. What did Adler say is the goal of human beings? How does that lead to the most important goal of a parent?

3. What are the four goals of misbehavior? How can a parent identify each goal? How does Adler recommend responding to each? Can you think of an example of each?

4. How can limits be soft? Firm? Which is more effective, and why?

5. When should natural consequences be used? What are the best practices for their use? When are natural consequences inappropriate? Can you think of an example of natural consequences in your life?

6. What are the steps and best practices of logical consequences? Can you think of an example of logical consequences in your life?

7. When should either/or choices be given? When should when/then choices be given? Why?

8. Why are consequences in the danger zone? Why is it dangerous? Why use it, even if it is dangerous?

9. How quickly do consequences work to change behavior?

10. Are time-outs a logical consequence? How can you tell?

11. Is there evidence that Adlerian programs are effective?

Terminology to Know

- Danger zone
- Democratic family
- Discouragement
- Either/or choice
- Encouragement
- Firm but friendly
- Firm limits
- Goal of attracting attention
- Goal of displaying inadequacy
- Goal of obtaining power
- Goal of retaliation
- Individual psychology
- Inferiority
- Intentionality
- Logical consequence
- Natural consequence
- Social belonging
- Social discipline model
- Soft limits
- When/then choice

Names to Know

- Adler
- Dreikurs

References

Baumrind, D. (1971). Current patterns of parental authority. *Developmental Psychology Monographs, 4*, 1–102.

Berrett, R.D., & Ramos, K.D. (Eds.) (2006). *Engaged parenting.* Pearson Custom Publishing.

Cline, F., & Fay, J. (2006). *Parenting with Love and Logic: Teaching children responsibility.* Boulder, CO: NavPress.

Dreikurs, R., Cassel, P., & Ferguson, E.D. (2004). *Discipline without tears (rev. ed.).* Toronto, Canada: Wiley.

Dinkmeyer, D., & McKay, G.D. (1996). *Raising a responsible child.* New York: Fireside.

Kohn, A. (2006). *Unconditional parenting: Moving from rewards and punishments to love and reason.* Atria Books.

Lindquist, T.G., & Watkins, K.L. (2014). Modern approaches to modern challenges: A review of widely used parenting programs. *Journal of Individual Psychology, 70, 2,* 148–165.

Mackenzie, R.J. (1998). *Setting limits: How to raise responsible independent children by providing clear boundaries.* Random House.

Masud, H., Thurasamy, R., & Ahmad, M.S. (2015). Parenting styles and academic achievement of young adolescents: A systematic literature review. *Quality and Quantity: International Journal of Methodology, 49, 6,* 2411–2433.

McVittie, J., & Best, A.M. (2009). The impact of Adlerian-based parenting classes on self-reported parental behavior. *Journal of Individual Psychology, 65, 3,* 264–285.

Mullis, F. (1999). Active Parenting: An evaluation of two Adlerian parent education programs. *Journal of Individual Psychology, 55, 2,* 225–232.

Nelsen, J. (2006). *Positive discipline.* New York: Random House.

Orgler, H. (1976). Alfred Adler. *International Journal of Social Psychiatry, 22, 1,* 67–68.

Popkin, M. H. (2014). *Active Parenting: A parent's guide to raising happy and successful children, 4th edition.* Atlanta: Active Parenting Publishers.

Shulman, B.H., & Dreikurs, S.G. (1974). The contributions of Rudolf Dreikurs to the theory and practice of individual psychology. *Journal of Individual Psychology, 34, 2,* 153.

Sleddens, E. F. C., Gerards, S.M.P., Thijs, C., deVries, N.K., & Kremers, S.P.J. (2011). General parenting, childhood overweight and obesity-inducing behaviors: A review. *International Journal of Pediatric Obesity, 6, 2,* e12–e27.

Stein, H.T., & Edwards, M.E. (1998). Classical Adlerian theory and practice. In P. Marcus & A. Rosenberg (Eds.), *Psychoanalytic versions of the human condition: Philosophies of life and their impact on practice.* New York University Press.

Watkins, C.E. (1992). Birth-order research and Adler's theory: A critical review. *Individual Psychology: Journal of Adlerian Theory, Research, and Practice, 48, 3,* 357–368.

7. Applied Behavior Analysis

Introduction

We have now arrived at the very top of the parenting pyramid. We have studied the formation and maintenance of relationships and the use of communication strategies to teach and to solve problems, as well as natural and logical consequences to teach personal responsibility. Now we are at the last set of strategies on the pyramid: applied behavior analysis.

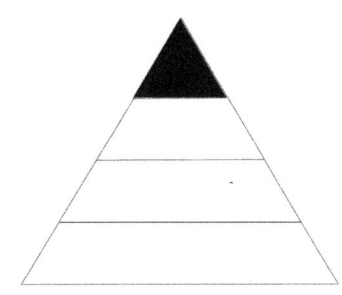

Figure 7.1 Behavior Analysis on Pyramid

Behavioral strategies are often what parents hope to get out of a parenting class. The tools are powerful and yield immediate results. Conceptually, they are easy to understand, and parents (as well as teachers, employers, politicians, etc.) rush to use them because they are intuitive and the exercise of power is sometimes gratifying. But they are overused and very often not used correctly. Therefore, they do not live up to their promise, and instead often become a mechanism for the destruction of the parent-child relationship, as well as the maintenance of undesirable behaviors. Behavioral strategies need to be limited in their scope and applied according to specific guidelines, and then they can be a useful part of parenting.

Theory and Background

Applied behavior analysis is a collection of strategies based on the theory of behaviorism, including conditioning, extinction, reward, and punishment. These are last-resort strategies in parenting, to be used sparingly and only under the strictest of circumstances.

Behaviorism

Behaviorism rose to prominence in the United States in the early 20th century, coincidentally just when expert parenting advice was first emerging. Much of the earliest expert parenting advice, therefore, was based on the principles of behaviorism. John Watson himself wrote a popular (i.e., nonacademic) book of advice about parenting (Watson, 1928). In it, Watson recommended emotional distance between parents and children, suggesting that warmth and affection are rewards that should be offered discretely only when the child's behavior deserves to be rewarded. The effect of the early prominence of behaviorism in professional parenting advice has lingered and shaped mainstream parenting advice. This is where the idea that picking up a crying baby will spoil him or her came from, as well as the notion that young children shouldn't be coddled but rather toughened up for the real world. These ideas are generally considered by developmental psychologists and family scientists to be problematic bits of folklore that damage children and family relationships.

The essential argument of **behaviorism** is that human beings are shaped largely by their socialization (nurture rather than nature) and that their behaviors are determined primarily by the consequences of those behaviors. In the early 1900s, they made this argument in opposition to the eugenics movement, which was popular at the time. Behaviorists made the case that much (or most) of human behavior is learned through the mechanisms of reward and punishment. Children (all people, really) learn to engage in behaviors that are rewarded, and they learn to avoid behaviors that elicit punishment or that simply fail to provide any reward. An assumption of behaviorism is that behavior is completely dependent on this process of rewards and punishments, such that power is the ultimate determinant of behavior. In its most radical form, advocated by B.F. Skinner, behaviorism entails the belief that free will does not exist. All behavior is therefore shaped by contingencies and does not reflect the choice of the actor (Skinner, 1971).

If this is true, then parents are ultimately responsible for their children's behavior and supremely capable of transforming their children into responsible citizens. Accepting this theoretical premise can both induce parent blaming and help parents to feel empowered. I think it is too extreme. Parents are simply not as powerful as the theory would suggest. However, there are strategies derived from behaviorism that can be useful.

Pavlov: Classical Conditioning

The story of the theory of behaviorism starts in the early 1900s with Ivan Pavlov, a Nobel Prize–winning Russian physiologist. He studied digestion in dogs and noted that over time, the dogs began to salivate before food was presented to them, suggesting that they had been conditioned to know that it was coming (Pavlov, 1927). He confirmed this suspicion by pairing an auditory stimulus (he used buzzers and whistles, among other sounds) with the food, thereby producing the natural biological reaction of salivation. Then he presented the auditory stimulus with no food and elicited the same biological reaction. He called this a "conditioned reflex" because salivation is a biological reflex and thus innate, but it could be generated by repeated pairing of the natural, or **unconditioned, stimulus** (food in this case) with a neutral stimulus (in this case, the sound of a bell or whistle or buzzer) to condition the animal to salivate even without the natural trigger. (See Figure 7.2.) Once the neutral stimulus elicits the biological reflex, it is then a **conditioned stimulus**. This process has come to be known as **classical conditioning**, and its discovery effectively launched the new theory of behaviorism.

Because there must be a natural stimulus of an unconditioned, biological response to start with, the intentional use of classical conditioning is limited to these circumstances. The physiologically driven responses of hunger and tiredness provide opportunities for intentional conditioning around mealtimes and bedtime, but it is hard to imagine other uses. Instead, conditioning is something that generally happens accidentally. In fact, Pavlov only discovered conditioning

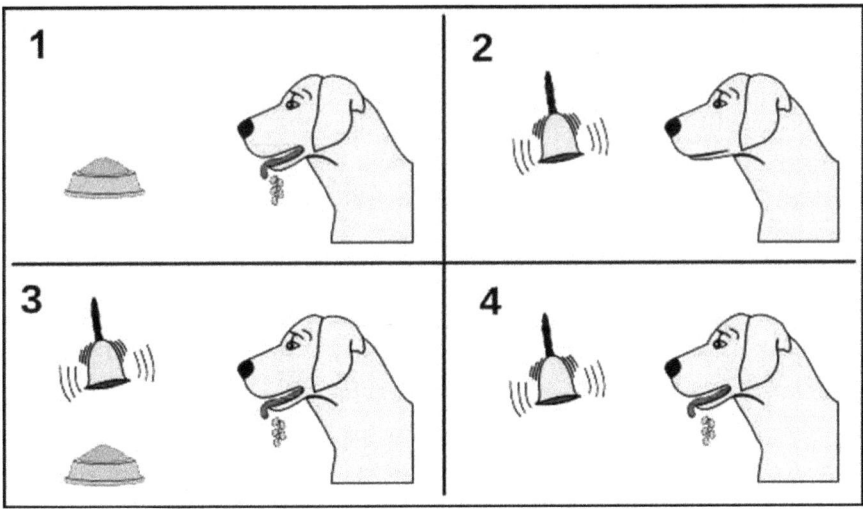

Figure 7.2 Classical Conditioning

when he noticed that the dogs he studied started salivating when the food handler appeared before any actual food had been presented. This gave him the idea to intentionally pair a neutral stimulus with the food. But originally, it happened unintentionally (Crain, 2010). Pavlov's genius was that he recognized how this had happened and its significance for understanding learning.

Conditioning often happens accidentally in a family environment when patterns of behavior are noticed by the child, even though the parent didn't intend to create an association. For instance, when my youngest daughter was a toddler, she started crying every time I put on my tennis shoes. Eventually, I realized that I had conditioned her to cry when I donned my tennis shoes because I had paired that with my leaving the house to exercise, which naturally triggered her sadness because of her developmental stage. She had grown to expect that if I put the shoes on, it meant I was leaving and she wanted her mommy at home, as is developmentally normal for a toddler. This **accidental conditioning** is done far more often than any intentional conditioning.

Contemporary behavior analysts are very concerned with identifying antecedents of problematic behaviors such as accidentally conditioned associations, and so we will return to this concept in more detail below.

Extinction is a strategy employed to intentionally unlearn something that has been accidentally conditioned. With extinction, the conditioned stimulus (in the case of Pavlov's dogs, the bell or whistle) is offered multiple times without being associated with the unconditioned stimulus (in the case of Pavlov's dogs, the dog food). After multiple events disassociating the stimuli, then the dog will stop salivating at the sound of the bell or whistle (Pavlov, 1928). The learned behavior can therefore be extinguished. In the case of my shoes, if I had purposely donned the tennis shoes and stayed home and done this multiple times, I could have extinguished the conditioning that caused my child to cry when I put on the shoes. After a behavior has been extinguished through the process of extinction, it can be reconditioned (relearned) quite easily.

Watson: Application to Parenting

Contemporary to Ivan Pavlov, a psychologist at Johns Hopkins University in Baltimore named John B. Watson was eagerly working toward transforming psychology into a science by objectively studying behaviors rather than speculating about mental processes. Watson is credited with successfully establishing the psychological school of behaviorism (Bolles, 1993), in no small part through publication of an article that outlined the features of this new position. He wrote in that article: "Psychology as the behaviorist views it is a purely objective experimental branch of natural science. Its theoretical goal is the prediction and control of behavior. Introspection forms no essential part of its methods" (Watson, 1913).

In the years that followed, Watson recognized the significance of Pavlov's work on classical conditioning as the exposition of some of the first behaviorist principles. He was also the first to apply psychological learning theories, primarily classical conditioning, to the domain of parenting. For instance, he wrote that babies are conditioned to love their mothers because "love" is an unconditioned response to the unconditioned stimulus of being touched tenderly. Therefore, babies are conditioned to love their mothers because mothers begin as a neutral stimulus that is frequently paired with the unconditioned stimulus of touch. As a result, the baby learns to associate the mother with affectionate feelings and thus is conditioned to love her (Crain, 2010).

Watson applied classical conditioning to human infants most famously with his Little Albert experiment. He demonstrated that an infant could be conditioned to show fear of a small furry animal and by extension, many furry things, just by pairing the furry thing (which was initially a neutral stimulus; he used a rat, a rabbit, a dog, and others) with something that the baby was inherently afraid of (the unconditioned stimulus; in this case, a loud noise). Little Albert grew to associate the furry animals with the loud noise and began to demonstrate fear of those objects, which were thereby converted into conditioned stimuli. Little Albert generalized his conditioning by showing fear of other furry things as well (Watson & Rayner, 1920), as in Figure 7.3.

Now he fears even Santa Claus

Figure 7.3 Little Albert Experiment

Watson was forced to leave academia in 1920 after a widely publicized extramarital affair with his research assistant, whom he later married. The scandal forced him out of his chosen career as a scientist, and he was forced to turn to find alternative ways of making a living. One such alternative was his work in the realm of parenting education with a parent advice book based on the principles of behaviorism (Watson, 1928). The book recommended treating children as if they were little adults, withholding love and affection so that they do not have unrealistic expectations of the larger world. The emotional detachment that he recommended has been roundly criticized, and Watson later said he regretted giving parenting advice, saying that he didn't have enough knowledge specific to that application (O'Donnell, 1985). Nonetheless, his advice was well received, his book was very popular (Hergenhahn, 2005), and the behaviorist perspective dominated parenting advice of the early 20th century. We still live with this legacy.

Skinner: Operant Conditioning

B.F. Skinner was an American psychologist who was influenced by the work of John Watson to study psychology, and he continued to define the theory of behaviorism in the decades following the departure of Watson from academia. He shared with Watson a radical emphasis on observable behavior. He considered internal processes (thoughts and feelings) to be forms of behavior. As such, he believed that thoughts and feelings do not *cause* behavior; they *are* behavior. Just as Watson conditioned Little Albert to feel fear, all human feelings might be the product of such conditioning.

Behavior, according to Skinner, is a response to a stimulus. An **operant response** is simply a behavior that occurs spontaneously in response to some stimulus. Skinner identifies the process by which operant responses can be intentionally conditioned and subsequently modified by reinforcement and punishment. He discovered that complex behaviors could be shaped and strengthened by teaching the subject to expect a consequence of that behavior. This allows for modification of a much wider range of behaviors than does classical conditioning. Skinner calls the use of reinforcers and punishers **operant conditioning** and describes how it works (Skinner, 1953).

Rewards, more technically called reinforcers, are desirable outcomes of a specific behavior that increase the likelihood that the behavior will be repeated (Skinner, 1953). (I will use the terms *reward* and *reinforcer* interchangeably.) A reward can be getting something desirable, called **positive reinforcement** (for instance, getting dessert if you eat dinner, getting a dollar if you wash the dishes), or it can be getting out of something undesirable, called **negative**

reinforcement (for instance, you don't have to take the final exam if you already have an A in the class, or you don't have to wash dishes if you work on that homework assignment). Reinforced behaviors can be extinguished in the same way that conditioning can be extinguished (Crain, 2010).

Punishment is an undesirable outcome of a specific behavior that decreases the likelihood that the behavior will be repeated (Skinner, 1953). A **positive punishment** is something aversive (a scolding or a spanking, perhaps), while a **negative punishment** is losing something pleasant (losing the use of a cell phone or the car, for instance). Skinner describes punishment as a mechanism of operant conditioning but does not advocate that it be used intentionally. He thought punishment should not be used because it produces only short-term behavior change (Skinner, 1938) and leads children to avoid the punisher but not necessarily to avoid the behavior that induces the punishment (Skinner, 1953). Behavior analysts generally recommend that instead of using punishment to reduce an undesirable behavior, parents use extinction combined with positive reinforcement of an alternative, more desirable behavior (Crain, 2010).

Please note that operant conditioning through reinforcement and punishment can occur accidentally, just as classical conditioning can. These are powerful mechanisms for learning, and they sometimes happen independently of the parent's wishes. Just as with accidental classical conditioning, it is an important skill for parents to be able to identify when **accidental reinforcement or punishment** has happened. For instance, kids are sometimes rewarded accidentally for misbehavior. Imagine a teenager who is supposed to come home by 11:00 p.m. but misses the curfew. If he comes home at 11:10, just a mild infraction, he encounters the angry parent and suffers the punishment of the parental scolding. But if he decides to just party on and doesn't stumble home until 2:30 a.m., the parent may be asleep by then. The teen has avoided the punishment and therefore been negatively reinforced for dramatically violating his curfew. This was not the parent's intent, obviously, but the parent is a fallible human being who got sleepy and dropped the ball. The result is an accidentally reinforced behavior.

This can also happen with punishment. For instance, I provide parent education to divorcing or recently divorced parents. They sometimes ask me why their children won't talk to them about the time they spend with the other parent. We often discover together that, during the few times early on when the children did bring up the other parent in conversation, the parent got angry or upset by what they heard. The children learned quickly just not to say anything because the parent's anger was unpleasant, maybe even scary for them, and so served as a punishment. This is an accidental punishment. Awareness of the principles of punishment allows us to correctly analyze that situation.

Reward and Punishment Overlap

Critiques of behaviorism generally include the observation that the operant conditioning concepts of rewards (aka reinforcers) and punishment are not as distinct as they might seem at first. Conceptually, a reward is something good and a punishment is something bad. That seems simple enough, and there should be no confusion of the two. In fact, Skinner was an advocate of rewards but was opposed to the use of punishment, suggesting that they must be clearly distinguishable, as one is useful and the other is harmful. But the distinction is difficult to fully maintain because it depends on perspective.

Is dessert a reward for eating dinner, or is not getting dessert a punishment for not eating dinner? Is allowance a reward for doing chores, or is a withheld allowance a punishment for neglected chores? What makes it hard to answer these questions is that both rewards and punishments rely on a power differential, whereby one person wields power over the other person and that power shapes the context of the exchange. The parent, in a position of power, has the perspective that he is giving something and believes that the child should be grateful for that. Therefore, from the parent's perspective, the dessert or allowance is positive reinforcement of desired behavior. But the child, in a position of less power, has a different perspective. Because the child has less power, the child is much more conscious of the threat of loss. To the child, the implied threat of the loss of the dessert or allowance is a threat of punishment. So is the parenting strategy reward or punishment? It would seem that it is both.

For this reason, I will argue that, in some very important ways, rewards are really no better than punishment. They are both limited in serious ways and incur serious risks, as described below. Both should be used with great caution and restraint.

Applied Behavior Analysis

Today, the discipline that began as behaviorism is known as **applied behavior analysis**. The premise is that all behavior is purposeful. If we assume that behavior always has a purpose, we can predict and even influence future behaviors, and we can do this in a specific setting for specific behaviors. The purpose or function of behavior is either to gain access to a reinforcer or to avoid a punisher.

Applied behavior analysis assumes that the purpose of behavior has to do with the interactive nature of behavior. It occurs in a very particular context, and that context can inform the observer of its purpose. Therefore, behavior analysis begins with careful observation and assessment of the context, generally using the **ABC model** of behavior. *A* is for Antecedents, *B* is for Behavior, and *C* is for Consequences.

Antecedents in the ABC model are the stimulus events that precede an operant response. These are the conditions that immediately precede the behavior of interest or concern. They can be considered prompts of the behavior. For example, if the parent is concerned about a child eating junk food and not eating a healthy dinner, the parent might want to consider all of the conditions that immediately precede the bad behavior. The child usually eats junk food when he gets home from school. He last ate a lunch, which was four hours prior and he is hungry. Parents are not yet home from work, so the house is empty and the child is bored, hungry, and unsupervised. Plus, the pantry is stocked with chips and cookies. A behavior analyst will consider that these conditions may make the operant behavior (eating of junk food) more likely to occur spontaneously. Hungry kids will want food, and they will eat whatever is most accessible and easy.

Behavior in the ABC model is the response that causes concern; in this case, the eating of junk food. Notice that the task of identifying the behavior requires that the parent state the observation clearly, objectively, and without judgment. This is very similar to the skill of stating behavior in an I-message clearly, objectively, and without judgment (see Chapter 5). The parent usually starts here, by identifying exactly what behavior is problematic and then considering the antecedents of the behavior.

The **Consequence** in the ABC model is what happens after the behavior. Behavior analysts use the term *consequences*, but they do not mean the same type of consequences that Adlerians mean (see Chapter 6). When behavior analysts use the term *consequences*, they refer to whether the outcome is punishing, reinforcing, or neutral. They do not attend to whether the consequence is natural or logical; that is simply not the conceptual framework they operate within. They may assert that it does not matter. The child only notices if it was pleasant or unpleasant. If the outcome is pleasant, then the behavior is reinforced; if unpleasant, it is punished. In the case of the child eating junk food before dinner, the behavior is rewarded by the reduction of hunger (a negative reinforcer). According to this theory, reinforcement is the key to motivation.

Applied behavior analysis involves a careful review of these three factors. The analyst is mostly occupied with critiquing and understanding why problem behaviors occur. With analysis, it generally becomes crystal clear why things are happening, and the solution is obvious. In the case of the child eating junk food before dinner, it becomes obvious that the antecedents of being unsupervised and hungry with a pantry full of junk food after school is clearly promoting the problem behavior. Given those antecedents, eating junk food before dinner is obviously going to be rewarding. So changing the antecedents to reduce the prompts that created the misbehavior is likely to change the behavior.

Best Practices

Applied behavior analysis is very popular. Many parents use some behavioral strategies in conjunction with other approaches on the parenting pyramid to no ill effect. Analysis of behavior is certainly a useful skill, and this theory provides a framework for understanding behavior that has a great deal of empirical support. Some behavioral strategies are perfectly compatible with approaches lower on the pyramid and are unlikely to produce problematic outcomes. But other behavioral strategies are inherently problematic.

Many parents seem to overuse behavioral strategies, especially when they fail to fully analyze the behavior and do not attend to antecedents, but instead focus only on the consequences part of the ABC model. Rewards and punishments may be quick and easy compared to other approaches on the pyramid, but in their overuse, the risks are highlighted. Consequently, it is my position that behavioral techniques have a "last resort" place on the parenting pyramid. They should not be relied upon very often or used for very long to address any given issue. When they are used, they should be accompanied by strategies lower on the pyramid in order to mitigate the risks. But they do have a place on the pyramid. Let us consider how best to use the strategies derived from applied behavior analysis.

Focus on Antecedents

Behavior analysts focus on the antecedent component of the ABC model. Once their role in behavior is understood, antecedents can be manipulated fairly easily. Altering antecedents does not come with any of the risks of rewards and punishments. Therefore, it is clearly the preferred behavioral approach. All of these behavioral best practices are summarized in Table 7.1.

Table 7.1 Best Practices of Applied Behavior Analysis

Strategy	Best Practices
Classical Conditioning	1. Pairing of stimuli is regular and frequent 2. Stimuli and response closely related in time
Shaping Behavior	1. Eliminate other rewards 2. Approximations 3. Reward immediately 4. Reward consistently to establish behavior, reward intermittently to maintain it. 5. Offer a variety of rewards 6. Social rewards have fewest side effects
Reduce Misbehavior	1. Offer no reinforcement 2. Reinforce incompatible behaviors

Punishment	1. Rare and short duration
	2. Used in conjunction with
	  a. warm, loving relationship
	  b. clear communication
	  c. reinforcement of incompatible behaviors
	3. Immediately after misbehavior
	4. Administered calmly
	5. No moralizing

Antecedents may be seemingly innocuous aspects of the environment, things that make it easy for a behavior to occur. For instance, if I have chocolate in the house, I'm much more likely to eat chocolate. Its presence makes the behavior easier, and when I see it there, that serves as a prompt. Children's misbehavior can also be triggered by environmental cues. Having a breakable glass item on a low shelf almost seems like an invitation to a toddler to come over and break it. This is what produces the "we can't have nice things" frustration of parents of young children.

Considered in this light, it is obvious that antecedents that prompt undesirable behaviors should be removed. We might think of this as removing the temptation. Once the breakable items are put up high, once the chocolates are gone, then there is simply less likelihood of the baby breaking the item or the mom eating the chocolate. Parents do this when they separate siblings at the dinner table to stop them from squabbling with each other or when they provide a healthy snack after school to stop kids from snacking on junk food. Allowing children to have reasonable choices eliminates the antecedent of powerlessness, thereby reducing the likelihood of a power struggle.

Antecedents can also be used to evoke desirable behaviors in children by placing **prompts** in the environment for that behavior. A prompt is a trigger for a specific behavior. Structure in the form of schedules, rules, clear expectations, and reminders all serve as prompts. For instance, a chore chart on the refrigerator and a reminder at the beginning of dinner about whose turn it is to wash dishes tonight are both clear prompts to help children do their chores. Modeling desirable behavior also serves as a prompt. This might be in the form of a parent who puts dishes directly into the dishwasher while preparing dinner, prompting the children to also clean up after themselves.

Furthermore, parents can set up the environment such that certain behaviors will be more or less rewarding. For instance, if the child is hungry when a healthy dinner is served, that healthy dinner is more likely to be rewarding (reinforcing) than if the child was full on potato chips and thus not very hungry when he sat down to dinner.

Readers will recall that the scientific consensus regarding parenting in Chapter 1 includes the role of parental supervision for reducing risk of misbehaviors. This reflects the use of parental presence as an antecedent. Parental supervision increases the likelihood that misbehavior will not be rewarded.

Another way to use antecedents to promote desirable behavior is to purposely condition a child to associate a particular antecedent with a specific behavior. For instance, if a parent wants her child to fall asleep every night at a given bedtime, she can pair a neutral stimulus (a bath, reading a book, a certain kind of music, etc.) with the end of the day, when naturally, biologically, the child will be driven to feel sleepy. That is a biologically driven response, one the parent didn't have to create. But the parent can intentionally pair it repeatedly with a bath, and soon the child will learn to respond to a bath by feeling sleepy. The parent can use a bath, cuddle time, reading, music, or any number of such strategies combined into a bedtime routine. In this way, bedtime routines help children (and adults, for that matter) fall asleep at the end of the day.

For parents who want to use conditioning intentionally, there are two best practices for this technique. First, the pairing of antecedent and behavior must be regular and frequent. Conditioning *can* happen with only one pairing of the conditioned and unconditioned stimuli if the unconditioned response is dramatic. For instance, many years ago, one of my daughters felt sick because she had a stomach flu, but chose to eat a hot dog nonetheless. The result was dramatic and excessively unpleasant. To this day, she starts to feel nauseated when she smells a hot dog. The pairing of the hot dog and the flu happened only once, but the resultant conditioning endures. However, it is typically only the extraordinarily unpleasant responses that are sufficiently dramatic to induce conditioning on a single event. Intentional use of conditioning by parents does not generally rely on dramatically unpleasant responses. Instead, parents are generally trying to condition antecedent-positive associations that are more subtle, such as associating a bath with tiredness and sleep. Therefore, the pairing of the antecedent and the behavior must be regular and frequent. Bath time must accompany bedtime every single night for a couple of weeks before the child will be conditioned to fall asleep after the bath.

Second, the behavior must be temporally related to the antecedent. This is called **immediacy** (Skinner, 1953). For the strongest and fastest conditioning, the antecedent is offered first, and then the behavior overlaps with it. To use the example of conditioning a child to associate bath time with sleepiness, the bath should coincide with or very slightly precede natural sleepiness. If the bath is offered an hour before natural sleepiness sets in, then the child will not be conditioned to see the two things as related to each other because the two things are not adequately temporally related. Therefore, the parent should be aware of early signs of sleepiness and begin the bath when they appear. Once the conditioning is achieved, then the parent might gradually move bath time earlier in order to induce a gradually earlier bedtime.

Reinforcement

Reinforcement is based on the simple principle that a child will do something if that behavior pays off for the child, if he or she is rewarded for it. A **reward** is a presumably desirable consequence offered in the hope that it will reinforce the behavior. Because a parent cannot always know if the reward being offered is truly reinforcing, the terms will be used interchangeably here.

Reinforcement can be used to make desirable behaviors more frequent or even to shape up some brand-new behavior. But it can also be used to reduce undesirable behaviors through extinction and differential reinforcement. The best practices described here are also summarized in Table 7.1.

Shaping Behavior

Skinner used the terminology of **shaping behavior** because the trainer (for our purposes, the parent) often wants to establish a behavior that is not already fully formed. For instance, if we want to teach a child in a diaper to use the toilet, we can't just reward her every time she uses the toilet because she's not using the toilet at all yet. Toilet use is not already in her behavioral repertoire, so the parent has to "shape it up" from its components. Therefore, applied behavior analysis is not as simple as "reward her for it." Let us consider some guidelines for shaping behaviors.

The first best practice is to eliminate the possibility of rewards from any other source. Skinner did this physically by placing his animal subjects in a Skinner box, a literal box with walls and only one source of reward, which was controlled by the trainer. Parents must find other ways to eliminate the possibility of rewards being obtained from other sources. If the parent decides to use candy to reward the toddler for using the toilet, then candy must not be available (during the training) from any other source for any other reason. If the parent wants to use allowance (money) to teach the child to clean her room, then the parent must be sure that the child has no alternative source of money. For this reason, reinforcement is more likely to work with younger children who are more fully dependent on parents because they will simply have fewer alternative sources of rewards.

Second, identify the component behaviors, called **approximations**, and reward them successively, step by step, one at a time. This is probably the most important guideline because a complex new skill does not materialize magically. If someone promised to give me a million dollars to build a clock, I would be motivated to build that clock, but I still wouldn't be able to do it because I don't know anything about clocks, and so I wouldn't know how to begin. A toddler is in a similar position with regard to toilet use. We must identify for them the first step, and reward that behavior. With toilet training, maybe that is recognizing that they have to go and telling the parent that it's coming, before they actually do. That is an approximation of toilet use, so we would reward that. Once that behavior is well established (the child is telling the parent every single time), then we stop rewarding that, and move on to the next approximation. This might be running into the bathroom. Now we reward the child every time he gets to the bathroom before he pees, whether he gets his pants down and makes it onto the toilet or not. Once he's getting to the bathroom every time, then we stop rewarding that, and move on to the next approximation, perhaps getting onto the toilet. Eventually we will reward only totally successful toilet usage, and later, we will reward going a full day with no accidents. We keep progressing in our approximations until we have fully shaped the desirable behavior from its component parts. The complex behavior that consists of discrete steps, each reinforced successively, is called a **behavior chain**.

Third, reward immediately after the desired behavior. It is critical that the child recognize that the reward is contingent upon the behavior that triggered it.

Therefore, it should be offered immediately after the behavior. The toddler being toilet trained, for instance, should not be told that he will receive his reward after lunch or even in ten minutes. He should get it right then and there. Sometimes, however, it's not possible to offer the reward immediately. For instance, I always cringe when I see a parent keeping a bowl of M&Ms in the bathroom to use them as rewards for a potty-training toddler. I'd rather the food be kept out of the bathroom. But keeping the food in another room means that the reward cannot be given immediately. How long a delay is too long? That depends on the child's cognitive development. For a toddler, it needs to be within the minute because toddlers are not cognitively capable of understanding time and thus inferring contingency over time.

Fourth, reward consistently to establish a behavior, then intermittently to maintain it. When the parent is shaping a behavior for the very first time, the child must get the message that the reward is contingent upon the behavior, as we just established. Part of that is that the reward must be offered immediately after the behavior. But in addition, the schedule of reinforcement is important (Ferster & Skinner, 1957). At first, the reward must be offered every time the behavior occurs. That makes it totally clear to the child that the events were related. This is a **continuous schedule of reinforcement**, and it ensures that the behavior is learned. For instance, the parent gives the child an M&M every single time he uses the toilet while the behavior is being shaped up. However, if the reward is offered every single time indefinitely, then kids get a little complacent about it, so the parent shifts to a **fixed schedule of reinforcement**, whereby the reward is offered regularly, but not every single time. Once the child knows what the goal is (in terms of toilet use), then the parent might reward him after five times in a row successfully using the toilet or at the end of each day without an accident. The reward comes after several demonstrations of the skill. Both continuous and fixed schedules of reinforcement will get a behavior established. The problem, though, is that behaviors controlled by regular rewards like this are very susceptible to being extinguished. If the reward is very regular and expected but then is not available for a few days (for instance, the parent runs out of M&Ms and doesn't have a chance to get to the store to buy more), then the behavior can easily be unlearned, and the child will stop. In order to make an established behavior resistant to extinction, the parent needs to shift to a **variable schedule of reinforcement**, which means that the reward is offered intermittently, with no predictable schedule. Behaviors that are rewarded on a variable schedule are quite resistant to extinction.

Fifth, offer a variety of rewards. When a stimulus is offered repeatedly, humans tend to become **habituated** to it, meaning that its effectiveness gradually wanes as the person gets used to it. If offered repeatedly, even desirable rewards will gradually be less effective as reinforcers because the child becomes habituated. Using a variety of rewards instead of the same one over and over can forestall that habituation. Furthermore, one of the limitations of applied behavior analysis described above is that the child may grow to see the reward as a sterile exchange of goods and services, which they might then evaluate logically and find it to be inadequate (say, for example, the child might decide that a $10 allowance just isn't enough money for him to do all of the chores assigned to him). This should inspire parents to question the strategy of using rewards at all, but using a variety of rewards is also a potential way around this problem. When an ice cream cone every time is replaced by an unidentified "treat," then part of the reward is the anticipation of not knowing and the thrill of surprise. This is why teachers in elementary school classrooms have replaced uniform gold stars with treasure boxes where kids reach in blindly to pull something out, knowing that there are a variety of treasures in there, and goodie "stores" where students accumulate points with which to shop for something they like. The surprise, or the choice, is part of the reward, maybe even more than the actual object. The variety prevents the businesslike nature of rewards to hijack the process.

Sixth, social rewards are the least likely to have unwanted side effects. Using rewards regularly and often is a strategy fraught with problems. Most have been addressed already, but some are specific to the actual reward chosen. Common problematic side effects include:

- Verbal praise, if it is evaluative or person centered in nature (see Chapter 4 for a reminder of what evaluative praise is) can effectively modify behavior, but it will simultaneously suppress motivation and learning.
- Money, because it is so uniform and standardized, is especially likely to require escalation and to inspire a cost-benefit analysis.
- Food, because it is directly related to health, can become distorted and unhealthy if used as a reward. If sweet treats are used as rewards, kids may develop an unhealthy attitude toward them (for example, conditioning to associate ice cream with good grades). If healthy foods are used as rewards, this means that healthy foods must sometimes be restricted, which is also problematic (it would be crazy not to let a child have a carrot if the child is hungry).

Using social rewards may be a way to avoid some of these troubling side effects of specific reinforcers. A social reward is a social activity offered to reinforce a behavior. For instance, a social reward might be a family outing to the movies to celebrate a good report card. A social reward has the advantage in that it provides an opportunity for relationship building and communication is built in, so that the reward is supported also by strategies lower on the pyramid, mitigating some of the risks.

Extinction

Applied behavior analysis includes two strategies for reducing undesirable behavior. The first is to simply NOT reinforce the misbehavior, to offer a neutral response. If a misbehavior is not rewarded, then it may simply stop on its own because it is not paying off. I remember complaining to my mother when I was a child that my sister was annoying me and she wouldn't stop. My mom would sometimes sigh in exasperation and say something like, "Can't you see that she's just trying to get a rise out of you? If you ignore her, she'll stop." It wasn't very satisfying to hear that as a child, but now I say the same thing to my daughters occasionally because it is sometimes so completely obvious that ignoring the behavior will make it go away. It was hard to see as a child, but easier to see with the experience of age. There are some behaviors that I find especially irritating, such as a child tugging on my sleeve. According to this strategy, I would simply offer no response (not a "Yes, honey?" but also not a "Stop doing that!") to the tugging.

Extinction is an intentional decoupling of the antecedent from the behavior or the behavior from the consequence. Extinction is, therefore, a process of unlearning a learned association. The parent must intentionally withhold the reward or punishment when the learned behavior occurs. If the parent has accidentally rewarded whining or begging in the grocery store (by taking the child to the store when the child is hungry and then buying him a snack when he whines), then the learning has to be extinguished by decoupling the stimulus of hunger and shopping (take the child shopping just after he's eaten a full meal) and/or by refusing to offer the reward (not buying him a snack when he whines).

It's not hard to imagine what will happen when the reward is no longer offered. The child will increase the behavior that he previously learned was rewarded. If whining usually gets him a candy bar, then he'll whine even louder. This temporary increase in the misbehavior is called an **extinction burst**. Behavior will continue and become exaggerated. The child might throw the most energetic fit he has ever thrown in a grocery store, but all of his behavior is an exaggerated version of the previously rewarded behavior. Then, when the child gets the message that the reward is truly not coming, he will abandon the misbehavior. Success! But it is a hard-won success for the parent who extinguishes a misbehavior.

The parent must hold firm during the extinction burst if extinction is to be effective. If the parent slips up and rewards the behavior after withholding rewards a few times, then the parent has effectively converted to a variable reinforcement schedule and made the behavior even more difficult to eventually extinguish. Therefore, it is critical that parents attempt extinction at a time and place when they will be able to follow through. For instance, if the parent withholds the candy bar reward for whining in the grocery store three times but gives in on the fourth trip because he is having a hard day and simply cannot tolerate the extinction burst, he has just undone the first three successful trips and made it much more difficult when he resumes the extinction effort.

Finally, extinction should only be attempted when the parent is sure that the behavior was learned in the first place. An unconditioned response is not amenable to extinction because it was not learned. Hunger, for instance, is a natural (unconditioned) response. It is physiologically based; it is not learned. If someone tried to extinguish their hunger by never "rewarding" it with food, that would be ridiculous, right? Hunger wasn't learned, so it can't be unlearned. Instead, it is a natural biological process that is adaptive for health. Similarly, natural behaviors of children can be annoying or inconvenient (crying when left alone, for example), but these represent unconditioned responses and thus cannot be extinguished. When extinction of unlearned behaviors is attempted, it will not be very successful, and it can be dangerous to the health of both parent and child.

The clearest example of inappropriate extinction attempt, to my mind, is cry-it-out sleep training for infants and toddlers. Babies are evolved (see Chapter 3) to expect close physical contact with caregivers for safety. When they find themselves alone, especially when sleepy, a survival instinct kicks in to prompt them to call out to the person who serves as their secure base, signaling distress. This behavior is built in, which is to say that it is unlearned, unconditioned. As such, it cannot be extinguished through extinction. But the strategy of cry-it-out sleep training, sometimes called behavioral sleep training or behavioral sleep management, is extinction. Sleep training may in fact teach children to suppress their distress signals but at great cost to the child's emotional health and the parent-child attachment relationship. Proper use of extinction is therefore limited only to learned behaviors.

Differential Reinforcement

The principle that ignoring misbehavior can make it stop is appealing. We can't always rely on it, however. For one thing, the misbehavior might have consequences that cannot be ignored for reasons of safety or human rights. For instance, a parent cannot simply ignore it when one child physically attacks a sibling, because it is unsafe and unjust. For another thing, the behavior may have an intrinsic reward (such as a child sneaking a cookie before dinner) and so ignoring it means allowing it to be reinforced. Additionally, some misbehavior is motivated by a genuine need that will not disappear when the misbehavior is ignored. Therefore, another form of misbehavior will probably pop up in its place. For instance, if a child whines when hungry or tired and the whining is ignored but the child is still hungry or tired, then the child will probably have a full-scale emotional meltdown. We know from attachment theory (refer back to Chapter 3 to refresh) that attachment-promoting signals such as these are biologically driven and universal among humans. They must be responded to for healthy emotional development. To respond with the behavior modification approach of ignoring the signal might work to suppress the behavior, but it would be very destructive to the child and to the parent-child relationship.

Therefore, a more useful strategy for reducing undesirable behavior is to reinforce a different behavior, which is called **differential reinforcement**. There are three forms of differential reinforcement (Cooper, Heron, & Heward, 2007):

1. Differential Reinforcement of Other behavior (DRO) means offering a reward when the child does anything other than the identified misbehavior. For instance, if the undesirable behavior is running around the pool, a parent concerned for her child's safety could use her attention as a reward. She could talk to him, tell him jokes, ask him to help her ... essentially offer her attention as a reward for anything else other than the running. This is an easy thing to do spontaneously; it can be implemented immediately without any planning. If the parent is desperate and frustrated with the behavior, she looks for anything else and starts rewarding that.

    The risk of DRO is that the parent may inadvertently end up reinforcing other undesirable behaviors. For instance, her attention might act as a reinforcer for the boy to start clinging and whining. He's no longer running around the pool, but she has simply traded one problem behavior for another.

2. Differential Reinforcement of Alternative behavior (DRA) offers a reward when the child exhibits a specific alternative behavior to the problematic one. The alternative generally is functionally equivalent, meaning it generates the same result, but it is more socially acceptable. For instance, the parent who is worried about a child running around the pool may start rewarding the child every time he walks around the pool. Both actions get him where he's going, so the parent will reward the action that she prefers and fail to reward the other. Teachers routinely use DRA when they attend to students who raised their hand to talk rather than to the student who just blurts out his comments. If the parent doesn't want the child to leave his dirty dish on the table, the parent might reward the child for putting the dirty dish in the sink while ignoring the dish left on the table. If the parent doesn't want the child to whine when hungry, then reward the child for verbally stating that he or she is hungry.

3. Differential Reinforcement of Incompatible behavior (DRI) is offering a reward when the child exhibits a behavior that is incompatible with the misbehavior that has been targeted for reduction. They need not be functionally equivalent; it's just that one makes the other impossible. If my daughters are arguing with each other, just bickering over small things, I may call one to my side and offer her reinforcement (through the social reward of my attention) for being in a different room as her sister. They simply cannot be bickering when one is in the bedroom and one is in the kitchen. If a parent doesn't want a child to put his shoes on the sofa, the parent can reward the child for taking his shoes off and leaving them by the door before he even gets to the sofa. If the parent doesn't want the child to jump on the bed, then the parent might reward the child for lying down on the bed.

Applications are almost endless. One can see why these strategies are so popular. Of course, differential reinforcement is subject to the same best practices of other reinforcement strategies.

Punishment

An aversive stimulus, an undesirable consequence of a specific behavior, is a **punishment** if it decreases the likelihood that a behavior will be repeated

(Skinner, 1953). It can be getting something undesirable (getting a spanking for talking back, getting a scolding for spilling one's milk) or being deprived of something desirable (losing the right to see one's friends this weekend because of sneaking out last weekend or losing one's cell phone for lying).

The original behaviorists (including Skinner), as well as contemporary behavior analysts, do not recommend the intentional use of punishment. It is less successful than reinforcement (e.g., Miller, Haas, Waschbusch, Willoughby, Helseth, Crum, Coles, & Pelham, 2014), and it carries enormous risks. One study of truth telling in school-aged children demonstrated that the threat of punishment actually increases the likelihood that a child will lie. That study demonstrated, furthermore, that the most honesty is elicited by making an internal appeal for honesty (reminding them that they will be happier with themselves if they tell the truth). The internal appeal loses its effectiveness if it is combined with the threat of punishment. This suggests two things: 1) punishment doesn't work to promote desirable behavior; and 2) persuasion might work better than behavioral approaches (Talwar, Arruda, & Yachison, 2015).

But there may be some small place for punishment. There is evidence that, while reasoning is usually more effective than punishment to reduce misbehavior, mild punishment is more effective than reasoning when the child's level of distress at the time is high (Larzelere & Merenda, 1994). Larzelere subsequently reported that mild punishment as an adjunct to reasoning about misbehavior is the most effective at preventing future misbehavior. The problem with this research, however, is that punishment is not compared to natural and logical consequences (which can also serve to place firm limits on children's behavior but without the risks of punishment) or reinforcement (which can be used to modify behavior but without some of the risks of punishment). The comparison here is between talking by itself and talking with behavioral limits. It ignores the other options for behavioral limits.

If we accept that there might be a place for punishment in a parent's repertoire of strategies, what are the best practices for it? The first is that it must be a small place. Punishment should be rare, and when it is used, it should be for a short duration. There are so many risks associated with punishment that it should never become a parent's go-to strategy. It is a last resort, to be used only after careful consideration.

Furthermore, it should only be used in conjunction with other strategies on the pyramid. The relationship must be a warm and loving one so that it can sustain the insult of punishment. A fragile relationship will be destroyed once punishment is introduced. In addition to the strong relationship, it must also be used in conjunction with communication approaches, especially the components of I-messages, including clear and nonjudgmental descriptions of the misbehavior and the effect of the misbehavior on others. These clear descriptions, along with clear expectations for future behavior, are essential to reduce the child's sense of powerlessness over the punishment. The use of punishment to correct a misbehavior should also be combined with reinforcement of alternative or incompatible behaviors. All of those other strategies remove the reliance on punishment and work to mitigate some of the risks of punishment.

Once all of those conditions are met, the punishment itself should be administered immediately after the misbehavior (for contingency). The parent must also remain calm during administration of the punishment in order to minimize some of the negative side effects of punishment, such as the damage to the parent-child relationship. Ideally, the child sees the parent as a neutral enforcer rather than as an antagonist or enemy. Furthermore, the parent must refrain from sending a moralizing message, which is a comment on the child's moral character (for instance, "Shame on you! How could you be so foolish? Bad girl!"). Moralizing messages violate the principle of behaviorism to focus entirely on observable behavior and so contaminate the applied behavior analysis with emotional content that is likely to interfere.

Limitations of Reinforcement and Punishment

In order to be effective, there are serious limitations regarding: a) the appropriateness of reinforcement and punishment; and b) the manner in which these tools must be implemented. Let us discuss each limitation in turn. (These limitations are summarized in Table 7.2.) First, what behaviors are appropriate to teach with reinforcement and punishment? These techniques address behavior—and only behavior. They cannot be used to change children's beliefs, attitudes, or feelings. For instance, a parent or teacher can use rewards to get a child to read a book, but rewards will not get the child to enjoy reading, or think about reading as a useful skill, or believe that reading is an important part of life. Only the behavior itself can be modified, nothing that is internal to the learner. This is a major limitation. We cannot use rewards to inspire a love of reading, or a commitment to education, or respect for one's elders. We can only use it to teach behaviors.

Table 7.2 Limits and Risks of Applied Behavior Analysis

Limits of Applied Behavior Analysis

Can only change behavior, not attitudes, beliefs, or feelings.

Only works in the short-term.

Only works in the presence of the authority figure.

Conditions have to be just right.

Risks of All Applied Behavior Analysis

Power must be escalated to maintain its effect. Parents eventually run out of it.

Children may see reward as payment and punishment as a price to be paid.

Can promote sneakiness and cheating.

Dehumanizing

Makes parents overly responsible for child's behavior.

Damages parent-child relationship.

Can incite rebellion in children with difficult temperament.

Additional Risks of Punishment

Children learn to imitate the aggression they observe.

Fears can be generalized beyond the intended scope.

Does not teach what behavior should replace the punished behavior.

In addition, rewards and punishment can only be used to change behaviors in the short term and in the presence of the authority figure. Skinner himself noted that punishment only changes behavior for the short term, but subsequent research has demonstrated that this is also true of reinforcement. Both rewards and punishments can establish or eliminate behaviors, but those patterns of behavior will be sustained only as long as the reward or punishment is sustained and only in the presence of the rewarder or punisher (Kohn, 1999). This is, of course, related to the first limitation described above: that rewards and punishment do not affect any internal mental processes. If a child learns to engage in a behavior but does not understand why that behavior is important or does not value that behavior, then he or she will only do it as long as it is necessary to meet external requirements.

Another major limitation of rewards and punishment is that conditions have to be precise for it to work. There are a great many rules for the use of these behavioral techniques, as outlined above as best practices. When best practices are not followed, the strategies do not work and even backfire. Strategies lower on the pyramid are much more forgiving in that parental intentions and attitudes can compensate for a strategy poorly executed. But higher up on the pyramid, this becomes less true. At the highest level of the pyramid, applied behavior analysis, there is basically no room for error. Parents must use all of the best practices, or the strategies will not have the desired effect.

Risks of Reinforcement and Punishment

Even when rewards and punishment are used properly, following best practices and applied only to behaviors and only for short-term change, they still carry some serious risks. (These risks are summarized in Table 7.2.)

First, power must be escalated to maintain its effect because children grow habituated to rewards and punishments. With habituation, the effect on behavior is gradually reduced. Therefore, it generally needs to be escalated. Consider rewarding a child with money to do a chore. When the child is a preschooler, she may be delighted to get a quarter if she helps put away the dishes, but before long, she'll want more than 25 cents for the chore. Rewards must be escalated to maintain their effectiveness. The same is true for punishment. The swat on the bottom that was so effective to control the toddler just doesn't faze him after a while, and so punishing parents must intensify their corporal punishment as the child gets older if they choose to use this strategy. This is obviously a dangerous game to play. And there is only one end to the game. Eventually, the parent simply runs out of power. The child grows in size until physical power evaporates because the child is just as big as the parent. The child gains the ability to make money until financial power evaporates because the child can get resources from alternate sources. If the entire parenting approach is based on power, then the parent sees his influence disappear gradually as the child ages, until there is nothing left. It is a foundation of sand.

Second, rewards and punishment look like a pure exchange of goods and services. After all, it's only about behavior, without considering thoughts, feelings, and values. So it can look like a very sterile exchange, and children will adopt that businesslike attitude toward the exchange. The desired behavior becomes an option only to be pursued if the reward is great enough. Instead of internalizing their duty to do chores as members of a family, they will see their chores as a job that they will do only if they think they're getting paid enough. Similarly, a punishment may not prevent misbehavior if the child calculates that it is simply a price to be paid. If the misbehavior is "worth it," then the misbehavior is chosen. If the reader has ever wondered how much a parking ticket would cost them knows about this calculation. If the parking ticket is only $5, maybe that's worth it, but a $50 ticket would be too much. That is an undesired side effect of the use of rewards and punishment to modify behavior.

Third, because rewards and punishment really only work for the short term and in the presence of the authority figure, it can produce sneakiness and cheating. When children have not internalized the reason for a behavior, their reason is external. Instead of avoiding the misbehavior, they will instead learn to avoid *detection* of the misbehavior. Similarly, instead of engaging in desirable behavior because it is the right thing to do, they will only engage in the behavior if they perceive that there will be a reward for doing so. They may even learn that the reward is worth having, even if they have to cheat to get it. Sneaking and cheating are more frequent when rewards and punishments are used to manage behavior.

Fourth, the use of rewards and punishment can be dehumanizing. This is because of the exclusive focus on behavior, as well as the inherent power differential. Thoughts and feelings are not factored in, so that people are seen as two-dimensional, without the context of their humanity. Human beings are treated, in the most "pure" version of applied behavior analysis, just as one might treat a dog being trained to beg for a treat. There is no consideration of feelings, of dignity or respect, or anything other than naked self-interest. A clear example of this is an article that was published in the *New York Times* called "What Shamu taught me about a happy marriage" (Sutherland, 2006). The author describes learning about the behavioral techniques used by exotic animal trainers. She writes: "I listened, rapt, as professional trainers explained how they taught dolphins to flip and elephants to paint. Eventually it hit me that the same techniques might work on that stubborn but loveable species, the American husband." This is a dehumanizing approach that I am personally uncomfortable with. The article is tongue in cheek and a nice overview of behavior analysis, but it illustrates an aspect of applied behavior analysis that I think implies a risk of the approach.

Fifth, rewards and punishment make parents overly responsible for their children's behavior. Children do not learn to internalize the reasons for engaging (or not engaging) in certain behaviors, and therefore, they are simply being controlled like puppets. The theory assumes that parents have power to solve all problems; hence, the parents are fully to blame when children's behavior is imperfect. I believe that this is not good for children or for parents. Children are exempt from accepting personal responsibility for their choices, which is not healthy for their development, and they are also prevented from pursuing their personal ambitions, which is also not healthy for them. Parents, if they believe this, are authorized to become tyrants over their children's lives and doomed to inevitable feelings of failure over the instances when they are not able to exert perfect control over their child's behavior. When taken to the extreme, applied behavior analysis is problematic for these reasons.

Sixth—and most importantly—rewards and punishment can damage the parent-child relationship. It is an explicit use of power. As such, it is inherently threatening to intimacy because it is difficult to feel emotional closeness across a power differential. The child begins to see the parent as a threat or as a source of goodies to exploit, and the parent begins to see the child as someone to guard against who might sneak or try to manipulate him. Each person in the relationship, then, has an incentive to withhold the truth, to hide their true thoughts and feelings so as not to lose whatever power they have in the relationship. The lack of authenticity drains the relationship. Soon, intimacy is gone. Trust is gone. Affection is gone. The relationship is compromised. And of course, in the job of parenting, relationship is the base of the pyramid, so if the relationship is gone, all is lost.

A related risk is that in children who have a so-called "difficult" temperament already, the use of power can incite rebellion. The child sees that reinforcement and punishment is coercion based on power; they resent being manipulated, and thus protest by exhibiting exactly the behavior that the parent wants to discourage. This is true with both reward and punishment because children feel the power differential with both and can resent it. Children with easier temperaments will be more malleable, but that does not mean that the relationship is not damaged.

In addition to these risks, which apply to all forms of rewards and punishment, punishment carries some additional risks. One such risk is that punishment models aggressive behavior. The parent may conceptualize the punishment as well earned and just, but the child may still see simply aggression. It may appear to the child that the parent gets her way simply because she is big enough and powerful enough to force the other to accommodate. The adult models such behavior, and the child sees that the parent is rewarded for it by getting her way. Therefore, the child learns that exertion of power is a strategy that will work, and they tuck away that knowledge for later use. This calls to mind the apocryphal image of the man scolded by his boss at work who comes home and yells at his wife, who turns her anger on the child, who eventually kicks the dog. Each person learns to use power against those who have less power than themselves.

Another risk specific to punishment is that it can create conditioning that is generalized beyond the intended behavior. Watson demonstrated this with the Little Albert experiment; he taught the baby to fear a furry rabbit, but the baby generalized the fear and was afraid of other furry things, including a man's beard. When parents use punishment to reduce a form of misbehavior, the child may develop a fear of the anticipated punishment but then generalize that fear beyond its intended scope. For example, a toddler who has his hand slapped for reaching for a specific object that has been designated as off-limits (electrical outlets, a kitchen knife, or a glass vase on the bookshelf) might generalize the lesson and reduce his exploratory play in general. This mechanism of generalizing fear could partially explain why, in one large longitudinal study, toddlers who experienced hand slapping had restricted cognitive abilities four years later (Straus & Paschall, 2009).

A final risk of punishment is that the subject of the punishment may reduce one specific behavior (the behavior that was punished), but that does not imply the establishment of a more desirable replacement behavior. It is not enough to know what NOT to do; kids must be guided toward what they SHOULD do instead. As any parent knows a couple of weeks into summer vacation, if kids don't have something to do, they're probably going to be getting into trouble. So punishment is only ever a half measure; it must be accompanied by efforts to build desirable behaviors.

When Should Applied Behavior Analysis Be Used?

Using the principles of applied behavior analysis to understand children's behavior allows parents (and others) to gain insights into many aspects of human behavior. As such, there is no reason to limit it as a tool of understanding. Furthermore, focusing on antecedents to prompt desired behaviors and to avoid prompts for undesired behaviors is fundamental to promoting smooth family functioning. It is harmless and can be operating at all times.

But sometimes the ABC model is not adequate to explain human behavior. Other theories of human behavior may provide better explanations of some human behaviors and relationships. Some behaviors are based on biological need and are driven by evolutionary forces rather than learning. Behavior analysis will not be the most helpful tool for understanding those behaviors, and changing the antecedents may not help very much.

As far as the consequences component of the ABC model, this should be used far less often; in fact, almost never. There are serious risks that accompany the use of behavioral techniques, as well as limitations to its potential effectiveness.

An important caveat of this broad assertion is that applied behavior analysis is widely used, and with great success, with children who have developmental disorders on the autism spectrum (Rogers & Vismara, 2008). It is possible that other forms of guidance (such as communication approaches, natural and logical consequences) are less effective with children with autism because those strategies rely on internal motivation, which may be reduced in this specific disorder. If so, applied behavior analysis may remain one of the few approaches available in the circumstance.

Among typically developing children, however, rewards and punishment are last-resort options. They should only be tried after other strategies have been attempted. Rewards are a better option than punishment and so can be resorted to earlier than punishment, but there are some additional general guidelines regarding when to use these strategies.

First of all, reward and punishment can only be used if the parent has adequate power, and this is something that should be considered before starting, due to the risks of such techniques. If it is a reward strategy, the parent must be sure that the child does not have an alternative source for the reward. Paying a teenager $5 to cut the grass will not work to establish that behavior if the teen has a job outside the home that pays minimum wage. The child could easily decide that the reward offered at home is not enough of an incentive to cut the grass. The parent should also be sure that the reward being offered is one that is desirable to the child. If the reward used in potty training is a big verbal "yay" and a high-five, but the child is shy and doesn't like being the center of attention, then that reward will not be sufficiently motivating.

With regard to punishment, the parent must also verify that he or she has adequate power to enforce the punishment. For instance, a parent cannot use grounding as a punishment if the child is about to return to the other parent's custody, so that the grounding parent will not be in a position to enforce the punishment. The reward or punishment should therefore be totally and exclusively within the control of the parent and should be sufficiently desirable (for a reward) or undesirable (for a punishment) to be motivating.

Secondly, the behavior to be modified must be a behavior, not a belief, value, or feeling. There must be no moral value judgments attached to the behavior. This is critically important. The parent must carefully consider whether or not it is enough that the behavior changes without any corresponding change to values or beliefs. Many times, parents actually want deeper-level change. For instance, they don't just want a child to do his homework. They really want the child to take some personal responsibility for his future and to appreciate the opportunity for him to have an education. Well, personal responsibility and gratitude are not primarily behavioral concerns: they are about emotions, values, and beliefs. Therefore, applied behavior analysis cannot help achieve these goals.

What does this leave? Not much. There are social norms that don't really reflect character, but they do help smooth out the process of living together. For instance, one might reward a child for putting down the toilet seat after use. It doesn't make him a morally better person, but the behavior is helpful to others in the house. Using eating utensils rather than eating with one's fingers is just a social norm and not related to moral character, so a behavioral technique could be appropriate.

Third, the behavior to be modified must be necessary only in the short term and only in the presence of an authority figure. Because applied behavior analysis does not change children's attitudes or values, it cannot be expected to work beyond the time when the reward or punishment is offered. Accordingly, it should only be used to shape behaviors or reduce misbehaviors when the need is time limited. Toilet training is a good example of this because it will happen naturally if no training is offered. By the time a child is about five, they will have developed their own reasons for wanting to use the toilet, whether they've previously been trained or not, so the training is only necessary for the year or two before the behavior would have appeared naturally.

But sometimes adults try to use behavioral techniques to train behaviors that they would like to continue far into the future, and this generally backfires. An example of this is when parents use rewards and punishment to shape healthy eating habits in children. The more controlling a parent is with regard to food choices, the poorer food choices the adolescent makes when finally out from under the parent's control (e.g., Loth, MacLehose, Fulkerson, Crow, & Neumark-Sztainer, 2013). The behavioral technique fails because there are no developmentally natural triggers for the behavior, and therefore, for a child to maintain healthy eating habits, reward and punishments are not appropriate strategies.

Another example of applied behavior analysis backfiring is the Accelerated Reader program, a system adopted by elementary schools all over the country to reward children for reading. Children read books in their designated reading level and then take a content quiz to be sure that they understood the content. This program has not been well evaluated, despite its widespread use, but it seems to increase reading, although it does not change children's attitudes about reading, nor does it promote reading outside what is strictly required (Boucher, 2010).

While these restrictions apply to both reward and punishment, there are a few additional restrictions to the appropriate use of punishment. Punishment is a last resort. It should only be used when other techniques have been tried and been ineffective. In addition, given the serious risks of punishment, it must be the product of serious consideration, never used as an impulsive reaction. I can think of two circumstances under which punishment may be the only reasonable choice.

First, when the intensity of misbehavior is a safety risk for the child or for others, it may be reasonable to think about punishment. The second circumstance is when reinforcing incompatible behaviors is not effective because other reinforcers of the misbehavior are overwhelming. These circumstances are often co-occurring. Consider this situation: I recently talked to a mother whose young teenaged daughter (14 years old) has been sneaking out of the house in the middle of the night after her parents are asleep. She was being picked up in a car by a 20-year-old man whom the parents did not know. The teenager and young adult were meeting other youth in a park to drink alcohol. The mother, having learned of these outings, was understandably horrified and desperate to figure out how to keep her child safe.

On the first point, this behavior is remarkably dangerous. The teenager did not seem to realize the extent to which her physical safety was at risk. For that reason, the parent might consider punishment. Punishment may be extreme, but the misbehavior is extremely dangerous. On the second point, the misbehavior was inherently reinforcing. Presumably, the daughter thought it was fun and very exciting to sneak out and hang with older people. She probably felt flattered and grown up. There were lots of reinforcers of the misbehavior that the parents could not control. Therefore, the parent was considering a severe punishment to immediately stop the misbehavior. If the parent decides to use punishment in a case like this, he or she should recognize that it is a risky approach and use the best practices described above.

Developmental Connections

Antecedents can operate at any age. Babies are learning from the moment they are born, maybe even before. So some conditioning is possible with children of any age. The major caveat, however, is that infant development in the first year after birth is mostly physiologically driven rather than being learned.

Biologically based behaviors cannot be extinguished. And behaviors can only be shaped if they begin with operant behaviors, which are behaviors that occur spontaneously at first. So parents are constrained in infancy to working within developmental limits. Furthermore, attachment formation is the critical developmental task of the first year, so anything that is dangerous to relationships should be avoided during that time. Rewards and punishment are thus off the table for infants.

At what age can parents consider starting to use rewards and punishment? It's difficult to settle on a specific age. As an attachment researcher, I am inclined to note that attachment relationships are fragile and easily changeable until at least 24 months, so I would argue against behavioral strategies until that point. Cognitive psychologists note that toddlers do not display intentionality until approximately 18 months, so rewards and punishment cannot be very productive until at least that point. The counterargument is that conditioning does not require higher-level cognitive skills, and that is why it works on animals like pigeons. So behavioral strategies might be used effectively on toddlers, but they pose a risk to the new attachment relationship that is still becoming established.

Therefore, rewards and punishment can be considered for children older than 18 months. There is no reason to think that it stops being effective at any particular age. However, as noted above, reward and punishment may become impractical when children move into the teen years because the parents no longer have adequate power to enforce them.

How Parents React

As a parent educator, I know that parents come in the door wanting to find out how to implement behavioral techniques, but I don't think it's typically what they *need* to know. I believe that parenting is smoother when sensitive responsiveness is increased and relationships improve or when parents listen with more empathy to child-owned problems. I believe that more family problems are solved with I-messages and consequences. I want to convince them to try these other techniques first, to take the time to learn the other strategies lower on the pyramid thoroughly and meaningfully, and then use them. I wish that they would believe me when I tell them that they won't need to know how to craft a good reward system very often if only they use the strategies lower on the pyramid more often. And so I go into this topic with some reservations. I tell them at the beginning that I will mostly be trying to convince them not to use these strategies.

But I don't believe I am very successful. First of all, the use of behavioral techniques often produces an immediate response in terms of behavior change, and second of all, it provides an emotional release to the parent. Both of these things are essentially rewards for the parent, increasing the likelihood that they will use rewards and punishment again. For instance, let's say the parent has used I-messages to convey frustration over a chore not being done, only to discover that the chore is still not done. At that point, the parent explodes in anger and yells a verbal reprimand (a punishment) at the child. The child's eyes fill with tears, and she mumbles a "sorry" while heading off to do the chore. The punishment seems to have made an impression right then and there, so the parent is rewarded for having used the strategy by the fact that it felt like it worked. In addition, the exertion of power over the child allows the parent a sense of relief and self-righteous indignation, which also functions as a reinforcer for the parent. It is quite likely that the child, feeling overpowered and resentful, may do a half-hearted job (or worse) on the chore and next time will be even more resistant to doing the chore. So all too soon, the parent is faced with the same issue again of the chore not done. Therefore, the punishment didn't work in the long term; it may have actually created more resentment, exacerbating the problem. But still, the parent felt rewarded in the short term and so is likely to keep relying on punishment in the form of angry outbursts. This parent is very likely to say to the parent educator (or just think it): "But punishment is the only thing that works with my kid!"

Please note that this parent is not following best practices of applied behavior analysis. But still, the approach might seem effective. So it is a pickle for the parent educator that parents often do not believe us that strategies lower on the pyramid could be more useful to them. This is a major source of frustration and challenge for anyone advising parents. I wish I had an empirically supported solution for this problem, but I do not. My suggestions are threefold.

First, I teach the other strategies before getting to applied behavior analysis. I start at the bottom of the pyramid and work my way up. My hope is that parents will discover and use strategies lower on the pyramid and those will become regular parts of their parenting practice, leaving less room and reduced need for applied behavior analysis.

Second, I explicitly warn about the limitations and risks of rewards and punishment. I am completely transparent with regard to my position. I hope that I have managed to build a relationship with the parents I work with such that they will take those warnings seriously because they have reason to trust me. I model for them sensitive responsiveness by the way I notice and respond to their needs in the class. I model for them active listening and I-messages, right there in the classroom. And very occasionally, I even model logical consequences for them in the classroom. But I try never to use reward and punishment as a teacher. I point all of this out to them. "If I have not used rewards and punishment with you, and yet you have been well behaved and learned something and maybe even enjoyed your time in this class," I say, "then please consider that your child may not need it either."

Finally, I have adopted a perspective on rewards and punishment that allows me to maintain my strong opposition to their overuse and simultaneously respect that parents may not agree or feel able to go along. I think of the job of parenting as one of the most difficult ones a human being ever assumes. It is hard. No one is prepared for it, partly because it's impossible to be prepared for such a complex job. There's more than one way to do this job. And what works for one child will not necessarily work for another. Therefore, most folks doing the job are struggling. They would like to be great at it, but they feel pulled in many directions as a parent and don't even know what being "great" at parenting really looks like. Therefore, my perspective as a parent educator is that I hope to put as many tools as possible into their toolkits, give them access to as many strategies as possible. If their toolkit is full, then they simply won't have to use the dangerous tools very often. I sincerely hope that this is true. My evidence is that virtually every form of parenting education ever studied has been shown to reduce harsh and abusive parenting. If parents feel competent because they have things that they can try, then they will be less likely to arrive at the "last resort" strategies. If I can maintain goodwill toward parents who do not agree with me, then I still have something to offer them.

Questions that parents often ask include:

Question: My parent (or my coach, or my teacher, etc.) was awfully harsh with me, using the punishment strategies you describe here. But it made me want to prove them wrong. It encouraged me to do better. Don't kids need that? We don't do them any favors by coddling them!

Answer: All of us have our own personal experiences, and we spend a lifetime making sense of those experiences, fitting them into a narrative that makes sense for us. This is important work for every human being to engage in. There is nothing wrong with it. But science offers us something different. Science offers us the opportunity to leave our personal life experience, to pull back, and to examine a particular issue as it pertains to a larger group of people. Sometimes the group coincides with our personal experience and so that feels "true" to us, but sometimes we learn that our experience is not exactly typical. That doesn't make our experience untrue; it just means that we must consider that our experience is not universal. Just because you felt challenged by a punitive teacher or parent does not mean that every child reacts that way. In fact, your experience may be unusual. It's important to note this kind of variety.

Question: If time-out is a punishment and we just learned that punishments are not effective to change behavior, why do so many experts advise using time-outs?

Answer: This is a great question and one I find myself asking as well. I believe that many parenting experts (just like many parents) get trapped into a punishment mode, and they simply look for a somewhat less dangerous punishment than spanking, rather than looking for a replacement strategy lower on the pyramid. In this way, the time-out bandwagon is a mistake. However, it is possible to use time-out as a logical consequence, as described in Chapter 6. That is a truly different thing.

Programs and Critique

Parenting education programs that rely on behavior analysis are numerous. Some seem to be based on fundamental misunderstandings of the theory and thus offer very damaging advice. Others are obviously informed by psychological research on the appropriate use of applied behavior analysis and so are far more helpful. Most in this second category also include strategies from lower on the parenting pyramid because, after all, that is best practice.

Misguided Programs

Some popular parenting books stun me with the degree to which they are misguided about behavior analysis. Usually, these books advocate a version of applied behavior analysis that could not be endorsed by anyone who understands the theory and the published research on behavioral techniques. One example is a book called *To Train Up a Child* (Pearl & Pearl, 1994). The authors describe their parenting approach as religiously motivated. The strategies that they describe are, in fact, behavioral strategies, but they are not informed by scientific knowledge of these strategies. They are generally punishment focused, despite the fact that behavior analysis does not endorse the intentional use of punishment. For instance, the authors suggest purposely exposing one's six-month-old infant to a forbidden object for a certain amount of time each day and then slapping his hand when he reaches for the object. So tempt him, then punish him. Repeatedly. Skinner himself would never have suggested such a thing, knowing as he did that punishment is not very effective and that it comes with risks attached. This is clearly terrible advice. They also recommend "switching" a seven-month-old infant. "If he is old enough to pitch a fit, he is old enough to be spanked" (p. 79). Again, this advice would not be advocated by behavior analysts.

Another example is John Dobson's *Dare to Discipline* parenting program (Dobson, 1996). In a nutshell, his argument is that parents must not be afraid to exert authority over their children because children suffer when there are no limits on their behavior. So far, so good. We have seen that there are problems with permissive parenting (see Chapter 2). But from there, he recommends punishment. For one thing, this is a false dichotomy. He assumes that there are only two options: 1) permissiveness; or 2) punishment. In fact, there are many, many other options, as have already been expounded in previous chapters. So this is a logical fallacy that leads the reader to a conclusion that is misguided. For another thing, this is the same mistake endorsed by the Pearl and Pearl book, that the behavior analysis preferred technique should be punishment. He does not alert his reader to the risks and limitations of punishment or to best practices for the use of punishment. This is not surprising, as Dobson acknowledges in the book that he has no training in family science but has used only his intuition and personal experience to conclude that punishment is the way to manage children's behavior.

Another example of misguided behavior programs are the behavioral sleep management programs for infants that are widely endorsed by the medical establishment. Richard Ferber, in his famous book on sleep training in infancy, *Solve Your Child's Sleep Problems* (Ferber, 1986), advocated that babies should be allowed to fall asleep in their own bed, alone, every night in order to create what he called **sleep onset associations** conducive to solitary sleep. Babies should learn to associate the feel of their bed, their solitude, and the sounds of their particular sleep space with tiredness, and so those stimuli will come to trigger sleep. This is clearly about the antecedents that serve as prompts for the desired behavior. This is not by itself problematic.

However, the problem with Ferber's method (called "Ferberizing") is that, given the natural, biologically based predilections of infants (see Chapter 3 to refresh), they don't usually like to fall asleep alone. Most do not do so easily or naturally. Falling asleep alone is never an unconditioned response. Therefore, infants cannot spontaneously create sleep onset associations desired by their parents, and so Ferber goes on to recommend extinction of their natural, physiologically based instinct to cry when left alone. He says that they should be placed alone in a room and the parent should fail to reward crying with attention. Let the baby cry it out. Even if we ignore the damage this will do to attachment formation, this is problematic from the perspective of behavior analysis. As we know, an unconditioned response (crying when left alone) cannot be extinguished through the process of extinction. Despite the fact that this advice contradicts known principles of applied behavior analysis, it is a common component of professional advice regarding infant sleep (Ramos & Youngclarke, 2006).

Evidence-Based Behavioral Programs

Other programs, though, are far more responsible in their endorsement of applied behavior analysis. These programs are very widely used for families with children who are already exhibiting signs of out-of-control behaviors and have been shown to be effective with those populations (Stolz, 2011). Consequently, while I would assert that they should not be used for more normative populations, they may be perfectly appropriate to help make children safe so that the other issues can then be addressed when the danger has passed.

One such program that is solidly evidence based is the Triple P Positive Parenting Program (Sanders, 1999). The program has several intervention levels, ranging from Universal Triple P, available to all parents who are interested in becoming better parents, up to Enhanced Triple P, which is an intensive program including home visitation for families with a child with persistent conduct problems. Consistent with the most up-to-date applied behavior analysis, this program emphasizes analysis and modification of the environment to assure that environmental antecedents promote success and that punishment is avoided in favor of reinforcement.

Another example is the *Incredible Years* program, frequently used with children identified as having behavioral problems. Consistent with the premise of the parenting pyramid, the Incredible Years program includes advice about consequences and communication because applied behavior analysis really only belongs in the context of a wide range of parenting strategies. In an effectiveness study of the program as used with child protection services clients (those who had been neglectful rather than abusive), it was demonstrated to reduce the most dangerous forms of behavioral techniques, such as physical punishment and other forms of harsh discipline, while increasing the less dangerous forms, including praise and other forms of verbal rewards (Letarte, Normandeau, & Allard, 2010).

Application: The Spanking Debate

Very few issues can polarize a discussion of parenting quite like the spanking debate. As spanking is a form of punishment, this may be the right place to broach the topic. Now that we have explored the theory of behaviorism and best practices for the use of applied behavior analysis, let us turn our attention to this societal controversy. Spanking is very common as a parenting practice in the United States. It is normative in all subgroups of US culture. And yet, it is almost universally disavowed by developmental psychologists and family scientists. The experts hate spanking, but US parents feel differently.

Arguments For and Against

What are the arguments in favor of spanking? Essentially, there is an intuitive, commonsense argument that parents simply must be able to exert authority over their children, for their own protection and to show them where the limits are. Children may not always have the cognitive capacity or maturity to accept guidance in the form of communication and consequences, but a spanking can alert them to a serious problem and they can always understand that a spanking means no. Advocates say that spanking may make a bigger impression than other forms of discipline and thus should be used for especially important lessons. Another argument is that it is normative and has worked perfectly well for all of human history (presumably) to produce fully functioning adults. This is the "I was spanked and turned out fine" argument.

What are the arguments against spanking? Intuitive, commonsense arguments include the confused logic of modeling a behavior (physical violence) that the parent says is unacceptable. For instance, spanking a child for hitting is ridiculous on the face of it, yet is widely espoused. As Haim Ginott wrote "When a child hits a child, we call it aggression. When a child hits an adult, we call it hostility. When an adult hits an adult, we call it assault. When an adult hits a child, we call it discipline." This is illogical. Another argument is that physical assault of a vulnerable person is a human rights violation, and spanking a child is exactly that. Opponents of spanking argue that children learn to model adult behavior. If we want them to be reasonable and kind, then we must be reasonable and kind with them, and exploiting our physical size and strength against a smaller person is neither.

So "common sense" might lead us to either side of this controversy. Clearly, evidence is required. Science to the rescue! Scientific research on the effects of spanking can only answer the empirical questions, not the moral ones. The word "empirical" means observable, testable, and objective. So empirical questions include: What effect (if any) does spanking as a form of discipline have on children's behavior, emotional health, and the parent-child relationship? Moral questions require a judgment and right and wrong, good and bad, and therefore cannot be answered by science. Moral questions include: Is it wrong to hit a child? Should I spank my child?

The Evidence

The empirical questions posed above (What effect, if any, does spanking have on behavior, emotions, and relationship?) can be answered by observation of fact; they are not moral questions. Ideally, when parents answer the moral questions for themselves, they will use answers to the empirical questions to guide their decisions. Too often, this step is skipped altogether, and people answer moral questions about parenting while remaining ignorant of the answers to the empirical questions. The question of whether or not to spank is a classic case. There are two opposing camps, and all too often, neither camp has consulted the evidence on the empirical questions. Let us consult the evidence here.

Types of Evidence

But first, let's make sure that we understand the nature of the evidence. There are two basic types of evidence, correlational and experimental, and it is critical to distinguish the two. We want to know whether something (let's call it A, an independent variable; in this case, spanking as a form of discipline) creates an effect (let's call it B, a dependent variable; in this case, behavior, emotions, or relationships). Does A cause B? That is our question.

The first type of possible evidence is **correlational**, meaning the researchers have simply observed A and B as they exist naturally in the world. If they are in fact correlated, it means that when A goes up, B also goes up (a positive correlation), or when A goes up, B goes down (a negative correlation). All we know from correlational evidence is that the two variables are related. The relationship could be there because A in fact caused B, or it could be that B caused A, or there could be something else (let's call it C) that caused both A and B. So for example, we know that spanking is negatively correlated with compliant behavior in children. It could be that spanking actually makes kids less compliant (A causing B), maybe because they resent the parent who spanks them, and so they misbehave more out of resentment. But it's also possible that noncompliance could cause spanking (B causing A). After all, who spanks a perfectly well-behaved child? Perhaps it is the rambunctious ones who drive their parents to desperation, and then those parents spank because they've run out of other options. It could also be that something else, maybe how stressed or depressed the parent is, causes both misbehavior in the child AND the parent's reliance on spanking (C causing both A and B). After all, children probably perceive their parent's stress, and it makes them needier and thus more prone to misbehave out of their anxiety. And parents who are stressed probably have less time and mental effort to put into constructing more positive parenting approaches. So stress could cause both.

So correlational evidence is limited because it's difficult to interpret. But it can offer hints. For instance, when longitudinal research separates A and B in time (let's say spanking frequency is assessed among toddlers, and behavior is assessed years later when the same children are school aged) then we can reasonably rule out B having caused A. We still cannot rule out the possibility that C caused both A and B, but the temporal relationship can help. This applies to correlational evidence on spanking because we do have longitudinal evidence that early spanking is correlated with later outcomes. For example, a recent study (just one of thousands of similar studies) found that the frequency of spanking at age three was positively correlated with externalizing behavior problems at age five and negatively correlated with receptive language at age five.

The more the young child is spanked, the worse the behavior and the worse his or her language skills are at age five. The effect was not moderated by parental warmth or the normativeness of spanking in the community (MacKenzie, Nicklas, Waldfogel, & Brooks-Gunn, 2012). This is correlational data, but it is longitudinal, so we know that either A causes B or something else is causing both of them.

Second, if the correlations always go in one direction (positive or negative), then we can be certain that causality does not actually go in the other direction. As it turns out, spanking children for discipline has been studied scientifically (using observations and producing correlational data) for several decades at this point, and it is virtually always correlated with undesirable outcomes (Gershoff & Grogan-Kaylor, 2016). All of the correlational research has found that spanked children or more frequently spanked children are worse behaved, have more psychological and emotional problems, and have worse relationships with their parents. The direction of the correlation is clear. We cannot know for sure if spanking is causing all of these bad outcomes (A causing B) or if something else is causing both of them (C causing A and B). But we can be absolutely certain that spanking is not causing good outcomes. It's just not an option, because the correlations all go in the opposite direction.

So correlational evidence leads us to the conclusion that spanking does not improve outcomes. We can be sure of that. But is it actually bad for kids? We don't know. Either A causes B, or C causes A and B. What do we mean by C—what else could possibly produce this correlation? Corporal punishment of toddlers is more common in families for whom spanking is normative in their community (MacKenzie, Nicklas, Waldfogel, & Brooks-Gunn, 2012), so there will be some racial/ethnic, social class, and religious groups that spank more or less than others. Those factors could also produce outcomes in children. For instance, African American parents, especially poor ones, are likely to endorse corporal punishment. If they were spanked, and all of their friends spank, and their in-laws recommend spanking, etc., they will very likely spank. But it's also true that African American kids suffer structural disadvantages that make it more likely that they will encounter difficulties in life not so likely for white children. So if their outcomes are worse, it could be because they were spanked, or it could be because of those structural disadvantages.

Another category of "other variables" that can affect both spanking and outcomes are personal ones. Spanking is less frequent when the parent has a supportive partner (MacKenzie, Nicklas, Waldfogel, & Brooks-Gunn, 2012). If the parent does not have a supportive partner, the parent is likely to be stressed and anxious, causing both spanking and child misbehavior as was described above. Again, this causes a problem with interpretation of a correlation. If spanking is associated with poor outcomes (and it is), that could be because spanking causes the poor outcome, or it could be because the parent's stress causes both spanking and the poor outcome.

Is there any way to rule out the possibility of "something else" (C), which could be structural, cultural, or personal factors, or potentially anything else, causing both A and B? Yes, there is a way to rule this out using another research method. The second type of evidence is **experimental**. The essence of experimental data is that the researchers don't simply observe what naturally happens in the world; they actively manipulate the variables. So while observational (aka correlational) research simply records who spanks and how much they spank, experimental research instead actively creates groups, randomly assigning some participants to a condition where they are instructed to use spanking and other participants to a condition where they are prohibited from spanking. If assignment to the spanking and no-spanking groups is random, then there can be no other variables (C's) confusing the issue. With random assignment to groups, if there is a difference between groups, we can be sure that A in fact causes B.

But wait a minute. Did I just say that we tell some parents they MUST spank and other parents that they MAY NOT spank? If that sounds ridiculous, it is. Experiments are possible in many areas of science but are prohibitively difficult in family science. For one thing, it seems immoral to intervene to this extent in parents' choices for the well-being of their children. For another thing, it's downright impractical. Parents simply will not comply with instructions that are this intrusive. Therefore, it is extraordinarily difficult to get experimental data on spanking. And this means that science cannot tell us finally if A causes B (or if C causes A) because experimental study designs are so limited. That is the state of the science on this question. We don't know, and we can't know for sure.

Correlates of Spanking

So we have correlational data only, but at least it is **longitudinal**, meaning the same children have been followed through time to measure their outcomes. That way, we can at least see if the spanking came first in time or if the presumed outcome was already present when the spanking started. What are the correlates of spanking that have been discovered by decades of observational research on the topic? There is little doubt about the direction of the correlations. Basically, spanking is associated with poor outcomes for children.

A meta-analysis of the large body of evidence in 2002 concluded that physical punishment of children was correlated with lower levels of moral internalization, lower quality of the parent-child relationship, poorer mental health both in childhood and adulthood, higher levels of aggression both in childhood and adulthood, antisocial behavior both in childhood and adulthood, higher risk of becoming a victim of domestic physical abuse, and higher risk of becoming a perpetrator of violent domestic abuse (Gershoff, 2002). Another meta-analysis soon after also reported that spanking was associated with mental health problems, suicidality, low self-esteem, poor academic achievement, disobedience, and hyperactivity. (Paolucci & Violato, 2004). Furthermore, spanking has also been negative correlated with multiple measures of intelligence and academic performance (Straus & Paschall, 2009).

Types of Spanking
These associations virtually always go in the direction of poor outcomes, and they are wide ranging, including short-term and long-term outcomes and covering multiple domains of development. However, because the data are observational (and thus correlational), interpretation is tricky, and some family scholars have suggested that not all spanking is equivalent. Larzelere and Kuhn (2005), for instance, published a meta-analysis exploring the existing published data from a different point of view. They proposed that only when spanking is particularly severe or when it is the primary form of discipline in the home will it be associated with such poor outcomes. They used the same published data as had been reported already (and summarized in the meta-analyses described above) and found ways to categorize spanking in those studies according to its severity and whether it was used with other strategies or not. Essentially, they found that the rarely and mildly spanked children have outcomes that are identical to the never-spanked children. So the spanking didn't really help anything, but it didn't hurt anything, either. The real problem is with frequent and exclusive spanking.

This is an important caveat to the spanking debate. Children who are spanked are at increased risk of being the victims of physical abuse by the very same parents who spank them (Gershoff & Grogan-Kaylor, 2016). It may be that physical punishment opens the door for parents to lose control and accidentally abuse their children. But it also could be that parents who are abusive spank abusively, and that is what damages children, but that parents who use physical punishment without being abusive are simply not placing their children at increased risk of anything; that they are simply using the technique of punishment according to proper guidelines. I don't know which it is. And due to the difficulty in obtaining experimental data in family science, it simply cannot be known. This remains an open question about which scholars continue to debate and pursue new lines of research in order to resolve.

Conclusions

Based on the research reviewed briefly above, we can conclude a few things so far:

- Spanking is almost certainly not helpful. It's not correlated with any good outcomes. Despite the "common sense" that spanking works and that spanking is sometimes necessary to help kids learn important lessons, decades of research has not produced a shred of evidence that this is true. There is no type of spanking and no frequency of spanking that is associated with improved outcomes.
- Frequent and harsh spanking is clearly correlated with many poor outcomes. We can't know for sure that it *causes* those poor outcomes, but it certainly cannot be ruled out. The family science discipline, by and large, is convinced that frequent and/or harsh physical discipline is damaging to children and to the parent-child relationship. A lot of parent education efforts are geared toward reducing harsh parenting, which typically means frequent and harsh spanking.

Remember the scientific consensus regarding parenting that was offered in Chapter 1? One point of consensus is the ineffectiveness and harm done by harsh punishment. This research on spanking is part of what created that consensus.

The remaining controversy in family science with regard to spanking is whether or not mild and infrequent spanking also increases the risk of poor outcomes. One camp says (with some correlational evidence to support them) yes, that since there is no benefit of spanking, then all it can possibly do is add unnecessary risk. Parent educators should, therefore, aim to reduce violence against children by eliminating any and all spanking. The other camp says (with some correlational evidence to support them) no, that mildly spanked children have the exact same outcomes as never-spanked kids, so this is not something that parent educators need to be worried about.

I invite students to consider which camp they are in and to recognize that they must do so from a position of a gap in scientific knowledge. Family science simply cannot answer this question yet. It's not that there is no answer. It's not that both answers are correct. It's not that it's a moral question rather than an empirical one. No. This is an empirical question with a right answer. But our science is not yet adequately developed to give us the answer. So we should attend carefully to the research on spanking in the near future, watching and waiting for an answer. In the meantime, we must make curricular decisions in the absence of the answer. It's a dilemma.

I will make one final observation here about this dilemma, in order to link it back to applied behavior analysis more generally and suggest a possible solution to the curricular dilemma. We have learned that all rewards and punishment are risky—punishment more so than other behavioral strategies—so we should not be surprised to learn that spanking in particular is risky and controversial. I often hear parenting experts say that parents should consider other strategies before spanking. The argument goes something like this: "If we can't convince you to give it up completely, then please, just try other things first." I agree with this strategy, but I notice that their suggestions for what to try instead are usually also punishments. They say to use time-out instead of spanking, to take away privileges instead of spanking, to scold instead of spank. But please note that all of these are punishments and so will also be quite risky.

Instead, I suggest that parent educators recommend moving down the pyramid. Get out of the level of applied behavior analysis. Move down into consequences, and try allowing the child to learn naturally or logically from their own choices. Or move down into communication, and try active listening to respond to the child's feeling, or try offering an I-message to convince the child to cooperate. Parents generally spank out of desperation. They don't know what else to do, and they feel at the end of their rope. If the parent educator reminds them that they have other tools, other strategies to try, then they might not feel so powerless. But we have to move them out of the behavior analysis level instead of recommending alternative punishments.

Review and Reflection Questions

1. What is the essential argument of the theory of behaviorism? If it is true, what does it imply about parenting?

2. How are classical conditioning and operant conditioning similar? How are they different? Can they be done accidentally? Can you think of any conditioning in your own life?

3. How do rewards and punishments overlap? What does that imply about the use of rewards?

4. What is the ABC model? What is it used for? Can you apply it to one of your own behaviors?

5. How can antecedents be used to promote desirable behavior? How can they be used to reduce undesirable behavior?

6. What are the best practices of using conditioning intentionally?

7. What are the best practices for shaping behaviors?

8. How is extinction accomplished? Why is it a problem not to follow best practices? Can you think of an example from your own life? When is extinction not appropriate to get rid of an undesirable behavior?

9. How can differential reinforcement be used to reduce an undesirable behavior?

10. What are the best practices for the use of punishment?

11. What are the limitations of the usefulness of rewards and punishments? What are the risks of these strategies, even when they are used appropriately?

12. When is it appropriate to use rewards or punishment?

13. Why do parents continue to use rewards and punishment even when they are not effective?

14. What mistakes do misguided behavioral parent programs typically make? Are behavioral parenting programs that follow best practices effective?

15. What is the difference between correlational and experimental evidence? What are the limitations of correlational evidence? What does correlational evidence about spanking suggest? Is it possible to get experimental evidence about spanking?

16. What are the correlates of spanking? Do we find them with all spanking, or just certain forms of spanking? What conclusions do scientists make regarding spanking?

17. How do you think parent educators should respond to mild and infrequent spanking?

Terminology to Know

- ABC model
- Accidental conditioning
- Antecedents
- Applied behavior analysis
- Approximation
- Behavior chain
- Behaviorism
- Classical conditioning
- Correlational
- Differential reinforcement
- Experimental
- Extinction
- Habituation
- Immediacy
- Longitudinal
- Negative punishment
- Negative reinforcement
- Operant conditioning
- Positive punishment
- Positive reinforcement
- Prompts
- Reinforcement/reward
- Schedule of reinforcement (continuous, fixed, variable)
- Shaping behavior

Names to Know

- Little Albert
- Pavlov
- Skinner
- Watson

References

Bolles, R.C. (1993). *The story of psychology: A thematic history*. California: Brooks/Cole Publishing Company.

Boucher, H.E. (2010). Participation in Accelerated Reader programs and reading pursuit in 11th grade. *Dissertation Abstracts International, Section A: Humanities and Social Sciences, 70*, 3743.

Cooper, J.O., Heron, T.E., & Heward, W.L. (2007). *Applied behavior analysis, 2nd edition.* Englewood Cliffs, NJ: Prentice-Hall.

Crain, W. (2010). *Theories of development: Concepts and applications, 6th edition.* Saddle River, NJ: Prentice Hall.

Dobson, J. (1996). *Dare to Discipline.* Tyndale Momentum.

Ferber, R. (1986). *Solve your child's sleep problems.* Fireside.

Ferster, C.B., & Skinner, B.F. (1957). *Schedules of reinforcement.* New York: Appleton-Century-Crofts.

Gershoff, E.T. (2002). Long-term effects of child punishment by parents and associated behaviors and experiences. A meta-analytic and theoretical review. *Psychological Bulletin, 128,* 539–579.

Gershoff, E. T., & Grogan-Kaylor, A. (2016, April 7). Spanking and child outcomes: Old controversies and new meta-analyses. *Journal of Family Psychology.* Advance online publication. http://dx.doi.org/10.1037/fam0000191

Hergenhahn, B.R. (2005). *An Introduction to the history of psychology.* Wadsworth Cengage Learning.

Kohn, A. (1999). *Punished by rewards.* Mariner Books.

Larzelere, R.E., & Kuhn, B.R. (2005). Comparing child outcomes of physical punishment and alternative disciplinary tactics: A meta-analysis. *Clinical child and family psychology review, 8, 1,* 1-37.

Larzelere, R.E., & Merenda, J.A. (1994). The effectiveness of parental discipline for toddler misbehavior at different levels of child distress. *Family Relations, 43,* 480–488.

Letarte, M.-J., Normandeau, S., & Allard, J. (2010). Effectiveness of a parent training program "incredible years" in a child protection service. *Child Abuse and Neglect, 34,* 253–261.

Loth, K.A., MacLehose, R.F., Fulkerson, J.A., Crow, S., & Neumark-Sztainer, D. (2013). Food-related parenting practices and adolescent weight status: A population-based study. *Pediatrics, 131,* e1443–e1450.

MacKenzie, M.J., Nicklas, E., Waldfogel, J., & Brooks-Gunn, J. (2012). Corporal punishment and child behavioural and cognitive outcomes through 5 years of age: Evidence from a contemporary urban birth cohort. *Infant and Child Development, 21,* 3–33.

Miller, N.V., Haas, S.M., Waschbusch, D.A., Willoughby, M.T., Helseth, S.A., Crum, K.I., Coles, E.K., & Pelham, W.E. (2014). Behavior therapy and callous-unemotional traits: Effects of a pilot study examining modified behavioral contingencies on child behavior. *Behavior Therapy, 45,* 606–618.

O'Donnell, J.M. (1985). *The origins of behaviorism.* New York: New York University Press.

Pavlov, I.P. (1927). *Conditioned reflexes.* New York: Dover Publications.

Pavlov, I.P. (1928). *Letters on conditioned reflexes, volume 1.* New York: International Publishers.

Paolucci, E.O., & Violato, C. (2004). A meta-analysis of the published research on the affective, cognitive, and behavioral effects of corporal punishment. *Journal of Psychology, 138,* 197–221.

Pearl, M., & Pearl, D. (1994). *To Train Up a Child.* No Greater Ministries.

Ramos, K.D., & Youngclarke, D. (2006). Parenting advice books about child sleep: Cosleeping and crying-it-out. *Sleep, 29,* 1608–1615.

Rogers, S.J., & Vismara, L.A. (2008). Evidence-based comprehensive treatments for early autism. *Journal of Clinical Child and Adolescent Psychology, 37,* 8–38.

Sanders, M.R. (1999). Trip P-Positive Parenting Program: Towards an empirically validated multilevel parenting and family support strategy for the prevention of behavior and emotional problems in children. *Clinical Child and Family Psychology Review, 2, 2,* 71–90.

Skinner, B.F. (1938). *The behavior of organisms.* Englewood Cliffs, NJ: Prentice Hall.

Skinner, B.F. (1953). *Science and human behavior.* New York: Macmillan.

Skinner, B.F. (1971). *Beyond freedom and dignity.* New York: Knopf.

Stolz, H. (2011). Parenting Education. In S.F. Duncan & H.W. Goddard (Eds.), *Family life education: Principles and practices for effective outreach, 2nd edition,* pp. 191–210. Thousand Oaks, CA: Sage.

Straus, M.A., & Paschall, M.J. (2009). Corporal punishment by mothers and development of children's cognitive ability: A longitudinal study of two nationally representative age cohorts. *Journal of Aggression, Maltreatment & Trauma, 18,* 459–483.

Sutherland, A. (2006). What Shamu taught me about a happy marriage. *New York Times,* June 25, 2006. http://www.nytimes.com/2006/06/25/fashion/25love.html Retrieved 4/9/2016.

Talwar, V., Arruda, C., & Yachison, S. (2015). The effects of punishment and appeals for honesty on children's truth-telling behavior. *Journal of Experimental Child Psychology, 130,* 209–217.

Watson, J.B. (1913). Psychology as the behaviorist views it. *Psychological Review, 20,* 158–177.

Watson. J. (1928). *The psychological care of infant and child.*

Watson, J.B., & Rayner, R. (1920). Conditioned emotional reactions. *Journal of Experimental Psychology, 3, 1,* 1–14.

Credits

- Fig. 7.2: Copyright © 2014 by Maxxl2 / Wikimedia Commons, (CC BY-SA 4.0) at https://commons.wikimedia.org/wiki/File:Pavlov%27s_dog_conditioning.svg.
- Fig. 7.3: John B. Watson / Copyright in the Public Domain.

PART III
Teaching: Strategies for Parenting Education

Part I of this book reviewed the context of parenting and parent education. Part II discussed the content that is often included in parenting education programs. Now in Part III, we turn to the task of implementing parenting education.

Anyone who works with children and/or families may be called upon to provide parenting education, whether it is their career objective or not. I teach in a department that is mainly comprised of child development students. My students generally want to work with kids. They want to teach preschool or elementary school, they want to be school counselors, or they want to be administrators of child care programs. A smaller number of my students are studying family science, often because they want to pursue a career in family counseling. Very few of my students come in wanting to provide parent education. However, they tell me after graduation that they do in fact teach about parenting in the jobs they have chosen.

Anyone who works with children necessarily has contact with adults who parent those children, and those caregivers see that person as an expert. The parents bring to the expert their heartfelt questions, such as: "She's having a hard time with the new baby at home. What can I do to make that easier?" or "Ugh! I can't seem to get him out of the house in the morning. Do you have any ideas for that?" This is an opportunity for informal parent education.

Child and family professionals also sometimes notice patterns of interaction that concern them, even if the parent doesn't ask for help. For instance, they might see a sullen and worried child in the classroom who will confide that her parent is making her play volleyball even though she doesn't like it. Or they may witness parents during pick-up or drop-off who willfully ignore their child's cries, explaining that he needs to toughen up. Professionals often see these things and want to advocate for the child by helping the parent see the situation differently.

Furthermore, child and family professionals build relationships with parents and see them occasionally at their most heartbroken or stressed and want to offer any help possible. Professionals in counseling very often help clients manage normative developmental challenges, a primary one of which is parenting. All of these circumstances call for informal parenting education. Matching the problem at hand to a relevant, helpful, and evidence-based suggestion requires the professional to have mastery over parenting strategies (Part II of this book). But it also requires that the professional consider his or her method of delivery of the parenting advice.

More formal parenting education is sometimes necessary, even in jobs such as those described above. For instance, when there is a "rash" of babies born into families in a given child care center, the center director may ask an employee to offer an evening session for parents to distribute information about this developmental milestone. Or when several parents ask a first-grade teacher for advice about how to help their children with reading, that teacher may set up an evening to meet with parents for this purpose. Professionals who conduct home visitations in families with children are essentially doing personalized semiformal parenting education with every visit. These are not full-blown comprehensive parenting classes, but they are short-term, targeted, parenting education interventions. Teachers and school counselors should be prepared with content they would like to share and training for how to administer such an intervention.

Formal parenting education is offered in a surprisingly wide variety of contexts. Parents often ask for help with parenting, so many organizations attempt to offer such a service. Churches, government agencies, and hospitals are some of the settings in which parenting classes are frequently offered. Again, students may not set parent education as their professional goal before finding themselves in a job that includes it as a component or being offered a job as a parent educator.

Therefore, we turn now, in Part III, to strategies for parenting education in the interest of informal parenting education, formal parenting programs, and all of the circumstances in between. Chapter 8 focuses on the emotional state of parents who need help. It addresses questions such as: What is the emotional response of parents to the difficulties of parenthood? Why do parents seem so surprised when things go wrong? How should the parent educator respond to a parent's grief?

Chapter 9 addresses the techniques used by parent educators. It will answer questions such as: Is it ever okay to offer unsolicited advice to parents? Can the strategies in Part II of the book also be used to help one teach? How is teaching adults different from teaching children? What makes for effective teaching? How might a student pursue a career as a parent educator?

Chapter 10 is a review of formal parent education programs. It deals with questions such as: Where do parents most likely go for help with their parenting? What are the advantages and disadvantages of support groups, classroom settings, online classes, and home visitation programs? Does it matter if the parent chooses to get help or is ordered by a judge in family court to do so? How do we know if a parent education intervention is working?

8. The Grief of a Parent

Introduction

We now begin to consider the strategies required to provide parenting education. The first step in this process is to consider the position of the parents involved. These are parents who informally ask for advice, who sign up for a formal program offered by their church or hospital, or who receive a court order to attend a formal class. What do they all have in common?

All of these parents are in a moment of need. They are at a point in their life where they do NOT have everything under control. Life is not going as they had planned or as they had hoped. It is a time of vulnerability, where they are facing something unanticipated for which they are not prepared. It is a time of unmet expectations. These are the pivotal moments in life, when things can change.

Unmet Expectations

Parenting involves the greatest joy and sometimes the deepest sorrow. This paradox is a difficult one to come to terms with. To illustrate, I begin with a personal example. As a child, when people asked me what I wanted to be when I grew up, I responded that I would be a mommy, of course. There was no question in my mind. I enjoyed school, excelled at it, and formulated expectations for my life in addition to motherhood, but I never relinquished my primary goal of being a parent. Through the years of my education and professional training, I dreamed about my future children and had names for them chosen and listed in rank order.

In my mid-twenties, I suffered my first miscarriage. It was a medically complicated situation, a ruptured ectopic pregnancy complicated by a blood clotting problem. I was rushed into emergency surgery and still I came close to death. My physical recovery was slow, and therefore I had many hours lying in a hospital bed to consider my loss and potential infertility. It was the first time it had ever occurred to me that parenthood might be a gift and not a birthright. I grieved not just for my lost pregnancy, but for the loss of my dreams, the loss of my innocent expectation that I was entitled to be a mother.

I have lost five pregnancies in all, but I have also given birth to four healthy daughters. For me, the pain of loss has been interwoven with the joy of new life so tightly that I cannot unravel the experiences. This was a profound lesson for me: parenthood makes us vulnerable to great pain in addition to great joy. While infertility, death, accidents, and injuries provide clear examples of the painful experiences of parenthood, a parent's pain is more universal than even those events suggest. It is not an unfortunate thing that happens to some unlucky parents; it is a central element of the experience of parenthood.

As my daughters have grown (the oldest is now an emerging adult), I have reflected often on the centrality of unmet expectations to my experience loving and caring for them. I have tried to relinquish expectations, but that has been impossible. There are many things we expect that we aren't even aware of. Just as I took for granted that I would someday be a mother, I became aware that I expect that my children would live to adulthood when I knew someone whose child died. I became aware that I expect that my children would be healthy when my best friend's child was diagnosed with a serious chronic disease and my nephew with a life-threatening allergy. I became aware that I expect them to be academically successful, finish high school, and pursue college educations when I watched friends whose children struggled with school and dropped out or failed academically. I became aware that I expect that they will share my political and religious beliefs when I listened to friends whose children did not share theirs. How many other expectations must I harbor of which I am even now unaware? This business of having expectations, it is what we humans do. Therefore, **unmet expectations** are central to the human experience.

As it turns out, my difficulty bearing children was only the first of many such unmet expectations that I carried into the job of parenting, and I'm nowhere near done raising my children. I expected that I would raise my children as part of a married family, until I got divorced and found myself raising them alone and then in a remarried blended family. I've had a child suffer with depression and one with scoliosis. I've seen them struggle with friendship drama, damaged family relationships, and academic failures. None of this is what I expected. There have been many times that I've thought that this job is harder than I thought it would be, more thankless, more desperate, and even unfulfilling. These unmet expectations—both the big issues (such as scary medical diagnoses) and the small ones (such as a failed driving test)—are ubiquitous in the parenthood experience.

Children's Health

Most of us expect our children to be healthy. How many times do we hear well-wishing friends of a pregnant couple ask "What are you hoping for, a girl or a boy?" only to hear the response "We don't care, as long as the baby is healthy!" This reflects a long human history in which children were quite likely to die in childhood or to suffer childhood illnesses that cause lifelong disability. But we live in a golden time, when most of us do not seriously consider the possibility that we won't have a healthy child. Antibiotics and vaccines have produced circumstances such that we can reasonably expect the vast majority of children born in the United States to survive childhood and to do so at a level of health unprecedented in human history (Centers for Disease Control, 1999).

Antibiotics revolutionized medical care in the early 20th century. Penicillin was discovered in 1928 and became widely available as a safe antibiotic medication during World War II. Now women could be treated easily for bacterial infections acquired during childbirth. Consequently, the maternal mortality rate plummeted, and women could reasonably expect to survive childbirth for the first time in human history. Now children could be treated easily for bacterial infections common in childhood. Now wound infections could be prevented and treated after injury. Antibiotics extended human life expectancy by making it possible to recover from infections that would have maimed and killed people in earlier eras. Very few people today even remember a time when we could not easily treat things like ear infections in small children with a simple antibiotic regimen. (See Figure 8.1.)

The other health-related revolution of the 20th century is childhood vaccination. We are now largely protected from viruses that in earlier eras routinely debilitated and killed children. For instance, the first polio vaccine became available in the 1950s, and not a single case of polio has originated in the US since 1979. Very few people today even remember a time when polio was a serious threat. Smallpox has been eradicated. Measles has been reduced to the point that most people in the United States do not know anyone who has suffered from it. This is a phenomenal success of modern medicine but one that is easy to take for

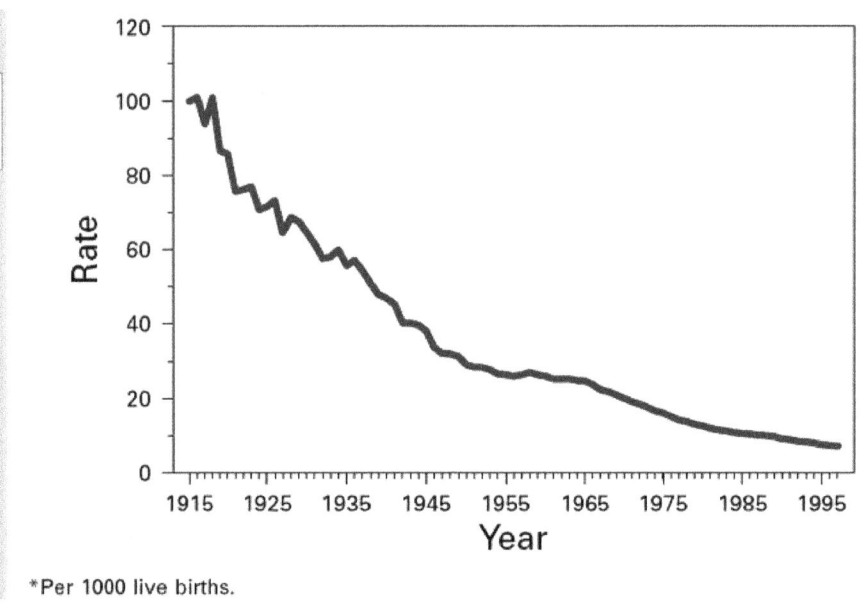

*Per 1000 live births.

Figure 8.1 Infant Mortality Rate, by Year—United States, 1915–1997

granted. We can now reasonably expect our children to survive childhood, and we don't even recognize how extraordinary this is.

So we expect our children to be healthy and our expectation is well founded compared to all of human history. But of course, there are still threats to children's health and well-being. For instance, congenital heart defects are the most common congenital birth defect and the most common cause of birth defect–related neonatal death (Mendis, Puska, & Norving, 2011). Sudden Infant Death Syndrome (SIDS) is another example of a threat to infant health. It is the most common cause of death in the United States for infants one month to one year of age (Centers for Disease Control and Prevention, 2012). Most parents do not expect to experience these things, and yet they happen.

I have a child with scoliosis (a condition where the spine is curved), and as a result have met several parents of similarly affected children. Many of them have children whose condition is far worse than my daughter's. All of us tell the same story, that we weren't even sure what scoliosis was until our child was diagnosed, and we never expected to have to face it.

Developmental delays, serious illness, accidental injury, physical and mental disabilities—the list of potential health problems that a child could face is seemingly endless. While the incidence of each one of these conditions individually is generally small, the chance that a child will suffer one of these health problems is not negligible. And since most parents have more than one child, the likelihood that a given parent will face a challenge related to a child's health is not small.

Other Expectations of Children

Health problems are only the tip of the iceberg. I have listed above some of my personal expectations about my own children. I hope the reader has been considering his or hers. Expectations are likely to vary by the personal values of the parent and family. Parents who are also teachers are likely to expect their children to value education. Parents who are also athletes are likely to expect their children to enjoy sports. Bookworms may hope for children who like to read, and artists may want their children to be creative.

Two areas that have received attention in family science research are sexual orientation and religious belief. Just as parents take for granted that their child will be healthy, they also take for granted that their child will be straight. Therefore, it is painful and disorienting when parents learn that their child is not (Saltzburg, 2004). Many parents of children who are lesbian, gay, bisexual or transgender (LGBT) children report that they themselves hide this information from their own social context to protect themselves as they take years to come to terms with what it means for their own identity (Phillips & Ancis, 2008).

LGBT teenagers report that telling their parents was extraordinarily difficult, and those are the ones who have done it. Others hide their sexual identity from their parents for fear of a bad response (Pew Research Center, 2015). Many LGBT youth receive as bad a reaction as they feared. Furthermore, a rejected response from parents is associated with dramatically higher rates of self-destructive behaviors such as suicide attempts (Ryan, Huebner, Diaz, & Sanchez, 2009).

The good news is that there is currently a shift in attitudes about this. As seen in Figure 8.2, it is only very recently that a slight majority of people in the United States say that it wouldn't upset them to learn that their child is gay (Gao, 2015a). We have yet to determine if this reported change in attitudes will lighten the actual burden of unmet expectations for parents or the implications of that for LGBT children.

The United States has one of the most religious populations of the world, especially among wealthy nations (Gao, 2015b). This has been changing in recent years, but it is still true. For many people, religious belief (or lack of it) is one of the most salient aspects of their identity. It is normal then to want and expect to

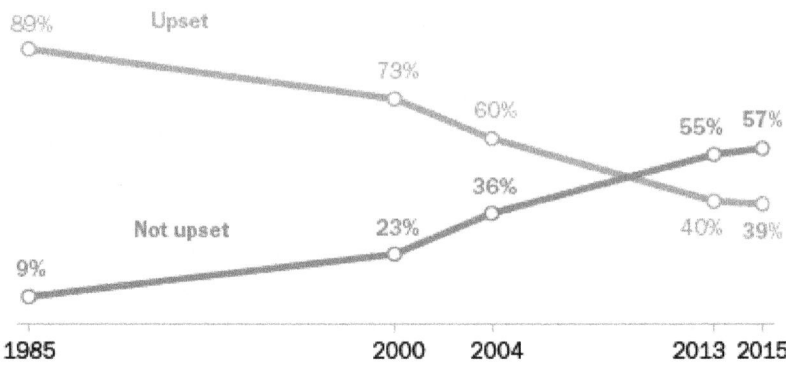

Figure 8.2 Changing Reactions to a Gay Child

share it with one's children. In fact, the vast majority of religious people share the religious beliefs of their parents. Families are generally the ones who teach religious belief, and most children retain the faith of their parents (Bengston, Putney, & Harris, 2013).

So imagine the dismay parents experience when their child abandons the religion of their childhood, either for a different one or for none at all. One small study (Martinez & Dyer, 2016) of young adults who stopped identifying with the religious faith of their parents found that most reported high levels of family conflict as a result. The young adults commonly reported that parents were angry and disappointed and that the parent felt like a failure as a parent to have an atheist child. Many also reported a new emotional distance with their parents. Data from the large National Longitudinal Study of Adolescent Health confirms that relationship quality is seriously damaged when children do not share their parents' faith (Stokes & Regnerus, 2009).

Parenthood

Thus, children are not always as their parents had believed they would be. So too does parenthood itself differ from expectations. Most prominently, it is far more difficult. Recently published research indicates that parents find the job to be utterly exhausting, even while they find it the source of their greatest fulfillment. Parents experience poorer physical health than nonparents; they are more stressed, anxious, and depressed. They are even less happy overall than adults without children (e.g., Hansen, 2012).

Not only is parenting a difficult job that takes a toll on the parent's well-being, parents aren't sure that they're doing a good job at it. About half of parents say that they are doing a very good job, but the other half can't bring themselves to say as much. Furthermore, the longer a person has been a parent, the less likely they are to report that they are doing a very good job (Parker, 2015). Perhaps parenthood keeps throwing challenges at them, draining their resources, and chipping away at their confidence.

Postpartum depression is a classic example of unmet expectations. Hormonally induced sadness after the birth of a baby is a well-known phenomenon that affects 10–15% of new mothers (Halbreich & Karkun, 2006). No one anticipates that depression will dominate their experience of new parenthood even though post-partum depression is a well-known phenomenon. How much less do they expect that depression will be a factor later in their children's lives. However, depression continues to be a risk of parenthood beyond infancy. One-tenth of mothers in the United States have suffered a major depressive disorder in the previous year. Women facing adversities such as divorce or unemployment are even more likely to suffer depression. Furthermore, only half of mothers who suffer an episode of major depressive disorder receive treatment (Ertel, Rich-Edwards, & Koenen, 2011).

Recent research suggests that mothers are most likely to suffer depression not when they have a newborn, but when their children are in middle school (Luthar & Ciciolla, 2016). The unhappiness of mothers of tweens seems to be related to their children's mood swings and behavioral acting out that become normative as they enter puberty, but also to the mother's own transition into midlife, concerns about her own competence as a parent, and worries about her child's future. Apparently, each developmental stage offers new sources of stress for parents, and many of them are not fully anticipated. It is well established that depression impairs parenting (Lovejoy, Graczyk, O'Hare, & Neuman, 2000), so the risk to parents' mental health is bad news for everyone involved.

Grief

Circumstances that do not meet one's expectations, such as the circumstances we have just reviewed, produce a sense of loss. What do parents do with all of those unmet expectations and the sense of loss that they produce? They grieve.

Grief is the process by which people come to terms with unmet expectations. It consists of an emotional component, a cognitive component, and a behavioral component. Emotionally, grief may include a wide range of feelings. Emotional experiences of grief often include sadness, yearning, fear, and anger sometimes accompanied by relief and even joy about the unexpected circumstance. Cognitively, grief may include ways of thinking about loss that attempt to either minimize or reframe the nature of the loss, and it may also include ways of thinking about the loss that embrace it. Behaviorally, grief may include personal behaviors such as crying, as well as social behaviors such as talking to friends or holding a religious service.

Grief is a process rather than a status. It is an activity rather than a state. It is something that we do. We feel. We think. We act. And in so doing, we grieve. It is an action verb. Therefore, it is possible to choose not to do it, to some extent. It is possible to get "stuck" and simply refuse to continue the process. I think here of parents whose relationships with their children are simply ruptured and never healed because the parent refuses to grieve the loss of their expectations and therefore meet the child—as he or she really is—in an authentic and meaningful relationship. I wish this was an extreme and rare thing, but it is not. For instance, one study found that, among parents of LGBT adolescents who were very rejecting when their child disclosed, only half became more accepting of their child over time (Samarova, Shilo, & Diamond, 2014).

Consequently, it is a process and to some degree an optional one. But it is an activity that human beings can often do naturally and often do well (Bonanno, 2004). Grieving is not an indicator of mental illness; rather, it is something we do best when we are healthy. Grief can deepen relationships and help people make meaning in life, and it usually does (Bonanno, 2010). I think here of the parents who take an active interest in their child's life, in their hobbies and professions, even when they did not share those interests originally. I think of the parents of gay children who advocate for the legal rights of all LGBT people after grieving their own unmet expectations. In fact, among people who have changed their mind on the issue of support for same-sex marriage, the explanation most commonly offered is that they know someone who is LGBT (Pew Research Center, 2013).

Additionally, grief is personal. People experience it differently. They do it differently. We cannot say even generally what the process is like. When Kübler-Ross (1969) wrote about grief in the 1960s, bringing unprecedented professional and cultural attention to the subject, she proposed that there were stages of grief that people move through in an orderly fashion. But research has not supported a stage theory of grief (Neimeyer, 2001). Instead, it appears that grief is a deeply personal and variable process.

Implications for Parent Education

We see that grief is a process, a natural one and a variable one. It is also integral to the experience of parenthood. How are parent educators to make sense of this omnipresent grief, and how can they help?

Perhaps the simplest explanation is that few jobs are so completely all consuming and for so many years. Parenting consumes most of a parent's time and identity for many, many years. Even when they do other jobs simultaneously, those jobs are, for most parents, less important than the care of their children. And few jobs define adults' identities so completely as does parenthood. In addition, it's an identity about which parents feel uncertain much of the time. As one friend complained to me when her first child was born, she wouldn't even know if she had done a good job until years after it would be too late to change! This is disempowering, even as the job is considered the most important one of a person's life. Parents have a sense that they MUST do this well, but they really don't know how, and they feel powerless about that.

When parents arrive at a parenting class, either chosen voluntarily or court mandated, grief is likely to be front and center. They have been confronted with painful feelings of powerlessness, failure, and desperation. They often feel vulnerable and lost.

Parent educators might begin to help by understanding how common those unmet expectations are for parents and thus how prevalent is the subjective experience of grief. If grief is normative, then we must be unafraid of it. We must see it in the parents we work with and recognize it for what it is: a normal and painful part of the job. Sometimes it is so deeply disturbing that it prevents parents from taking positive steps toward improvement or growth. What do we do with the normal painful experiences of childhood when we see children experiencing them? We accept those experiences, and we let children know that they can talk to us about them. We help them process those feelings. This has been called active listening (Gordon, 2000) or emotion coaching (Gottman & DeClaire, 1998). This is what we offer to children when they suffer. Refer back to Chapter 5 for a refresher. Perhaps parent educators can offer this to parents too when the parents are suffering. This is **acknowledgment**, where the person's emotional state is recognized, and **validation**, where the person's state is seen as reasonable or understandable, even if it not ideal.

A parent educator must therefore be willing to acknowledge unmet expectations and reflect back to the parent his or her feelings associated with grief. They might say things like: "That must be difficult to accept … It seems that this is an ongoing struggle for you … By your facial expression, it seems that this is causing you a lot of pain." This acknowledgment can be remarkably powerful. Validation is equally powerful. The parent educator might simply say: "You are in a very difficult situation; I can see why you would feel that way," or "What an exasperating kid! I wouldn't know what to do either!" Acknowledgment and validation will not, of course, solve the underlying problem. But it does free parents to explore the problem fully because their own emotions have been permitted into the conversation.

Conclusion

When parents ask for help with parenting or when parents are forced to seek help, they are in an emotional state that makes them both vulnerable and resistant. They are certainly facing unmet expectations regarding their children or the job of parenthood. Unmet expectations are very painful, yet they are an integral part of parenthood. Grief is how people come to terms with them. Therefore, the parent educator must be ready to acknowledge, with compassion, that the parent learners are probably grieving and have respect for that process.

Review and Reflection Questions

1. What are your expectations of children you love? Of your relationships with them? Can you imagine the emotional impact when those expectations are not met?

2. Why does the author assert that unmet expectations are a central element of parenthood? Do you agree?

3. What medical advances created the circumstance that we live in, that most of us expect children to live into adulthood and to be generally healthy?

4. What are the potentially damaging outcomes associated with unmet expectations regarding sexual orientation and religious belief? Can you think of other subjects that might also cause the same outcomes?

5. What are the implications of grief being a natural, but optional and variable, process rather than a fixed state? How have you grieved? Does this chapter reflect your experience with grief?

Terminology to Know

- Acknowledgment
- Grief
- Unmet expectations
- Validation

References

Bengston, V.L., Putney, N.M., & Harris, S. (2013). *Families and faith: How religion is passed down across generations.* New York: Oxford University Press.

Bonanno, G. (2004). Loss, trauma, and human resilience: Have we underestimated the human capacity to thrive after extremely aversive events? *American Psychologist, 59, 1,* 20–28.

Bonanno, G. (2010). *The other side of sadness: What the new science of bereavement tells us about life after loss.* Basic Books.

Centers for Disease Control (1999). Achievements in public health, 1900–1999: Healthier mothers and babies. *MMWR Weekly, 48, 38,* 849–858. https://www.cdc.gov/mmwr/preview/mmwrhtml/mm4838a2.htm Retrieved 1/3/2017.

Centers for Disease Control and Prevention (2012). Infant Health. http://www.cdc.gov/nchs/fastats/infant-health.htm. Retrieved 12/17/2016.

Ertel, K.A., Rich-Edwards, J.W., & Koenen, K.C. (2011). Maternal depression in the United States: Nationally representative rates and risks. *Journal of Women's Health, 20, 11,* 1609–1617.

Gao, G. (2015a). Most Americans now say learning their child is gay wouldn't upset them. http://www.pewresearch.org/fact-tank/2015/06/29/most-americans-now-say-learning-their-child-is-gay-wouldnt-upset-them/ Retrieved 12/17/2016.

Gao, G. (2015b). How do Americans stand out from the rest of the world? Pew Research Center. http://www.pewresearch.org/fact-tank/2015/03/12/how-do-americans-stand-out-from-the-rest-of-the-world/ Retrieved 1/15/2017.

Gordon, T. (2000). *Parent effectiveness training.* Harmony.

Gottman, J., & DeClaire, J. (1998). *Raising an emotionally intelligent child: The heart of parenting.* New York: Simon & Schuster.

Halbreich, U., & Karkun, S. (2006). Cross-cultural and social diversity of prevalence of postpartum depression and depressive symptoms. *Journal of Affective Disorders, 91, 2,* 97–111.

Hansen, T. (2012). Parenthood and happiness: A review of folk theories versus empirical evidence. *Social Indicators Research, 108,* 26–64.

Kübler-Ross, E. (1969). *On death and dying.* Routledge.

Lovejoy, M., Graczyk, P.A., O'Hare, E., & Neuman, G. (2000). Maternal depression and parenting behavior: A meta-analytic review. *Clinical Psychology Review, 20,* 561–592.

Luthar, S.S., & Ciciolla, L. (2016). What it feels like to be a mother: Variations by children's developmental stages. *Developmental Psychology, 52, 1,* 143–154.

Martinez, C., & Dyer, K. (2016). "She calls me her lost lamb": Emotions and family relationships associated with the loss of religious belief in young adulthood. Paper presentation at the 37th Annual Central California Research Symposium, Fresno, California, April 20, 2016.

Mendis, S., Puska, P., & Norving, B. (2011) Global Atlas on Cardiovascular Disease Prevention and Control. World Health Organization in collaboration with the World Heart Federation and the World Stroke Organization.

Neimeyer, R.A. (2001). *Meaning reconstruction and the experience of loss.* American Psychological Association.

Parker, K. (2015). Parenting in America. http://www.pewsocialtrends.org/2015/12/17/parenting-in-america/ Retrieved 12/17/2016.

Pew Research Center (2013). Growing support for gay marriage: Changed minds and changing demographics. http://www.people-press.org/2013/03/20/growing-support-for-gay-marriage-changed-minds-and-changing-demographics/ Retrieved 12/17/2016.

Phillips, M.J., & Ancis, J.R. (2008). The process of identity development as the parent of a lesbian or gay male. *Journal of LGBT Issues in Counseling, 2, 2*, 126–158.

Ryan, C., Huebner, D., Diaz, R.M., & Sanchez, J. (2009). Family rejection as a predictor of negative health outcomes in white and Latino lesbian, gay, and bisexual young adults. *Pediatrics, 123, 1*, 346–352.

Saltzburg, S. (2004). Learning that an adolescent child is gay or lesbian: The parent experience. *Social Work, 49, 1*, 109–118.

Samarova, V., Shilo, G., & Diamond, G.M. (2014). Changes in youths' perceived parental acceptance of their sexual minority status over time. *Journal of Research on Adolescence, 24, 4*, 681–688.

Stokes, C.E., & Regnerus, M.D. (2009). When faith divides family: Religious discord and adolescent reports of parent-child relations. *Social Science Research, 38, 1*, 155–167.

Credits

- Fig. 8.1: Centers for Disease Control / Copyright in the Public Domain.
- Fig. 8.2: Source: Pew Research Center.

9. Effective Teaching

Introduction

We have reviewed the context and content of parent education programs. We have begun to consider the emotional state of parents when they find themselves in need of direction. Now we turn to the subject of how best to teach parenting. As readers surely know from their own experience of having both excellent and cringe-worthy teachers, teaching is not easy. And it does not necessarily flow automatically from knowledge. Teaching involves a skill set that is separate from the understanding of content. Therefore, we must discuss methods of instruction and principles of effective teaching.

Unsolicited Advice

Gaining insight into the challenges and processes of parenting is a powerful experience. Students generally see their own parents in a different light by this point in the semester, typically softening toward their mistakes and feeling more gratitude for their efforts and appreciation for their successes. But something else happens. Student often begin to recognize destructive parenting practices in family members and friends and wonder what to do about it. Non-responsiveness to tender needs, evaluative person-centered praise, overuse of punishment … these are commonly observed. Students want to know what to do about this. Should they make recommendations to people who didn't ask for help? That is, should they offer **unsolicited advice**?

It's a tough question. In general, my suggestion is that they say nothing unless the treatment rises to the level of abuse. Why say nothing? Well, most parents see parenting as the most important job of their life and are therefore so defensive about it that direct and unsolicited feedback will go unheeded at best, but more likely will be resented so deeply that relationships will be ruptured.

Most parents are extraordinarily sensitive about what people around them think of the job they are doing. To be challenged on this, especially by someone who has just taken a college class seems unbelievably insulting. Most parents do not accept unsolicited advice with equanimity. They get defensive and angry. Commonly, in response to unsolicited advice, parents explain that real-life everyday parenting is different from what is in a textbook, and/or they may argue that their child or circumstances are unique. Either way, this defensive posture means that they are not willing or able to hear the advice that their friend is offering.

First of all, let's acknowledge that the parent is absolutely right. Textbooks generally present information in the clearest way possible, while real life is far more muddled and confused. And the book could not possibly have been written about the specific individual circumstances of a particular family. Consequently, a textbook cannot possibly have the exact right answer to every problem. This is perfectly true of this book just as for every other book written on the subject of parenting. However, let us also acknowledge the content of the book is not invalidated by the fact that this is a textbook. And a student is not necessarily wrong just because he or she is a student.

Very good insights and helpful advice are commonly rejected as a result of defensiveness. That is a shame, but it is understandable. Unsolicited advice is heard as criticism, as an indictment that the parent is a failure at the most important job imaginable. It is humiliating. It can be devastating. So most parents defend against criticism by invalidating it. I don't blame parents for resisting advice in this way. For one thing, the vulnerability of parenting is like nothing else in life. Most parents are highly motivated to have others see them as good parents (Parker, Horowitz, & Rohal, 2015). They want their children to thrive, of course, but they also have a deep need to maintain their identity as a competent person. Parenthood is threatening in that way. The outcomes are important, yet out of a parent's control in meaningful ways.

Parents and nonparents alike see children's behavior as a reflection of parenting. It reminds me of the song from the musical *Willy Wonka & the Chocolate Factory*. One of my daughters played Violet Beauregard in the musical, the girl who turns into a giant blueberry when she tries Wonka's bubble gum. The lyrics of the song (Bricusse & Newley, 1971) say:

> Who do you blame when your kid is a brat?
> Pampered and spoiled like a Siamese cat?
> Blaming the kids is a lie and a shame,

You know exactly who is to blame:
The mother and the father.

Ouch. Mothers and fathers know that they are being blamed when their child is a brat or badly behaved in any way. And it doesn't matter if the child's behavior is developmentally normal. They feel judged (and let's face it, they ARE being judged) anytime the child's behavior is inconvenient to others ("Those parents shouldn't take him out if they can't keep him under control!") or the child mistreats others ("You know where she learned that!") or anytime the child suffers ("Why didn't his parents protect him from that!?").

And then there is the risk of a child not getting his act together in time to meet adulthood. I feel a twinge of performance anxiety when one of my kids goes to school without her lunch, again. Or forgets to take her musical instrument to school, again. What must that teacher think of me? When the dentist reports a new cavity, it feels as though he is silently scolding me: "Why don't you teach her to brush her teeth better?" Most parents know that they will feel like a failure if they have a grown child who cannot navigate adulthood meaningfully. Since there is no second chance, the stakes are high, and parents are supersensitive about being seen as bad parents.

Given the sensitivity of parents, are child and family science students ever able to share their expertise about parenting outside of formal training programs? My answer is yes, and that the skills required to do so can then be translated for use in formal parent education settings. Here is my suggestion: Instead of verbally offering unsolicited advice, students would do better to model the skills that they think the parent lacks. If the parent is insensitive to tender needs, the student can try to demonstrate what it looks like to respond sensitively to tender needs—the tender needs of the child, but also the tender needs of the parent. If the parent tends to use communication roadblocks, the student can demonstrate active listening, both with the child and with the parent. If the parent offers person-centered feedback, the student can offer process-centered feedback. Parents will watch, and if it appears to be effective, they will copy the behavior. Sometimes they will even pull the student aside and ask them to explain what they just did. Modeling like this works best when the person doing it is known, liked, and trusted by the parent.

This is not immediately fulfilling. Friends and family do not generally gush with gratitude. They just quietly notice and try it later when they are alone. They almost never come back with thanks later. But this may be the most powerful mechanism a student in child and family science has to share his or her expertise with folks in an informal setting.

At times however, modeling a behavior with the child is not practical. For instance, a friend might explain that she tried cry-it-out sleep training last night. The child and family science student might be concerned about her lack of sensitive responsiveness but is not in a position to model more sensitive caregiving. Therefore, the student needs a **nonconfrontational opening**, a way to broach the subject without being directly critical of her. Often, the best way to open up a conversation about something without offending the parent is to do it in the form of a question.

"I wonder" questions are a way to invite the parent to consider the child's point of view. For example, "I wonder what she thinks is happening when you leave her alone at night?" or "I wonder why she's reacting so badly to the broccoli? Do you have any idea?" Such questions invite the parent to consider a perspective other than the one she has been using. When life gets hectic, kids get out of control, and parents get tired, it is easy for them not to take a moment to consider the child's feelings. And this is a nonconfrontational way to invite the parent to do so. The "I wonder" technique is used by pediatricians, whose job requires that they use nonconfrontational openings in the context of a short doctor's visit when they want to help parents gain insight into their child's problematic behavior (King, 2009).

The key to a nonconfrontational opening is to open up the conversation on the topic of the parenting practice in such a way that the parent does not feel attacked but instead has a chance to carefully consider his or her behavior. Another strategy I use is to express sympathy when the parent appears to be overwhelmed or exasperated. "Oh man, some days are hard!" I might offer, or "What are we supposed to do when they act like that?" Then, if the parent wants to tell me about it, I've created an opening for that to happen. The reader may be able to generate other types of nonconfrontational openings.

My final recommendation is that when offering parenting advice, it should be offered in the spirit of "just something to try" rather than being presented as the best, most obvious, correct approach. It is just one option, something that may or may not help, one way to think about it. All of these caveats lower the stakes. Parents are free to try this or not without this being a test of their parenting skills.

These strategies for offering unsolicited advice can also be used in a formal parent education setting. People may have chosen to be in class, or they may have been forced to be there by a court order, but they are quite likely to still feel sensitive about being judged. In fact, if they are already facing unmet expectations regarding parenthood, their feelings of being a failure may be heightened. These principles may help the instructor ease them into the learning environment without triggering a defensive reaction.

Parenting Pyramid = Teaching Pyramid

The parenting pyramid that we spent so much time discussing in Part II (see Figure 9.1) can also be considered a teaching pyramid. Many of the principles pertain to teaching just as well as to parenting. I don't mean that the jobs are identical; they are obviously different in important ways. But many of the principles operate in both settings.

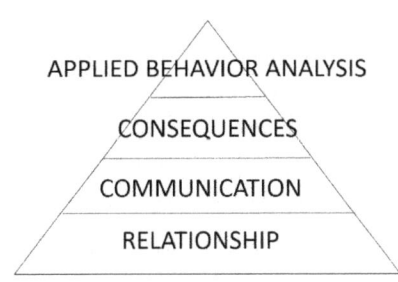

Figure 9.1 Parenting Pyramid

The reader may recall from our earlier discussion of the pyramid that the strategies at the bottom form the foundation upon which all else rests, and that strategies higher up should be used less often than those near the bottom. If we apply these principles to teaching, we begin by considering how a teacher builds relationship with learners. We also should restrain ourselves from overuse of rewards and punishment while teaching, in favor of building authentic and responsive relationships.

Relationship

Just as children trust a parent with whom they have a secure attachment, learning also happens in the context of warm relationships. How is that accomplished? Parent educators should not dismiss or minimize the role of introductions. He or she must spend time to build relationships at the beginning of a formal parenting class. It is an investment, not a waste of time, to allow each person a chance to share something of their personal story. In a large class, they might be offered the chance to share with someone sitting next to them rather than with the whole group. In a case where details are legally sensitive or where former partners are in the same classroom, the instructor may ask for a written introduction/explanation at the time of registration rather than doing so verbally in class. In all cases, they should be allowed to introduce themselves and have their story responded to with empathy and kindness.

Remember from Chapter 3 that secure-attachment relationships are built by sensitive responsiveness to tender needs. When parents tell their story at the beginning of a parenting class, they are presenting their unmet expectations and their vulnerability. This is an emotional task that deserves to be recognized as such by the instructor. In my experience providing parent education to divorcing parents, these introductions are generally offered with quavering voices and sometimes tears. An introduction in this context is no small task. The instructor must respond gently and with the unconditional positive regard we read about in Chapter 5.

The emotional tone of the introductions is a critical component of successful relationship building. All humans are sensitive to judgment but especially people who already feel vulnerable, such as parents in a parenting class. And learning cannot happen so long as hypervigilance and defensiveness are maintained. As Haim Ginott wrote: "Truth for its own sake can be a deadly weapon in family relations. Truth without compassion can destroy love. Some parents try too hard to prove exactly how, where and why they have been right. This approach cannot but bring bitterness and disappointment. When attitudes are hostile, facts are unconvincing" (Ginott, 1972, p. 38). It is true of parents in the home with their children and equally true of teachers in a classroom with their students.

Furthermore, during introductions, the instructor should take note of specific details of each parent (for example, the gender and age of each of the children) and use that information to shape future discussion. The instructor should also use whatever strategy is necessary to learn names. To be called by name helps people feel that they are known. The effort for the instructor is worth it because it helps build a relationship upon which all else rests.

Communication

The parenting pyramid also taught us that we can use communication to teach new skills if we use process-focused feedback rather than person-focused feedback. Recall from Chapter 4 the work of Carol Dweck. Some parents will come into class with a helpless orientation to learning due to their fixed mindset. They will believe that their parenting skills are a fixed entity, not going to change.

They will have the goal of performing for the judge who ordered them to come and thus will not want to take any risks by trying anything new. They will be defensive, bored, or anxious. And (unless we can change their orientation to learning) they will not learn. Others will have a mastery orientation due to their growth mindset. They will hope for an opportunity to learn something and be excited about it.

The parent educator should consider how to move folks toward a mastery orientation. We learned in Chapter 4 that this is done through process-focused feedback. The parent educator should notice the parent's efforts ("It sounds as if you have tried many things; you've really been working on finding a solution to this); describe the parent's approach objectively and without moral judgment ("You thought maybe setting up a reward would motivate your son to work harder"); and focus on progress. Language that notices—rather than language that evaluates—is very powerful to help parents move toward change.

Remember, the skills that the educator wishes to teach need to be modeled with the learners. If the parent educator suggests that the parent use process-centered feedback but then offers person-centered praise to the parent, he is sending mixed messages. The parent will probably learn what was experienced rather than what was heard, so the lesson has just backfired. As such, parent educators must feel very comfortable practicing the same skills that they are teaching.

Teaching new skills is obviously the heart of an educational program, and hence the material on mindset is probably the most relevant here. But we might also consider the PET strategies (active listening, I-messages, and win-win problem solving) as they apply in a classroom. Active listening is helpful when a parent in the classroom comes to class with a difficult circumstance from home. Parents often feel helpless and frustrated and scared when their children are acting out. The parent educator can reflect those feelings and help the parent problem solve.

For example, I once had a student who brought up her 19-year-old son's behavior in a parenting class. She repeatedly stated how little she sees of him. She said things like: "He lives with me, but I go for weeks without seeing him. Sometimes he comes home late, but he's still sleeping when I leave for work in the morning, and he hates it when I open up his bedroom door, and then he's gone when I get home. Ha, ha! I assume he still lives with me but I can't really be sure!" Somehow, under her attempt at humor, behind her anger at him, I recognized something else. I asked her "I wonder if you miss him?" There was silence for a moment. Something had happened. I had managed to reflect her feelings in a way that helped her see them clearly. "Yes!" she cried. "He's my baby. He's all I have right now. We used to be so close, and now it feels like I've lost him."

There may not have been a dry eye in the house as this mom described her sorrow and her sense of helplessness. Then she told us what a sweet boy he is and how much she enjoys his company. She had needed help seeing the situation clearly, and a little bit of active listening allowed her to get the insight she needed. She resolved that when she does see him, she will stop scolding him for how he neglects her. She suggested that she might construct an I-message to tell him her feelings in a way that is less confrontational than the snarky comments she has been making. That situation is not something that happens every class period. And it cannot necessarily be planned in advance. But if the parent educator knows how to use active listening, it is a skill that can be demonstrated quite powerfully in the classroom.

I-messages and win-win problem solving can also be utilized in a classroom setting. When the parent educator uses one of these strategies, he or she should take a moment afterward to point out what has just been illustrated. Making these connections explicitly helps the learner see them clearly.

Consequences

On the parenting pyramid, we sometimes have to move into the Danger Zone, beginning with consequences. This is necessary to build personal responsibility or when communication has not worked to solve problems. If all goes well, a parent educator need not spend much time this high on the pyramid, but he or she must be capable of this if necessary.

For example, if a parent is court ordered to attend a specific number of hours of parent education, the parent educator is obligated to keep track of attendance in class and to honestly report that to the court. The parent is free to make his or her own decisions regarding attendance, but the parent will also face the logical consequences of those decisions. The parent educator must be prepared to use active listening with the parent when the consequence is enacted.

Behavior Analysis

The final level of the pyramid has to do with behavior analysis. Analysis and manipulation of antecedents of behavior is very useful for the parent educator. Prompts of appropriate behavior will surely include clear expectations, a schedule, and reminders of tasks, as well as modeling of desired behaviors.

Other prompts may include the physical layout of the meeting room. Allowing students to sit in rows of desks creates the association with passive receipt of information as in school. If I want a discussion to happen, I will put the chairs in a circle to convey that all will actively participate.

As for the behavioral techniques of reward and punishment, it is dangerous to rely heavily on rewards (food, prizes, etc.) to entice participation in a parenting program. It is certainly even more dangerous to use punitive methods (scolding, humiliation) as a form of instruction in a parent education setting. Neither of these approaches is conducive to authentic and long-lasting change. So the parent educator should guard against the temptation to use these strategies.

Adult Education Theory

So far, we have reviewed some of my personal insights about teaching that are specific to parent education. To metaphorically step back and consider the broader area of adult education yields additional insights for the parent educator.

Formal education has generally been directed toward children. Children typically enter into formal education around six years of age and complete it by their late teens. As a result, strategies for effective teaching are based on the cognitive development and other developmental needs of children. The practice of teaching has been termed ***pedagogy***, a word of Greek origin meaning "the leading of children."

But not all formal education is for children. Adult education is a specialized field that explores the strategies for effective instruction of adults rather than children. Malcolm Knowles has proposed the term ***andragogy*** to describe this. The term is derived from the Greek, meaning "the leading of adults" (Knowles, Holton, & Swanson, 2015).

Pedagogy

Knowles begins his exposition of andragogy by first specifying the assumptions of pedagogy against which andragogy can be compared. He argues that pedagogy is a model of education that is based on the status of the learner as dependent, which is generally true of young children. Due to the learner's dependence, several assumptions (Knowles, Holton, & Swanson, 2015) can be made:

1. **The young learner does not know what he or she needs to learn.** Consider young children starting elementary school. They have no idea what the requirements of adulthood will be. Hence, they must trust their teachers to determine their curriculum. They simply don't know what they need to know. Children in kindergarten, for instance, do not question why they need to know their colors. A first-grader never suggests that they can probably get by just fine without reading. If the teacher teaches it, then they will learn it. They have no alternative but to trust the teacher completely.

2. **The young learner's self-concept is based on feedback from the teacher.** Very young students simply have not had the time or experience to construct an academic self-concept. No kindergartner walks in the door and announces that she has math anxiety but really enjoys literature. They just haven't developed that kind of self-concept. They don't even know the categories yet. Therefore, education of young children is wide open and not threatening to the way kids think about themselves.

3. **The young learner does not have experience that is relevant to learning.** Not only do children not have an academic self-concept, they also don't bring a lot of personal experiences that shape their learning. Teaching children means starting from scratch. Introducing a concept to them typically means introducing something they have never heard of or thought about before. It's remarkable, really. To be a true novice can be an advantage, because there are no misconceptions to clear up. But it can also be a disadvantage because it means the student cannot make meaningful connections to help them remember things.

4. **The young learner must be prompted by the teacher to be ready to learn.** Children don't have experiences to help or hinder their understanding of new material, but that also means that they are not particularly primed to be ready to learn anything in particular. They don't come in the door desperate to know something. They really don't seem to think about how subjects build on each other, that lessons have direction. I'm always amazed when I ask my children what they are studying in school. They act like it's

a ridiculous question, as if they couldn't possibly have any idea what will happen tomorrow at school. They don't leave school one day eager to see how the subject will be resumed the next day. They just take each day as it comes. Even if they enjoy school, they just take it one day at a time.

5. **The young learner is focused on a subject matter (rather than on a specific task).** Because they don't have a particular need to know and they don't know what it is they need to know, children accept what their teachers offer to them. And that tends to be driven by subject matter because it is general background information rather than a specific task. This is a defining feature of pedagogy that is easy to see in elementary school education. We divide up the day among reading, math, and social studies. These are the subjects. These are the categories that we teach them. We add subjects gradually as kids move through elementary school, but we continue to divide up the day by subject matter rather than by tasks.

6. **The young learner must be motivated by external pressures, including the approval or disapproval of the teacher.** The issue of motivation to learn may be the quintessential feature of pedagogy. When Knowles says that children are dependent learners, he gets directly to the source of their motivation. Their motivation comes from their teachers, not from themselves. They might not mind learning, they may even enjoy it, but they do it because someone else created that experience for them. Therefore, the teacher must find ways to maintain motivation, even when the task is difficult.

When learners are totally dependent, as they are in early childhood, these assumptions seem to hold up. They naturally lend themselves to particular teaching strategies, which has been called pedagogy. We are all familiar with pedagogy, having been brought up in a formal education system that uses it. We went to school because it was required, not because we had a gap in knowledge that we needed to fill. Our parents signed us up and dropped us off. The teachers decided what we would do in school. They divided the day into subjects. We worked to get passing grades or even good grades. We were pleased when the teacher was pleased, and we were dismayed when the teacher was unhappy with our performance.

As we got older, however, some of these assumptions probably started to chafe. How many of us ever said (or thought), "I don't see why I have to know this! When will I ever use this in real life?" We may have resented studying things we weren't interested in for reasons we could not fathom. We did start to develop an academic self-concept, and we started saying things like "Ugh! I'm not good at English!" or "I'm always good at science, I don't even have to study hard in that class!" These newly developed aspects of our self-concept actually started to interfere with our education, as we didn't want to work hard on subjects we believed ourselves to be bad at. And we started to exercise our choice of electives to avoid those subjects entirely. For high school students, some of the assumptions of pedagogy are still true, but many are only partly true. And yet mainstream teaching strategies continue to be pedagogical.

By the time a student arrives in college, are any of the assumptions of pedagogy still true? I would say that there is a lot of variety in a college classroom. Some students remain very dependent academically. They may have chosen a major, but they really don't know what their job will entail, so they must rely on their professors to tell them what they need to know. Their habit of being externally motivated is so deeply engrained that they do not abandon it. They want to please their parents, who may be paying for college, by getting good grades.

But many other students are no longer very dependent at all. None of these assumptions fit them very well. They are fully functioning adults, working a job to make their way through life and doing school at the same time. Their schedules are tight, their time precious. They might even work in their field of choice already. Many of my students work in child care centers or after-school programs, applying the course content on a daily basis. They feel a need to know what they learn in their child development classes. They are internally motivated to do the job they have chosen.

So there is wide variety. Most college students are somewhere in between these two extremes. And they may lean in one direction in one class but toward the other direction in a different class. Or they clearly meet some of the assumptions of pedagogy but clearly do not meet others. It is a mix.

Andragogy

Knowles argues that pedagogy does not work very well with adult learners because they arrive at the learning experience with a different set of characteristics than children do. I was introduced to this principle when I spent a few months teaching in an adult literacy program after I finished my bachelor's degree. I had a classroom full of adults, people older than I was at the time. People who had jobs. And children. Sometimes grandchildren. But they didn't know how to read. I assumed that I would teach them to read in the same manner that I had learned to read, but I had been a child when I learned.

Thankfully, I had a wonderful mentor who explained to me exactly why my flashcards and worksheets wouldn't work. She said that our students had more pressing concerns than "See Spot run." For instance, I had an adult student who had been eating beans for years because beans often come in a clear plastic bag, so he knew what he was buying at the grocery store. He wanted to know how to read what was on opaque food packages so he could have a more varied diet. We brought in food packages for a few weeks. Another student had recently taken over the bill paying in her house as her husband was sick. She needed help writing checks, so we practiced that for a week.

The time I spent teaching adults to read really made me think about how adults learn. (See Table 9.1.) When I read Knowles's theory, it resonated with my experience. He argues that the following assumptions (Knowles, Holton, & Swanson, 2015) can be made of adults as learners:

1. **The adult learner will make an effort to learn something when they need to know it.** Most adults spent at least 12 years in formal education experiencing pedagogy. Some continued their schooling after high school and have therefore spent a majority of their life in a classroom. That's a lot of time in school. Even for those who loved school, they outgrew the assumptions of pedagogy. Now that they have arrived at adulthood, they are no longer willing to subject themselves to someone else's curriculum if it does not match their learning goals. They simply have to be on board if they are going to participate.

   Therefore, adult educators must invest time making sure that the learners feel a need to know what is being taught. Otherwise, they simply will not participate. If they can't leave physically, they will close down emotionally, and they don't even bother faking interest. A bored adult learner is a painfully obvious presence in a classroom. The instructor may have to engage in some consciousness-raising activities to help an adult learner recognize his or her areas of need.

In a parenting class, consciousness raising might involve asking the parents to explicitly identify their areas of concern. I often ask every single parent in the room to state (either to the group or to a discussion partner) a problem they are currently experiencing in their household on today's topic. I provide paper or I list the problems on a whiteboard because writing things down can make them feel more real.

2. **The adult learner needs to see him- or herself as competent and self-directed.** As we have already discussed, parents are remarkably sensitive about being judged as a parent. That is because their self-concept is profoundly attached to their role as parent, and they need to see themselves as competent. This is a huge challenge for parent educators: to help parents feel comfortable enough to relax their defensive posture so that learning is possible.

Table 9.1 Pedagogy versus Andragogy

Assumption of Pedagogy	Assumption of Andragogy	Implication of Andragogy for Parent Education
1 The young learner does not know what he or she needs to learn.	The adult learner will make an effort to learn something when they need to know it.	Consciousness-raising
2 The young learner's self-concept is based on feedback from the instructor.	The adult learner needs to see him/herself as competent and self-directed.	Unconditional positive regard
3 The young learner does not have experience that is relevant to learning.	The adult learner has experiences that affect future learning.	Active listening
4 Thee young learner must be prompted by the teacher to be ready to learn.	The adult learner is ready to learn when that skill becomes required.	Developmental changes
5 The young learner is focused on subject matter.	The adult learner is oriented to learning tasks.	Problem-based learning
6 The young learner must be motivated by external pressures, including the approval or disapproval of the teacher.	The adult learner is most potently motivated by internal pressures.	Avoid external motivators

Sometimes, parent education is marketed as a "parent discussion group" instead of a "parenting class" because the word "class" triggers a defensive response because it implies that the parent needs to learn something. Adults are, in this way, far more fragile as learners than children are! It may be helpful to congratulate parents for the courage it takes to be in class, to acknowledge that the act of showing up is an act of love for their children.

3. **The adult learner has experiences that affect future learning.** Adults have had years of experiences, and it is impossible for them to leave their past at the door when they come into a classroom. This simultaneously makes learning easier (because they are often inherently interested in, and invested in, the content) and harder (because adults tend to "know" a lot of things that are not true that must be unlearned). In the realm of parenting, someone who has already spent years caring for children has lots of experience to draw upon. They know exactly what the problems are, and those problems are likely to be quite painful for them, motivating them to want to learn. But they also may have formed habits that the instructor knows are counterproductive that they should unlearn. But the parent can't always see that what they've been doing all along is a problem. I very often see parents who have an authoritarian style who simply cannot see that cracking down even harder on their misbehaving children won't help if the authoritarian style is what has produced the misbehavior in the first place. So prior experience is both good and bad. But it cannot be dismissed. It must be embraced in adult education and met straight on.

Because adults bring prior experience into the classroom, adult learners are not able to simply abandon those experiences and sit passively to receive knowledge. No, an adult learner must learn actively. **Active learning** involves strategies by which the learner uses their existing knowledge and skills to help construct new knowledge for themselves. Active learning teaching strategies include group discussions, simulations, and problem-solving activities; that is, pretty much anything other than passively listening to a lecture. Adults are active participants in their own learning. They cannot simply be told something and be expected to accept it unquestioningly and move on. They need to compare it to what they already know, consider it in light of experiences they have had, test it out, and adjust it.

The parent educator must be willing to accept this quality of an adult learner, to see it as an asset for meaningful learning, and to embrace it and use it. One illustration of how a parent educator can use this to great effect is to require parents to go home and try out a skill discussed in class. The teacher might announce that the next class period will consist of every single member of the class reporting one attempt they made to use the skill discussed today (active listening, process-focused feedback, logical consequences, etc.) and allowing the group to discuss it. This is hands-on, active learning. The processing in the group is where each parent actively constructs his or her understanding of the concept after trying it out. The learning may start with a mini-lecture about the skill, but working through examples of attempts is where most of the deep learning occurs.

So this is the feature with the most potential for deep learning. But this is also the area where a skilled instructor will take note of different levels of experience in the group. I have taught parenting classes that included parents who had full custody of multiple children, as well as parents who had only one hour of supervised visitation per week with only one child. Their experiences and their ability to meaningfully participate in the active learning are vastly different. And yet they participate in the same group. The instructor must be able to identify these discrepancies and somehow individualize their instruction to some degree so that both parents can make meaningful progress within their particular context.

4. **The adult learner is ready to learn when that skill becomes required.** While children become "ready to learn" when the teacher says it's time to learn, adults are not so easily put in the mood. Instead, readiness to learn is generally triggered by a developmental change. Just as college students sometimes magically become "ready to learn" in the days before an exam, all adult learners are more open to learning something when they are on the cusp of needing it. I am often asked why we don't teach parenting skills to high school students so that they will be ready when the time comes. Well, that doesn't work. They wouldn't learn it in high school because they don't realize that they need it until they are on the brink of parenthood. The time to teach parenting skills is right before those specific skills become desperately needed. So ironically, there is no way to learn the necessary skills in advance. Parent education is, for all parents, really on-the-job training.

This raises the question of how to tell that a skill is required. To some degree, this comes from the parents themselves. They can identify the areas of their parenting where they feel helpless or frustrated. But with court-mandated parent education, the parent does not necessarily feel ready to learn because they do not see that something is lacking. The court order itself becomes the indicator that skills are needed. And that is often not very convincing to the parent. Such parents may need the parent educator to focus their attention on the well-being of their children as the appropriate indicator of whether skills are needed. This can be accomplished by encouraging the parent to identify ways that their child's well-being is impaired. It is uncomfortable, maybe even painful, but parents need that kind of focus if they are to become ready to learn.

5. **The adult learner is oriented to learning tasks rather than subjects.** This was the lesson that my adult literacy students taught me. They had no interest in learning the subject of "reading." But they did need to achieve tasks of everyday life such as grocery shopping and paying the bills. They would learn to read because it helped them with those tasks. But to teach them, we had to focus on the tasks, not the subject.

   A focus on tasks rather than subjects has been called **problem-based learning**. Medical schools in Canada and the United States have recently shifted toward problem-based learning because it is much more effective than a subject-based curriculum (Barrows, 1996). Similarly, when parents come into a parenting class, they generally come with a specific task that they want to learn or that a judge thinks they need to learn. Parent education does best when it focuses on the tasks rather than the subject. People do not usually sign up for a totally generic "parenting" class. They sign up for a class on a specific task, such as "improving communication with your teenager" or "getting baby to sleep."

6. **The adult learner is most potently motivated by internal pressures.** I have already addressed the risk of using rewards and punishment in a parenting class. We know from Chapter 7 that behavioral interventions tend to change behavior only in the presence of the rewarder or punisher. We do not want parents performing for their instructor (either to earn praise or to avoid scolding) because that leads to sneakiness and to temporary behavior change that will revert back to the old ways after

the class is over and the judge has been placated. We want parents to be inspired to improve their parenting for their own reasons, for love of their children, or out of a sincere desire to have a more peaceful and loving home. Therefore, parent educators should resist the temptation to rely on external motivators with adult learners.

The andragogy model is widely accepted in adult education. Some have suggested that andragogy can and should be applied to education of children too, that things like active learning, developmental readiness to learn, and problem-based learning are good for everyone (Knowles, Holton, & Swanson, 2015). The extent to which the andragogy model can be applied to children is an open question. But it is unquestionable that it is helpful when preparing an educational intervention with adults.

The parent educator must consider these aspects of andragogy to decide how to facilitate learning. It seems that some conditions (a parenting class for teen parents, say) may include learners who are very dependent despite their status as parents and therefore could tolerate (or even require) some pedagogical interventions. Other conditions (court-mandated interventions, for instance) will exacerbate things like the parental sensitivity to one's self-concept as competent and the limitations of external motivation. The parent educator needs to consider these issues when constructing and implementing an intervention.

Research-Based Best Practices

A review of court-mandated parent education (Myers-Walls, 2011) identifies several characteristics of the most effective programs. The most effective programs use active learning (Pollet & Lombreglia, 2008). This is not a surprise; the andragogical model predicted this. Effective programs also utilize collaborative agendas (Pollet & Lombreglia, 2008). This means that parents should participate in the selection of topics for the course, rather than having it completely standardized and determined in advance. This also is predicted by the andragogical model, as adults learn best when they need to know something. Finally, leader characteristics are related to program success. The characteristics that seem to help are a positive disposition, compassion, and authenticity (Bundy-Fazioli, Briar-Lawson, & Hardiman, 2008). Notice that the qualities of the leader that have been identified as helpful are not academic training or credentials but instead reflect interpersonal skills. This reflects the role of relationships as foundational to learning, as the pyramid model suggests.

A meta-analysis of program evaluations (Kaminski, Valle, Filene, & Boyle, 2008) found that the most effective parent education programs have three components, two of which are related to content and one that is related to the method. The content of the most effective parenting programs include 1) parent-child communication (the communication level of the pyramid); and 2) instruction in positive parent-child interaction (the applied behavior analysis level of the pyramid). The methodological best practice is the inclusion of a practice component. Simply lecturing about skills is insufficient; parents must also have opportunities to try them out, to practice and get feedback for skill building. This is to say, of course, that active learning is required for successful adult education.

Parent Education as a Profession

While parent education has its roots in several fields (family science, education, social work, health care, mental health, human services) it has emerged as a distinct discipline. But it is a discipline with appallingly few professional standards or safeguards.

Essentially, there are almost no legal restrictions on the practice of parenting education or use of the term "parent educator." I say "almost" because one state (Minnesota) requires a teaching license in order to work as a parent educator. Minnesota requires parent educators to pass the same basic skills tests for licensing as all other teachers and to have completed 27 units of specific coursework, including some child development, some family science, parenting and parent education, and student teaching in parent education.

But Minnesota is very much alone in this. In the rest of the United States, parenting programs are offered widely, but there are no standards for who can teach them. In 1996, a report on the status of the field noted the need for a set of standards for preparation for parent educators (Carter, 1996). Ten years later, Cooke (2006) reiterated that call, noting that well-intentioned but poorly prepared parent educators are routinely placed in positions that call for expertise and skills they simply do not have.

In 1984 the National Council on Family Relations (NCFR) established standards and criteria for certification of family life educators. Family Life Education is a discipline that includes relationship education, marriage enrichment, sex education, and parenting education. Certification is achieved by meeting standards for academic preparation in several relevant areas and maintenance of continuing professional education standards (Duncan & Goddard, 2011). This is an attempt to standardize and professionalize a field that includes parent education. Students who are interested in parent education should consider pursuing certification in family life education.

The National Parenting Education Network (NPEN) is a professional association of parent educators. It is another organization that has been working to identify care competencies for parent educators and provide opportunities for professional collaboration among parent educators (Bowman, Rennekamp, & Wolfe, 2012). NPEN has acknowledged that parent education is a field that thrives with the participation of peer educators, paraprofessionals, and professionals in parent education (Jones, Stranik, Hart, McClintic, & Wolf, 2013). Students who are interested in working as parent educators should consider membership in NPEN.

Parent education is different from other potential interventions for parents. We can think of it on a continuum of intensity. The least intensive would be informal advice that is often shared between family members, friends, and neighbors. Parent education is an intermediate level of intensity. It is more professional than the casual advice offered by friends and family, but not as intensive as that offered by licensed mental health providers. It is considered a psychoeducational intervention, meaning that it is an attempt to change behavior by way of providing information, insights, and skills rather than by treatment of mental disorders.

It is important to distinguish family life education from the most intensive interventions, which are clinical interventions such as psychotherapy or counseling. Psychotherapy is individually tailored and must be administered only by a licensed mental health professional. Therapists are qualified to identify and treat psychological disorders and mental illnesses. This is not in the domain of family life education. It is very important that parent educators, who need not be licensed as mental health providers, can identify the boundary between psychoeducational interventions and therapeutic interventions. Therapy involves diagnosis of disorder, whereas psychoeducation deals with normative family problems. Those family problems might be very serious, including things like domestic violence and child abuse, but they do not require that the perpetrator has a mental illness. Once mental illness enters the equation, the family life educator is ethically obliged to refer the case to a licensed mental health practitioner.

Conclusion

Parent education is an exciting field. It is young and vibrant. Every parent educator has the potential to shape the discipline, as we are currently developing into an independent profession. We retain our connection to several existing disciplines, and much work remains to be done in terms of finding the connections between our multiple related fields. I look forward to the day when a chapter on teaching methods in parent education can be more evidence based than it is today. A great deal of research is currently being conducted on parent education, so we are on the cusp of important growth and development.

Review and Reflection Questions

1. Why are parents so resistant to unsolicited parenting advice? How can a student or new professional offer help to a parent in need? Have you ever offered unsolicited advice? How did it go?

2. How can the parenting pyramid be applied to teaching?

3. What are the assumptions of pedagogy? Of andragogy? Where do you fit on these six continua in your college classes?

4. What are the implications of andragogy for teaching parenting classes?

5. What are the characteristics of effective parenting classes?

6. How would one pursue a career in parent education?

Terminology to Know

- Active Learning
- Andragogy
- "I wonder" questions
- Non-confrontational opening
- Pedagogy
- Problem-based learning
- Unsolicited advice

Names to Know

- Knowles

References

Barrows, H.S. (1996). Problem-based learning in medicine and beyond: A brief overview. *New Directions for Teaching and Learning, 68,* 3–12.

Bowman, S., Rennekamp, D., & Wolfe, J. (2012). Finding from the National Forum on Professional Development Systems for Parenting Education. Hallie E. Ford Center White Paper. Oregon State University. http://npen.org/wp-content/uploads/2012/06/2011-Findings-from-the-National-Forum-on-Professional-Development-Systems-for-Parenting-Education.pdf Retrieved 1/3/2017.

Bricusse, L., & Newley, A. (1971). "Oompa Loompa." *Willy Wonka & the Chocolate Factory.*

Bundy-Fazioli, K., Briar-Lawson, K., & Hardiman, E.R. (2008). A qualitative examination of power between child welfare workers and parents. *British Journal of Social Work,* 1–8.

Carter, N. (1996). See how they grow: A report on the status of parenting education in the US. Philadelphia: Pew Charitable Trusts.

Cooke, B. (2006). Competencies of a parent educator: What does a parent educator need to know and do? *Child Welfare, 35, 5,* 785–802.

Ginott, H. (1972). *Between parent and teenager.* New York: Macmillan.

Duncan, S.F., & Goddard, H.W. (2011). *Family life education: Principles and practices for effective outreach.* Sage.

Jones, S.T., Stranik, M.K., Hart, M.G., McClintic, S., & Wolf, J.R. (2013). A closer look at diverse roles of practitioners in parenting education: Peer educators, paraprofessionals, and professionals. NPEN White Paper. National Parenting Education Network. http://npen.org/wp-content/uploads/2012/03/diverse-roles-in-PE-white-paper_-12_17_13.pdf Retrieved 1/3/2017.

Kaminski, J.W., Valle, L.A., Filene, J.H., & Boyle, C.L. (2008). A meta-analytic review of components associated with parent training effectiveness. *Journal of Abnormal Clinical Psychology, 36, 4,* 567–589.

King, H. (2009). 20 Psychosocial pediatrics interview questions that work. Children's Emotional Health Link. http://www.cehl.org/20interviewquestions.html Retrieved 12/31/2016.

Knowles, M.S., Holton, E.F., & Swanson, R.A. (2015). *The adult learner: The definitive classic in adult education and human resource development, 8th edition.* Routledge.

Myers-Walls, J. (2011). Family life education with court-mandated parents and their families. In S.M. Ballard & A.C. Taylor (Eds.), *Family life education with diverse populations,* pp. 61–90. Sage.

Parker, K., Horowitz, J.M., & Rohal, M. (2015). Parenting in America: Outlook, worries, aspirations are strongly linked to financial situation. Pew Research Center. http://www.pewsocialtrends.org/2015/12/17/parenting-in-america/Retrieved 5/17/2016.

Pollet, S.L., & Lombreglia, M. (2008). A nationwide survey of mandatory parent education. *Family Court Review, 46, 2,* 375–394.

10. Parent Education Interventions

Introduction

We have arrived at the last chapter. We're almost finished. So far, we have reviewed the context of parenting and parenting advice in the United States, we have surveyed parenting strategies as devised by several decades of theory and research in child and family science, and we have considered teaching strategies for working with adults. Now we finish off by turning our attention to a review of current parenting advice and education interventions.

Sources of Parenting Advice

To begin, we must consider where parents go when they need help with parenting. Parents report that they want information about child-rearing (Young, Davis, Schoen, & Parker, 1998). The vast majority of parents agree that even good parents might need help or advice sometimes. They report being willing to seek help from books (93%), family (88%), friends (81%), or a parenting class (84%). They are quite open to getting help from a health care provider (74%), school personnel (69%), or clergy (56%) (Keller & McDade, 2000). It is reasonable to conclude that most parents are open to parenting advice and education.

And as it turns out, they do seek help, but not quite as often as they say they might. And their sources are almost always informal. Parents report using an average of five sources, typically books, friends, and family members (Radey & Randolph, 2009). One study found that parents are equally likely (approximately 70% of parents) to use other parents and parenting books for help with both child development questions and discipline issues. Parents were somewhat less likely (40%) to go to their own parents for help in these areas and less likely still (20%) to use a parenting class as their source of help (Ateah, 2003). Other studies that are focused more broadly find a slightly higher rate (approximately 30%–35%) of parents who have attended a parenting class or group (Fuligni & Brooks-Gunn, 2002; Young, Davis, Schoen, & Parker, 1998).

The use of friends and family members for parenting advice and support has numerous advantages. They are accessible. The parent has direct information about their credentials. The friend knows the individual circumstances of the parent asking for help, and they often even know the children about whom the parent refers. They generally are committed to the best interests of both the parent and the child, so they can offer advice that is sensitive and well intentioned. All of this means that they can offer individualized and relevant advice.

But there is a downside, of course. When people share the same social context, they already know each other's thoughts and habits. Therefore, friends and family members will probably be unlikely to offer a new insight that can change the parent's perspective. And they may not know any better than the parent what to do. They are quite likely to have no expertise on which to base their advice. Parents are quite likely to get more of the same from a close friend or family member.

Books are also consulted widely. They have the advantage and disadvantage of being completely unresponsive to the parent. This is an advantage because the parent will not be judged by the book. The parent will not have to face a human being and admit failings and fears. That might reduce their defensiveness and allow them to hear new ideas. But it is also a disadvantage because the parent cannot get misconceptions cleared up. He or she cannot ask how the idea might apply to a very specific case.

Another characteristic of books that is both an advantage and a disadvantage is that they can be written by anyone. Books allow parents to get insight from people who they might not ordinarily invite into their homes or have access to. As a result, parents can be exposed to ideas that are truly revolutionary for them, and they can get access to knowledge gained through scientific study that would otherwise have remained the sole domain of the highly educated. But as I reviewed in Chapter 2 of this text, there has been an explosion in the availability of parenting advice books such that the market is flooded. Parents are just as likely to pick up a book full of nonsense as to find one written by a true expert. So books are hit-or-miss.

Parent Education: What Format?

A smaller number of parents pursue more formal parent education or are compelled to do so. I tend to think of parent education as something that occurs in a classroom. But that is not necessarily the only format for it.

Support Groups

The earliest form of parent education may have been the **support group** format, where small groups of parents (mothers exclusively, at first) meet up for discussion in each other's homes to help each other problem solve the difficulties of motherhood. The **intensive mothering ideology**, the pervasive belief that motherhood should be the dominant and all-encompassing role of a woman's life and that the mother is really the only person able to provide for her child's needs (Hays, 1998), took off in the United States in the Victorian era (Coontz, 2016). Middle-class women assumed a great burden of responsibility when they accepted the intensive mothering ideology, and that was accompanied by a commensurate amount of anxiety related to parenthood (Stearns, 2003).

Perhaps in response to these pressures, middle-class women started to form groups called "maternal associations" where women would discuss their concerns about parenting. These groups came together to form the National Congress of Mothers in 1897, which became the Parent Teacher Association (PTA). Today's PTA is unrecognizable as a parenting support group, but that is how it started. It was aligned with the brand-new **child study movement** of the time, which became (under the academic psychologist G. Stanley Hall) the scientific study of child development (Ponzetti, 2016).

A current example of parenting education in the form of a grassroots support group is La Leche League (LLL), which offers support to breastfeeding mothers. The stated mission of La Leche League is to "help mothers worldwide to breastfeed through mother-to-mother support, encouragement, information, and education …" (La Leche League International, 1993). The mother-to-mother support is the essence of LLL. Ordinary women who breastfeed become leaders of small groups. The small groups meet in homes or other community-based settings. While they may invite experts to talk to the group, the groups are not directed by experts; they respond directly to the needs and interests of the mothers who comprise the small group. The organization was founded in 1956 and has maintained its relevance by responding to the lived experiences of mothers even through significant cultural changes (Blum & Vandewater, 1993). An ethnographic study of an LLL group suggests that the group shares, and effectively teaches a philosophy of natural mothering through processes of modeling rather than explicit instruction (Merrill, 1987).

Another example of parenting support groups were the neighborhood discussion groups formed in the 1950s and 1960s by Rudolf Dreikurs and his followers (Ponzetti, 2016). The groups were based on Adlerian principles of parent education, which we discussed in Chapter 6, but the predominant method was small groups of mothers who met in their own homes, with discussion facilitated by a trained group leader. Expert guidance was critical, but the topics of discussion and the direction of the discussions were generated by the mothers. The group leader was trained to facilitate discussion so as to help the mothers consider Adlerian/Dreikursian concepts.

Support groups are powerful because they are driven by grassroots forces. They respond to the specific needs of parents in their own specific contexts. They also draw upon the strength of existing social support systems. The quality of help in support groups is variable, of course, and depends on the facilitator (if there is one) and on the people who make up the group. As the curriculum is not standardized, there is no way to predict if it will promote the scientific consensus regarding effective parenting or not.

Small-Group Format

The move toward professionalizing parent education, which shifted some of those private support groups into formal organizations, triggered an explosion of parent education in the United States. Group-based parent education became popular in the 1920s (Campbell & Palm, 2004). In 1930, the US Office of Education found over 400 organizations offering parenting programs (Croake & Glover, 1977). These programs were primarily in the form of classes in small-group format. Surveys of parent education in the 1980s noted that it was embedded in community-based human services. Parenting classes in small-group format were being offered by hospitals, schools, churches, and multiple other agencies. The instructors of these programs were not primarily parent educators; they were social workers, nurses, psychologists, or preschool teachers. The same remains true today (Campbell & Palm, 2004).

Therefore, it is impossible to really have a grasp of the scope of small group parent education: who is providing it and what exactly is being taught. Due to the dispersal of parent education among many settings, we do not have a way to measure how many such parenting classes are currently offered in the United States. We assume that it is a lot, and that most small-group classes remain unevaluated.

According to Campbell and Palm (2004), small-group parent education is powerful because it allows parents to have access to information and develop a sense of community through connection to other parents. The social connections that may have been inherent in communities prior to the Industrial Revolution can be replaced to some degree by small-group parenting programs.

When groups are led by talented and well-trained parent educators, they have the potential to be responsive to individual needs and to convey scientifically sound principles of effective parenting. If they are done well, they can be the best that parent education possibly can be. But since there are no standards outside of Minnesota, they can also be offered by uneducated, untrained, and incompetent facilitators sharing information that is not consistent with the scientific consensus about effective parenting. There is no way to know.

Commercially Packaged Programs

There are many **commercially packaged parenting programs** that are designed to be delivered in a small-group format. These are proprietary programs that have a standardized curriculum that is provided to the parent educator along with materials needed to implement it. The Parent Effectiveness Training (PET) workshops, which target communication skills (discussed in Chapter 5), were originally designed to be offered in a classroom setting, although research finds that parents can complete the activities with the book alone and still see benefit. As discussed in Chapter 6, the Systematic Training for Effective Parenting (STEP) program, which is based on the Adlerian model, is also designed to be delivered by a trained leader in a classroom setting.

Many of these commercially packaged programs involve the use of videos. The first to do so was Active Parenting. The Adlerian/Dreikursian neighborhood discussion groups described above changed form in the early 1980s to take advantage of the new technology of videocassette recorders (VCRs). Video-based parent education retained the form of a small-group discussion, but prompts for discussion topics were no longer provided by the participants themselves, and the groups no longer required a highly qualified and talented group leader. Instead, the prompts were video vignettes of common parenting problems. In place of a well-trained group leader, anyone can pause the video at the appropriate time and restart it after some discussion. The producers of the videos insert expert analysis (Popkin, 2014), and discussion guides and workbooks are provided.

These programs generally cost several hundred dollars for videos, workbooks, and discussion guides. They can sometimes be offered with minimal training (for instance, Active Parenting, STEP); other times they require more substantial training (such as Nurturing Parenting, Triple P). The quality of help in commercially packed programs is far more standardized. They are generally offered by people with minimal training or expertise, but they have been designed by people who are true experts. The commercially packaged programs have been subject to formal evaluation research, although that research is usually done with the intent of promoting the program rather than making improvements, so interpretation of the results is complicated by the influence of commercialism.

Fully Online

Technology has now developed to the point that it is no longer even necessary for parents to be together in a physical place or even together at the same time to participate in a small group. Some fully online programs allow parents to be part of a virtual group, and others have parents interacting with the program individually without interaction with other parents.

Fully online parent education may come in the form of a parent support group, such as Internet-based discussion groups. One format is parent-submitted questions that are answered by experts or other parents and compiled into a newsletter that is distributed by e-mail. Another format is the discussion board or forum, where parents post comments and questions and respond directly to one another in an online forum.

Hall and Irvine (2009) note that these fully online, but social, venues may be a very important resource for rural parents who do not have ready access to personal sources of support and guidance. Support groups that are fully online may also increase access to support for parents who work full time or who prefer the emotional safety of a group that is anonymous in some ways but deeply personal in others. Online parenting support has been found to help parents feel supported rather than judged (Sarkadi & Bremberg, 2005).

These fully online supports are sometimes created and run by experts, but sometimes they have no expert involvement at all. Mothers using these venues have reported that sometimes they use the Internet group specifically to escape or combat the expert consensus on issues that they struggle with (Madge & O'Connor, 2006). This feature make them vulnerable to being hijacked by people whose agenda directly contradicts the scientific consensus regarding effective parenting. Therefore, the quality of help in this format is wildly variable.

There is currently a push toward providing more formal parent training online produced by true experts, such that parents can access the program individually, on their own time line. They can go to a website, register and pay for the course, and then work through the modules at their own pace. Advantages are that qualified and available instructors are not necessary to maintain the program, but all of the (considerable) costs are incurred upfront by the agency or organization that plans to offer the intervention. Therefore, if the program is effective and investment can be made, it can pay dividends indefinitely. For parents, the fully online program is flexible. They can do it whenever it is most convenient for them. If they are court ordered, they do not have to wait for a program to cycle through and risk the possibility that it will not be offered again before their next court date. Instead, they can just complete the course in their own time with no restrictions. Furthermore, the parent can complete the education without being forced to endure the public humiliation of a parenting class with strangers. The privacy may help protect parents' self-concept as competent from the grief that may come with public exposure.

Parenting Wisely is such a program, offered fully online to individual subscribers. It was designed for families with children who are at risk of problem behaviors such as delinquency and dropping out of school (Lindquist & Watkins, 2014). The method of the Parenting Wisely program reflects problem-based learning. It shows video vignettes of common problem behaviors (getting kids to help with housework, sibling conflict, drugs in the child's bedroom, and so forth), and pursues possible solutions to the problems. The parent learner selects one of three possible solutions to each problem and watches a video of what happens when that solution is chosen. The possible solutions reflect authoritarian, permissive, and authoritative parenting. Clearly, this program is designed to promote authoritative parenting. The videos include skills that fall on the communication and consequences levels of the parenting pyramid. The Parenting Wisely program has been shown in randomized controlled trials to reduce problematic child behaviors (Pushak & Gordon, 2016).

In Chapter 6, we discussed the Love and Logic program, which focuses on the use of natural and logical consequences. It is available fully online. It was originally designed to be taught in a classroom setting, but it has been converted for fully online administration.

There are currently substantial efforts to identify or create an effective coparenting program for court-ordered couples that can be administered fully online. Several models exist for such a thing. Driving school programs are fully online for people who have a traffic violation. These are most in demand for parents who are court ordered to parenting class related to custody proceedings. Some states require parent training for all divorcing couples with minor children, regardless of whether there are indications of risk. Those situations seem conducive to relatively short (one or two hours) online parenting programs that can be completed individually.

The success of Parenting Wisely suggests that fully online programs may be promising, even for coparenting classes. But fully online coparenting classes have not yet been adequately evaluated.

Home Visitation

Home visitation is an individualized and intensive strategy that is used with very specialized populations, especially the highest-risk families or as an intervention after problems have been detected. It involves sending a professional with advanced training into the family home to watch interactions between parent and child, to assess the environment directly, and provide face-to-face individualized feedback. Most home visitation for parent education is in the area of pregnancy and newborn care (Stolz, 2011). Home visitation programs are incredibly intensive and expensive but are quite effective (Casillas, Fauchier, Derkash, & Garrido, 2016).

A few parenting education programs, including Triple P (Positive Parenting program) and the Nurturing Parenting program, are designed to provide intervention for families with identified problems according to a tiered system. Some families can be served by a minimal level of intervention offered online or through a classroom experience, but the most intensive level of intervention requires individualized home visits (Sanders, 1999; Nurturing Parenting, n.d).

Home visitation programs, because of their individualized nature, stray farther away from the model of a psychoeducational intervention. Many require licensing and are implemented by nurses or therapists.

Parent Education: For Whom?

Another way to conceptualize formal parent education is to consider the target population. We might consider three types of interventions distinguished by the population of parents involved.

Enrichment

Some parent education is voluntary; it might be considered **enrichment** because it is usually designed to improve on strengths. These are typically free classes or discussion groups offered in hospitals, churches, bookstores, or other open community settings. Some enrichment parent education is narrowly focused because parents often seek help around specific family transitions. There are childbirth and newborn infant care classes, as well as classes about parenting adolescents or helping kids adjust to a new sibling or starting school. Programs sometimes target specific needs of individual children (based on their temperament, their abilities, etc.) or reflect the parent's circumstances (stay-at-home moms, dads who travel with work, Christian parenting, etc.).

Another kind of enrichment parent education is a general parenting class, such as those often offered in church settings or adult education programs. General programs like this are often weekly or monthly meetings, and each session is focused on a specific topic. I have taught a church-based course like this for many years. Research on parents who voluntarily attend a community-based parenting class offered to the general population suggests that they are highly educated and employed full time; their children are quite young (average age younger than four years), and the parents are stressed (Reedtz, Martinussen, Jørgensen, Handegård, & Mørch, 2011).

This coincides with my experience. I will also note that the kinds of parents who actively seek help with their parenting, who attend these community-based voluntary programs, are easy to work with. They are typically conscientious and hardworking, committed to their children, eager to learn, curious about new ideas, willing to engage meaningfully. In short, they are the kind of learner that every teacher wants to have in class. Consequently, teaching a voluntary class like this is a pleasure. I regularly have parents waiting to talk to me after class to thank me for the insights I've offered. It's like having a fan club.

A systematic review of studies evaluating the impact of parenting programs in the United Kingdom found that, on average, parenting programs do in fact improve children's behavior, improve parent-child interactions, increase parents' confidence, and reduce parental depression and stress (Bunting, 2010).

Furthermore, developmentally specific interventions also have evidence of effectiveness. Parenting education with those who are on the brink of the transition to parenthood have been shown to be effective in multiple domains, including reducing parental stress and child abuse, increasing health-promoting behaviors and the child's health, and maintaining adult relationship quality. The effect sizes are small but consistent and significant (Pinquart & Teubert, 2010).

Is enrichment parent education necessary? Well, if we consider the notion of "good-enough" parenting raised in an earlier chapter, we might say no. The parents who attend these classes are already doing a fine job as it is, and our efforts are somewhat wasted here. On the other hand, their eagerness and their appreciation suggests that, even if we have not altered their children's outcomes, we have helped make their experience of parenthood more meaningful or fulfilling. That is parent support. And that has to be worth something.

Preventive

Sometimes parent education is offered to a population that is at risk, even though the individual parents have not demonstrated any particular incompetence or problems. It might be considered **preventive**, designed to help reduce risk. Some adoption agencies require preventive parent education before a parent is allowed to adopt a baby. This happens specifically with international adoptions more often than domestic adoptions. Preventive education might be required of adults seeking to become foster parents or accept a foreign exchange student (Myers-Walls, 2011).

The most common risky situation that leads to court-mandated preventive parent education is parental divorce. In fact, the majority of parent education offered in the United States is specifically for this circumstance (Myers-Walls, 2011). This is necessary because anywhere from 10 to 25% of divorced couples continue to remain high-conflict long after separation (Maccoby, Mnookin, Depner, & Peters, 1992).

Divorce-related parenting classes generally focus on how important it is for children to maintain their relationships with both parents, as well as the reduction of hostile conflict between the parents. Because divorce education programs are so commonly court ordered, there are a great many commercially packaged divorce education programs, and evaluation of these programs is more common than other parenting programs. Parent education for divorcing parents is generally effective at reducing parental conflict and increasing parental knowledge of children's reactions to divorce (e.g., LaGraff, Stolz, & Brandon, 2015).

Divorce-related parent education has the advantage that it occurs at a time when parents are developmentally "ready" for it. They are open to change because so much of their life is changing. This can produce a readiness that is simply not usually present. But it has the disadvantage that it is typically externally motivated. Parents are generally eager to meet the judge's requirement through attendance but afraid that what they say will be reported back to the judge. Therefore, active learning is difficult in court-mandated divorce education.

I have been involved for several years with a program that provides divorce-related parent education to a court-mandated population. I find this population to be resistant at first but then to move toward active participation rather quickly, and they are grateful by the time it is over. However, because in California this education is only mandated for families who already have signs of trouble, it is a population for whom problematic behaviors are deeply entrenched. The parents are typically in a great deal of turmoil and emotional pain.

This is a more difficult population to work with then those who voluntarily attend enrichment programs. I am both gratified for the opportunity to work with parents who so clearly need support and have the potential to make improvements in their lives, and sometimes overwhelmed by the magnitude of the problems they face. Clearly, preventive parenting education requires more thoroughly trained parent educators than do enrichment programs.

Intervention

Other times, court-mandated parenting education is a targeted **intervention**. Parents are ordered to an educational intervention when their children display problem behaviors or when they have a history of domestic violence or conflict has already been routine (Myers-Walls, 2011).

Circumstances that commonly lead to court-mandated parent education include parental substance abuse, child abuse and neglect, and domestic violence (Barth, 2009). Parent education is very commonly mandated for families in these circumstances, and yet the programs have only rarely been subjected to research for evidence of effectiveness (Barth, Landsverk, Chamberlain, Reid, Rolls, Hurlburt, Farmer, James, McCabe, & Kohl, 2005).

A meta-analysis of parent education intervention of court-mandated divorce programs found that such programs are generally effective. Outcomes were, on average, 50% better in participating than nonparticipating families (Fackrell, Hawkins, & Kay, 2011).

Parent education for purposes of intervention very often includes a clinical component. These programs are more likely to be delivered by licensed mental health practitioners and are somewhat beyond the scope of a typical parent educator with a background in child development or family science.

Effectiveness of Parent Education

In order to address the question of whether parenting education does any good—**effectiveness**—we must address two preliminary questions. First, do we know what should be taught? Second, does teaching it actually change behavior?

Can We Know What to Teach?

First, do we know what should be taught? Many parents seem to have the idea that the "experts" don't really know what they are talking about; that they change their minds frequently and therefore they must not actually know much. An example that I often hear is about infant sleep. Experts used to recommend a prone sleep position for babies (sleep on their bellies). That way if he throws up, he won't choke on his own vomit. Makes sense. Anyone who has cared for a newborn knows that they spit up more than seems reasonable. So this admonition really made sense to parents, and they complied. It is also true that babies sleep a bit more soundly on their tummies, so parents are rewarded with a longer sleep this way.

But then the data came in on reducing the risk of Sudden Infant Death Syndrome (SIDS). Babies who died of SIDS were significantly more likely to be put to sleep on their tummies than on their backs. The experts changed their tune and started recommending the supine sleep position (babies on their backs). The **Back to Sleep** campaign, launched in 1993, recommends that babies always be placed to sleep on their backs. Parents around the country threw up their hands in exasperation. I have heard this complaint more times than I can count: "First they say to put him on his tummy, that his life was in danger if I did otherwise. Now they say to put him on his back, that his life is in danger if I do otherwise. I don't think they know what they're talking about!" The skeptics seem to think that either the so-called "experts" are just guessing and they really have no idea of the truth, or that there is no truth, that sleep position really makes no difference at all, and the experts just like having something to say, but it's all gibberish.

But this pessimism is unwarranted. This is actually a nice example of how science works. First, experts make reasonable hypotheses. They reasoned that supine sleep was dangerous and had a perfectly plausible explanation for why it would be so. But then they subjected it to empirical investigation; they tested the hypothesis that prone sleep was safer by collecting data in the real world. Much to everyone's surprise, the original hypothesis was wrong. Completely wrong. Exactly the opposite of the truth. So now we have an evidence-based recommendation for supine sleep in infancy. The first recommendation was wrong; the second recommendation is right. We know the answer now. So this is not reason to disbelieve the experts; it is reason to *believe* them. The family science experts continue the scientific study of children and families and so they continue to get closer and closer to the truth.

But another objection is often raised. It might be true that supine sleep is safer than prone sleep for preventing SIDS, but that is a very narrow issue. Parenting as a whole is much bigger, much more complex and multifaceted. It reflects culture, personal beliefs, and family values. Maybe the experts don't know what they're talking about because, on something as big and complex as parenting, no answer is really possible. Perhaps no matter how much scientific investigation is conducted, no clear answers emerge because children are all different, parents are all different, and everyone's life circumstances are complex and varied. What works for one parent of one child simply will not work for another child of a different parent.

This objection is typically voiced by parents who are defending themselves against a perceived criticism. "Look," they might say, "you don't even know me. You certainly don't know my child. This is working for us. Maybe something else works for you, but this is fine for us." They will assert that there is not a one-size-fits-all solution because people are too complex for that.

This objection is also easy to refute with scientific evidence. It is a reasonable hypothesis to predict that parenting practices would have no systematic effects on children. If everyone is different to the extent that no patterns can be found, then empirical investigation would find no patterns. If this hypothesis is correct, then there would be no difference in outcomes when parents use an authoritarian style compared to a permissive style compared to an authoritative style. But we know that this hypothesis is incorrect, because empirical investigation *does* find patterns in outcomes. Those patterns are not absolutely determinative, of course. We cannot say with 100% certainty that a child with authoritative parents will come out a certain way. But we can say that it is significantly more likely.

There are some areas of scientific investigation that have turned out not to matter very much. For instance, I started my research career exploring the relationship between parent-child cosleeping and attachment status. But it turns out (as I discovered during years of collecting data), there just is no relationship between this particular parenting practice (cosleeping) and that particular outcome (attachment). It does not matter. As this example illustrates, the hypothesis that parenting has no systematic effect on outcomes was possible.

But in many other domains, family scientists have collected a body of evidence demonstrating that certain aspects of parenting do have predictable outcomes on certain aspects of child outcomes. This body of evidence comprises the scientific consensus on parenting, as described in detail in Chapter 1. The scientific consensus includes these patterns:

1. Authoritative parenting produces the best outcomes.

2. Psychological control is damaging to children.

3. Secure attachment in infancy lays the foundation for emotional health and relationship success.

4. Harsh punishment is harmful.

5. Parental supervision and monitoring help prevent problem behaviors.

We didn't know these things a hundred years ago when parent education was in its infancy, but we know them now. As family science continues to pursue questions related to parenting, we will probably know more in the future than we do now. So, yes, we do know what should be taught. These five points should be taught. It turns out that they are all quite complicated. That is why we spent Part II of this text discussing the details.

Can We Know if It Works?

So we know what to teach, but that's not the same as knowing that teaching it does any good. I regularly hear people argue that parenting is just one of those things that you have to learn on the job. It is all trial and error. Parents simply have to try things and see how they go. There's nothing for it, they say—it's one of those things that can't be taught.

Given my status as a certified family life educator, as someone who devotes much of her professional life to parenting education, it must be obvious that I disagree. But let me explain how I can be so sure that parent education is not just possible but also demonstrably useful and effective.

Program evaluation is the process by which effectiveness of an intervention is studied. It is a specialized area of applied research. Interventions can be evaluated at several levels, starting with need. If there is no need for the intervention, then evaluation can stop there. But we established at the beginning of this chapter that parents have a need for parent education. They *want* help with parenting. They claim to need it and want it, and they seek it out. They talk to friends. They buy books. They show up when parenting groups are held. So there is a demand. All of these are indicators of need.

But unfortunately, that does not necessarily mean that those interventions do any good. A lot of people diet and exercise to lose weight too. We have an epidemic of obesity in the United States; many adults claim to want to lose weight; they sign up for gym memberships and many are lifelong dieters. But most of those New Year's resolutions fade, and the weight comes back on. Most weight-loss programs are ineffective. So once we know that parenting programs are needed, we then move on to the second level, the implementation of the program. (See Table 10.1 for a summary of these levels.) Implementation is evaluated by the administrators of the program. They note how many sessions were offered, how many parents attended, and what costs were incurred. This is basically just evaluating feasibility. This happens by default because programs can only be offered if they make sense financially and if people attend.

If there is a need and the program is feasible, the next level of evaluation is **customer satisfaction**, or the participant's subjective reaction to the program. Participants can be given surveys at the end of the program to determine if they enjoyed it and felt it was worthwhile. If not, the program should end right there. Just enjoying something does not mean that it worked, but if parents do not enjoy it, then they will not come and will not meaningfully participate. Parent

Table 10.1 Levels of Program Evaluation

Level of Evaluation	Relevant Questions	Method of Evaluation
1. Need	Do parents want the help that is being offered? Do they need it?	Needs assessment in community.
2. Implementation	Is the program feasible? Can parents show up when it is offered? Are qualified staff available? Is it cost-effective?	System analysis
3. Satisfaction	Do parents enjoy attending the class? Do they feel that it is worthwhile?	Satisfaction survey at the end of the program
4. Knowledge or Attitude Change	Do parents have a better understanding of their children's needs? Did they gain knowledge of parenting strategies? Did they adopt more authoritative beliefs? Was their anxiety reduced?	Pre-test and post-test questionnaire; ideally with a comparison group
5. Behavior Change	Does parenting behavior change to reflect new skills, implemented according to best practices? Are behavior changes sustained over time?	Self-report and direct observation of parenting behavior
6. Outcome	Did the behavior change produce tangible improvements in the parent-child relationship? Or a reduction of problem behaviors in the child?	Objective indicators, or third-party reports of child behavior.

education is adult education, after all, and the andragogy model asserts that adults will only learn when they essentially consent to the agenda. So if parents are not satisfied, there is no point going any further.

Satisfaction is the first level of program evaluation that requires data to be collected directly from the participants. It is simple and easy. On the final day of the program, participants are asked to complete a survey or to write an evaluation. They are typically asked if they enjoyed it, if they would recommend it to a friend, if it met their needs. They may be asked for suggestions for improvements to the program.

But customer satisfaction is not enough to be convinced that the program is helpful. For one thing, **social desirability**, the tendency to provide a response that will please the person asking, may inflate customer satisfaction scores. The parent may not want to hurt the feelings of the instructor or may not want to risk a critical report being sent back to the judge. The parent may also just not want to put any energy into completing the evaluation and so just mark "very pleased" down the line in order to move on.

Even if the parent honestly completes the survey and is very pleased with the class, that might not mean much. Sometimes it is just the act of seeking help that alleviates some of their anxiety. This is called the **placebo effect**, the relief provided by simply acting, regardless of what the action is. Is the education what felt so good to them, or was it the satisfaction of feeling like they were doing something? Or could it have been simply getting out of the house once a week? Maybe if they had not signed up for the class but had instead had coffee with a friend one night a week, they would have enjoyed that too.

It's also true that most people seek help when circumstances are at their very worst. Maybe the situation had reached a peak of difficulty and things would have calmed down no matter what. This is called **regression to the mean**, the tendency of many problems to resolve on their own and return to a more normal state. For example, people often suffer with the common cold for five or six days until they can't stand it anymore, and then they make an appointment with their doctor. They go in, feeling like they got hit by a truck. But the natural course of the infection is that they are on the worst day. They'll soon start feeling better. They will feel better tomorrow whether they go to the doctor today or not. But they go to the doctor and perceive that it helped because they soon start feeling better. So too do parents seek help for their parenting problems; they did not realize that they were in a bad patch and things might have gotten better anyway.

So parents must like the class to make it worth continuing. But just liking the program is not enough to know that the program is effective. The next level of evaluation is to determine if the parent learned anything, or if the parent changed his or her attitude in a meaningful way. These are more objective indicators of effectiveness. To determine if a program is effective, we have to measure the knowledge or attitude before the class and again after the class to look for change.

This is the first level of evaluation that tells us anything directly about effectiveness. It is more difficult to implement because the evaluation requires a valid and reliable measure of knowledge or attitude, and it must be administered both before and after the class. So the evaluation plan must be in place before the program is started. It is surprising to me how few programs evaluate themselves in this way, even though this is not very onerous to implement.

But I am not surprised that most program evaluations that do use pre- and post-tests do not include a **comparison group**. A comparison group is necessary in order to determine if the program is responsible for any improvement noted from the pretest to the post-test. If knowledge is gained, that knowledge could have been gained by parents talking to their friends and family. People do that regularly, and they might have landed on the same information as was presented in the class. Parents might also have figured it out for themselves by trial and error. If they can do it without the class, that is a lot less expensive and a lot easier, so we need to know if the program was necessary. The only way to know if the knowledge or attitude change is a product of the program is to compare the participants to similar parents who did not participate. But it is not usually easy to find a comparison group who matches the participants meaningfully. So this is not often done.

The final two levels are also rarely completed. But a truly effective intervention will change the way parents actually behave. This can be partially assessed using self-report of behaviors (for example, "How often in the past week have you spanked your child?") but parents may not answer such questions honestly. It's also true that they may not be able to judge how well they are using skills. For instance, they may self-report that they are using I-messages frequently, but a trained observer might see that their attempts to use I-messages are fatally flawed. For these reasons, observational data are required to determine if behavior change has occurred. And finally, all of this really only matters if it produces the desired final outcome, which is usually a change in the child.

Behavioral assessment of parents and children requires some consideration of change over time. It is not enough to change parental behavior during the program; those changes must be sustained over the next weeks and months at least. And outcomes on children generally do not appear immediately; they take weeks or months to become apparent. Therefore, these high-level evaluations are longitudinal in nature. This makes them expensive, and they require sophisticated research skills. As a result, these levels of evaluation are rare. But they constitute the gold standard of evaluating parenting programs because they get to the ultimate purpose of offering parent education.

Does It Work?

So program evaluation is both necessary and difficult. What do we know from program evaluation research that has been conducted? Does parent education actually change behavior and thus child outcomes?

In a word, yes.

Parents generally enjoy parent education. This is true even when the program is court ordered (Myers-Walls, 2011). Parents like having a "space" to process this most meaningful part of their lives. Parents often feel overwhelmed and anxious about parenting, so they like having a time set aside to get help, to talk to others for emotional support, to have access to ideas that might be helpful. This is great news, and it is even a little surprising. Resentment and resistance tend to melt away after a short time, and most parents emerge with appreciation for the experience.

Furthermore, published evaluation studies show that parent education can increase knowledge, can decrease depression and anxiety, and can shift parents' attitudes toward their children. Studies also show that parental behavior can be changed, and those changes can be sustained over time. And children's lives can be improved measurably by providing parent education (Medway, 1989; Stolz, 2011).

Not every program accomplishes all of this, of course. But all of this is possible. It is well worth it to invest our time, our professional energies, and our money in parent education programs. We know that it can work, and it very often does. The programs reviewed in this text, in fact, have demonstrated effectiveness (Collins & Fetsch, 2012).

Evidence-Based Programs

The National Registry of Evidence-Based Programs and Practices (www.samhsa.gov/nrepp) is a database that collects information about commercially packaged parenting (and other) programs. The California Evidence-Based Clearinghouse for Child Welfare (www.cebc4cw.org) also has a searchable database. Both provide summaries of the programs in the database, along with an analysis of the quality of evidence supporting the program. These resources can be used to explore the evidence base for a program that is being considered for use.

Conclusion

This very brief review of parenting education reveals that it varies considerably in form and content. But a few things are clear. Parents want and need support in the job that they do. In virtually every format and context in which it has been studied, parent education is associated with positive outcomes. Much work remains to be done to fully understand the conditions under which parent education is most effective, but the body of evidence suggesting its utility is large and growing.

Review and Reflection Questions

1. Where are parents most likely to go for help with parenting? Why? What are the advantages and disadvantages of possible sources of advice? Where would you go?

2. What should a parent educator consider when deciding the format of a parenting program? In what ways do the formats fit various circumstances? What format most appeals to you as an instructor?

3. What are the advantages and disadvantages of enrichment, preventive, and intervention parent education?

4. Why is program evaluation necessary for parent education? Why are the higher-level evaluations done so rarely? What do we know about effectiveness from parenting program evaluation?

Terminology to Know

- Back to Sleep campaign
- Child study movement
- Commercially packaged parenting program
- Customer satisfaction
- Effectiveness
- Enrichment
- Fully online program
- Home visitation
- Intensive mothering ideology

- Intervention
- La Leche League
- Placebo effect
- Preventive
- Program evaluation
- Regression to the mean
- Small-group format
- Social desirability
- Support group

References

Ateah, C. (2003). Disciplinary practices with children: Parental sources of information, attitudes, and educational needs. *Issues in Comprehensive Pediatric Nursing, 26*, 89–101.

Barth, R.P. (2009). Preventing child abuse and neglect with parent training: Evidence and opportunities. *Future of Children, 19, 2*, 95–118.

Barth, R.P., Landsverk, J., Chamberlain, P., Reid, J.B., Rolls, J.A., Hurlburt, M.S., Farmer, E.M.Z., James, S., McCabe, K.M., & Kohl, P.L. (2005). Parent-training programs in child welfare services: Planning for a more evidence-based approach to serving biological parents. *Research on Social Work Practice, 15, 5*, 353–371.

Blum, L.M., & Vandewater, E.A. (1993). "Mother to mother": A maternalist organization in late capitalist America. *Social Problems, 40, 3*, 285–300.

Bunting, L. (2010). Parenting programmes: The best available evidence. *Child Care in Practice, 10, 4*, 327–343.

Campbell, D., & Palm, G.F. (2004). *Group parent education.* Sage.

Casillas, K.L., Fauchier, A., Derkash, B.T, & Garrido, E.F. (2016). Implementation of evidence-based home visiting programs aimed at reducing child maltreatment: A meta-analytic review. *Child Abuse and Neglect, 53*, 64–80.

Collins, C.L., & Fetsch, R.J. (2012). A review and critique of 16 major parent education programs. *Journal of Extension, 50, 4*, https://www.joe.org/joe/2012august/a8.php. Retrieved 1/3/2017.

Coontz, S. (2016). *The way we never were: American families and the nostalgia trap, rev. ed.* Basic Books.

Croake, J.W., & Glover, K.E. (1977). A history and evaluation of parent education. *Family Coordinator, 26, 2*, 151–158.

Fackrell, T.A., Hawkins, A.J., & Kay, N.M. (2011). How effective are court-affiliated divorcing parents education programs? A meta-analytic study. *Family Court Review, 49, 1,* 107–119.

Fuligni, A., & Brooks-Gunn, J. (2002). Meeting the challenges of new parenthood: Responsibilities, advice, and perceptions. In N. Halfon, K. McLearn, & M. Schuster (Eds.), *Child rearing in America: Challenges facing parents with young children.* New York: Cambridge University Press.

Hall, W., & Irvine, V. (2009). E-communication among mothers of infants and toddlers in a community-based cohort: A content analysis. *Journal of Advanced Nursing, 65,* 175–183.

Hays, S. (1998). *The cultural contradictions of motherhood.* New Haven, CT: Yale University Press.

Keller, J., & McDade, K. (2000). Attitudes of low-income parents toward seeking help with parenting: Implications for practice. *Child Welfare, 79,* 285–312.

LaGraff, M.R., Stolz, H., & Brandon, D.J. (2015). Longitudinal program evaluation of "Parenting Apart: Effective Co-Parenting." *Journal of Divorce and Remarriage, 56,* 117–136.

La Leche League International (1993). La Leche League Mission. *LLLI Policies and Standing Rules Notebook, May 1989, Revised April 1993.* http://www.lalecheleague.org/mission.html Retrieved 11/7/2017.

Lindquist, T.G., & Watkins, K.L. (2014). Modern approaches to modern challenges: A review of widely used parenting programs. *Journal of Individual Psychology, 70, 2,* 377–394.

Maccoby, E.E., Mnookin, R.H., Depner, C.E., & Peters, H.E. (1992). *Dividing the child: Social and legal dilemmas of custody.* Cambridge, MA: Harvard University Press.

Madge, C., & O'Connor, H. (2006). Parenting gone wired: Empowerment of new mothers on the internet? *Social and Cultural Geography, 7,* 199–200.

Medway, F.J. (1989). Measuring the effectiveness of parent education. In M.J. Fine (Ed.), *The second handbook on parent education: Contemporary perspectives,* pp. 237–255. Academic Press, Inc.

Merrill, E.B. (1987). Learning how to mother: An ethnographic investigation of an urban breastfeeding group. *Anthropology and Education Quarterly, 18, 3,* 22–240.

Myers-Walls, J.A. (2011). Family life education with court-mandated parents and families. In S.M. Ballard & A.C. Taylor (Eds.), *Family life education with diverse populations.* Sage.

Nurturing Parenting (n.d.) Programs/Prevention levels. http://www.nurturingparenting.com/ecommerce/category/1/Levels%20of%20Prevention Retrieved 1/7/2017.

Pinquart, M., & Teubert, D. (2010). Effects of parenting education with expectant and new parents: A meta-analysis. *Journal of Family Psychology, 24, 3,* 316–327.

Ponzetti, J.J. Jr. (2016). Overview and history of parenting education. In J.J. Ponzetti Jr. (Ed.), *Evidence-based parenting education: A global perspective*, pp. 3–11. New York: Routledge.

Popkin, M.H. (2014). Active Parenting: 30 years of video-based parent education. *Journal of Individual Psychology, 70, 2*, 166–176.

Pushak, R.E., & Gordon, D.A. (2016). Parenting Wisely: Using innovative media for parent education. In J.J. Ponzetti Jr. (Ed.). *Evidence-based parenting education: A global perspective*, pp. 161–175. New York: Routledge.

Radey, M., & Randolph, K.A. (2009). Parenting sources: How do parents differ in their efforts to learn about parenting? *Family Relations, 58*, 536–548.

Reedtz, C., Martinussen, M., Jørgensen, F.W., Handegård, B.H., & Mørch, W.T. (2011). Parents seeking help child rearing: Who are they and how do their children behave? *Journal of Children's Services, 6, 4*, 264–274.

Sanders, M.R. (1999). Triple P-Positive Parenting Program: Towards an empirically validated multilevel parenting and family support strategy for the prevention of behavior and emotional problems in children. *Clinical Child and Family Psychology Review, 2, 2*, 7190.

Sarkadi, A., & Bremberg, S. (2005). Socially unbiased parenting support on the internet: A cross-sectional study of users of a large Swedish parenting website. *Child: Care, Health, and Development, 31*, 43–52.

Stearns, P.N. (2003). *Anxious parents: A history of modern childrearing in America*. New York: New York University Press.

Stolz, H. (2011). Parenting Education. In S.F. Duncan & H.W. Goddard (Eds.), *Family life education: Principles and practices for effective outreach, 2nd edition*, pp. 191–210. Thousand Oaks, CA: Sage.

Young, K.T., Davis, K., Schoen, C., & Parker, S. (1998). Listening to parents: A national survey of parents with young children. *Archives of Pediatric Adolescent Medicine, 152, 3*, 255–262.

Index

A

ABC model 241
Abuse 5, 56, 122, 274, 301, 320, 335
Accidental conditioning 236
Accidental reinforcement or punishment 239
Accurate interpretation of signals 83
Acknowledgment 296
Active communication 192
Active learning 315
Active listening 158
Active parenting 121, 142, 192, 200, 229, 329, 330
Actualize 151
Addenda 208
Adler, Alfred 142
Adlerian 142
Adopting OR adoption 54
African American OR black 14, 272
Agricultural revolution 70
Ainsworth, Mary 69
Ambivalent attachment 80
Andragogy 309
Anger OR angry 78, 86, 90, 95
Antecedent 241
Antibiotics 289
Anxiety 55
Applied behavior analysis 67, 240
Appropriate response to signals 84
Approximation 246

Asian American 14
Attachment 72, 100
Attachment parenting (AP) movement 100
Attachment-promoting behaviors OR attachment-promoting signals 72
Attachment theory 69
Authoritarian parenting 9
Authoritative parenting 27
Autism 260
Autocratic 200
Awareness of signals 83

B

Baby boom 34
Baby trainers 104
Baby-wearing 102
Back to Sleep campaign 336
Balance 104
Baltimore study 79, 80
Baumrind, Diana 9, 25
Bedding close to baby 102
Behavior chain 246
Behaviorism 234
Berrett, Rich 15
Best practices 67, 126, 154, 193, 214, 216, 219, 223, 224
Binuclear family 42
Birth bonding 100, 113

Birth order 228
Birth rate 34
Bonding 72
Bowlby, John 69, 70, 78
Brazelton, T. Berry 26
Breastfeeding 101

C

California Evidence-Based Clearinghouse for Child Welfare 343
Causation 41
Childlessness 37
Child-owned problem 153, 154
Child study 327
Choice 93, 200, 210, 212, 215
Circle of Security 99
Civil rights movement 24
Classical conditioning 235
Client-centered therapy 150
Coach OR coaching 154
Cohabiting OR cohabitation 40, 49, 50
Commercially packaged programs 329, 330
Common sense 22, 270, 275
Communication roadblocks 156
Comparison group 341
Conditioned stimulus 235
Conflict 13, 42, 52, 53, 57, 175
Conflicted coparenting 51
Conformity 21, 22, 45
Confrontation 167, 169
Congruent communication 185
Conservative 44
Consistent non-responsiveness 85
Consultant 200
Contact comfort 77
Contingent 133
Continual feeders 73

Continuous schedule of reinforcement 247
Contraception 33
Cooperative coparenting 50
Coresidential 54
Corporal punishment OR physical punishment 27
Correlation OR correlational 271
Co-sleeping 102
Court ordered OR court mandated 308, 331
Critical period 113
Criticism OR criticize 135, 136, 141
Crying 27
Cry it out 104, 268
Cues 125, 127
Culture 11, 19, 123, 337
Culture of poverty 47
Curiosity 44, 45, 76
Custody 40, 42, 49, 54
Customer satisfaction 339

D

Danger Zone 223
Dare to Discipline 267
Dehumanizing 257
Demandingness 9
Democratic 200, 201
Dependent learner 311
Depression 34
Descriptive praise 135
Dictator 200
Differential reinforcement 251
Discouraged OR discouragement 199
Disguised you-message 171
Dismissing model 95
Disobedience 46, 203, 274
Displaying 88, 231

Diversity 4, 5, 19, 27, 39, 44, 46
Divorce 41
Doormat 200
Douglass, Frederick 69
Dreikurs, Rudolf 198
Drugs 13, 14, 122, 331
Dweck, Carol 127

E

Earned secure 96
Economic hardship 47
Education OR educated 295
Effective OR effectiveness 336
Effect size 53
Either/or choice 215
Emotional availability 87
Emotion coaching 158, 192
Emotion-disapproving emotional parenting style 158
Emotion-dismissing emotional parenting style 158
Empathy 45, 82, 83, 91, 109, 219, 220
Employment 6, 24, 46
Encourage OR encouragement 143, 199
Engaged parenting 65
Enrichment 333
Environment of Evolutionary Adaptedness OR EEA 70
Eugenics 234
Evaluation 67, 100, 133, 138, 143, 192, 229, 330, 334, 341, 342
Evaluative praise 132
Evolution OR evolutionary 70, 71
Experimental OR experiment 273
Expert OR expertise 17
Extinction 236, 249

F

Family court 57, 285
Family science v, 1, 3, 6, 25, 26, 27, 54, 267, 273, 275
Family size 35, 36, 44, 56
Family structure 35, 40, 42, 43, 49, 56
Father OR fathering OR fatherhood 48, 49, 59
Faulty beliefs 206
Ferberizing 108, 268
Ferber, Richard 108, 267
Firm but friendly 217
Firm limits 210
Fixed mindset 128
Fixed schedule of reinforcement 247
Freudian 75
Freud, Sigmund 198, 228
Frightening parental behavior 86

G

Gayby boom 54
Gender 11, 12, 49, 164, 306
General fertility rate 34
Generalist species 19
Ginott, Haim 132, 137, 185, 270, 306
Goal of attracting attention 201
Goal of displaying inadequacy 205
Goal of retaliation 204
Goals of misbehavior 201
Good enough 4
Gordon, Thomas 150
Gottman, John 185, 192
Government 284
Grandparents 1, 2, 3, 20, 36, 50, 92
Grief 294
Growth mindset 129
Guidance vii, 9, 28, 328, 330

H

Habituated OR habituation 247
Hall, G. Stanley 327
Happiness 6, 7, 82, 93, 120, 127
Harlow, Harry 76, 77
Harsh punishment 27
Health 6, 53, 270
Helicopter parenting 88
Helpless orientation 127, 128
Hispanic OR Latino 46
Holt, Luther Emmett 20
Home economics 20
Home visitation 332
Hostile conflict 53, 54, 334
Hostility 51, 89, 270
How to Talk So Kids Will Listen 26
Humanistic psychology 150

I

Immediacy 245
Immigration 46
Imprint OR imprinting 75
Income 46, 213
Inconsistent responsiveness 86
Incredible Years 269
Independence 44, 45, 47
Individual psychology 198
Industrialization 20, 21
Industrial Revolution 20
Inferiority 199
Insecure attachment 81, 94
Insecure avoidant attachment OR avoidant attachment 80
Insecure disorganized attachment OR disorganized attachment 81
Insecure resistant attachment OR resistant attachment 80
Instinct 19, 73, 74, 223, 250, 268
Intensive mothering ideology 48
Intentionality 223
Intergenerational transmission 96, 112
Internal motivation 124, 260
Internal working model 79
Intervention 335
Intimacy 26, 133, 151, 223, 258
Intrusiveness 11, 88, 94, 153
Irrational fears 107
"I wonder" questions 304

J

Joint custody OR shared custody 42

K

Knowles, Malcolm 309

L

La Leche League 327
Language of acceptance 150
Lareau, Annette 47
Latino OR Hispanic 38, 39, 40
Learning goals 128
Lecturing 157
Lesbian baby boom 54
LGBT 24, 54, 291, 294
Liberal 44
Little Albert 237, 238, 259
Logical consequences 214
Logically related 216
Longitudinal 273
Lorenz, Konrad 75
Lose-win problem solving 177, 178, 189, 193, 204
Love and Logic 142, 200, 331

M

Main, Mary 81, 86, 95
Marital satisfaction 7, 8
Mastery orientation 127, 128, 130, 139, 307
Maternal associations 20, 327
Maternal mortality 72, 289
Maternal Sensitivity Scales 88
Meta-analysis 80, 83, 192, 274, 319, 335
Middle class 6, 20, 45, 47, 327
mindset 128
Mirroring emotions 185
Miscarriage 287
Modeling 126
Monitoring 27, 132, 338
Mother-in-law 18, 96, 154
Motivation 15
Mutual sensitivity 87

N

National Council on Family Relations 320
National Parenting Education Network 320
National Registry of Evidence-Based Programs and Practices 343
Natural childbirth 92, 100, 112
Natural consequences 210
Nazi Holocaust 21
Negative punishment 239
Negative reinforcement 238
Neglectful parenting 10
Nighttime parenting 102
Nonconfrontational opening 304
Nuclear family OR nuclear families 43
Nurturance 9

O

Obedience OR obedient 13
Online 100, 192, 229, 285, 330, 331
Operant conditioning 238
Operant response 238
Orientation to learning 306

P

Paradoxical theory of change 151, 190
Parallel parenting 52
Parental demandingness 9
Parental goals 44
Parental responsiveness 9
Parental supervision 27
Parent Effectiveness Training OR PET 149
Parenting advice 2, 18, 19, 20, 22, 25, 48, 55, 65, 149, 234, 284, 325
Parenting pyramid 69, 90, 109, 119, 125, 197, 207, 233, 242, 305, 306
Parenting strategies vii, viii, 51, 65, 197, 269, 284, 325
Parenting stress 39
Parenting style 8
Parenting wisely 192, 331, 332
Parenting with Love and Logic 229
Parent-owned problem 165
Parent Teacher Association OR PTA 327
Pavlov, Ivan 235
Peale, Norman Vincent 24
Pedagogy 309
Pediatrician 4, 18, 20, 154
Performance goals 127
Permissive parenting 9
Personal responsibility 198, 203, 206, 219, 223, 233, 257, 260, 308
Person-centered feedback 131

Physical punishment 26, 27, 47, 56, 269, 274
Placating 157
Placebo effect 341
Polarization of fatherhood 48
Positive Discipline Parenting 229
Positive parenting 142, 268, 271, 332
Positive punishment 239
Positive reinforcement 238
Postdivorce OR divorce related 49, 51, 112
Postpartum depression 293
Power 203
Praise 143
Pre-attachment phase 91
Preoccupied model 95
Preventive 334
Primary drive 75
Primary feeling 172, 173, 191
Problem-based learning 317
Problem ownership principle 153
Process-centered feedback 131
Program evaluation 339
Prompt response to signals 83
Prompts 244
Psychoanalysis 198
Psychoanalytic theory 75
Psychoeducational 320, 332
Psychological control 27
Psychological size 170
Punishment OR punisher 252
Pyramid model v, 65, 319

R

Racial/ethnic OR race/ethnicity 45
Ready to learn OR readiness to learn 310, 316
Reality 150

Reflective listening 192
Regression to the mean 341
Reinforcement OR reinforcer 238
Religion OR religious 292
Repartner 49
Replacement level 35
Responsibility 67, 198, 203, 206, 214, 219, 308, 327
Responsiveness 83, 97
Retaliation 204
Reward 238, 245
Rhythmicity 84, 88
Rogers, Carl 150

S

Same-sex relationships 54
Sane message 186
Sarcasm 157
Scaffolding 125
Scientific consensus 25, 26, 28, 45, 169, 244, 275, 328, 331
Sears, William 26, 87, 100, 102, 142
Secondary drive 75
Secondary feeling/emotion 172, 173, 182
Secure attachment 27, 80
Secure-autonomous model 95
Secure base behavior 77, 78
Self-actualization 150
Self-concept 310
Self-esteem movement 120
Self-help movement 25
Send a put-down 168
Send a solution 168
Sensitive responsiveness 83
Sexual orientation 54, 55, 58, 291, 297
Shaping behavior 245
Shared problems 175
Single parent 43, 314

Skinner, B.F. 234, 238
Sleep consolidation 106, 111
Sleep onset association 267
Sleep training 108
Small-group parent education 329
Sneakiness OR sneaky 257, 317
Social belonging 199
Social desirability 340
Social development theory 124, 144, 145
Social discipline model 198, 199, 231
Social revolution 24, 25, 29
Social reward 248, 252
Socioeconomic status OR social class 46
Soft limits 208
Spaced feeders 73
Spanking 207, 215, 226, 239, 253, 266, 269, 270, 273
Specialist species 18
Spitz, René 76
Spock, Benjamin OR Dr. Spock 22
Spock generation 24
STEEP (Steps Toward Effective Enjoyable Parenting) 99
Stepparent OR stepfamily OR stepfamilies 42
Stranger anxiety 92
Strange Situation 79
Structural variables 12
Sudden Infant Death Syndrome 290, 336
Support group 100, 327
Supportive coparenting 50
Systematic Training for Effective Parenting OR STEP 142

T

Tangible needs 179
Teen birth rate 39
Temperament 107, 258, 333
Tender needs 78
Time-out 226, 266
Toilet training 246, 261
Tolerance 44, 45
Total fertility rate 35
Triple P 268, 330, 332

U

Unconditional positive regard 152
Unconditioned stimulus 236, 237
Unemployment 46, 293
Uninvolved 10, 154
Unmarried women OR unmarried parents 40
Unmet expectations 288
Unrealistic expectation 55, 238
Unresolved model 95
Unsolicited advice 301
Unsupportive coparenting 51

V

Vaccination 289
Validation 296
Variable schedule of reinforcement 247
Voluntary 5, 49, 192, 333
Vygotsky, Lev 124

W

Warmth 9, 46, 272
Watson, John 234, 238
What to Expect 26
When/then choice 215
White OR White American OR European American 38, 48, 134, 272
Win-lose problem solving 176, 194, 203
Winnicott, Donald 4

Win-win problem solving 154, 176, 178, 180, 183, 188, 194
Withdrawn parenting 10, 29
Women's movement 24
Working class 45, 47
World War II 24, 34, 76, 289

Y

You-message 171, 190

Z

Zone of Proximal Development (ZPD) 125, 134

CPSIA information can be obtained
at www.ICGtesting.com
Printed in the USA
BVHW02s1641020218
506830BV00004B/179/P